D1797186

MEMORIES OF A SHARED FRIENDSHIP: IDEAS, MUSINGS, AND MEDITATIONS

THE COLLECTED LETTERS OF STEVE KOGAN & TED SITEA

1987 - 2015

Volume I

TED SITEA

Memories of a Shared Friendship:
Ideas, Musings, and Meditations

The Collected Letters of
Steve Kogan & Ted Sitea
1987 - 2015
Volume I

First printing: October 2016

Copyright © 2016 by WildFive Publishing LLC.

All rights reserved. No part of this book may be used or reproduced or transmitted in any form or in any manner whatsoever without written permission of the publisher, except in the case of brief quotations embodied in critical articles or reviews.

The views expressed in this work are solely those of the author and do not necessarily reflect the views of the publisher, and the publisher hereby disclaims any responsibility for them.

WildFive Publishing LLC
P.O. Box 515
Mayer, AZ 86333

For information write:
TedsBooks@cox.net

ISBN- 978-1-36-724406-1 (sc)
ISBN- 978-1-36-724407-8 (hc)

Printed in the United States of America

For information regarding author interviews, please contact Ted Sitea.

MEMORIES OF A SHARED FRIENDSHIP: IDEAS, MUSINGS, AND MEDITATIONS

THE COLLECTED LETTERS OF STEVE KOGAN & TED SITEA

1987 - 2015

Volume I

CONTENTS

Dedication

I would like to thank Carol Rusoff and Ruby Sitea for making this book come to life; were it not for their inspiration and support I could not have started, let alone completed, this labor of love.

Acknowledgements

My deepest bow goes to Steve for allowing me the privilege of proofreading his essays and letters. Hats off to Carol Runoff (Steve's wife) for assistance in finding many of the letters and editing, to Mel Hausner and Len Jenkin for pinning down dates and events, to Nancy McClure, a fellow colleague of Steve's at BMCC, for her support in this endeavor, to Ruby Sitea, my wife, who, for years, had urged both of us to publish our correspondence and greatly helped with putting it all together for publication, and to Shawn Dell Wildman and Owen Wildman, editors and publishers of the *Coffee Gram* in Mayer, AZ, who brought this book to life in the real world.

Preamble

MEMORIES OF A SHARED FRIENDSHIP:
IDEAS, MUSINGS, AND MEDITATIONS

The Collected Letters
of Steve Kogan & Ted Sitea
1987 - 2015

The 1970s:

The collection of our letters in book form is in furtherance of the wishes of friends, family and loved ones to share our correspondence with others. For those of you who did not know or do not know Steve or me the following is a brief, but necessary, review of the historical context of how we met and who we are.

I met Steve in the winter of 1970. Some of you may recall that this was a time when feminism was on the march and 'women's groups' were popping-up throughout Manhattan. Well, Warren Farrell (a name fairly well known on the Upper West Side of Manhattan) posted a number of broadsides in the neighborhood announcing that this was the time for men to meet with him and learn how to form "Consciousness Raising Men's Groups". I decided to answer the call. A number of men showed up at the scheduled meeting and were soon circulating in an effort to get to know each other.

One of the men was Mark Solomon. As Mark and I were both from Brooklyn, (unlike most of the men there), we started talking, quickly determined that we were of like mind and left the meeting to find a diner where we could talk comfortably over coffee about how to form our own group. Within a few weeks two other acquaintances were interested in joining our group and additional members were recommended by the new recruits. The initial two new members were interviewed by Mark and me and each new member, once admitted, participated in the interviewing process. Steve, a friend of Mark's, was the third member.

The new men's group was composed of: two math professors from NYU, a third math professor from Pratt, a physicist from Bell Labs, Mark Solomon, businessman and Ph.D., graduate of Columbia University, Steve, an English professor at BMCC with a doctorate from Columbia, and me, a B.A. in History and Philosophy from UCLA, a Master's Degree in History from Berkeley, a teacher at Pacific Alternative High School in Brooklyn.

The 'group' met on Thursday evenings and over time developed enough trust and friendship so that discussions of our personal problems were free and easy. We all agreed that politics, religion and women's groups were verboten topics. Amazingly, for twenty some-odd years, we talked with gusto and rigor - and enjoyed ourselves so much that we vacationed together in various parts of the country.

That Steve and I should become the dearest of friends for forty-five years is astounding to me. Steve was born and raised in a middle class, residential section of Brooklyn to well-assimilated, immigrant parents, attended the best public schools, and, *"gravitated" as he always wrote, toward the humanities teachers at Columbia College in the 1950s.* At some point in his life Steve took a break from school - I cannot recall exactly when, but probably in the late 60s or early 70s. He and some friends left New York and headed for San

Francisco, exploring the Southwest along the way. San Francisco was the home of the new literary and jazz scenes and it is where Steve developed an interest in the Beat writers and jazz performers - especially Kerouac and Chet Baker. Coincidentally, I was living in Berkeley at the time attending graduate classes, but we did not meet. Upon his return to the east Steve moved to the backwoods of Connecticut, built himself (out of hand-cut timber) a 'Phantom Hut' and, essentially, disappeared from the academic world. (The Phantom Hut is a tale written by Basho, a Japanese poet in 1690. It is a tale both of us admired.) But Steve never gave up being a scholar. He read voluminously, attend many cultural events and wrote a number of essays which were published in academic journals. Sometime later Steve 'walked his way back' to Columbia College and fulfilled his 'gravitation' by getting his Ph.D. in English in 1980. He taught English for thirty years at the Borough of Manhattan Community College.

One of the things Steve and I shared was being a child of 'Lefty' parents. In those days the children were often called 'Red Diaper Babies', at least by other Communists. Steve's father was active politically and travelled to Israel in the 1940s to participate in creating the independent nation of Israel.

[Of possible interest to readers of this book is Steve's new book titled *Against The Grain: Essays and Arguments (posthumously published in 2015.) It is a fine collection his favorite essays and available on Amazon.*]

Ted's Family Story

My parents were immigrants as well, but from Rumania. My father, Theodor (or Toadoa, as friends and relatives called him) received his formal education in Rumania, regarded himself a poet, a writer, and a journalist. In the early 1930s, he started a quarterly journal called *The Earth/Pamantul* formatted along the lines of Ezra Pound's 1920s journal *Blast,* Pamantul featured poems my father had written, translations of Lenin, Trotsky, etc., and contributions by fellow Communists, pundits, writers and poets. My father claimed on the masthead that *The Earth Pamantual* was "The Only Publication in the Roumanian and English Language on the Planet" and , in fact, it was. According to Douglas Wixson, in his book *Worker/Writer in America,* University of Illinois Press, *The Earth/Pamantul* attracted a number of worker/writers, such as: John Rogers, H.H. Lewis, Hugh Hanley (aka Emerson Price), J. Henry, George Weiss, Edward Potts, Lucia Trent, Jack Conroy and Upton Sinclair.

My mother, Octavia, was born in Seibu in 1907, a small cow town in Transylvania. She had very little formal education, and taught herself English after she arrived here in 1917. Like many immigrants who could not afford to pay for the passage of their children, Octavia's parents had left their ten year old daughter and twelve year-old son John with relatives in Europe. My mother worked as a chamber maid to support herself in Budapest. In the U.S., Octavia lived with her family in East Chicago, Indiana Harbor, Indiana (or Steel Town as I later called it). The main attractions of Indiana Harbor were Bethlehem Steel and Inland Steel, two huge factories that jutted out from Lake Michigan. I would guess that at least eighty percent of all the Rumanians worked in one of these two factories. My father had immigrated a few years before my mother and they met in Indiana Harbor, married, had two children, my older brother Oliver and me.

For the first seven to eight years of my life I lived in a completely Rumanian environment; I wore hand-stitched Rumanian style clothing, spoke Rumanian and basically thought everyone in the world was Rumanian.

Odd Facts: A meditation on Steve & me

   Some odd facts. Not only did Steve and I share many sensibilities
regarding our appreciation of, say, literature, art, history, philosophy, music,
movies, and alcoholic beverages, it now seems to me that we were sharing in
a common Destiny - if you believe in such mystical things. I don't know
what reasons Steve would have to explain his life-long dedication to
teaching. What I do know is that it gave him his greatest happiness in life.
(When it came to writing an essay, however, Steve knew he was embarking
on a spiritual/intellectual journey that could last months or years before he
thoroughly grasped its fulfillment.)

   Years later, when Steve returned to academia from his "Phantom Hut"
disappearance, he became a teacher and chose to teach English to 'marginal
students' precisely because he had earlier felt himself to have been just such
a student.

   My commitment to teaching began the day I was booted out of a High
School in Cicero, Ill. (in Al Capone's home town), at age 16. I soon took a
vow to become a teacher and rectify the ills that would beleaguer future H.S.
students. Like Steve, I, too, took a long, seven year break from any further
education. I spent most of my time reading Russian, French and American
novels, philosophy, history, Medieval theology, Marxist theology/theory,
listening to classical and jazz music and, of course, watching the art movies
pouring out of Europe. Also I hitchhiked across America and, with a friend,
hitched down to Mexico City for a month. I had a grand time.

   Eventually, I found my way to Los Angeles where my brother lived and
started working as a bus boy in a cafeteria on the UCLA campus. It was
really a small, wooden shack supported on stilts on a slight hill overlooking

I enjoyed the Rumanian festivities, especially the foot-stomping dances, the music of violins, accordions, trumpets, whistles and, of course, the food at picnics in the forest preserves outside of town. I wasn't allowed to wear long pants for many years.

When my father died after returning from the Soviet Union (where he marveled at the wonders of the Russian Revolution) I could no longer straddle his shoulders to watch union strikes against the steel mills nor could he make me laugh with his magic wand. My life had radically changed. Within a year or so after his death my mother married a Depression - era Welsh/Irish hobo, Lloyd, who had been riding the rails looking for work. As his train was passing through Indiana Harbor he jumped off to eat lunch in a restaurant where, by chance, my mother was waitressing, and, as my mother told me, it was love at first sight. Much later, I found it was not so much love at first sight as it was her need to get out of the house of her Seventh Day Adventist mother who gave her nothing but grief. Her husband's death had left Octavia in dire straits and we were forced to live with her parents. Her mother's strident religious way of life infuriated my atheistic mother. After winning a local beauty contest and becoming "Miss Romania of East Chicago" my mother's only wishes were to wear perfume, lipstick, sleek dresses and be a 'twenties' flapper, all of which my grandmother would not allow in her house. Lloyd, my new stepfather, was her ticket out.

Within months we were indeed out; first to LaGrange, Illinois and then to Berwyn, Illinois. The consequences for me were both dire and promising as I was rudely wrenched out of Romania and into America. But my journey out of Steel Town is a story best left for another time.

"The Corsican Brothers" (based on a novel by "Alexandre Dumas pére), starring Douglas Fairbanks Jr. and Ruth Warrick.

Essentially, *"The Corsican Brothers"* is a tale of twin brothers born as Siamese twins and separated at birth. One brother is immediately sent to live with a rural family while the other is sent to an urban center on the Isle of Corsica to ensure that they should never meet. As the children mature, each begins to experience events and feelings (including pain) which are not their own. Each is unable to determine why they suffer this vexing problem, but learn to live with this quirk as best they can. One day, quite by chance, they run into each other on this small Isle and the mystery eventually unfolds. The movie is delightful although the tale is impossibly silly.

However, several years after Steve and I met we too were mysteriously able to communicate somewhat in this fashion - though not quite with the precision or the frequency of the Corsican brothers - we did regard ourselves as non-identical Siamese separated twins. Hence the title of this book: *Memories of a Shared Friendship.*

Humble Beginnings

My mother wins the Miss Roumania Beauty Pageant in 1929

My Father [second from left] dancing. 1918

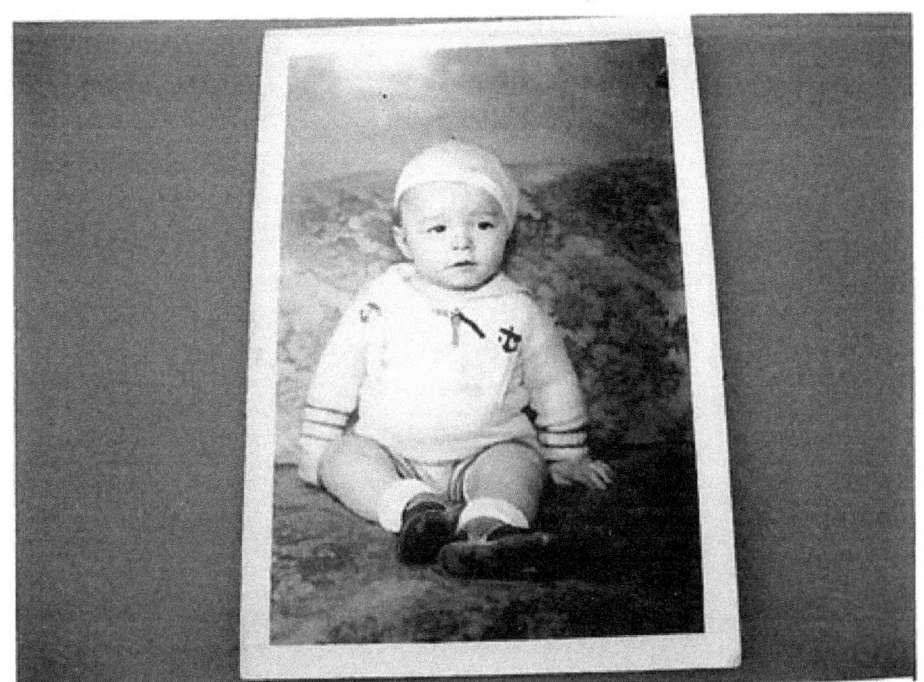

Me, as the youngest and proud member of the Industrial Workers of the World ; other wise known as: the Wobblies in 1938.

My brother Oliver and me while
living in Berwyn, Illinois

Picnicul dela 1" Iulie,
1934. cu sosirea Tov.
Teodor Sitea din
U.S.S.R.

The street where, as a child, I lived and played
in East Chicago/Indiana Harbour, Indiana

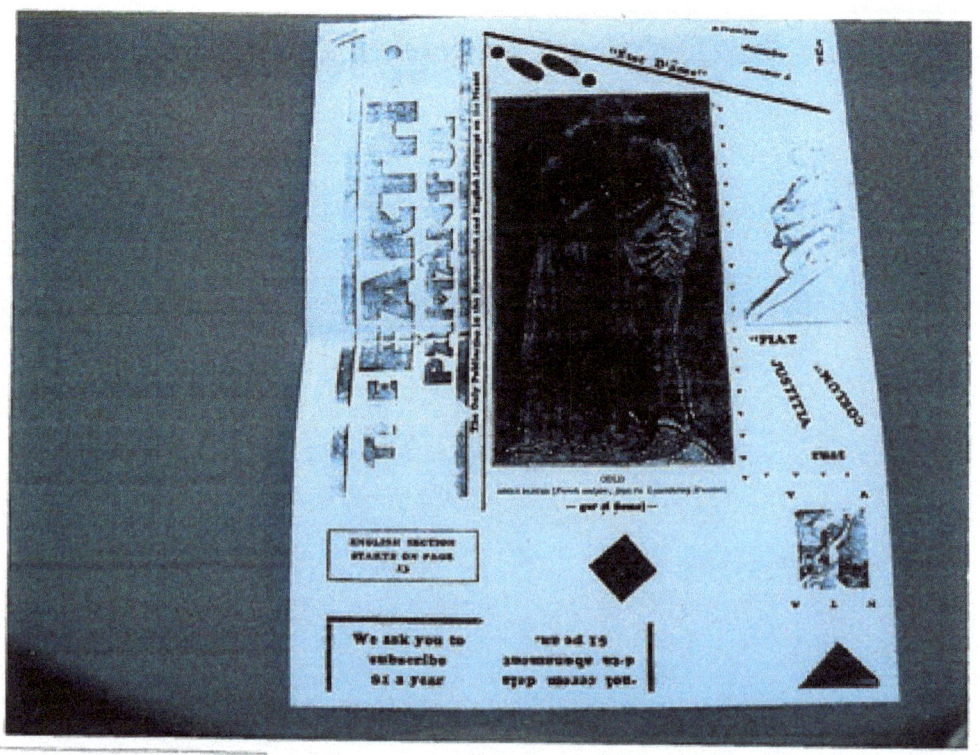

An edition of *The Earth Pamantul* in 1932.

My friend Stan and I after hitching from El Paso, Texas to Mexico City for a mon...

Alexander Vraciu, my uncle, after the "Marianas Turkey Shoot" in June 1944 and becoming an "ACE" pilot and my hero. (Photo in "Top Guns" by Joe Foss and Matthew Brennan; 1991)

Some of my students at Pacific H.S..

A student receiving good news about passing a college admission test.

This is the image of Steve his publisher placed on the dust jacket of his book: the scholar, glancing up from his work, head cocked after the manner of yearbook photographs, looking directly and intently at you. But it's Steve, and lurking at the corners of his mouth is that puckish pursed-lip grin, almost a blown kiss... Perhaps he is wondering, as he wrote in his inscription, "how the Elizabethan court masque could ever have entered the mind of a young man who had been born and raised in the heart of once-Russian-Jewish Brownsville and East New York."

Carol having fun as opera Diva Carmen in a LaScala production of Bizet's *Carmen*.
(In the spirit of Nadar.)

Steve's take on *The Man Who Would be King* in India. (Inspired by Nadar photos of Toulouse-Lautrec)

Letters: The Early Years

1987 - 1995

**1987
to
1990**

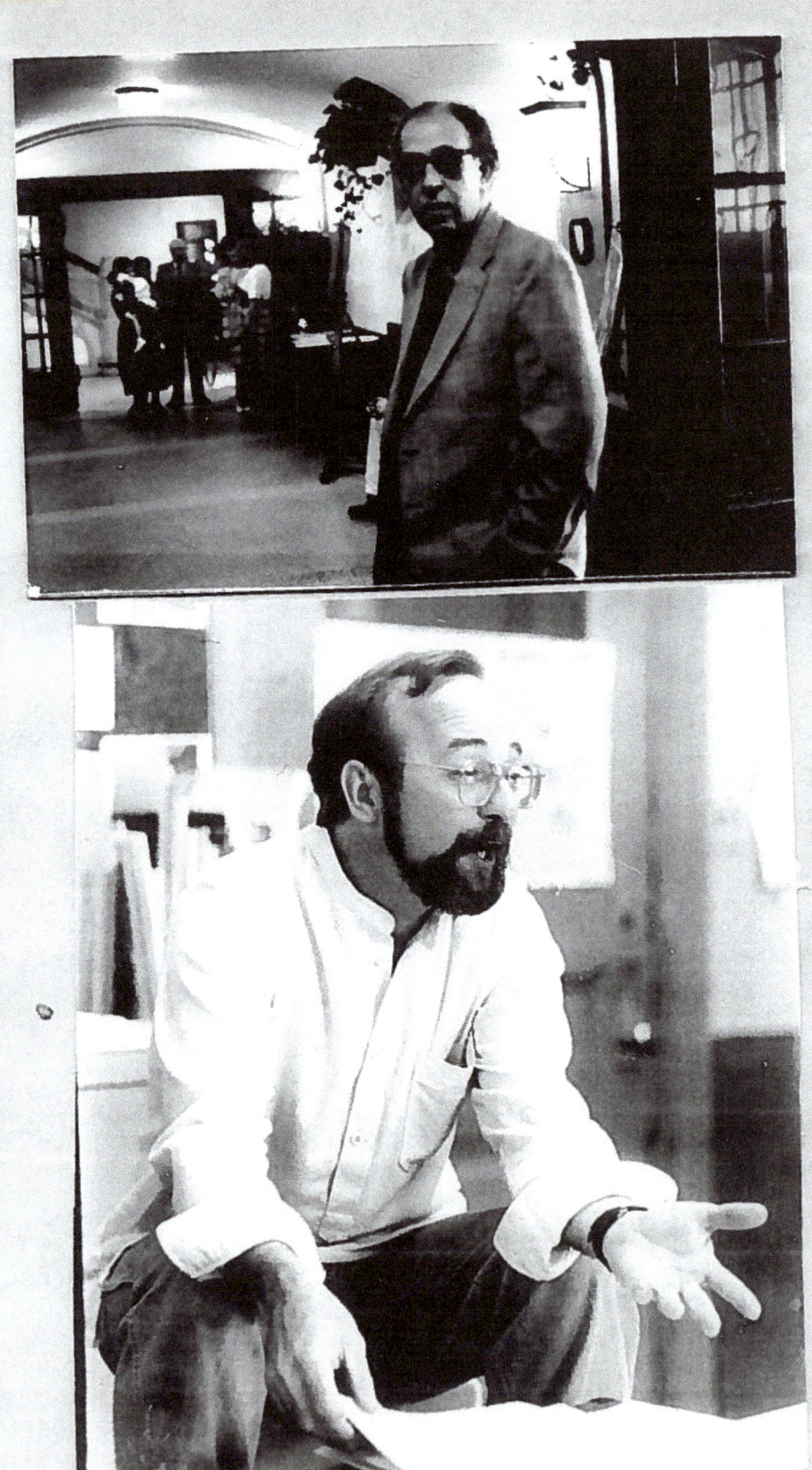

Dear Ted,

How nice! A literate literary letter in my mail. And on Spengler too, and much else besides. I don't know what to make of the Huizinga. I respect him too, but these capsule reviews are hardly ever good. Every time I read a historian who's summarizing different views the remarks seem to be squeezed into narrow / wrong limits. It's *very* hard to hit the nail on the head. Here's one I read the other day by John Constable, straight from the heart of romanticism, that expresses the whole sense of "historicism" from Goethe to Spengler, Croce, and Trevelyan: "A good thing never happens twice." That's ½ of the <u>Decline of the West</u> right there, and Herder too. The other half comes from Goethe, and Spengler says it over and over that <u>this</u> is the basis of his interpretations: "Everything transitory is only a symbol." That is to say, everything is unique and irrecoverable, and in its uniqueness there lies a symbol -- not a cause, not an idea leading toward a final goal -- but a symbol of a relationship, a feeling, an experience. Goethe again: "There are relationships everywhere, and relations are life." I still think that people object to Spengler because they don't have a compelling vision of their own.

The Campbell is nice. I like writing that has personal narrative in it -- something definite and actual.

I'm reading the libretto for <u>The Flying Dutchman</u> -- German/English. I know enough German/Yiddish to see how poor the translation is and how straightforward and symbolic the original is. There's the romantic gospel right there -- vivid, dramatic clarity of specific moments, which are symbolic at the same time.

Two sea captains meet on a rocky coast during the subsiding of a storm. One says: "Xxxxxxxxxx" "Can there be a more welcome son-in-law?" (thinking of the gold treasure in the Dutchman's ship). The other says: "Eternal oblivion, carry me away." Ditto for the women in the prosaic sea-captain's house. The maids are spinning and spinning out their fantasies of love. Senta, the daughter, spends all her time in dreamy contemplation ("träumerischen Anschauen" -- Goethe's word for the contemplation of symbols in events) of a portrait of a ghostly figure in black that is hanging on the wall, along with other paintings of seascapes. And as she tells her "normal" suitor Eric, "Xxxxxx "Are you afraid of a song, a picture?" It's all too wonderful.

Why all this reading of the Germans, I wonder? I've been doing it all year. I must be trying to learn something, for some reason.

Many thanks for the letter, and keep those Spengler reviews coming!

Steve

enlivens the shit-balls the world throws at us without remorse, namely, love of the gift of (our) life. That we keep sealed as though, were it to get out, it would contaminate the world, and because we mistakenly think we can better - objectively - understand the world without it, but mostly because it has been forsaken. (Perhaps I use "we" to loosely, but your <u>Ordeal At the Dentist's Office</u> - a magnificent 2 reeler - has stayed with me in very unexpected, important ways. Perhaps I see to much of me in it, or see it incorrectly. Excusa, excusa, excusa.)

Wordsworth once wrote that art takes its source from "emotion recollected in tranquillity"; that emotion (past experience) is contemplated until "by a species of reaction the tranquillity disappears, and an emotion, kindred to that which was before the subject of contemplation, is gradually produced and does actually exist in the mind", and these emotions are made into art (the representation of experience) by our capacity to trace in them, "truly though not ostentatiously, the primary laws of our nature." I stop, as it were, at the 'contemplation' of experience and seldom reach that 'species of reaction' which traces in them the laws of (my) nature. I feel forbidden to do so, condemned to tranquil contemplation not setting off fusion's of self and experience. In modern lingo, I am condemned to the objective rationalizing of my subjectivity. This is the 'missing' self I always complain about in my letters, in my writing in general. Experience cut from the flesh, dehydrated in the mind, then forgotten.

Once again I gaze at the row of faces lining my window ledge; Kafka, Tolstoy, Dostoyevsky, Proust, Flaubert, and Rimbaud. They have all been where I am and I hear their voices calling me over a great distance. Weil is there too, she with the burning eyes, trying to cup her hands round the flicker of light within me. I am in good company, but the gift of love remains in critical condition from its ancient, head-on collision with the world. (One has only to first look upon the pre-teen, beautiful Weil and the later twenty year old bespeckled woman of a hundred to witness the time-bomb of childhood experience. Talk about nuclear reactions when contemplating in tranquillity!) I want them to be my mother and father, but they are too old and tell me I must be my own.

In my childhood (to make this all strictly personal) I learned this lesson: in me, experiences go to waste. I bungle, misunderstand, botch, distort, corrupt, and, in general, degrade them. I always have the wrong ones as well, ones I shouldn't have, one's that have no 'objective correlative.' Learning this lesson I soon hated my experiences of things, nor did I want them. Indeed, I fought them, disavowed them, repudiated them, mocked them, pilloried them, and spit upon them. I wished no more than to be free of my experiences of the world. It got to the point where I couldn't stand being alive precisely because I was me. I then summarized my lesson: Who am I, after all, to experience wind, sand, and stars, let alone Tom, Dick, and Mary? These are sacred things best left unviolated by my experiencing them, better I teach myself to behold them as they are, wholly independent of me. Further, beholding the world in this state of awe will also place me in the unique position of being able to instruct others on the true nature of the world as it exists on the other side of human experience - something they are all selfishly ignorant of and totally oblivious to. In other words, I (as not me) would teach them a lesson or two! As a side benefit, if I succeeded in pointing toward the world which lies beyond experience, others will perhaps leave me alone and stop laughing. In short, I learned that though I was unworthy to experience the world I was a saint nonetheless - even one who could fly backwards if need be - two dreams dialectically sustaining each other in the tranquil ether of my mind. My childhood was a brief, syllogistic attempt to re-define self-abasement as self(but not me)-glorification. (I chose the worst interpretation of Christianity and Buddhism around though I was scarcely aware of either as doctrines at the time.) As Jack Lemmon said, as you often point out, there is no Ministry of Logic to look after one when one has been forsaken. Or, rather, as you also said, there is only logic, but a logic unmoored from life.

We are related to history as a shark is related to the ocean depths. History surrounds us just so, supporting and conditioning every move we make. Under and above us, in front and in back of us, we inhale it's currents through the gills of our minds and hearts. Though we can not escape it, we do guide our suspended destinies within it with purposeful cunning. And I kid you not, saints are quite cunning even though they live *sub specie aeternitatis*. They are like faceless Bufano sculptures of St. Francis raising an admonishing finger pointing nowhere in particular. They drift along the bottom unnoticed, rocking to and fro in ocean currents.

Would you believe I actually ran across a living historian who postscripts his latest book on things Medieval with:

> *In the late twentieth century, a truly large amount of new work - about 100 titles a year - continue to appear on medieval dissent. Predicting what new angles of vision the twenty-first century will produce would be rash, but the variety will point us gradually toward the truth, provided they include the following: continued search for new documents relative to dissent; a review of already well-known documents with an eye to seeing new implications for dissent; a use of new conceptual approaches to an understanding of dissent; a continued rootedness in the tradition of solid work already accomplished; an increased awareness of the multiplicity of lenses through which we seek to understand dissent and orthodoxy and the tension between them; a firm moral and loving commitment to the men and women of the*

7 ?

past whose lives and thoughts are as real and as
important as our own. (Jeffrey Burton Russell:
Dissent and Order in the Middle Ages: The Search for
Legitimate Authority.)

A thoughtful man!

Received your letter dated April, 97 today! Ah, a joy
and a pleasure. And, as you must already know, given Carol's
remark about my writing, I love her already! (Was that a
photo of her on the envelope? If so, it could have been
clearer! Or is the light-gathering strength of my eyes
diminishing?)

And while I am hot on the trail: your questions "Is it
just a matter of forgetting 3/4 of what you want to say, or,
like me when faced with something I want to write, that you
grow instantly fatigued? Some passivity that allows your
thoughts and impressions to slip away?" and comment, . .
."and grew immediately exhausted at having a desire," are
precise!! What you call "fatigue," however, I called
disassociating oneself from one's own experiences then
feeling bludgeoned by them. Long-winded. Experience taxes my
sense of worthlessness. Challenges my forsakeness which I am
loath to give up. Resistance, yes! But of a singular sort. An
Ur-resistance.

"(filled with five-ton Danielle model trucks, six
Allison 75mm field guns, half a ton of Clover nerve gas, a
dockload's worth of small caliber Lee machine guns, and steel
plating for six Janet Waterhouse heavy armored tanks, not to
mention a complete installation of a Stealth Mother-radar and
the history of western civilization)" - magnificent! And
everything around this parenthetical remark as well. "My
heart soars like an eagle," Chief Joseph once said. Well,
yours soars like that Strato-Cruiser you mention.

I agree, Talleyrand was right in a sense, but if the
world had not lost its sweetness it is doubtful if you and
Carol would be "nuzzling into each other before Reynaldo and
Armida and red-robed madonnas." Everything has its price.
But, a nuzzle is a different kind of sweetness, after all,
just a small sweetness as befits a democracy where it must be
spread very thin indeed (Talleyrand, I am sure, had plenty of
big ones).

You capture the essence of Paglia beautifully: "reveling
in her one-sided sixties persona," says it all. "Strength and
limitation," she has not the lethargy which plagues us, but
experiences the present through her past without remorse or
apology. We tend to imagine we live either sub specie
aeternitatis or in the future - looking down upon or glancing
backwards upon the present - not as racing to keep up with
it. But she is limited for she only goes back to the sixties
not the forties or thirties. She equates her intelligence
with her education and does not include her formation by
life. She begins as an adult. (Similar to the way Marx always
writes as though because he never had a childhood no one else

acts as a depressant.) Or, do we regard ourselves as unworthy of our own experiences and so, when we have one, especially a good and true one, we feel instantly burdened, as though we had stolen gold from the treasure chest of humanity and were staring at it on the kitchen table waiting for the cops to come?

The key word here is 'disassociation.' Do we somehow separate ourselves from our experience of the world: sense experience itself as rocks thrown at us from a vacant lot, as a heaving, suffocating bosom landing on or face, or from Cezanne himself flinging green and blue paint at us, rather than as an external wisp of a sensation hungrily feeding itself on our historical, psychological singularity and becoming strong, a contender among men? The dental assistant straddling you, like W.C. Fields straddling that poor woman, is the way I imagine we experience having an experience. Not that all our experiences need be felt so physically or violently, but we experience experience as invasive ℳ nonetheless, invasive of an inner sanctum that would otherwise be resting in eternal peace and harmony. It's not for example, that I felt I fashioned the experience of the nation as ill, but the illness of the nation itself which rudely pushed itself upon me, beating me up on its way in. If I experience my experiences in that manner it is to perpetuate my childhood fantasy of being bludgeoned by life, and I have no choice but to feel either called upon to be a weaponless crusader against the monstrous or an aesthete prostrated by the breath-taking - in the sense that all such experiences come with a tag which reads: you have nothing to do with how the world works and are powerless before it - thus I sink back into that depressing, fretful eternal peace and harmony waiting for the next experience to come slamming in - I have long given up being a crusader.

But, to deny the active role one plays in fashioning experience is to be like Mercury who refuses to deliver a message for Jupiter because he might put his skates on backwards causing the other gods to laugh at him. In my case, it is the refusal to be mortal on grounds of having been forsaken. It is not our experience of the world we experience, but (we imagine) the world experiencing itself, by itself, in us, that we imagine we feel. We do not understand our experiences as a mother or father would, we do not see in them the likeness of our loved off-spring yearning to be set free to mingle in the concourse of men, but tear at them as though we were imposter cousins being handed a will which excludes us, or clumsy oafs being handed a Ming vase coated with vasoline. We loose ourselves in our card-shark shuffle of reality.

It's us against the world! Throw at us what it will we "WILL TAKE IT LIKE A MAN!" But we can do this only because we have given up being in it - we are not of this world, but of another, our own, which we live in far away. We do not yet comprehend the second half of Goethe's sentence, namely; ". . .by means of the world within me." Which I take to mean by means of that which predates, conditions, shapes, molds, and

Dear Steve

Received your last two letters with glee. Oh, how I loved "He died in the gutter, admired"! That says it all. And yes, what does time matter in letter writing? Ours are of a piece - in one way or another! Any word, at any time - not to mention a flirtatious smile or a dried tea-bag - leads right into our concerns. Valery once said: ..."such is the definition of the self. It can never be lost"...

Speaking of 'admiration', it is precisely your 'letting off steam', your refusal to always be a servant without right of speech (in a world that would, it seems, fall apart without them), your refusal to "hop to it, to jump, to sidestep", that stuns me. I seem able to enter the world only through the back-door and am unable to stop jumping, hopping, and sidestepping.

The weariness you speak of is, I believe, anger. But the anger of a servant (speaking of servants) disappointed in his masters behavior (i.e., 'Aieee', you seem to say, 'again they did not notice me after I brought in all the food, set the table, and poured the wine!) Your recourse is to quietly wander back into the kitchen - somewhat disgruntled - to wait until they come to their senses, or call to include you in the festivities. When you are in the kitchen, and can no longer "tell if, in this clinging to whatever sense of self I have,...I am developing or thwarting myself", you return to helplessness (mother), and a recognition of reality ('others' are either "stupid, nuts, or full of shit". Yet, you are also able to recoup, to set aside mother, reality, and come out of the kitchen ranting: 'Fuck momma, fuck reality - there is a self at stake here.' Wonderful!

A. Bloom speaks of political behavior as the essence of man; the only arena in which man expresses his existential freedom in the face of necessity and reality. It is only after man has built his civilizations, and, by personal extension I add the details of his civilization: his art, his music, his ordinary letters, his allowing himself "to see and feel a moment of crisis", his saying, "we'll do this or that today", etc., that psychologists, historians, anthropologists, etc., can rush in to explain him (as though, by so doing, they explain reality). But none of the disciplines can reduce him to their determining explanations, for the true politician (read: human) deals with experience in the raw, not musings over the acts of others. Explanations are always ex post facto, and less than the Act. For Bloom, there is no room on the pinnacles of freedom for critics! Nor for anger. Only individual humans clashing with reality. Below the pinnacles however, in the coliseum of Brooklyn, where there are few creators of civilization or its details, and everybody sees themselves as free from experience, or, as you say, see themselves in a world where "no one is in charge", is where we, you and I, live. Down here, few want self-proclaimed adventurers coming back from the zoo in Dresden telling of their skirmishes with the Beast. Most are in "paradise", farting under strain of their spectator pleasures.(Either "stupid, nuts, or full of shit.)

(So why, when D. Thomas shouts at the dinner-table: "Man, be my metaphor!", do I fall back into the kitchen, so as not to be included?)

Ah, Sonya - she too is one angry chick! You, having refused to be her master, but a servant/supplicant in search of favors acceptable to a Queen, and she the mother-degraded, tormented chimmney-sweep Cinderella from Portland. From gunny-sack to silver-threaded gowns. Pointing to the Knight who just served her tea (which she must pretend to dislike) she cries: "Off with his head!", and the confused Knight, thinking perhaps it should have been gold threads, raises the hair from his neck to give the blade a clean swipe. How glad I was to hear that you drew your sword - not for her sake, but for yours. Once again you prove - to me - that you can summon yourself to battle on a real battlefield, not merely to shadow-boxing in the servants quarters.

What I don't understand, is how you can unrobe, put on dress-jacket, mingle with the best, yet keep returning to the kitchen. I do not own a dress-jacket. You say I see the "oppresive aspect of others and therefore stay away from them." Murderous, might be more apt.

While I simply revolve in mid-air, you seem to revolve around a single, existential situation, embodied, this time, in the Eliot-Nancy affair. For me this affair all hangs - where else - on that "cup of coffee". For me, Ghengis Khan could not have been more defiant or assertive than you in asking Nancy for that "cup of coffee". A true servant - like myself - would have rushed to bring it to her. Over-turning my desk in haste to meet her emergency, I would have fled the room in desperate search for that "cup of coffee". But you, grasping her by the throat, demanded she bring it to you. And as a good servant, she did. Imperially, you dash it to the ground.(Had she been there, her eyes would have flashed, her vagina would have erupted, and she would have been yours. But she never is, or never as you would want her to be. Unable, as is Don Giovanni able to command his prey to recognize his superiority before taking them, - indeed, uses that recognition as his seduction - you are yet not content with servants acquiesing in what they see as needs equal to their own, i.e., the needs of the ignored. Thus, unable to release the command of a master, to let them know just who who are, you find youself ignored and in ex post facto rage - a rage that forfeits its object to find its expression. It is moments like these however, which spell the difference between us: you at least have a self to which you can repair.

But somehow, the scene is determined. Even the imperial gesture. It is one you live over time and time again. Each time experiencing the agony of 'being ignored', and then the recapturing of self in isolation. Then the rage. This time at Eliot. Charles Atlas on the Beach. Yet, the ex post facto anger even if expressed directly to him, never seems to compensate for his having ignored you in the first place. Or even to prevent him from doing it again. How does he sense 'the right' to do so? Would he do if it were Hercules talking to Nancy? Somehow you wait for the Eliots of the world to come in? You leave the bold unbolted? Or does Eliot think he knows that you won't fight for Nancy? Does Eliot think he knows that you are not a human building your reality, piece by piece, but merely a spectator serving in a reality which has been built by others - as he?

I disarm my presence wherever I am. I struggle to be ignored by others. It is precisely being recognized by others that upsets me - I do not know what they are recognizing, and am at instant loss to either explain myself or to hang on to it. I rush to disown whatever it is they recognize, and to re-claim my non-presence. It is a disappearing enterprise in which, in my stupidity, I think I have succeeded. You however, expect to be not ignored (a negative) - thus, you are taken by surprise, never quite knowing who will or when. (A version of, "I have always relied on the kindness of strangers." Only here the pivot word would be 'respect'.) You place yourself in their hands. But recognition is something that must be commanded, it is never given. The command must be ever present and clear, for most think of others as they think of themselves - disposable dishrags to be used by who ever needs them. They are formless, bleeding pulps of need, forever thinking that the world is (or should be) a charitable organization. They never expect Don Giovanni to walk in (or even the likes of you and me, for that matter).

I can not tell you how weary, disappointed, and frustrated I am in being simply uninterested in anything other than trying to explain myself to myself. If your epitaph is "Died in the gutter, admired", mine would be "Died talking about himself - elliptically". It is truly a sickness. I don't know what it is with me. I wouldn't mind if I could occasionaly realize a feeling, but to always be trying to explain why I can not is pathetic. I am pure interior. A self-negating proposition. The way I emotionally conceive myself - my being-in-the-world, to speak existentially - doesn't make any logical or human sense. I can talk about myself all I want, but all I will accomplish - all that I have accomplished - is to say what it is not, never, in fact, being able to prove that it even exists. Indeed, by never finding a positive attribute, I always come closer to proving that it doesn't. A Cheshire Cat in the flesh - or rather, not the flesh.

Clinically, I suppose, I suffer something like total, perpetual amnesia. Musil wrote of a man without qualities. I write as a man without the capacity of memory. An eternal nomad seeking an identity, but never able to remember where he came from, where he just was, or what he just wanted to do. Everyone and everything is always strange and new to me, no matter how often I have been in its presence. Every instant of my life I probe everything with my robot-like senses as an unwanted intruder never seen before. There is no feeling here, just

desperate, hurried gropings to orient myself to the backdrop of
things and presences before the nomad in me is questioned. Yet,
though a nomad, I do not move. I understand myself as standing
at the center of a revolving stage upon which the world turns,
presenting me with different scenes. As a man without memory, I
can want nothing, can not desire to go anywhere, can not
express hope, nor purposefully move even my own hands. The
world swells up before me as a monstrous stage from whose
ceiling drop the puppet strings which painfully jerk me about.
My robot-like senses, seeing all and hearing all, are unable to
guide my actions. My movements are random. Just as I can not
cause anything, I can not prevent anything, though it might be
a fist flying into my face. I pull my disappearing act, and
don't feel a thing.
    I too saw "Between Two Worlds" on TV. A long time ago.
Although I had forgotten it, your quoting Garfield's line,
"Here lies"... brought Garfield's smirking face vividly back to
mind. Somehow I remembered that line. It stuck in me. So too
did your mentioning of the "fog" - I remember a dreary,
one-room ship, many close-up's of intense faces, and no one
being able to walk more than twenty feet at a time without
being enveloped in fog. "No Exit".
    America is "stupid" now. No one talks except in skewered
philosophies: 'objectivity doesn't exist', 'words have no
literal meaning', 'God denies humanity, Allah makes it whole',
'honor the soldiers, but hate the war', 'blacks are superior,
but whites are racist', 'loving women is an act of violence',
'good people are the ones who hate bad people', 'be weak for
the oppressed are strong', etc... Even my relatively educated
(white) co-workers say things as "Aborigines are smarter than
any white", or "The one good thing about 'Son of the Morning
Star', is that it shows how evil America is". Unless we are
approaching Armageddon however, this feeble attempt at
patricide will pass, two years at most. It will strangle
itself while threating world destruction. Exit to heaven.
    Saw "Coney Island" tonight on PBS. America when it was
America! Can you imagine bringing in primitive people from the
Phillippines, Africa, plus an entire Eskimo village and putting
them on display in 'natural habitat' settings? Manufacturing
an Alpine village, made to scale, housing 300 midgets? Running
450 movies at a time. Staging the eruption of Pompeii and
burluesques. And then executing an elephant. And charging
admission fees? All this while broad-grinned immigrants from
around the world - rich and poor - dropped from parchutes and
danced together on the shores of the Atlantic? A country like
no other: warm, big, generous yet cruel, pitiless, degrading. A
huge instinct in love with itself. Then reality (boredom) set
in. Formless, not yet civilized, boredom plays havoc with our
instinct. We have not yet realized what we want our nation to
make us. Civilized or instinctual? Coney Island is only of the
mind. But we have not yet formed our instinct into nation. Or
have we? Are we a people of disciplined - not civilized -
instinct? Animals with a constitution? (Is this what Hobbes was
talking about?) If so, then it is as animals that we must wrest

our selfs from nature, in an eternal Renaissance of the self in combat with reality. The political man of Bloom. The artist struggling with his art, the letter writer with his letters, the ignored with the bold, the memoryless with ... the past?

To feel the above as flowing out of my childhood, out of remembered, felt experience - as expression - would be, for me, my passport into humanity.

Thank you for the Baker, the "New York" article, and, of course your letters! Did you receive my little gift? I shall see Len on Friday, and give him your 'blessing'.

Yes, please do try to make it out! I can not tell you how much our fortuitous intersecting on the streets of Brooklyn has meant to me! The desert is merely a scrim placed between me and the plot there begun.

Love
V

Note: What is David's Apt. #? And two, the windshield repair is $40.00 bucks - do you believe it?

Dear Stan

Spiritual exhaustion - the Destiny of the West.
Ossification and entropy after 400 years of vigor and growth.
Surrounded by Gothic cathedrals luminous with stained glass,
towering symphonies wafting out of apt.windows, wonderous
poems visible at the flick of a finger, recorded deeds of
valor bursting from library shelves, and magnificient art
tearing our eyes with their beauty, we are also surrounded by
the graves of those who created them. We walk concrete
streets, hands in pockets, witnessing rampant confusion,
unable to comprehend ourselves.. Our souls are frozen in the
Arctic air of civilization. The Big Chill has set in. What
is Spengler's advise? Become engineers. Build dams spanning
a continent, cyclotrons encircling the Atlantic, space-nets
that will harvest the energy of the solar system - but do not
paint a painting, write a novel, or ask fifty bald men to
toot your new tune - they only know honky-tonk.

In the 1880s Ambrose Bierce ("Bitter Bierce," they
called him back then), defined Birth as: *The first and direst
of all disasters. As to the nature of it there appears to be
no uniformity. Castor and Pollux were born from the egg.
Pallas came out of a skull. Galatea was once a block of
stone. Peresilis, who wrote in the tenth century, avers that
he grew up out of the ground where a priest had spilled holy
water. It is known that Arimaxus was derived from a hole in
the earth, made by a stroke of lightening. Leucomedon was
the son of a cavern in Mount Aetna, and I have myself seen a
man come out of a wine cellar. (The Devil's Dictionary)* Could
Bierce and Spengler be talking about the same thing, but from
different angles? If so, Bierce's response was to slink out
of the wine cellar to primitive Mexico, and get shot - no
dams, cyclotrons, or space-nets for him! ▬▬▬......

According to Osborne Russell, mountain-man and trapper
in the 1830s, the Crow Indians were warriors who conquered
their land and lived from its game. But once the enemies are
no more and the game is gone, what then would their chiefs
recommend they do? Who would be the Spengler among them?
What would he say? Put on a suit and go to work? Or, drink
fire-water and go crazy?

Speaking of Bierce, did you know that somewhere between
1881 and 1906 (probably closer to 1881) Bierce spoke of the
"Afro-American" as though the phrase were in the common
parlance of the day? e.g.: *Razor:, n. An instrument used by
the Caucasian to enhance his beauty, by the Mongolian to make*

a guy out of himself, and by the Afro American to affirm his worth ? (Or, for that matter, that in 1917 the 42nd Division of the American Expeditionary Forces was widely known as the "Rainbow Division" because of its multi-ethnic composition?) Who needs multifuckyouism or Jessie Jackson? (And I love Bierce's definition of Self-esteem: *An erroneous appraisement* - that definition should be plastered over all public school entrances. As well as his definition of Selfish: *Devoid of consideration for the selfishness of others.* One last gem, Righteousness: *A sturdy virtue that was once found among the Pantidoodles inhabiting the lower part of the peninsula of Oque. Some feeble attempts were made by returned missionaries to introduce it into several European countries, but it appears to have been imperfectly expounded. An example of this faulty exposition is found in the only extant sermon of the pious Bishop Rowley, a characteristic passage from which is here given: Now righteousness consisteth not merely in a holy state of mind, nor yet in performance of religious rites and obedience to the letter of the law. It is not enough that one be pious and just: one must see to it that others are in the same state; and to this end compulsion is a proper means. Forasmuch as my injustice may work ill to another, so by his injustice may evil be wrought upon still another, the which it is manifestly my duty to estop as to forestall mine own tort. Wherefore if I would be righteous I am bound to restrain my neighbor, by force if needful, in all those injurious enterprises from which, through a better disposition and by help of Heaven, I do myself refrain.* Instead of showing smokers hanging out of high-rise office buildings taking a quick drag, the cover of the New Yorker should have placed this quote under a photo of a congressional hearing on public smoking. Russell Baker did a good job on this issue in today's (6/3) paper, though)

Now, to return to the impossibility of art - i.e., me. I am an ignoramus! Not only am I ill read, I still write to ghosts; "the outward and visible sign of an inward fear," i.e., to childish projections onto the world. I write to put to rest the inner demons which torment me - and pretend I am sending missiles into the real world. I am truly full of sound and fury signifying nothing. A tempest in a closed tea-pot. One day, long ago, I remember Jim taunting me, calling me a "mommy's boy". Furious, I lashed out at him, but he put his hand against my forehead, keeping my fists from hitting him, laughing the entire time. Classic, no? His friends, sitting on the front porch steps, were amused - I was mortified. I am still fighting this battle. Each paragraph I write is but a small, futile fist flying through the air, bringing embarrassment to me. Nor do I grasp the fact that I am no longer in front of 3232 Wisconsin Ave. fighting Jim. I cannot conceive of leading a different life, of doing something else. I am stuck there as Bill Murray in the movie *Groundhog Day* was stuck in Punxsutawney, Penn., only it is I that remain the same while the world dances through normal time. Those who know me can set traps for me, for they know I am doomed to walk to 3232 Wisconsin Ave., raise my fists, and begin to fight every day at "cinco de la tarde" (Jim doesn't even to be there; it can be Joe, Pete, or Moe. It doesn't really matter, since I can't see them through my tears.). Writing under these conditions is not only unfruitful, it is unbearable. How many variations on a single, convulsive act can one invent ("thousands apparently," you say warily)? I can't break the spell. In other words, it will take me a long time to chart the subtleties of Spengler, Gaugin, and Stephen King - I have yet to find my way out of my dream of battle on Wisconsin Ave..

C-Span panned (with a camera) the German cemetery at Normandy. Black, Druidic crosses carved out of pitted lava-rock. Massive in proportion, yet only four feet high. Fields of them. Overlooking them all stands a huge cross made of the same material, but under whose outstretched arms stand two tall, gaunt figures as stern and unforgiving as Brunhilde and Wotan. It is the burial ground for ancient, mythic barbarian warriors whose evil ferocity matched the evil of monsters sent from Hell. It gives no indication of who won the battle. Indeed, it imples the battle is eternal and must be fought again. Hell will be back and the dead shall rise. It is errie, cold, magnificient, tragic, mournful, victorious, and malevolent at each beat of the heart. The American cemetery is trim, and seemingly tended by meticulous monks. Rows upon rows of polished, white marble crosses almost translucent with purity; the burial ground of devout knights early defeated in their innocent search for the Grail. The promise of ultimate, eternal and redemptive victory hangs in the air. The entire history of the war is here, clear as a bell. (My amateurish tendency to favor alliteration would make Flaubert vomit.)

These cemeteries are symbolized battle-dreams. The great dreams of nations formed in sculptured stone. Thus, it is not so much my battle-dream which holds me back from reality - we all, after all, must have dreams. It's the fact that I hate my dream.and want to crawl into someone else's. Some have the motto "I gotta be be," others, "I don't want to be me." One would think I am a holocaust survivor who couldn't remember the holocaust: I seem to myself to have arrived in the world defeated and born with the "mile long stare." I do not expect more.

When I do expect more, than a nervous lethargy sets in, and I don't know what to do with myself. My thinking becomes frothy, bubbly, and flits around my brain like lightening. Write without anger, cynicism, irony, sarcasm? Without someone taunting me to fling my fists? How is such a thing possible? Write what I feel? How absurd! Why, I don't know what to write then! No, set before me my protean opponent, the evil demon who scoffs at me, laughs at me, and jeers me. The opponent who will always defeat me - then, then I shall write into the wee hours of the night, lighting each page from the burning fire of the last, and sink into exhaustion when dawn breaks, with nothing. That is what I expect! To meet my nemesis at every turn in the laybryinth. (I am my own mortification. Recordare, Jesu pie. I summon demons to life with each word I write. Sanctus Sancti. Each night they leap from the page and devour me. Resurectum infinitum & Mysticum hocus-pocus. Consorting with demons. Jubilata Morte. I write to be devoured. Requiem Humiliumdolores. Ave Maria. Amen.{ I hear Berlioz in the background: Ahhh-men, Ah, Ah, Ah, Ah, Amen, Ah, Ah, Ah, Ah, Amen, etc..The howling handshake on the outer fringes of hell, and then the ride through thundering clouds, straight into perdition. In my case, into a blank piece of paper!}.)

Never underestimate the day-dreams of children. They are Time Machines, and children who have them are the Lords of Time, determining its flow and on what experience to stop it. It is all a trick, a magician's illusion, of course, which tricks only them.

Bierce on 'emancipation': *A bondsman's change from the tyranny of another to the despotism of himself*. From the tyranny of Reality into the clutches of one's own mind!. Now you know why not all become the builders of bridges, areoplanes, and space-nets - they prefer mental constructions and punching someone else's time-clock (it's their way of making sure they enter Reality everyday at precisely 8 o'clock).

Self-expression - what is that? A luxury of the rich? A past-time of amoral hedonists? Why, I do not even turn on the air-conditioning in my own home when the temperature reaches 106º in order to replicate the atmosphere of my childhood when such conviences did not exist for the poor. Someone must shake me first, to wake me from my wide-awake slumber. Then I wander to the switch, a pauper feeling the arrogance of a Prince, i.e., not myself. I write for the same reason - to replicate the struggles of childhood. Who has emotions to squander on new experiences? Riches enough to plan the future? The few morsels handed out to one in the past should be enough to last lifetime! Crumbs will allow one to survive! A penny not spend you can keep forever. And no one will think you are putting on airs. Let artists expressive themselves away, I will remain in the basement, with drawn curtains, hammering my penny in to forms no one dreamt possible.

In describing the original Buffalo Bill Museum in Cody, Wyoming, Peter Hassrick, present Director of the Buffalo Bill Historical Center, writes: *Once, seven or eight generations ago, when practically all of America was a frontier, a fledgling museum in the burgeoning cultural center of Philadelphia fashioned a wonderfully ordered view of the world for its visitors. The galleries were referred to collectively as Peale's Museum . . .What Mr. Peale's museum provided fir its bewildered through eager audiences was not a finite view of the universe, but rather a broad picture of the manifold facets of human interest in the order of the world. Combining the fields of art and history and science, the museum charmed, educated, and enriched native and foreign*

*visitors through a potpourri of Americana. The museums
guests were invitd to see and enjoy not an art exhibition nor
a history lesson nor a science demonstration but rather a
union of these forums, each sharing in equal measure with the
other to provide a window on to the world and to reveal the
essence of the developing American experience. The
propensity for such eclectic acquisitions has found less
favor with recent generations of museums professionals. . . .
Rarely these days, . . . are art, material culture, and
literature joined equally in celebration of history. As
disciplines they have kept their distances, presumably for
the sake of maintaining the integrity of each. Yet, common
ground for the union of these three forces was laid in the
American experience in 1803, shortly after Peale founded his
museum, when Lewis and Clark bridged the Mississippi and
confronted the Far West.*

The US of A, of course, is dotted with museums of this
nature, and every major museum in the Far West has at least
one room set aside in honor of the material past (though they
are not quite the same thing since these rooms exclude
"art"), but isn't there something magical about the way
Hassrick describes Mr. Peale's museum (which Buffalo Bill's
museum is in imitation of)?. By assembling all of its
paintings, pencil stetches, farm implements, pots and pans,
nails, wheels, guns, baskets, blankets, signs; i.e.,all the
tools of life people used, these museums recreate the vision,
the order, which people of the past expressed in the world.
In this attempt, they are far more ambitious than say, the
Whitney or MOMA which maintain "professional distances" from
life. When a Charlie Russell (the "cowboy artist") is placed
between a well curved sythe and a photo of three upright
coffins containing dead bandits then people can understand
it; why it was fashioned, and from whence it came: humans,
under certain conditions, figuring out life. (I can imagine
a museum curator, 100 years from now scouring junk shops for
pieces to put in such a museum of the late 20th century and
running across a twisted, dark something that he can't make
out. No one he asks seems to remember what it was used for.
He returns it to the junk shop - but that was the last
remaining expression of my soul!)

One of things about me is that I can gab. It seems I
find the least thing fascinating, pregant with meaning, then
can't wait to prattle on about it. Of course, everything
tumbles into the funnel that I am - like the medieval devil
devouring everything in sight while sitting on the toliet.
To paraphrse Churchill, I am a cliche wrapped in the words of
others.

Do you realize I can stand nothing I do? Everything is
unbearable. I do not like any pen I buy, and don't
understand why I didn't buy the one next to it - it would
have been so much better. I don't like the way I leave books
lying around - either they are the wrong books, or they are
not scatterd the way scattered books should be scattered, or
they should be neatly stacked and not scattered at all. I

don't like the way my fingers move across the keyboard -
others move theirs so much better, more efficiently. I don't
like the way I look at paintings - I should have looked
closer, stood farther back, made notes. I don't like the way
I leave a tip on a resturant table - it should not be so
prominent, nor placed under the wet water glass, it should
have been larger, no, smaller. I don't like the last
sentence I wrote - it should have been more concise,
impressionistic, no, brutal. Why did I buy <u>that</u> pair of
shoes, black would have been better. Why am I interested in
this or that, there are so many other, more interesting
things to be be interested in. Why did I go here, rather
than there, there is so much better. Why am I eating this,
when I could be eating that?   It seems I always make the
wrong decision, conscious of its wrongness even while doing
whatever it is I am doing. But, if I change my mind, that
too will be the wrong thing to do. I should have been
consistent. The brown shoes whould have been better, why did
I change to black? Oh, how stupid! My solution - I rush
through everything, knowing I will dislike whatever I do.
But even that thought I don't like, so I rush through that
one as well. Think, think, think that last thought. Think
until you've thought yourself to death. Tell Saint Peter at
the Golden Gate he's just got to wait till I have that last
stinking thought. And never do anything you want to do!
(Ray Milland had this down pretty well in THE LOST WEEKEND.
Like him, I gussy-up a sordid fixation.)
     The last thought about Phoenix, the intellect, and
Nietzsche: Patrick Hamilton - who ever he was was - said
sometime ago that "there is no region on the globe, not
excepting the Italian peninsula, that can show such grand
effects of light and shade, such gorgeousness of coloring, or
such magnificent sun-bathed landscapes." (In *American
Nicknames*, G.E. Scankle, H.W.Wilson, Co., 1937,) So much for
the Mediterranean! Nietzche and his intellect would have
loved it here! Bare-chested, in shorts and tongs, with that
moustache, he would have been a knock out at the pool!
     In reading my letters you are essentially watching me
pick at an infected boil. This time a little pus squirted
out - perhaps next time you can witness me remove even more
encrustation. Oh, Joy! Right?
     Do you think I will ever face the fact that I am me:
husband, father of Ezra and Joshua, career teacher, son of
Dorothy and Theodor, climber of trees, cut-up of the streets,
ditcher of school, thief and coward of the block, righteous
prig, and vagabond of America (and Mexico) - all those things
I forget - rather than living the life of an unborn, Ill-wind
from Berwyn, the life of The Swirling Monad from Hell? Oh,
self, where is thy sting?
     Is there truly nothing in the world that interests me
other than myself? Is my sentence (judiciously and
literally) to make myself as interesting as possible so as
not to bore either myself or my listeners, readers, etc.,...

Do I offer only panoramic vistas of my nose? Cinemascopes of my eyeballs? Is that the job of a human? Or a lunatic? (out of the corner of my eye, I caught a PBS special of a young movie maker (black) who got funded to do a film about his rural, southern family. The first ten minutes he is complaining about his equipment and photographing himself in turmoil - all the while talking about how important his family is to him. At least I am not that stupid. But, then again, I am not funded my anybody. This show was preceded by another in which the narrator, sounding like Rosenblatt [can you imagine someone sounding like Rosenblatt for an hour!], was recommending that America give up "these mysterious things called borders" so immigrants wouldn't be found illegal when they emerged on the US of A. side of the sewer running under the Rio Grande. And he, I bet, considers himself educated and a "good citizen". When the world turns to dreck right before your eyes, on the tube, perhaps the self is all that's worth picking apart. {Have you ever noticed that 'narrators' on TV, whether it be 20/20/. PrimeTime, or PBS, never say phrases like: "It seems to me," "I may be wrong,"a radically different way of seeing this," but always embed "contrary views" into the narrative flow (usually with a clipped interview), as though their narration is beyond question and incorporates all possible "contrary views"? It's an amazing sleight of hand, and explains why one always leaves the TV feeling as though one has learned nothing - like the hunger following a chinese dinner - empty and drained, that is, nothing has been presented objectively, in an educational context, i.e., through the legitmate, objective comparison of different texts or points-of-view.)

Oh, well, the world remains hovering about me like a nightmare that I want to crash into.. Meantimes, I sit in my room content fighting imaginary demons as though it all meant something. I suppose I love feeling small, stupid and inconsequential - its my idea of freedom (and won't get me in trouble!). Who else but a capitalist would smile down on such unacknowledged luxury? Where else but in America? Well,   the gulag is another possibility.

Had it not been for that first fight in Berwyn, Charlie, I coulda been a contender!

ps, I include a copy of another, zany, letter I sent off to one of my enemies of sanity.

Dear Prof. J. Gray Sweeney

   I purchased your book *Masterpieces of Western American Art* remaindered at $3.99. Normally, I buy art books just for the illustrations, but when I inadvertently noticed that you spelled the author Owen Wister's name "Owen Whister", not once but several times (and in the index!), I knew something was dreadfully wrong. And sure enough, I was right.

   It all became clear to me when I then also noticed that the historians you mention as the source of your views on art history were none other than those "imagist historians" which Frederick E. Hoxie long-ago branded as 'historians of hate,' namely, Roy Harvey Pearce, Richard Sloktin, Reginald Horsman, Robert Berkhofer, and Brian Dippie. You picked up some bad habits from these historians, i.e., the habits of not paying attention to facts and a marxist aesthetics.. (By the way, Pearce's seminal *The Savages of America* [1953] one should not typify as "recent".)

   I don't know how many times you inarticulately (and pompously) use the words "romantic," idealistic," "mythic," and "nostalgic," (it probably numbers in the hundreds), to describe the paintings in your book, but after a while one catches on.. They are not used to convey your feelings about the paintings, but as tools of moral propaganda, i.e., as ways of referring to the supposed glosses you maintain western artists put on their paintings to justify American rapacity, greed, imperialism, and racism. In brief, your major "superstructure aesthetic" point is that all but the most contemporary western artists (after all, you do not want to offend their living relatives and friends), were liars, or worse, dupes of land-grabbing, profiteering capitalist. You learned from the teachers of hate very well. (Too bad you never absorbed Nietzsche on art - but he is probably over your head - not to mention, heart. I suggest you read Francis Paul Prucha, William McNeil, Page Smith, Paul Johnson, and Oswald Spengler before you pick-up another history pen - for you obviously have little historical awareness of Romanticism and Idealism as historical forces. Baudelaire may be of some help to you here, as well as Blaise Cendrars. Delacoix or Constable I think would overwhelm you.)

   If you are unhappy with the historic American character, his culture, technology, and religions, and feel morally comfortable in degrading her artists, I suggest you buy a very long, black whip and begin to lash yourself for you are, you know, a product of that history, consuming her trees, ink, and printing arts and technologies indistinguishably from those who were convinced of the rightness of Manifest Destiny (and you probably make more money off it than all of them put together!).. Indeed, since it is obvious that you hate everything you naturally are - being naturally "white" and rapacious and all - why don't you just keep your self-hatred to yourself, eat bread and water, and let the paintings speak for themselves. Which, by the way, is what art historians are supposed to allow art to do. How you ever got the jobs you did is beyond me - not really, for your scholarship and art appreciation is abysmal and institutionally fitting..

The old Soviet Union would have loved you. Lenin would probably would have placed your censorious body between every brush and canvas in Russia, telling you to send him the cleaning bills. You should be on a soap-box preaching the evils of racism and civilization - for free! (The tomatoes that Remington, Moran, Stanley, Bierstadt, Russell, and Wimar would throw at you, however, you would have to have cleaned off your clothes at your own expense - capitalism is nasty to do-gooders that way)

Dr. Hieliopolitan
10817 Sarabande Circle
Sun City, AZ, 85351

steve —

    Unlike in N.Y., where the air is thick, oppressive, dirty and makes its presence known between objects — if only as a carrier of noise — the air here is thin, almost non-existent. Except for an occasional wind, I _feel_ as though I am talking through, sitting in, and walking through nothing — that literally, there is nothing between me and, say, that tree down the road. Distance collapses in the clarity. I feel vulnerable to things, more intimate. People's faces and expressions are sharply detailed, more present and alive — and thus, more demanding of a (my) response. Without recognizing it, I have somehow made or used the air of N.Y. as a barrier, insulating me from the world or rather, the air of N.Y. has isolated me from the world by its thickness, its opacity, its noise, its diffused, unnatural light and its consequent distortion of vision and separation (by its noise) of sight from hearing (the one must inform the other). There is, _in fact_, something between me and the world, something I can not wave away, push aside, talk out of existence (for the experience is pre-verbal), — it is _there_ and I am _powerless_ to remove it.

    Off hand, one might say I was overly sensitive, but the experience of ...

    I came to this probable insight (and probably trivial to boot), not because I suddenly experienced 'liberation', the 'joy of closeness', the 'beauty of the desert', etc., but because I found myself feeling uncomfortable in the clear landscape, in the street, in talking to people; I found myself feeling inexplicably oppressed by an unusual vulnerability and much called upon need to respond — very unlike N.Y., where the humidity alone causes one to ignore what one sees, to withdraw from others, to cast the eyes inward, and to see all human expression as though a ~~they~~ silk-stocking had been stretched over them.

23

went to Los Alamos on the way to San Ildefonso Pueblo. Los Alamos looks like the army barracks and officers quarters you might expect to see surrounding a concentration camp, - ala 1940. Simply disgusting - the degeneration of human intelligence to a concern with things - not life. The entire town bears witness to the Pit Indian saying: 'The Indian believes everything is alive. The white man believes everything is dead'. I do not understand the scientific mentality - to see Los Alamos as a Pueblo, i.e., as another Indian village inhabited by a distinct, local tribe, one could only say that this particular tribe must have suffered great humiliation or shame in front of all the other, surrounding tribes, and so has built a myth enabling them to destroy all the other tribes in anger and righteousness. Unfortunately, the anger is blind and so will end by destroying itself as well — once its' task is over. And then there will be nothing. Los Alamos breathes their death. To enter the town, passing between the towers of 'check-point-charlie', it would not be out of place to see a the sign: 'Hiroshima will make you Free'. (Los Alamos)

Descending from its' lofty perch in the Jemez mountains (height is power - right? Even its sense of symbol is banal, nazi like), to the valley of the Pueblo - with its adobe houses encircling a Kiva - out of the hidden, high center of which protrudes the two long, wooden end of a ladder, is to descend into a place where there is nothing but life - where indeed the entire world is a stage and everyone and everything is an actor in an infinite dramatic play without end, without plot but full of meaning and symbol which resonate with the universe. In fact, however, the Pueblo is empty, the great Kiva sits desolate in the center. A few children walk or ride by on their bicycles. All is quiet. The road encircling the Kiva and upon which the circling adobe house front, is wide, dusty and hot. We speak to a few Indian artists - friendly and informative. But, they will not reveal what goes on inside the Kiva, the steps of their sacred dances, the words that contain themselves, the secrets they hold among themselves, their grasp of civilization, their humanity.

No, its not like Los Alamos at all. I can not help but feel that what they know is so much greater than what we know. That what we know would require only one breath skin - helpful but boring, limiting, and full of fear and loathing. (I should mention - as an aside - that when one does in fact enter Los Alamos, there _is_ a large sign which reads: "Fireworks Prohibited" - only A-bombs allowed.)

Today I wandered into a rehearsal for a piano recital to be given in a few days. He, Swann, was rehearsing the "Waldstein". As he played the soaring lyricism - ~~fingers~~ fingers flying and arm weaving - tears came to my eyes. The beauty - which I have heard many, many times - was astonishing. Not ~~his~~ playing of it, but the beauty of the music itself was ripping me apart. I didn't know what to do with myself, I wasn't myself - for a moment I _was_ those ~~_produce_~~ notes sounding simultaneously in a blaze of profound complexity. It was painful, it was joyous. It was like ~~_being_~~ the entire history of Western civilization; the ~~summation~~ summation of my life, my soul, anything and everything I could possibly know, want, desire, feel, be. (I can hear the notes now.), as well as what everyone who preceded me could possibly know, want desire, feel and be. He stopped playing. Then repeated the passage. Leaned over and told the manager that the piano should be more centered on the stage. Played part of the beginning. Complained about the middle c - which ~~_was_~~ strident rather than fortissimo. etc.. By then my mind had wandered and was re-creating the sounds of a Navajo chant - sounds I often spontaneously imitate while cooking, walking or whenever I am alone - strange as _that_ may sound. My body was pulsing with the phantom chant in my head. I wanted to stand, arch my back, and raise my knee to the beat. (all other music, jazz, pop, folk, etc slices in between the above two and never affects me strongly - they seem never _to_ grasp the basic element of being and time - or, rather, _my_ basic, dichotomous elements.)

Knowledge is power - and, as Valéry said, is payable in gold. But it is singularly limited to that (exhilarating) posture. That is _all_ it has to offer - and there is no human reason for pursuing it other than for power

The 'critique', the most prized form of western writing, is only so because it seems to offer power over power; the supreme power. But what if one is not interested in having power? As an old hunter in Africa said: "the difference between the white man and the black man in Africa is that the white man 'has' and the black man 'is'."

Beethoven 'has' (power), the Navajo chant 'is'. And being can never be translated (known) or felt by those who 'have'. (the reverse, however, may not be true). Yet power permeates our lives: knowledge is embodied (is, in fact) in TV sets, cars, sneakers, missiles, refrigerators etc., (even $E=mc^2$ was not knowledge until light was seen to bend and thousands incinerated), but it is also in words — our great words of such abstract power: 'civilization', 'history', 'culture', 'good', 'time', etc., these too are the embodiment of power allowing for control, manipulation; are, in fact, control and manipulation, but of what? of what meaning? Progress? (the concept of 'self' is itself a power concept — a unit of self-interest, desire, etc., and a fortress of defense.)

Music seems to take aspects of linear, scientific time (forever progressive and continuous) and to emblem and miniaturize them — unlike words, which disappear into the past before they are completely uttered, i.e., the sounds of language (the music of spoken language), the notes of music suspend time and recreate it; recreate its scientific unstoppable flow, while all around it scientific time continues continues uninterrupted. It (music - Beethoven's type) is crystallized power; gems of transparent power held as it were in the air — which proves that power and time are myths, for if time were real this could not be done. If time were real, there could be no music. Chants have no time, take up no time, interrupt nothing. Like words, chants dissolve into the past, and as a language, whole and complete at every moment, contains the entire universe of a people, it can go on endlessly in a moment. there is no power in chant, simply being

What is the joy of listening to Beethoven? what is it precisely primitive can not attain in their music? are chants 'biological', reuniting man with the rhythm of eternity? Is the "Waldstein" (when heard) a super-organic intelligence (non-biological) unifying man with the non-sensible world myth of abstraction (knowledge)?

Visiting, one by one, the twenty pueblos — now discrete villages separated by miles of privately owned land and cities — it is difficult to reconstruct the time when only the Indian populated these mountains, mesas and deserts and lived in a universal culture (different, but more alike than different; essentially the same world round — 10 – 12 thousand years ago)= that recognized the pit-falls of knowledge (abstraction) and shyed away from it with all their humble might. and still do!

Perhaps there is a great pendulum in the sky: 40,000 years in the building of culture (reflected in the way, the Hopi, the aborigines, the bushmen) and so many thousands of years in its destruction, and then — what?

Today, — saw a full rehearsal of Stravinsky's 'History of a Soldier (in English)! Tonight — saw 'Full Metal Jacket' — aah... from civilization to white-man triumphs over the moral delirium of his conquering myth; what a come down. (the movie actually insults the enemy by wondering: 'Gee, how could we, the most advanced military nation in the world, be so cruel and barbarous to such sweet people — imagine that!? We better stop fighting wars — our guilt and confusion will tear us in two and we don't want to feel pain. I, S. Kubrick, in my 8 million dollar house, don't want pain staining my living room floor.')

But- enough! Let me read this rambling letter off.
P.S.: I am sorry for the quality of the print — but I "dropped the ball".
By the way — the city of Santa Fe is plastered all over with the names of all the christian martyrs that died in the single Pueblo revolt of 1680, but not one of the thousands of Indians — the true martyrs, that died. Pass the hemlock, Sherlock

Ted
the Wasichu

Stanely Diamond in In Search of the Primitive, on Spengler:

"This would seem to imply that myth is the science of primitive peoples and science is the myth of civilization. In turn, that leads to the conclusion, more frankly arrived at by Spengler, that the scientific worldview must be understood as an ideology." (p 304)

Hence, Levi-Strauss acknowledges his debt to Marx, Freud, Kant, Rousseau, modern physicists and empirical American anthropologists among others. By allying himself with them, he makes them partially responsible for his vision; that is, he interprets them as determinists, universalists, and reductive or analytic rationalists. Structuralism is thus rationalized as the ideology of our time, the logical denouement of western reflection on self, society and nature, until Levi-Strauss sounds like Spengler, a predecessor to whom he acknowledges no claim". (p. 319)

Stanely Diamond — an anthropologist turned poet — is a valuable writer, one of the few I can read without screwing up my face. I believe he is now at the New School. The above book was out in 1977 — reprinted in '8?. by Transaction Books.

I think you might find Walter Ong's Interfaces of the word interesting. (Published by Cornell.) especially the essay ~~Bronson related~~ "From Epithet to Logic: Miltonic Epic and the closure of existence".

posture, down to the rumpled suit and open white collar with red necktie, steady, self-assured--Sunday morning, 11:30, no one but myself in the place (Sonya waiting in the car), and he simply cannot stop telling me things--slow, steady pointing out of details, coming to one set of tools and a photograph of the old timer who worked them all his life, telling me that the guy was so crotchety that he couldn't even accept the coming of the band-saw, which he called "the devil's instrument." This kid was stunning. I mentioned that I'd seen a picture in the paper of a naval museum in Kuwait City that the Iraqis had burned down, including a 14th-century dhow, whereupon he says to me that he's not just a ticket taker at the museum. He's been in the merchant marine and was in Dubai and Kuwait a few months before the war broke out, found himself standing on the docks in Dubai one day staring at a dhow, not knowing how the crew would respond, not knowing a word of Arabic or a thing about the people at all, and suddenly they're waving him on board. They know exactly what his staring means, invite him down into the hold, turn on the light, 10,000 cockroaches disappear into the woodwork, and he sees workmanship exactly like what he knows from Essex and Gloucester shipping, takes 4 rolls of film in an hour, is invited later that night to dinner by the crew, and though he's never taken drugs, sits down to their food and their hookah, the opium laying everyone out. He volunteered that perhaps there was an article in it all, with photographs and story on the order of National Geographic. All this and more in about 3/4 of an hour in that doll house of a museum. And the funny thing is that as we were driving into Essex and I spotted it, I told Sonya I had to stop, because I knew that small museums in odd places generally have something wonderful to see. When I came out, it wasn't just that I was blown away by the kid (who reminded me of some twenty year-olds I used to know in Maine, kids who ran their own shrimp boats and went out on Norwegian ships to the Grand Banks by the age of 19), but even more, I had it confirmed once again that the moment I see things clearly, the moment I connect, I find.

The whole weekend with Sonya was wonderful. Allison showed up with Rick, and I was actually friendly without opening myself in any way, a combination I've rarely been able to bring off, so that there were simply no problems at all. Everything was understood. They left an hour after the ceremonies, and that was that. It felt wonderful to be able to have given Sonya that school experience, and then the graduation, and then a really nice motel--better than nice-- with swimming pool, great little library, superb 19th-century English color engravings in the dining room and lounge, and the place filled with other Endicott girls and their folks. I didn't have a twinge of anxiety the whole three days and felt remarkably, unusually centered in myself. Trieber says that, among other things, I'm working out my relationship with my mother in my dealings with Sonya. I don't have any liturgy, but I pray a lot.

Many Thanks for the goodies. Looking forward to Scheinbaum's gallery and most especially to you.

30

Notes: To Start

One of the more remarkable features of anthropological writing is its certainty and surety of hand in not only describing, but in explaining primitive culture. There is seldom a moment of doubt in the writings of Malinowski, Evans-Pritchard , Levi-Strauss, E. Wolf, P. Farb, etc.. Each of these authors, no matter the method or model of explanation, used, seems to be pretty cock sure that he has finally 'gotten it right'. The notion that primitive cultures are simple, i.e., 'elemental' or, worse, 'elementary', assists in this confidence. There is something like a compulsion to understand the 'primitive', as though unless it is understood, the present cannot be understood. Analogous to: calculus cannot be understood unless arimethic is understood first? There is almost no attempt to see a qualitative difference between the primitive and the present. Merely a quantitative difference. Social compexity and encephalization. (Hence, the continuing astonishment over the continuing discoveries of the technological inventions of primitive man: the Baghdad battery, the Antikythera Mechanism, the Giant Balls of Costa Rica, the Crystal Skulls,the source of the Piri Re'is map, the 'digital computer' of New Guinea, etc., as though these were pre-mature break-throughs, smashing through som e kind of sound-barrier).

Another remarkable feature of writing in this field - though not exclusive to it - is the equally pervasive notion that clear, lucid prose is what makes reality clear and lucid; i.e. if the description of say, a particular ritual is clear, then the ritual is clearly understood. But isn't this like confusing Hollywood realism with the actual, real world? If not, what is the difference?

The fact that primitive cultures have proved highly resistant to being 'explained' (and seem to be becoming more so) - despite a much larger technical vocabulary capable of great abstraction and precision - does not in the least seem to interfere however, with the above notions. Generally, there is not a hint in anthropological writing that something could be wrong, or skewered. C. Geertz thinks he can restore complexity to reality by complicating his descriptions and explanations - but matters are not so simple. It may be only his mind that is complicated or, rather, his delight in his mind may be complicated.

By analogy: just as the 8 tone musical system seems to have become exhausted by the turn of the century, i.e., anything written using it could only be a repetition, technically more proficient, but a repetition nonetheless, perhaps the written/printed word has reached such an impasse, and all that is left is sheer technical brilliance, verbal virtuosity; Debussys' and Ravels' of the dictionary. Hermeneutics - Socrates in a vacuum? (He at least saw the world as text, not just the word in contextual strings.).

Perhaps the location of the bursting through of the process of secularization in Biblical times has something to do with the qualitative change from the primitive to the present. Whatever 'the process of secularization' means.

If there is no difference in 'time' between the primitive and the present, i.e., it is not the passage of time that separates us (time for evolution to occur, for inventions to happen, for social complexity to develop, etc.,) then what is it that separates us? An invisible kind of dimension? Holes in space that we could. theoretically, walk through?

To try to capture the 'world of the primitive' in our language - is this like trying to have a computer visualize objects, to recognize objects? Like a computer programmed with a million and one forms super-imposing each one upon an object until it 'recognizes' it, is an anthropologist running through the dictionary, super-imposing every word upon a ' foreign' word until one seems to fit? But, what does a computer 'see' and is the anthropologist any different in what he comes to understand? (Are computers making intelligence artifical?- the ultimate desacralizing force?) I.Q. tests measuring not so much intelligence, so much as the absence of the sacred? Is this why intelligence has not yet been defined - because it is testing for what is absent? (And rewarding it).

How difficult it must have been to organize a society with only a primitive mentality - a society designed to meet emotional needs - and to satisfy them. The will not to rationalize must have been very strong - as strong as the will not to invent the alphabet?

What if our high technology could have been invented 40,000 years ago (at least, have begun to be invented), and did not require evolution (the brain was already fully developed), or progress? Are the two concepts of evolution and progress rationalizations to mark the un-extraordinary achievements of science. Do these achievements 'require' a positing of an age of ignorance (what ever ignorance is - it seems to have been invented itself), to precede them not because man had to struggle, to develop to get here, but because they were easy, requiring only a change in the way one wants to see the universe? What if science is easy, whereas 'humility'(the emotions, contingent, unjustifiable and responsible), is difficult, demanding the utmost discipline and rigor?

Is experience an avenue into reality? Which one? What reality? An ontologically more pure one - because it is not instumental? Does emphasis upon experience resuppose a world, a universe, that is sacred; i.e., tacitly assume the universe to be sacred? Or does paying attention to experience reveal the universe as sacred?

What is the sacred? That which commands awe - an ireducible aura which premeates all experience - if one pays attention to them; i.e., treats them as 'ends', not as 'means'.

> How wonderous this,
> How mysterious!
> I carry fuel,
> I draw water.

> (old Haiku)

The sign that we are not paying attention to our experience is anxiety, dread, 'the five-mile stare'. Our experience of meaninglessness - does this experience reveal awe?

> Where am I, or what? From what causes do I
> derive my existence, and to what conditions
> shall I return?... What beings surround me? And on
> whom do I have influence (or do I?), or who has
> influence on me (or, more fightening, do
> they?).I am confounded with all these questions, and
> begin to fancy myself in the most deplorable
> conditions imaginable, envirnone'd with the deepest
> darkness and utterly deprived of the use of every member
> and limb.

> Hume

35

people upon recognition of mutually felt awe (primitive

groups), is a major human feat. How did they do it?

Steve —

The odd meanderings of a futile mind
with a sense of nothing to do. Of passing
interest — I hope. As you read, I did not
push any of these musings too far; certainly
not even to the edge of a cliff. Perhaps
to the pond just beyond the forest where I
stopped to rest, but no further. I am not
sure what would happen were I to push
them over the cliff's edge — would I go with
them? And into what abyss? Ay, there
the rub

Not a letter to me exactly but he did send it to me

A Night in the Desert

Steve Kogan

I was on vacation one summer outside Grommet, California, south of Needles in the Mojave Desert. After five years of research, I had finally completed a Freudian analysis of hermetic flower symbolism in Spenser's <u>The Faerie Queene</u> ("Gather Therefore the Rose"). A month before, while looking at some New Age notices in a bookstore near Central Park, I found a listing for a cabin outside Grommet, offering as its chief attraction a nearly perfect plant-free environment.

When I arrived one week later, I stopped at the local gas station/convenience store, stocked up on spring water and groceries, and looked through a bin of T-shirts with typical southeast California slogans, such as "Grommet, The Edge of the World," and "Ludlow, A Place Where Nothing Ever Happens." I paused by a circular rack of postal cards and turned it slowly around, wondering which to send to friends back home. I skipped over the photographs of London Bridge at Lake Havasu City and picked three copies of a cartoon card showing a man staggering past a cactus with a buzzard sweltering on top, a bright yellow disc in the sky beating down in the 120 degree atmosphere, and a road sign with three arrows, one above the other, which read, "Grommet 10 miles/ water 600 feet/ 2 steps to hell."

The environment suited me perfectly. The drive through southern Arizona had already beaten Caesare Ripa's <u>Iconologia</u> out of my mind, and the following day promised to temporarily destroy all memory of Spenser's neo-platonic plant imagery (I had specialized in garden symbolism). I wanted a landscape as far away from the Bower of Blisse and the Garden of Adonis as possible. On the ride out of Grommet, I began to lose all contact with my five years in the libraries and research abroad. It was a typical beginning for a vacation, but now I see it as a symbol foreshadowing my experience at the cabin on the first night itself, in which the entire course of my life was changed.

I drove south off the highway onto a dirt road just past the store for about three miles and came to the cabin, a Woodstock architectural fantasy left over from the days of '68 and the summer of love. It consisted of a Buckminster Fuller dome connected to a wooden shack painted pink and blue. On the overhang of the door were wind chimes from Paolo Soleri's city of the sun. The walls inside were lined with Guatamalan fabrics and old Filmore posters of concerts by Quicksilver, the Dead, and Vanilla Cream. In the dome, I found a fouton on the floor covered with a madras print, a bookcase with underground literature from Berkeley and San Francisco bookstores, and another set of books which might have been in my own library and included a copy of Monasteries and Priories of England, Richard Brome's The Weeding of Covent Garden, An Elizabethan Garland, the anonymous Nero (c. 1624), Ficino's Platonic Theology, and The Faerie Queene itself in a rare edition. On a low coffee-table by the bookcase, I noticed a manilla envelope with the initials "E. K." neatly written on the front. Surely this was not the E. K. who wrote the dedicatory epistle to Spenser's The Shepheardes Calendar, I chuckled to myself, though slightly apprehensive about the closeness of it all and what I might find inside.

I pulled out a fairly small ms. stapled in the upper left-hand corner, but immediately set it down and went to the refrigerator, poured myself a glass of spring water, and returned, dropping into an arm chair by the table and picking up the ms. to see if there was anything in the writing that might pique my interest, or failing that, to browse through the pictures in Monasteries and Priories.

It took me the better part of an hour to read the ms. Every page exploded in my mind with thoughts that shook the fabric of my mental world. The desert night came on. A wind picked up as the air turned cold outside. The Soleri chimes tinkled in the dark. Vast forces of consciousness seemed to be moving back and forth across the sky. The orbits of the universe began to pick up speed. The solid foundations of my life dissolved into shadows that laughed at me and disappeared. The revelations of E. K. have blown away my mental furniture and filled me with their light. I have become a messenger. I spend my days in the convenience store in Grommet making copies of the ms., which I mail to newspapers, periodicals, and private homes throughout America.

_____

1987(?)

Steve,

I have led the life of a minnow. Believing I was swimming
in the deep, profound, and philosophic darkness of the ocean and
that I was capable of causing great, earth-shaking (but
anonymous and humble!), tidal waves, the shades have been
raised, and I discover myself in a bowl on my mother's bedroom
table flitting about in three inches of clear water. How do I
get from here to the ocean?

Here is the book I mentioned to you on the phone. It is
amusing (and bitter), if a bit to long and repetitious. But it
is nonetheless interesting, and full of marvelous sentences.

As to the 'Bloomsbury group', I already feel like I'm
beating a dead horse. To gather around it would be like getting
together to smell devotional incense. I want to move on, for
once, in the direction in which Bloom is pointing - out beyond
the frontier of (my) psychology (but, of course, dragging it
along as one must). Changes are in the wind.

I want to thank you for helping me back home - to myself.
I needed that. The high altitude of 'cultural relativity' was
getting to me. I had confused - or rather made one of - it's
destruction of the West with my own attempts at
self-destruction. I was trying to disappear (unnoticed) along
with the West it is trying to dispose of. Myself as the
illusionary, evil, awful and down-right neurotic West.
"Cultural relativity' provided the heavy-duty morality to
accomplish (and hide) my personal task.

Well, anyway, here is the book. Enjoy it (please send it
back).

Take care. Listen.

Love,

Ted

41

P.S. I have been quite busy — churning out another 50 papes of my research paper. This note is to just to get the book off to you before a year passes by. Please write (to me) about whats on you mind — you know, Clover, the other, wild and exotic one, and of course, reality — I'll try to do the same.

12/8/89

Dear Ted and Ruby,

My friend David Herman just came in today from Rio (so naturally it started snowing) and I got your card from New Mex. My mantelpiece now has 8 feather necklaces from the Matto Grosso (they are absolutely beautiful) and your Congolese axe photo, all that, plus yr. address and #, a bottle of firewater from Brazil, and half a dozen cassettes of Brazilian pop (and it's my day off too).

Whatever did happen to Josh and his million dollar date? We were left hanging on that story. The last I knew his car blew up or melted down before she arrived (if she did). The story is too good to leave hanging in mid-air, unless that's actually how it remained.

Sonya seems to have gotten herself a job for January with Connoisseur, of all things (screening photographs). She called them from school, set up an interview, came down with 2 portfolios of work and some black leather clothes. I took her up to them last Friday late afternoon, rush hour traffic, etc -- I was not in a happy mood -- she spent an hour with them and apparently got the job. This is the "retarded" kid Allison always criticized! God knows what lies I would believe about myself if I took that woman seriously at all. So Sonya will be with me for Jan — what a turn around that is. She was down the last two weekends and it was nice times all the way. She even went with me to 2 exhibits on Madison Ave (American painting), so things are looking up. Gerson is still making the long Island circuit. One woman asked him if he knew any single men. I appreciated what he said about me. He said he did know someone but that even though he was free, he wasn't available, "in some way." That about sums it up.

Are you living in a tent? A trailer? A garage? A house? I guess it's actually an apartment, from the looks of your address. Is it all new and strange for you out there? Oddly enough, I found myself both missing you and yet feeling adjusted to the change. Maybe things just get more matter-of-fact as time goes on. On matters of fact when things are basically O.K. (and weird when they're bad). Anyway, part of me feels good to know that you're trying something new on for size. Actually, from what my friend David says, New York can't hold a candle to Rio for filth and violence. He actually finds mid-town quiet and mellow sun by comparison. From what he says, all of Rio is chaos and gunfights ("bangee-bangee"), although he's found a comfortable niche for himself.

Between his arrival and your card, I'm reminded of how stuck I feel right now, although it's not altogether a bad stuck. There's just more stuff left to get squared away -- I'm sure I'll feel differently once Sonya has finished her first two years of school.

I am about to get myself a word processor, the car is winterized and the steering is a bit better (will have the whole front end done up right pretty soon), so if I can just keep chugging along. Things should be ok.

Thanks for the card and the info. Keep in touch. It'll be great to get out there and see you, assuming all the outer and inner forces ~~available~~ will behave as they should and I don't get a special revelation to go to Labrador and write. I don't quite feel strange about myself, but I still felt that Kafka struck a chord in me when I thumbed through his letters a few weeks ago and found one that ended like this. "I am going to Dresden and will see the zoological gardens, in which I belong." As for me, I'm already in a zoo and take advantage of every opportunity when the gates mysteriously open and I'm left to roam outside for a few hours at a time. Take care. Hope you settle in OK — Love, Steve

Jan.19,1990

Steve,

Thank you, thank you, thank you for the offer of your spare
room. I cannot tell you how much it helps me -spiritually as
well as practically! I am in your debt - and will take you out
to dinner countless times - where we will recapitulate the past
invigorate the present, and fashion the future after our own
tastes. Fertility is not only in the prick, it is more
importantly in the worlds and visions that the mind can pluck
out of its infinite darkness. The world is as it is; a Great
Mystery. Apprehended only in unexpected moments of utter
inarticulateness. Inaccessible except inarticulately, the world
is there, I mean really there - mountains, wolves, wind, whales
and ocean - whatever they are when experienced in awe. Because
of this steadfast, inaccessible mystery, we are existentially
free (the only nonpolitical definition of that word possible) to
create worlds and visions of worlds unhinged from the mystery of
the ways things really are, with and without consequence for our
lives. Life occurs in an enchanted, unchartable location - we
are in a dream, we know we are in a dream, and when we come
close to waking up we lo se speech (ourselves), and fall back
asleep. At any rate, thank you again for your offer.

Life is a bitch. I once wrote a haiku complaining that
while sucking on Ling Wing's cunt, I had to pause because a
haiku just occurred to me. Now, I feel that way every moment: I
am always on the verge of enjoying myself, the desert, the
mountains, the sand, that wisp of fading rose sun on the edge of a
disappearing cloud when something comes up - and its not my

prick. Neurosis and captialism - my mother and money - rule my life. One uses the other to sustain each day, hour and minute. I must contend with two dreams, one real the other my own. Yet, aside from the neurotic pleasures my neurosis gives me (self abnegation, the secret, savoury greatness of powerlessness, the cloak of invisibility of being), I also feel a great, abiding and growing happiness within me.

In any case, the house we bought will make you come. It is simply outstanding in all aspects - craftmanship, location and accessibilty to civilization. You must see it - and soon! (I am writing this letter to you listening to the Pathetique, a symphony which mirrored and encouraged my despair as a teenager. I relished every note of its exquisite pain, sunk into the deepest, darkest depression one could imagine(if one were crazy). I dreamed of committing suicide to its lyric darkness. Memories flood me though the performance is not not as good as Guido Cantelli's - I will stop and sent this off before I start writing of my unending past I must go now and conduct).

I thank you.

Steve,

   With the old Chrysler mud-caked and metallically clanging,
I arrived at the Albuquerque airport and immediately flew off
to Phoenix. After a week or so there - extended because of a
debilitating flu- Ruby and I - after buying a new, firered
Mazda pick-up truck - drove wonderously via Flagstaff/ Gallup
back to Albuquerque. Since then, under mystically beautiful
skies, randomly placed extinct volcanos far to the west,
looming, majestic mountains to the east and white snow
everywhere, have been busy finding places to live, jobs to
wither in, various insurances, driver's licenses, bank
accounts, etc., etc., and etc.. I don't know wether it's simply
me or reality, but scurrying around seems to be epidemically
very post-modern.
   Enjoyed your letter immensely, and yes, as time goes on it
fills the present with freshly concentrated facts that become
'the way things are', and seemingly destined to be the sole
determinants of the way things will be - leaving the facts of
the past in a hard-to-hold-on-to vibrating limbo of
ineffectualness, rememberance and 'strangeness' with pounds of
overwhelming feeling occasionaly oozing out and drowning one. I
do miss you and the guys. I recall dimly Gide's ode to
friendship and Socrates' praise of it, but if I were to reread
them now I might be more impressed by their faggoty quality
then their truth to manliness.
   The saga of Josh remains the first page of a short story -
difficult to determine anything but the style. He has moved to
Greeley only to shortly move onto Boulder for the Spring term -
to be closer to Kristen, of course. Before leaving Plattsburgh
however, he revitalized the relationship with ChrisAnn - he too
has a hard time with 'separations'. Will keep you informed -
especially if I come into the millions I deserve!
   Glad to hear about Sonia - Allison - despite her inspiring
name - is the retard! (Ah, a name. What's in a name? An Allison
by any other name, remains a retard.)
   Tell Gerson he should go to father the West - Sandoval
county - where(with the aid of a good telescope), in the bright
morning, one can see scantily clad women climb geologic mesas
looking for raw, horny men. Red-lipped they brush their golden
hair away to look intently, longingly for the long, erect prick
casting its shadow against the mountain wall. By noon, under
the heat of the sun however, they melt and become cool, wet
stains on the white rock. He had better hurry.
   Well, this is just a brief note to let you know all is
well. More to follow.

your till the last Indian

Ted

Dear Steve,

Happened to find this review of Bloom's book while looking
through my mountains of research. Don't quite remember why I
copied it - perhaps because it had something to do with ed
(Can't believe I didn't 'date' it). Any way, among other
things, notice the sub-title that S. Hook gives the book. Is
this an earlier edition? Did Bloom change it in later ones?
Why? Read the review before reading the next paragraph - if you
feel like it.

Hook seems to miss the point altogether. I can't believe
he said that Bloom ... "confuses {from first page to last}
subjectivism with moral relativity.", and that he ... "seems
not to have heard of the notion of objective relativism." For
me, it is just that point that Bloom wants to make. In fact he
says most people have made that mistake! Hook seems not to have
noticed that Bloom is trying to objectively describe something
- our culture and its students - and is not simply waging a
cosmic war in which 'Absolutism v Relativitism'. Hook doesn't
seem to realize that there are whole flocks of people out there
who think that 'subjective relativism' is the whole of
(non-relative) Truth. Bloom does not say that we must turn to
absolutism - the truths of the Great Books, the Founding
Fathers, and the Word of God - to dogmatically correct the
'subjective relativists'. Indeed, I think Bloom would agree
with Hook; there is a healthy relativity in the quest for
truth, but, unlike Hook, would go on to add that this quest
depends upon there being a world, a nature, really out there,
whose reality human reason can more or less, through heavy-duty
thought and debate, on ocassion, penetrate (using the 'great
books' because they are full of heavy-duty thought and debate -
which is what makes them great). The only 'absolute' I see in
Bloom is the belief that questions such as "who are we?", "What

is man?", "Who am I?", "What is good?", "What is evil?", and "What is knowledge?", can be asked of nature or of other humans who have previously asked and wrote about it. Answers to these questions can not be asked in the arena of 'subjective reelativism' or 'historicist/cultural relativity'. And if they are, and the relativist premise is accepted, the only answers possible are the answers of the deconstructionists; i.e., these are the questions of oppressors, there is no nature, no world out there only the cries of the oppressed seeking freedom from the realities of nature and the world(as created and imposed by the 'white man). All is sunlight and warmth.

I don't get it. I thought of all people S. Hook would have understood Bloom. Am I an asshole - or what? More, perhaps, to follow.

At any rate I took the ocassion to write this review of a review only to send back the pictures you left behind.

Give my love to Clover. Hope to see you both soon. (I felt I was just beginning to 'know' Clover on the eve of your departure. Hated to see her go.)

As always, it was a great, great pleasure to see you. See you soon I hope.

Say hello, of course, to all the guys. And tell David that I miss him.

from a duck who can never find
the pond

1586

$ 100

American Fighter Aces
Series 1

"THE MARIANAS TURKEY SHOOT"
(original oil painting by Roy Grinnell)

The weather was clear with scattered cumulus clouds off the coast of Saipan on the morning of 19 June, 1944. As part of Task Force 58 protecting the Marianas landings, Fighting Squadron 16 was expecting an attack from the 400-plane Japanese carrier force. At 1030 bogeys were picked up on radar approaching in several large groups and twelve Hellcats were launched from the USS Lexington to intercept the Japanese force. Twelve-victory ace, Lieutenant (jg) Alex Vraciu was one of the pilots in that group.

Leading a division of four Hellcats, Vraciu experienced engine problems and couldn't climb past 20,000 feet, but requested a vector from the fighter director and was put onto a line of Yokosuka D4Y2 "Judy" dive bombers. In the eight-minute tail-chase, Vraciu splashed six. The air battle became known as the Great Marianas Turkey Shoot — Task Force 58 Hellcats destroyed over 300 Japanese aircraft. The following day, Alex Vraciu claimed his 19th and last victory, a Zeke.

9/1/90

Care package for Ted!

Do you have the cover for Bloom?¹ I think I took it off to protect it, and now . . .? Hope you have it. I have a big cleaning to do at home, so maybe it'll turn up. Whenever I go off on vacation, no matter how neat I've left the place, I simply can't find things when I return.

I picked up a complete solo piano music of Ravel today for $7 (3 records, Philip Entremont on Columbia--'75) and a complete Karl Bohm of Beethoven's symphonies--Deutsche Grammaphon--<u>wonderful</u> recordings--for $4!! This was at the flea market on Columbus near the Nat. History. I'm sending you a taste of the Ravel. (Clover and I had lunch at a cafe on Columbus in which the menu was sometimes barely comprehensible, something like: "Raclete of mushrooms, tomatoes, onions, snails galmonte, and olives turpinade," along with "Tuscan three bean salad" and shit like that.

> The river Phasis
> Cannot afford them fowl, nor Lucrine lake
> Oysters enough: Circei too is searched,
> To please the witty gluttony of a meal!

> (Ben Jonson, <u>Cataline</u>)

The papers are totally awful. I mean really dreadful. Weird murders in N. Y. that stop you in your tracks while you're reading and having breakfast. <u>Unreadable</u>.

On different subjects, I thought you might like the clippings I enclosed. Couldn't resist making comments on <u>Sexual Anarchy</u>. Russell Baker had a piece on Ted Koppel in Baghdad: "Koppel in Arabia." Then television went to "Rather of Arabia" and "Brockaw of Arabia." He's waiting for Kaitie Chung of Arabia. Actually, you have to say "Chung of Arabia," because it wasn't "T. E. Lawrence of Arabia."

My letter to Prof. Fred also enclosed. I sent a cover letter to the editors of <u>AHR</u> with a copy for them too. I believe I'll send one to Bloom while I'm at it. It's the year of the letter for me. I'm getting close, though. Maybe next year I'll start talking to people more.

Clover and I saw a wonderful show of masks, drums, pots, etc. from the Congo--c. 1910. It was from the permanent collection at the Nat. History, made by two guys who went there for 6 years--one guy 29 and a kid from Columbia College--18. According to the review in the <u>Times</u>, it was one of the best-made, best-recorded expeditions of its kind, ever. 18-- can you imagine? African stuff is <u>scary</u>, nothing at all like the light and air I see in American Indian work. But who knows, right? Spengler says that it's real easy to get other cultures totally wrong. He mentions a story of a Chinese man listening to a symphony orchestra tuning up, who thought the

First sentence gets a footnote! I found the cover next day --

51

Dear Ted,

First the light stuff--some clippings of this, our daily life in NY--all from today's Times! The headlines may be enough for you, but once in a while, the absurdities in the articles are wonderful, like the street vendors who hang their stuff all around newsstands, so that eventually you can't see the newspapers, or those who get a little window space inside a store and make a store inside a store. (That one is almost Baroque, like the Mannerist painters who used to paint pictures on frames and surround their paintings with other paintings).

As for "crime in the city," Clover's son went up to Yale to check out the grad. school and found out that New Haven's crime rate is even worse than NY's (which is a little like saying that you might as well stay in Calcutta because it's only worse in Bangladesh). One city official here actually calls it "the third worldization [sic] of NY" (read: sick of N. Y.).

Anyway--a little something from a day in the life, as if you didn't know what you're missing. It's the communal talk of the town, the latest patter. People talk about crime and fear in a kind of chit chat. I heard one woman in Balducci's today talking to the meatman behind the counter about, "Well . . . we just got back from Hawaii and," etc. etc. And then there are the clowns who write these Op-Ed pieces about how many gin mills and whores there were in NY in 1852 and how it's really all the same. It's not just that I drive a rusted-out Duster. The whole place around me is falling apart. The roads are even worse than my car, in fact, which at least still works. Con Ed decided to plow up 6th Ave (honestly), so there's only one lane on each side still open. The whole center is simply plowed up--which means there's no parking on 6th, from about 3rd St on up, past 23rd. This started two or three days ago. I'm curious to see how Balducci's and the Jefferson Market are going to get their truck deliveries. To get up to the men's group or my therapist now means that I have to go up Hudson, cross at 14th or 16th and then go back down on 6th--or something. They're going to get to get to the point where people will wake up one day and find themselves paralyzed. That's exactly what will happen.

All this is still rather amusing, mostly because I don't have to live in it that much and can still worm my way around. I'm sure some joker will write an Op-Ed piece about how London was clogged in 1662 or Samarkand in 1280.

Speaking of rusted Dusters, my Cousin Boris already has a better car than I have ('85 Pontiac for $3000). True, he washes cars on Long Island, but as you said, these people are going to have it all doped out. They all have carpets already, and couches and lamps and beds--the kids are in school-- Yeshiva, that is--not "the government schools," as they call them. How did one of them put it to me? "If I keep my kid in a government school, he'll be a criminal in three months."

Actually, my students have learned something. Maybe I'll be pissed at them later on, but right now they don't seem so bad, at least not worse than the usual. In fact, it's a miracle that they've learned anything, but the truth is that they have learned something about writing. They've done about as well as they could with what they got, although in two weeks, they've already made amazing leaps in my class; so on the one hand, I feel a kinship with their other teachers, and on the other hand, totally estranged. I teach what others teach, and then again, I don't. In the normal course of things, this is exactly as it should be: we're like other people in some ways, and in some ways, we're not. In my case, though, everything gets exaggerated. I'm just the way I should be, but I don't know it, so everything feels stretched in opposite directions. If I think of myself teaching more or less to the same goals as everyone else, which I do, then I start to feel imprisoned; and when I think of how I work, which is different from others, then I feel estranged. Each position can sometimes feel like a mask for the other, so that I end up feeling duplicitous either as a member of the department or as myself. Now, all this would be fine if it were the reality itself, as it was in the 19th and early 20th century--endless Dr. Jekyll and Mr. Hyde situations in literature, all the way up to T. E. Lawrence, who felt like a fraud either as an Englishman or an Arab. But the sad fact is that this is not my reality, or rather, these conflicts exist only where I still haven't worked things out. In the men's group or my poker group, I feel perfectly fine, comfortable with others and with myself. So I don't <u>believe</u> in the conflicts I face at school. It's just that I have them, and they're a fucking drain. There's something about school that acts like an enchanted magnet, attracting all the negative influences in the air around--absorbing and radiating them out again, so that it's almost impossible to hear oneself.

The other day it occurred to me that this was one reason why I feel so impossibly stuck about making contact with Pam--the sheer fact that she's a student at the school. The place simply clouds my mind--not that I couldn't attach my difficulties to any external reality, but all the same, school doesn't help. I just associate it with too many awful scenes in my life, and can't seem to separate her in my mind from the place itself. So at this point, I'm fairly well removed from women altogether. Clover has problems, Nancy has problems, Catlin, whom I ran into a few weeks ago, doesn't respond, and I simply have to stop putting myself into a world of troubled ladies. So there's another fear--that if Pam likes me, in fact, all the more because she had such an outpouring for me, she's responding to me because I'm basically sick--that what she finds attractive is my propensity to give myself away, which is another way of saying that it's only depressed women who are attracted to me. At the end of Marlowe's <u>Dr. Faustus</u>,

Faust sees Christ's blood streaming across the firmament. That's how it is with me and my mother. I see her stretched across my universe. I am <u>very</u> mistrustful of myself these days. Trieber tells me this is a good thing, that it's a sign of change to mistrust oneself and not simply "go with one's feelings." Interesting, no? Do you know the scene in <u>War and Peace</u> where Kutuzov's generals are sitting around the battle table hammering ideas at him, and he falls asleep on them? "There's nothing to do," he tells them. Napoleon will just keep coming on. That's all the Russians can do--let him keep coming on--and that's how he prepared for Borodino, by falling asleep. Well, I feel the same sense of onslaught. I simply can't do a thing, and it seems worse than senseless-- impossible--for me to try to do something when nothing clear is coming through. There isn't one guy I've spoken to about Pam who hasn't said it's too bad I didn't pick up on her, which only serves to feed my sick sense of specialness. But then I think, am I really that removed from ordinary reality that I can't see the obvious? But it's not as if I don't see what they mean. Her story pleases me too, yet <u>something</u> holds me back. I was the same way on Carpenter Hill in Vermont. I simply couldn't leave, as much as I wanted to, until the time was right, and then I simply left. Some days I used to gyrate inside so ferociously between wanting to leave and wanting to stay I thought I'd vibrate into a thousand pieces. Those were the times when I simply disappeared, and as a matter of fact, my friend David Herman, whom I got to know on the Hill, told me that when he first met me, I was simply not talking at all. It's a hell of a way to start a relationship, but in fact I've had several long-term friendships that began by my keeping away, especially if there were strong attractions going on. They tell me that's the way I learned to walk. I simply didn't move, barely crawled, and as though learning how to walk <u>inside</u>, I never practiced in the ordinary way--crawling and standing and falling, but one day around the age of three or three and a half, I simply got up and walked.

9/28

And speaking of getting up and walking, I've had close to a month of the vertigo again. I ought to give it a name of my own, it's <u>so</u> familiar to me now. Another irony, that this all too familiar problem, which has been with me way beyond the pale of any other illness I've ever had, is also entirely disconnecting, so that I end up feeling in the grip of something that is deeply ingrained and deeply alienating, all at once. In any event, it started clearing this week (9/28), and for some reason, as bad as it is, it hasn't affected the rest of me, in which I'm simply chugging along, finding my clarities as I go. I have a sliding door on my big closet in the little center room, which has had one of the rollers torn off these 15 years, and for 15 years I've been <u>pulling</u> the door. Can you believe it? It's astonishing how many burdens I live with, which I'm aware of, but just below the surface of consciousness, so that I end up putting up with things instead of changing them. It's always the same with me. One day, I see. And the change is immediate. As soon as I saw, for myself, what I was doing all these years, I fixed it. Took about 20 minutes all told. And then I painted the doors and the frame. And then I made some big readjustments in Sonya's room and my rear sitting room, and tomorrow I get a bed. As Trieber would say, how can I get to Pam if I can't even fix a castor on a sliding door, let alone get to a woman when I don't even have a bed (I bought a good mattress for myself but have been sleeping on the floor in the main room these three months). But I never really had a bed in the apartment. I don't exactly know how these things work, but not having a bed (which was ok for me alone) really meant I didn't want a woman in the house. That's exactly what it's meant. And another thing. My car. You know what might make me go out and get another one? The fact that the other day I realized that if I did want to see Pam, I'd feel uncomfortable driving out to Queens. It's as simple as that. Car + bed = women. You know how I mean it too, not externally, but internally. I could live with the car, fix it here and there, and keep it running. It's what the car is keeping me from, inside, which is really the problem. And that's the reason to get another. You see, it's only when an issue hits me on the inside that it makes any sense. It's really not the car itself that I've been holding onto. The other day, I made a new telephone/ address directory for myself, the old one being frayed. I was amazed to find names of women I had never called. Pam is just the end of a long line of people I never contacted. My problem isn't with her at all.

10/4

"But now, in the sunset of the scientific epoch and the rise of victorious Skepsis, the clouds dissolve and the quiet landscape of the morning reappears in all its distinctness": 1) My vertigo started lifting; 2) I decided to call Nancy in spite of it all--to have a real feast--took her to a small but absolutely the most wonderful Japanese restaurant in N. Y. (the Omen on Thompson St.), where we spent three hours in wonderful eating and talking--Nancy telling me loud and clear to take risks, of whatever kind, and if I crashed or went into fits, I simply had to remember that her place was always open for me to be as crazy as I wanted (how they love blind Samsons--but all the same . . .); 3) My platform bed has arrived , and my place has undergone radical changes--a couch is coming soon--the chest of drawers and white shelf are gone from the small room (the bed has a huge drawer underneath)-- the small bed is nestled in the niche in the small room between front and back--the area cleared of all bookcases and junk, a light now making that room part of the entire place; 4) Sixth Ave. has been repaired and is back to what it was;

5) Sonya sent me $1,500, Allison $1000, with another $1000 coming, my words finally got through to Endicott and I got a student loan for Sonya for $2,2000, and instead of a bank loan for my chunk of the bill, I discovered a tuition payment plan with extremely low interest and other fine features; 6) My Mss. are ready to go out (the Brownsville boogie-woogie and a reworked essay on Oswald); and 7) I'm finally about to start making calls to those women in my address book I totally forgot about all last year.

So there it is for now. David Herman called me from Rio the other night, and once again, he'll be coming up in December and Sonya in January if she lands a job for the month. I feel that I'll be harvesting the fruits of our five months together for a long time to come. A big hello to Ruby and regards to Oliver next time you talk to him.

P. S. Prof. Fred replied! I guess I got to him. Notice what he thinks I ought to look at--Neo-Thomist attempts to reconcile the irreconcilable. Ecumenism in everything! I heard his problem a long time ago in one of my college seminars, when a student complained that Kafka was too negative, and I realized one could complain about everyone along these lines: Milton is too Latinate, Dante too Catholic, Frost too rural, etc. etc. Listen to this, John Constable to a friend: "[Callcott] has another large work, not so good, rather too quakerish, as Turner is too yellow; but every man who distinguishes himself stands on a precipice."

Much love,
Steve

11/2/90

Dear Ted,

Enclosed, for your amusement, upset, or total lack of
interest, the letter from the State Ed. Dept.

Yes, I know that Bougeureau well. It's at the Clark Art
Institute in Williamstown, Mass., where I spent many hours
during my visits to Sonya up north in the old days. It seems
the painting ended up somewhere c. 1890 in a bar in N. Y. and
thence into the museum--something like that. And yes, that's
me, unable to move--on my Mss. as well. But I tell you, I'd
rather be stuck than Mel. His Tales of Frieda are horrendous.
I have been making gallant attempts to help him see himself as
he is in the situation, for which he is grateful. But what a
scene he's in. And nary a clue. As for my "seamless stitch"
called "myself" (some deconstructionists use quote marks
around author's names: "Milton," for example, who is really an
interpretation, according to them)--I'm reminded of Orwell's
passage where he says, "What have we in common with that
photograph of ourselves when we were five years old? Nothing,
except that it happens to be us."

Yes, your Indians as you describe them are very much like
my mother, and I am also much moved by your closing words. I
too miss you a great deal and am up against myself in
unfamiliar ways.

Love,
Steve

Dear Ted,

A'right. You want sick? I'll give you sick. Got yr. letter the other day and said to myself, "No, Cogan, you mustn't reply soon. Delay, delay as long as you can. A quick response indicates too much _desire_." You ask about the transcendent mother. Well, there she is. Any spontaneity was for her 1) a sign of vulgarity, and 2) an opening to be taken over and wiped out. Even delay is already an indication of my self, an expression of desire and possibility, which is why my procrastination and geological slowness are for me nevertheless tinged with hope. But today I rebel. I take fate into my hands, and respond. It's better this way. It's as if I'm talking to you, and if the pages pile up and you are busy and cannot write back for as long as you can't, it's OK by me and a treat for me to keep talking to you all the same.

Napoleon. Yes, indeed. I have a love affair with him, and the funny thing is that I wasn't aware of it in my description of Kutuzov's sleep. It was the sleep itself that interested me at that moment. But do you know that Kafka himself was absorbed by Napoleon, and in particular, Napoleon in Russia? He read a number of memoirs by Napoleon's officers of the Russian campaign. Here's a detail I remember from K's _Diaries_: it seems the horses were so swollen with illness (or whatever it was) that men had to ram their arms into the horses' ass holes up to their shoulders to get the shit to come out. Linger over that one, and they did it in that terrible winter campaign. Endless stories of that kind. These memoirs must be fantastic. I have a book of quotes by Napoleon himself-- extracts from letters, speeches, conversations overheard. People _wrote down_ what they heard at parties, staff meetings, etc. I've got another book debunking the whole Napoleonic legend, with fabulous descriptions of his generals during the early campaigns. At Versailles, there's a room I saw with portraits of those men, most of them under 25, and at the Louvre, Kafka spent time looking at the pictures of Napoleon himself. There's a famous one by Messonier showing Nappy leading the full retreat. Snow, if you remember, is often the central motif in Kafka's work. The land surveyor K. goes looking for employment at the Castle in wintertime (when all landmarks are obliterated)--there's "The Country Doctor" and "The Bucket Rider," both taking place in "this unhappy, frozen time." And a marvelous entry in the diaries, the beginning of an unfinished story, "I was once employed as the manager of a small railroad in central Siberia." Delicious, isn't it? (Another good one would be, "I was once a replacement janitor in a house whose address I did not know"--your letter is indeed filled with stories. That's how Hawthorne did it--he kept a journal of those interior moments and later they became narratives: "A man once left his wife, took a room across the street from his house, and contemplated her comings and goings for the next twenty years."

Kafka was intrigued by Napoleon's iciness. "Daru is cold and withdrawn, and that suits me fine." You may remember the passages on N. from Chateaubriand I read to you. Something in my Russian fatalism draws me to the story of that winter campaign. The passive, sleeping, infinitely suffering Russian who burns his own land, retreats, and saves himself for the future. My sacrificial offerings took place on the psychiatrist's couch.

Well, I make my attempts with women, and it's the same story all over again: "Weird scenes inside the gold mine," as The Doors so rightly sang. 1) Serge was going to give me the phone number of a woman he said was interested in meeting men. He never did. 2) I finally called Pam. YES. I knew I would as soon as I got sick enough of myself. No reply, but a few days later shows up in my office. Would she be willing to go out with me? Yes (turns out not to be true). I call, get the machine. She calls my machine, leaves no message except that she's returning the call. Again I call, again the machine. My spontaneities drained dry. She finally reaches me on the phone, only to tell me that it's over for her. She went through all those feelings, and in the summer realized she had to get on with her life. There's no surmounting that (and no mounting either, apparently). She had some bad experiences, hasn't dated in years. We talked for a long time on the phone, but that's as far as it went. A little word, the merest nothing, and I take it for what it says. She has to get on with her life. I know I have to make these attempts, but I swear to God, it will never happen except Hamletlike, by happenstance. I will be carrying letters bearing the tidings of my own execution, unknown to me, and I will leap into the pirate ship and so escape and make my way, by the sheerest coincidences finding what I most deeply need, as you came into my life last spring simply by a series of random events. You see, the struggle is necessary, but it offers nothing, nothing but the struggle, and it is all a discipline for the spontaneities that must come. Whatever woman comes into my life will simply arise out of my unconscious, and that's all there is to say. There's that fatalism again, and it feels like the only truth. Marilyn Monroe said it all for me in "The Misfits," talking to Montgomery Clift outside a bar, when he asks her, "So tell me Rosalyn, who can you trust?" and she replies, "It's not fair to ask people for something they can't give. Sometimes I think the only thing there is is the next thing that happens."

Of course we feel we live against the grain of this American life, this life that is turning into everything the East Europeans have vomited out, this life of dire consequences and results and believing in experts who take you to the cleaners. Here's another story, told to me by a colleague in my department. It seems that the big Frenchman at Columbia, Prof. Michel Rifaterre, in all his gory, semiotic glory, used to keep a light on in his study all night to create the effect of deep study, so that rumors of his heroic research efforts would spread around the campus. <u>Exactly</u> like the scene in "The Sorrow and the Pity" when Ophuls shows a French documentary of the time, in which the light is burning late in Laval's home, and the newsman says that here is Laval, working night and day for the sake of France. They are liars, one and all. It's pathetic. Devin (Clover's son) went for a visit to Duke U. to check out their grad. lit. department and sat in on a class of Frank Lentrichia, another big boy in the field (Duke has lots of big names). Devin tells me that Lentrichia went on for about half an hour on a Wallace Stevens' poem, spinning out all sorts of ideas on his use of the term "The large," and Devin suddenly realized that it was old French for the sea ("l'appel du large"--the call of the vast--the call of the sea). There was the class, knee-deep in theories, and no knowledge of French, particularly where it was needed, with Stevens, himself deeply cultured in French art and poetry. But you see, they've done away with the study of foreign languages in comp. lit. at Duke. In fact, the primary readings are in the critics, not the authors. The actual study of literature is dead itself, let alone languages, at least in the places that make all the noise. And they plan out every move, every thought, every pose. There's nothing for its own sake any more. And gorgeous women sit home for five years without dating, or come on, but completely in their minds.

I loved your line, "You capture something, and you capture it beautifully, but I don't know what yet." It had me worried at first, but then I realized that's exactly where I am with it too. Maybe it needs a final tying of the knot. The pieces were all done separately, and for all my attention, I never really stepped away from it. But there it is, and I've sent it off to someone who may be of help. I've got a bundle of information on people to contact but am waiting on Ms. B. Plumb to tell me what she thinks.

Don't think of this as a letter so much as me talking to you. I love hearing from you, your lines fall out so deliciously (sorry to take your soul searching as an aethsetic--anaesthetic--narcotic medicine of words). Your beautiful line about maybe now wanting to go home. It set me to thinking about how much I could live making things all day, every day, anything--words, a set of stairs, a garden, but making things. Yes, we've lived among the cripples, you for sure at your school, but are they any less crippled at Duke? It frightens me to think that I'm rationalizing the handicaps away in order to remain. It's my enormous sense of panic in the classroom that keeps me locked inside, that and the sheer inertia of the thing, which by now has bred a pension, benefits, etc., all inadvertently, as it were. I simply find myself with these things, attached to me, but nothing that I was working for. It's mystifying.

I am reading a novel by De Maupassant--<u>Bel-Ami</u>. How in God's name could critics do anything but celebrate? What shit are they into anyway? It has nothing to do with me, nothing at all. De Maupassant is truly astonishing. Simple, utterly simple sentences. Paris in the 1880s--Lautrec's Paris--whores, the neauvau riche, the fading aristocrats, the sex, the endless sex, the use of women to gain power, the newspapers, a chapter on the death of a tubercular editor that was absolutely amazing and brought back to me, almost word for word, the scene of my mother at home as she was dying in her final weeks. Sunset streaming into Forestier's death-room on the Riviera: "The mirror over the mantelpiece, in which you could see the reflection of the horizon, looked like a pool of blood."

Mirrors everywhere in the novel. Like a dream, they appear at key moments in the plot. Why should I go anywhere but into books and art? De Maupassant. I don't have a clue about why I picked him up, and a novel at that. Not even his short stories, in which he made his mark. His novel <u>is</u> a mirror, in which I see myself drinking in everything at once--the world he describes, my own awareness of myself and the issue of women in my life, of writing, everything. I haven't felt anything like this since Chateaubriand. I am there, in Paris, 1880, but utterly. The thing itself. Not Balzac's Paris, 1820, or even Flaubert's, 1860, but this new, completely crass, decadent Paris, all built upon the world that came before, yet changed into something very close to us. The Bougueraeu of "Nymphs and Satyrs" (1873), by the way, is typical of De Maupassant's scenes--"elegant smut" he calls his characters' conversations. Nietzche says that Wagner went to school in Parisian decadence during his early years (and came out with "Rienzi"). De M's novel is fantastically Wagnerian--or perhaps it's the other way around. That Wagner is really Parisian, as Nietzche says. The ending of <u>Bel-Ami</u> is like a tornado. Picture this: a giant Victorian greenhouse in the new mansion of a newspaper publisher, who just made a killing on the stock market knowing some inside information on French colonization in North Africa. Inside the greenhouse the scene is strictly Baudelaire, real flowers of evil--sickly sweet smell of giant jungle plants, an immense gold fish pond with gold dust sprinkled at the bottom, weird Chinese gold fish swimming around with their bulbous eyes, and the wife of the publisher, seduced and abandoned by the man who is about to marry her daughter, writhing in agony in one corner of the greenhouse below a giant painting of Christ Walking on the Water! And that's not the end either! I am educating myself for something that I myself do not understand.

I send this off in pleasure at having heard from you. Matters of the heart indeed. I am for nothing if not the heart, the heart and words to put it in. I am so touched by your reading of my work and the time you gave to answer me.

Love,
Steve

Paving the Super Highways
of the Sky

Dear Ted,   10/19/99

Just came across your lexicon of deconstruction. Carol
thought this one was a stitch: "Homosexuals: different
from others only because the word 'different' is part
of the English language." Read a review today of yet
another book on T.E. Lawrence that goes "sifting
through the biographical record for inconsistencies and
contradictions." Here's a new wrinkle: It seems that
"Lawrence was homosexual by nature but probably never
consumated his passion, given the horror of physical
intimacy he developed as a child." In other words,
there are gays who have been so oppressed that they
never even made it *into* the closet (thus raising the
spectre of *empty iron cages*, the most insidious of all,
since the oppressed aren't even allowed to take their
rightful place in the system of oppression). The
reviewer says that Lawrence started his own myth "with
a theatrical self-portrait" in *Seven Pillars*, which is
obvious once you think about it, since everyone knows
how easy it is to blow up trains on stage, plus we're
all so hip nowadays that we can spot self-glorification
even when it's invisible, as when Lawrence rejected the
VC, changed his name, and went into hiding as a private
in the army. But it has been depressing indeed to go
through my newspaper clippings, letters to well-known
nobodies, and piles of *PMLA*, *College English*, etc., and
to see how much time I myself have spent "sifting the
record for inconsistencies and contradictions." Have
you heard of *The Ecological Indian* (W.W. Norton), just
published by an improbable Shepard Krech 3d?

Ted Sitea

Nov.28,1990

Dear Steve -

What a pleasure to hear from you! And two letters in a matter of days! Really - a great surprise.

Yes, by all means, spontaneity!: immediate release of the most ancient of feelings inside oneself is the triumph over the dreams of childhood. It is to walk on the brezzy slopes of Olympus conversing with mighty Zeus; with him who knows the value of self and can respond to its slightest whims with the greatest of concentration - for in them is an entire self resplendent with its own important history.

Oh, for the taste of it! Oh, for the feel of it! - Sometimes I think I would rather get a free Toyota than be spontaneous - a true American fighting for the right to have his imprisoning childhood dream come true, even if it means that on the two chairs remaining of the furniture of the universe there would only be me and my mother haggling it out. Whata life!

Your image about digging the shit out of horses by hand is enormous. Now that's spontaneity! (It makes mincemeat out of most things that concern me - mostly me.) The mechanical (phone) nature of your pulling a feeling out of yourself-Pam broods darkly over the immediate energy which muscled shit out on the white, icey plains of Russia. And that was so long ago, Pam is today. Spontaneity, once expressed, is eternal!

-----Several days later -----

Mensonge and Small World, arrived today. Thank you. I will tackle the Lodge soon.

Did you read John Searle's article "The Battle over the

University", in the Dec.6 issue of N.Y. Review? Interesting, but somehow flat - he doesn't seem to have any real feeling for anything: 'oh hum, here is the way things are in this state of crises, oh hum. Honey, is there any more coffee in the pot?", type of sophisticated writing. Also some nonsensical, irrelevant comments about Bloom and Kimball. Can't anyone write anything accurate about Bloom?

Am sending you a tear-out from Time magazine - thought you might find it interesting. A new men's group to join perhaps? Also a brief editorial by Rasberry - I found it encouraging.

I don't know about you, but I keep waiting for me to start living my life. Not only that, I am so very tired of compulsively pursuing that elusive thought, that soul-bending experience, that always-just-about-to-emerge-insight (I never imagine a person) that will take me directly into myself, that I am in a constant state of self-induced exasperation - and boredom. It is as though I hype myself up every day in anticipation of the arrival of that long-awaited event, and every day I retire incomplete and with a bad taste in my mouth. But for fifty years!

I think it was your line: "I am educating myself for something that I myself do not understand.", that promted the above paragraph. It is a great line. Only what I don't understand is myself: I am educating a self that I don't understand yet.

-------a day or so later----

Still deeply embroiled in my paper - not that I haven't completed the first draft, and know quite definitively what it is all about - but my knowledge of all the things I talk about - nineteenth century Indians, Indian policy, anthropology, history, and textbooks (none too strong to begin with) - is everyday being increased by interesting details that are "just perfect" for the paper. Why I ever picked 'textual representations' of the Indian in nineteenth century American intellectual and governmental life is now quite beyond me. Its not really what I should be doing.

In rereading the above - Searle does ask one interesting question: why is it that 'radical political views' are birthing in departments of English, French, and Comparative Literature and not sociology or political science? One answer is that these are the only disciplines that assholes think are easy to understand, and to which 'minorities' might respond - English now including pictures and fiction without logic. Another is that it was English departments that had to deal with the first waves of 'open admissions' students, and in order to stay alive in the classroom, they had to 'take the students side'. To hell with the universe. Any thoughts?

Did you know that Johann Herder said:

"It is but just when we proceed to the country of the blacks that we lay aside our proud prejudices, and consider the organization of this quarter of the globe with as much impartiality, as if there were no other. Since whiteness is a mark of degeneracy in many animals near the pole, the Negro has as much right to term his savage robbers albinoes and white devils, as we have to deem him the emblem of evil, and a descendant of Ham, branded by his father's curse. {Well} might he say, I, the black, am the original man. I have taken the deepest draughts of the force of life, the Sun: on me, and everything around me, it has acted with the greatest energy and vivacity. Behold my country: How fertile in fruits, how rich in gold! Behold the height of my trees! the strength of my animals!...let us enter the country appropriate to him with modesty." (Outlines of a Philosophy of the History of Man; T Churchill,trans.1803)

Perhaps this is where Malcolm X got his lines! Jefferies(?). Perhaps my students were secretly reading Herder, only claiming to be reading the Koran.

There was once a boy - fair but pained -who could no longer bear the cruelty and nastiness of humans. First placing minute sensors in the shubbery, he sealed all the doors and windows to his house, turned out the lights, and sat in the darkness vowing never to be a human. He began to purge himself of all human desire, thought, and reason, in search of pure and gentle sources of being which, he was sure, were located somewhere within - unharmed and uncontaminated. Deprived of all sensory experience - as though submerged in an enclosed tank of tepid water - he began to float about his dark room. He knew however, from information gotten from his external sensors, that humans were constantly moving his house from one place to another. He could hear them talking, wondering what to do with it, where to place it, and in what state of repair or disrepair it seemed to be in. It thus travelled to many places - saw the world as it were, but the boy inside was scarcely interested. The exotic, but all too human, places to which it travelled were more like rumors to him than reality. Today excavators are poking about, wondering what to do with this old 'haunted' house. The sensors are crakling. As they lift and let fall one corner of the house after another, testing the foundation, the floating man/thing inside crashes into one wall after another. What will happen? Will one of them open a door? What will he find?

The West - its heritage, its traditions, its artistic, philosophic and scientific splendor - are just beyond my door. All I need do is step outside and assume my humanity. When will I dare to put my hand on that fateful knob? How much pain does it take? How long does the resentment of the 'insulted and injured' endure? How long does it take to understand that mommy, daddy (and step-daddy) are not the essence of the universe? How long indeed? A single moment of spontaneity!

Dear Ted,

I got your letter and looked at it with trepidation. "Here it comes." I swear, I had an instant fantasy of getting chewed out for my quick replies. Tense. I was actually tense: "Here it comes: 'Cogan, slow down. Slow down.'" Why do I do this to myself, Ted? And it goes on and on. I must be living honestly, but it's a hell of a way to tell myself I'm being real. We're 50s cats, eh? Cigarettes, manhattans, martinis--life on the edge--beauty and death--Lenny Bernstein smoking himself away-- We were weaned on Kerouac and abstract expressionism and all those paperbacks and old friends getting hepatitis and electric shock therapy. We were right there, weren't we, in that whole litany of craziness Ginsburg starts off with at the beginning of "Howl." But do we have to keep that shit alive in us all the way? Penance for survival? I think that's part of it--the guilt at having learned how to survive our mothers. Survivor's guilt. It's a hell of a fix. The war was over a long time ago. We won, and it drove us nuts. What matters how we survived? My friend John Short said that he and I at school were like a couple of Japanese soldiers on a coral island in the Pacific 40 years after Hiroshima, still fighting the war and living on seaweed. You and I tell each other combat stories. Mine take place in the junkyard landscape I talk about in my book. You see it as you and your mother on the only two chairs left in the universe. For me it's a railroad shack in Maine with Cynthia White in dungarees and a blue polk a dot blouse drinking a glass of cheap sauterne.

And then I open your letter, and there's a great sigh of pleasure and relief. You're still there. I seem to trust nothing past the instant. The next moment is a canyon away and not a bridge in sight. But you were there all the time, right on the money. That's what it's all about, isn't it: when I act from within, will anyone else be there? Will I be there? Or will everything crack and self-destruct? Trieber told me a nice Zen story today: the initiate goes to his master and asks for direction, and the master tells him to go to the sage. He goes and asks, "What is my way? Give me my direction." And the sage replies, "Go."

"Pam broods darkly." How right you are. She is a darkness that glows in the dark. The cliche is "sultry," but her darkness is amazing. Black hair, dark skin, but tinged with light. To sit with her is literally to feel a glowing darkness right in front of me. In fact, however, I don't think anything will come of it, but I tell you, I have traveled far in the last two months. Painfully, painfully, my voice is coming through.

I know about your feeling of resentment, "the insulted and the injured." I experienced it first hand. I am still amazed that I walked through it to the other side. Remember that night at the Chinese restaurant a hundred years ago when I came late, or you came late, 10 minutes or so, and I gave you an argument, or you gave me an argument. Then the other guys came, but you glowered and I withered. This went on for weeks and weeks. And then I was stuck with you at Lake Huntington. I remember it as clear as a bell. I took the long walk over to your bungalow (now _that_ was a trek--one foot in front of the other across the grass, with me feeling that I was already beheaded, the headless professor, carrying it under his arm-- an offering). You had just found an old Daily News behind a mirror, something like that. And then the nightmare ended-- not so much induced by you as me. You see, I _wanted_ to talk to you. I didn't care any longer what you felt or what I thought you felt. I'm proud of that moment and feel all the gratitude for your having been right there to talk to me. We seem to do both things at once, or one right after the other--first the two chairs alone in the universe, and then an act of some kind, and the world returns. I feel ten feet taller for having gone out with Pam. She drops by my office now and then. I call her at work. We chat. But you see, once I take that walk, relations change for me. I become myself, or rather, I give myself a chance to be myself. Everything gets clarified (this is so fucking obvious, isn't it?). I think I dropped by your place the next two nights, you did the same, and we started talking. That's where it happened, that's exactly where we really began. We both went through all our private shit viz-a-vis each other in that experience, and then the shit was all over for good. Amazing, isn't it, the way we carry it inside ourselves and then dispose of it all at once, but there's just _so damn much_ of it.

People have been telling me for several weeks now--Nancy, Pam, my cousin Roza, Serge--that I sometimes give the impression of wanting to be left totally alone. They often don't know when or how to reach out to me. It's a bad dream of some kind. Here I am, ostensibly wanting to touch the world, and the world tells me I give the impression of wanting it to go away. It's hopeless. I swear to God, it's hopeless. It's _sometimes_ hopeless, only this sometimes seems to have an eternal life of its own. I have more sense of my mother's continuity than my own. In fact, I generally have a sense that only she continues. I am a discontinuity. A thousand times a day, I reappear to myself, as if by magic. I think of Dylan's lines: "You disappear, you reappear/ You finally find you have nothing to fear/ When a distant trembling voice, unclear/ Startles your sleeping ear to say they think they really found you." As you say, whata life.

As for John Searle, he represented nearly everything I detested in graduate school. Marty's like that. You never know where he is. It's a false front of balance and objectivity, except that he isn't there. Reading him makes you wonder, "so what's all the fuss about?" No insight, no passion, no point of view. He says Bloom's book is "implausibly" entitled "How Our Schools of Higher Education Have Impoverished our Students, etc." And Page Smith's title bothers him too--he seems to smirk at their "apocalyptic views." It can't be as bad as all that, he says. "Killing the Spirit"--how alarmist, how sophomoric, really. And not a word about the books themselves, mind you. I had the feeling that he hadn't read them. And then he dithers into a finale in which he presents a program of education he's already said that others hate, but he's forgotten what he wrote about them, and then presents the same tired words.

Yes, it is interesting that those yo-yos have latched onto literature. The same thing happened in Russia. I don't know about elsewhere, but I know that in the 20s and 30s, the arts in Russia became a battleground for the politics to come. In France too, come to think of it. You know that Genet was so weirded out by Sartre's book on him that he stopped writing for a time. He said that Sartre had sucked his life away. After he won some prize or other, he went out and committed a robbery, just to remind himself who he was.

In high school, I was reading the communist aestheticians, can you imagine? Zhdanov, Herb Finkelstein. I tell you, I've heard it all before--Rembrandt, Goya, Daumier, these were the proto-socialists. Mozart, Joyce, the Cubists, these were the bourgeois "lackeys," the panderers of oppressive taste. Lenny Bruce does it funnier: Goy--one not of the Jewish faith. Second definition--barbarian. Ray Charles is Jewish. Marlboro, Camels, Lucky Strikes are goyish--Salems is Jewish. Esoteric battles, like the raging controversies about the dual body of Christ at the Council of Nicene, when eastern and western christianity fought it out. You had to be part of a select circle in Moscow and Leningrad to know what the hell they were at each other's throats about, but the ripples would be felt around the country in a hundred different ways. Suddenly the posters were different, the films changed direction, novels and poetry went into another mode. But the populace wouldn't know why. All they knew was that they'd better shut up and disappear as best they could. The critics and commissars were tearing at painting and literature to glean the tiniest mileage out of a scene, or character, or plot, arguments piled on top of a literary text to prove some allegory of a current political point of view. Nadezhda Mandelstam talks about it all in <u>Hope Against Hope</u>. Then they shot the writers. That came after the barrage had softened the terrain. I had a first-hand experience of what is going on through Clover's daughter, Ariel, over Thanskgiving. She was in from Clark U. in Mass., and she poured out a torrent of the stuff, as though she were reciting the Gospel at top speed. Here it is: All western literature is male oriented (white male oriented), phallic, thrusting, teleological, mechanical, controlling-- from Plato right on up. Notice all that light imagery in Platonism, medieval doctrine, the Enlightenment? Well, those images of light are phallic thrusts of a superman God, and nature is the mother, the passive, receiving, dominated, oppressed, raped mother. All of western civilization has brought us to this point of nature being destroyed by western, phallic thinking. The old curriculum was the instrument by which people were drained of their own agencies of power. There is nothing of value to learn from phallic consciousness. Schools must teach by reflecting that which the oppressed, the passive, the _feminine_, the silent victims have had to undergo. If it seems as if Ariel is demonizing western civilization, it's because western civ. _is_ demonic. The millions of voices never heard from must and will be heard. It is time to kill the tyrant male, the tyrant who brought us Christianity and Elizabethan poetry, with their images of male, spermatic grace, falling down upon a passive humanity, the same imagery by which men were conditioned to drop napalm on helpless villages (see Forest Wood's new book on Christianity). Linnaeus' system of biological classification is one step away from the mechanistic male mind that brought us El Salvador, the West Bank, and South Africa. Ted, I kid you not. This is how she spoke. I took her up on every point, and at the end, she said it was so odd. She'd never talked to anyone who disagreed with her before. My friend Black Steve up in Bennington (I was White Steve) told me years ago to watch out or I'd end up on 42nd Street walking around with a sign proclaiming that the end of the world was at hand. I told a woman at a party several weeks ago that I was counting on the morons of America to save the country from itself.

The CUNY station on cable TV is showing a series of 22 Russian documentary films made over the last few years, "the Glaznost Film Festival." I've been taping some of them. It's incredible. They are unravelling 70 years of their history, point for point, extricating themselves from what we are now plunging ourselves into. On Olympus, they are having one good laugh.

If your thesis is beyond you now, it probably means you're almost done with it. I had the same feeling when I was at the point of finishing the writing. It took me a long time afterwards to understand what had propelled me into it. And ditto with my present work. I almost don't understand what it was all about. It's finished, dead. Kafka said the same thing to Felice. He didn't care a rap about his finished works, only the moment in which they were made.

The quote from Herder is superb. And yes, that's Herder and the whole line from him right up: "let us enter the country appropriate to him with modesty." Spengler calls it "looking into an alien soul with a deep, wordless understanding." I wish I could find some complete Herder, not that I've looked very hard. No one reads Herder in America except the Herder Society. But he is the man. He and Goethe were friends and collaborators. Your passage illustrates precisely what Neff says about German historicism from Herder through Nietzche and Spengler. I was pleased to see the quote but not surprised. Actually, and although they don't know this at all, the radicals and yo-yo deconstructionists are on the very side they are supposedly in opposition to, not so much on the same

side as in the forefront of all that they oppose. In this as
in all his psychological insights into modern decadence,
Nietzche's remark holds good: He who fights with monsters
should take care lest he become a monster himself. And when
one stares too long into the abyss, the abyss will soon stare
back into him. Soviet communism merely perfected and
intensified the bureaucratic model of Peter the Great.
Spengler calls the bolsheviks the lowest rung on the ladder of
Petrine, bureaucratic resentiment.

Well . . . that's enough for the moment. I notice how much
verve there is in your writing when you focus on your mind-
numbing fatigue. That's like me and my mother in my book. Her
image gives me my wealth of emotional vertigo. Maybe I am
leaving her. We love the identification, and there's the hell
of it, but yes, I agree with you absolutely. There is life
apart from them. All we have to do is go, anywhere but go. The
smallest opportunity, the smallest step, is infinitely better
than where we were.

Love,
Steve

Many Thanks for your offer to Len J. and his wife. I don't
quite know what they plan to do, perhaps pick up on
the university's housing, if it exists.

oh yes -- I read that N-Y-Teacher article a while back.
But where do we all run when the shit hits the fan? Where
is an America?

Dear Steve,

Received the articles you copied. I especially liked the one on Patrocinio Barela - the home-made New Mexican peasant artist. Where there is Art - it will find a way to get out. (The sculptors name you can't remember is Alan Hauser - and yes, he does come straight out of the WPA.)

Liked your letter on Greg Tate. Isn't it amazing how much one can invent using the tools of ignorance? Tate must be a product of the 'new education' - where one learns that ignorance is not only a blessing, but a fountain for metaphysical truth. There is a new book out called Politics and Corruption in Higher Education: The Hollow Men, by Charles J. Sykes - we must read it. Together we will become the savants of education and it's ills in America!

Today, again, the cranes are flying south. To see their V formations undulating in mid-air, and to hear their harsh cries high in brilliant blue sky is sheer pleasure. Then to look down and take in the the Fall yellow leaves of the cottonwoods set off against the grey of the mountains in the distance - all in the great silence and sun-lit aloness of the desert - is enough to bring one very close to the boundaries of oneself, and to start the wonder of life all over again.

Sorry for not having written sooner, but my paper is occupying my head to the hilt - I think, eat, and sleep it - yet, at the same time, something in me, myself, is running alongside my thoughts, trying to come to realization in what I am doing. It is as though I am writing this paper in order to force myself into understanding myself. I am using it as the vehicle to force me to come to grips with myself. In that sense, the paper itself seems both important and unimportant simultaneously. But I must finish it to find, or come closer, to myself. There is a way in which, for all my life, life has eluded me. Perhaps I stopped growing, or consciously experiencing life, about the age of sixteen, and have, since then, been floating on the expectations of others. I am now trying to find and release all those feelings that I could not bear to feel back then. To finally resolve them, and get on with my life. I have been occupied!

The other day on PBS (the McNeil-Lehrer Show - what else?) someone said: stories only happen to those who make them. Well, you are full of stories, and I have nary a one. A significant difference betwen us. I am limited to intellectual excursions, halting excursions into self, and prattle - practical matters. But as to stories - ay, there's the rub. Or rather, the lack of rub between me and the world. For me, to venture out into telling a story is as momentous as venturing out into the 'coal, black night with harpies all around'. Frightening as hell. In other words, I scare the shit out of myself. I want nothing to do with revealing myself to the world or even to myself - the stories will only turn on me and humiliate me. You, if I may take the liberty, can tell marvelous stories, revealing yourself in every word and turn of narrative. You realize your reactions to the world - and more - you enjoy your realizations. For me, this is a gift of the gods. You must have made all the right sacrificial offerings!, whereas I must have stooped and ignorantly eaten them. (Yet, I too, am full of stories. Humble Romainian from the lower depths, belched out of the blaring furnaces of proletarian steel mills into the middle-class world of Protestant America - how else should I be? My stories have no place, and are stories of stupid people doing stupid things. And then, of course, the travesty on family life of my family life - secrets so brutal that even the Devil would not want to know. The gods did not favor me, and put no shrines along my journey North.)

Must everything I write these days be a searching of soul?

I have yet to digest your writings. As I read, I am intrigued and so turn the pages in anticipation of discovering what will happen, who will show up, and to understand the meaning of that image, this tale, etc., - but I am not sure what I have when I reach the end of this tale, the final focus of that image, etc... In some way, I think I am looking for the wrong thing. I need more time. Your repeated insistence of your mothers quite definite, emphatic, real, unmistakable, etc., illness is a little bothersome. Why so often? To make sure the reader knows that you know that she was really ill apart from your perception of her? But what is the point of knowing that - for the reader? And especially that, for nowhere else do you want to draw such a fine, clear line between reality and you. Elsewhere, the existence of such a line is even questioned - but not when it comes to your mother. Her illness emerges as the one really real thing - that no one, not even God, could question.

You capture something - and capture it beautifully - but I don't know what yet. Not a time. Not a locale. To say 'you', your mother and father, and so and so, etc., is true, but something more is going on; reflections on life, reality, the past, the present, the present as past and the past as present, the odd-ball things that can influence a life forever, the stillness of life, the eternity of a minute, the minute of eternity, the ghetto in the ghetto(one past upon another past) surrounded by sweet, beckoning America - Manhattan, a school, a magazine, a balsawood P51, a farm, a resort hotel, a baseball card, the wildness of night driving with headlights falling nervously on black asphalt, a San Francisco - to escape from the gulag, the phographs of death, the past, - only, once escaped into - offers no lasting relief either in itself or by itself, and (though filled with delights) turns out to be significant only when it reveals the themes and conflicts of childhood - which, in fact, is all the present really is anyway and so it is back to the ghetto in the ghetto, to once again over turn every rock, looking for the ugly centipede of truth which no sooner glimpsed flits beneath another - the place where the self exists scattered in a million microcosms - stored, but called upon daily - in oneself for eternity. But the mother - Queen Lear - transcends all this, or encompasses the eternity of self - she as the center which has no circumference - and her illnes somehow defines the limits of the reality you write about. But, as I say, I need more time. I am not at all sure that I have anything at all.

In a letter you speak of the sleep of Kutuzov. But he knew everything. There was not an inch of Russia he did not know and that wasn't in him or he in it. As he slept, the geography of Russia was in repose. Like an out-stretched hand waiting for the fly to walk from finger's tip into his palm for the final crushing, Russia/Kutuzov pretended sleep. We pretend the same sleep. Only America - from sea to shinning sea - isn't us. Mere mortals, we merely project our past onto the present - confuse it with the universe - and wait for the unwary to walk in. When they do, when they pass through our time-barrier, they enter our dreams, becoming dream-persons, Hindoo's to the core. They, as all dream-people, are unaware that were we to only shift our attention, or awaken, they should disappear in a puff. But it is we who need to awaken from the 'nightmare of the past', the illusion of an eternal self swirling in a gypsy crystalball.

Enter Pam. But without a passport filled with old photos and the smudged markings of ancient lands. Exotic, she recalls nothing. Beautiful, but in an unknown aesthetic. Animated, but robotically. Clumsily, she walks around knocking into things. She belongs in a different dream.

I too think of reality as such an extension of my past, only when Napoleon walks into my dream, I refuse to clench my hand into a fist. Rather, I suddenly claim to be only the subsitute janitor of the place, snigger at the palacial facade which decieved him, and apologize for the mess and dirt. In this way, not only do I deny my dream, I make him scratch his head wondering if he ever left France. This, to me, in all sickness, is victory. (For me, 'Napoleon' is anything that moves, hangs on a wall, or is projected onto a screen.)

Was glad to read that the Pope decided not to do away with celibacy. He argued that were the church to do so, it would be indistinguishable from Club-Med - or something like that.

Everybody, including the cars, are fine. Josh is doing terrifically in school, and enjoying life in Boulder. Ezra - whom I have asked repeatly to contact you - is, well, living a hermits life with Shira two blocks away from you. He has a good job, and is contemplating which graduate school to go to. Ruby is busy in law school - trying to wrench herself away from years of intellectual apathy and emotional isolation, i.e., putting new strains upon her self, wringing it to see what else it contains. Working with the crippled for so long, I think we have all suffered. Our identification with them is too strong, and they encourage the crippled outlook upon life.

The solitude - the sun, the sky, the quiet, the clouds, the wind, the cranes, the mountains - have been good for me. Each day I am forced to confront myself, to encounter its miserly joys with only the blank face of nature looking back at me. Surrounded by that indifferent, but powerful stare, I begin to realize that I, and I alone, have shaped the near meaningless universe I live in - all in the effort not to be myself, but another, a subsitute janitor working in a strange house whose address is unkown to him. For the first time in living memory I think I actually want to go home, to be myself.

Well, more anon. I wish I could respond more directly to you letter of 9/24, it is so full. Perhaps later.

Say hello to David, and, of course, to all the guys. I really miss our private rib and hearts of lettuce dinners. I miss you, and seem to need your guidance in matters of the heart.

Love
Ted

P.S. Enclosed is a copy of a photo of my father, mother, Oliver, and me. I am just begining to have a clue as to who that little guy was, and what happened to him.

P.S. Guess who they are?

Dear Ted,

My letters to you turn into running conversations over
several days and sometimes weeks, but I've decided not to date
the sections anymore. Now that I'm trying to familiarize
myself with the notion of spontaneity, my dating of separate
sections is an unnecessary formality that I no longer like or
even understand. I'll leave the archeological levels for the
scholars to decode. I'm tired of my compulsive, one-sided
attention to historical detail, my endless justifications of
my experience to a non-existent audience, a perpetual doctoral
defense and last judgment that rages in my head. I am weary of
my old ways, and this weariness is intensified by the way the
world goes round. Perhaps it was something about the news from
the middle east last week, or another article about multiculturalism in the colleges, or something about the N.Y.C.
scene--something about people acting blind and stupid and my
hearing about one event too many and suddenly feeling that all
the facts and truths are totally impotent against the blind
stupidity that passes for the world. I build up truths inside
my head, the way you do, I think, to defend myself from
ghosts. Can you imagine if Arnold Schwarzenegger had to make
"Total Recall" using our histories? His muscles would soon
turn into match sticks, and he'd end up being Charles Atlas
"Before," getting sand kicked in his face.

My weariness: perhaps I read one story too many in the news
about a horror in the public schools, or another shooting. Two
people died from smoke inhalation in a subway fire just
outside the Borough Hall station yesterday. I heard it on
national public radio while driving through a snowstorm on the
Massachusetts turnpike (bringing Sonya down for her month of
work in a photo studio). Imagine. I am driving through winter
snow along deserted fields, and my car radio tells me a story
about explosions, panic, smoke-filled subway cars at my stop,
Borough Hall, at 9:15 in the morning, rush hour time. The
firemen arrive in several minutes and are required to stand
around doing nothing for an hour because of how the subway
regulations operate. All trains have to be at a certain
distance away from the fire before they can turn the power
off. Every item in the story made no sense to me, yet that's
the way it was. It is frightening to realize that I am in a
situation where no one is in charge and everyone is afraid to
handle anything. I look around and see a thousand versions of
the sickness that enveloped me as a child, and to this date,
as always, I see myself desparately clinging to whatever sense
of self I have. And as always, there are the times when I
simply cannot tell if, in this clinging, I am developing or
thwarting myself, whether I am doing what I want or what my
mother wants.

In the midst of my usual bewilderments (I simply live with them), I'm ready to start peddling my Ms. and will have to put in time and effort to contact people, get names and addresses (I have a bunch already), make lots of copies, and send them out. There's going to be a big change coming for me when I finish that part of the project. This month of Jan. is going to involve several projects of that kind--my ms, money, Sonya's new college applications (she's going to transfer after this year), another essay to send out, things of that kind, paperwork that's real.

I drove up to Portland and the next morning picked up Sonya during the start of a blizzard--found myself driving along country roads outside of Portland almost completely whited out. There's something about that particular silence, white fields in the distance, a line of bare trees, a house here and there, and I'm home. I feel myself home. It's not the only place I belong, but I am so close to being back to myself when I'm in that scene. It's the memories of Vermont, but not only that. It's more whatever drove me to Vermont in the first place--the little cabins in the woods in my Russian book of fairytales, but something beyond that as well and not to be articulated or understood, just felt and lived.

For several reasons I'll spell out, I feel really down today. It was a bring down, as usual, to have to return to the city, especially from the winter landscape that I love so much. On the other hand, I had my years in the snow, and if I want them again, I know what it will take: a change that allows me to see myself clearly, so that I can finally recognize the world outside of me for what I want. Actually, I think the rhythm of things is pretty well spelled out for me-- the things I still need to do, mostly how I'm tied in to Sonya and the money I need to square away for myself, therapy, the bungalow apartment, other things. It's all there in the bud.

What's so dreadful for me in N. Y. is not just that the city I grew up in has all but disappeared but that it has been replaced by something utterly stupid, destructive, and incomprehensible, especially to itself. That's one of the lessons I get from the rap song you xeroxed for me (that wonderful copying toy of yours came back to me the moment I saw the curly paper in the envelope). Rakim feels all the horrible truth of his condition and his community's, and the appeal of his awareness blinds us to the fact that he's in complete darkness over what to do and how to be. My father was in that darkness. It had another style, but it was equally horrible to see someone so appealing, so filled with recognitions of injustices, nevertheless blinded by whatever he took to be the way out of those conditions. I know the appeal of wanting to "go all the way, to go the limit, right to the core." The impulse is at the heart of what the brothers are going through in Karamazov. I know that feeling right down to my toes. But the style nowadays seems so feeble, so unmanly. A leak-proof osterizer, by all means! That would at least be something, but Rakim and the deconstructionists want to insist, like deprived infants in a rage, that nothing but themselves is real, that there are no leaks, that there are no facts, that there are no limits to anything. It's insane. In an adult, at any rate, it's strictly speaking, insane. The world is telling us at every step of the way, to the last subatomic particle, that we encounter things through the limits they impose--or another way, that we are absolutely creatures of limit, simply through our separateness, through our very ability to move around. For Spengler, it's only the vegetable world that participates in the flow of things, that truly lives in the midst of cosmic processes, whereas all moving things have an inbuilt anxiety simply by their freedom to move--that simply being free to move lets the creature know, consciously or not, that it is separate from the universe.

Well, that's a way of expressing it. I don't care how it's said, as long as the consciousness of separateness is there. Even Islam is fine by me. Why not? But Rakim is unreal. He shouts "My identity!" with no sense of separateness at all, except as things intefere with him, like Chateaubriand's picture of Napoleon, for whom even a pesky gnat had no right to fly except by his permission. I don't believe what Rakim says, and what's more, I don't believe he does either. The nagging has to be going on inside of him, and to deal with it, he intensifies his rage. A tyrannical personality always ups the ante when confronted by the outside world, getting crazier at every turn. Rakim's words, after all, have other repercussions than the ones he intends. In fact, they arouse antagonism all the more, or they get co-opted and he gets to make a fortune. He learns how easy it is to jive the folks who pay him for shitting on their heads. And the easier it gets, the stupider he gets and the stupider he makes his community that also gives him his money by buying his records and his way of life. Go tell Rakim that his rap is fueling the fire that his rap is supposedly against. And it wouldn't matter if he knew. He loves the chaos he thrives upon. That to me is the worst of fascism or any of the modern ideologies. The people who use them don't even believe in their own raving ideas. They are merely the means they've found, depending on their own circumstances or quirks of unconsciousness, to live out the chaos they feel in themselves. What bewilders us is the notion of people living to destroy, to destroy themselves as well. The truly terrible thing is that we see no opposition to what is going on. We live with the old good guys in our heads and don't know what to do ourselves, and yet whatever is to be done must happen as simply as a ripe fruit falling from a tree. The only clean people in "The Sorrow and the Pity" are the two brothers, farmers, who don't even understand the question when Ophuls asks them why they joined the Resistance. All they can say is that there was no other way to be. It was as simple as that for them. Everyone else in the film is tortured with complications, or filled with reasons, lessons, family histories, anything but the notion of a simple deed. Even Hamlet acts with superb simplicity and spontaneity. Every time he does something, it is with swift, unerring grace. Everyone he kills doesn't know what hit them. Rozencrantz and Guildenstern hand the letters he's forged to the king of England, and bop! _their_ heads get chopped off. Polonius is killed behind a tapestry and never sees Hamlet coming at him, although he's spying on him at the time. The truth is that even when we doubt, you and I, we are striving to be real. I don't know how it is with others, but somewhere, those little boys we were learned how to keep themselves alive. Remember that question you used to ask about Mel and Gerson? You wondered how it was that they couldn't stand themselves, because even you, in your worst condition, still knew that there was a better way to live.

I read your letters two ways almost at the same time. They crackle with energy. Yo Steve! Like a splat of eyewash to clean the orbs. I know I'm in for a cleaning when I get your mail. Thousands of false words, piled up in my head over the weeks, just fall away, and I'm back there where the good things are. You envy my stories? I love your sharpness. You are so elliptically direct, it's marvelous. It would be so easy for me to be entranced by the style, _le mot juste_ for murky pain. From the Goon Show: "My God, someone is screaming in agony! Fortunately, I speak the language." You see what I mean? And then I think, no, this is not a question of aesthetics. Or is it? In a college seminar evening on Kafka, I remember how Dennis Flynn and I were the only students, two out of twelve, who were positively thrilled, laughing and meditating all at once, while the others were completely revolted by "In the Penal Colony" and "The Metamorphosis." How much do we mine our feelings for the sheer interest, the sheer life of it? How much more _interesting_ than the daily round. At least for us, the daily round becomes incorporated into our past, seen and understood through that railroad car lost in time and space. Sometimes, though, I wonder if I am reading your letters realistically or missing the point. This difficulty actually reflects a personal one, quite separate from your mail. I accomodate to experience, struggle to stick with what I know makes sense, take what I can, enjoy the aesthetics where I can, and yet underneath, there is the grinding, pulverizing feeling that I am barely alive, that there are others who really live their lives, while I can only make do, slogging through each day, taking my pleasures as they randomly occur. The pleasures themselves start to seem tainted--moments of relief, which are not grounded in anything real, simply fantasy escapes that somehow miss the point. A few hours after my first reading of your letter, I suddenly felt the pain of what _you_ were saying, and it brought me up short. The first time around, it was wonderful to read your letter. The second time, I was aghast, partly because of the pain itself that you were going through and partly because of the pain that it evoked in me, a reminder of how far away I can be from seeing things as they are, as I would need to see them for myself in order to live consistently, _deliberately._

An added problem is that I'm kicking myself unnecessarily for not experiencing everything about your letter all at once. On the second reading, I suddenly became aware of my own difficulties in the areas you describe (on second reading, you got to me!). May we come out of the antithesis and get both sides together all at once, the way Roebling did with his Gothic arches and the engineering of a steel suspension bridge, "Of the harp and fury fused."

Example of both sides: I live my life as receptively as possible to what needs to be done, to what I myself need to do, and then come up against those moments when I seem to disappear. I am not there at all, but simply hungering for a dedicated life, to be at home among the snowy woods, to live my life with the dedication of an artist hermit-monk. I have a video documentary off CUNY cable TV of a former Russian communist and soldier, an old man living in the forest and taking care of the trees. It's a stunning thing to see. And yet there is no way to plunge into one's life out of desparation. It simply does not work. ("There is a goal, but there is no way. What we call the way is simply wavering"-- Franz K.). It just has to happen through the way we actually live our lives and the struggles we must pursue. I don't know why it has to be that way, but it does. There is no way to anything worthwhile without the struggle and the discipline, and yet, in the end, the thing we want simply falls into our lap, often in spite of the struggle, or contrary to what we thought it meant. A slight turn of the mind and we too would be at home in the void, like my beloved Prof. Chiappe.

Anything happening in the way of jobs? Is everything sort of turning around in a big soup, the sludge refinery of your mind, distilling different products at different rates of speed? I see you having "world enough and time," mostly because of the space in which you live.

The literature, as always, for your amusement. I cannot help but pass it on to you, remembering how we used to pore over books and the news, debriefing each other as a way of making it through the day, revolving it all through our thoughts and memories. I too feel that those days helped to put me in the world, into some chunk of it I had not been before.

The Pam situation by now has gone through so many changes that I simply cannot write anything that would stay still on the page. Any conclusive thoughts I have at any given point turn out to be pieces of the unknown. I can't say anything right now except that I've been leading an active life. Lots of events, a swirl of feelings, but more than likely a tale told by an idiot, full of sound and fury, signifying nothing.

Will probably call before you get this letter. Len J. tells me he was pleased to talk with you. They've left already for Georgia, where, as he says, he will visit friends and then make a right turn for New Mexico. He also tells me lots of friends in NY told him about people they knew in the Santa Fe area, on the order of: "You ought to call my friends out there. He's a gestalt therapist and she's doing needlework."

Apparently I was the only one who put him in touch with people in a real way by calling and making it possible for him to feel an actual connection to you. And besides, you're not a gestalt therapist and Ruby's not finding herself in clay or needlework. Those people probably deserve the five second sound bites they get from friends of theirs.

Your card was beautiful. The long winding road indeed.

Pam turns out to be wound up tighter than a drum (this point seems to be holding true throughout it all), with a seven year old child she left to her husband, while she spent the first 6 months of its life in stupor on a couch! I'm beginning to think of my neurosis as an instrument of observation, an instrument Bell Labs couldn't begin to touch. A few more Pams in my life and I really will be ready for Basho's hut.

Much love,
Steve

PS   Enclosed Chet Baker tape after listening to my copy. WKCR did a memorial broadcast when he died a few years ago. I taped a few hours of it but never heard it till this xmas. "Heard melodies are sweet/ But those unheard are sweeter still." What a way to encounter the world!

**1991
to
1993**

Yo! Steve!

> Well, my name is Rakim. I am interested
> in where I came from, and who I am, and
> what's my duties on the planet earth.
> ....I want to speak the truth, since I
> know the truth.
> Well, I study Islam, and you know,
> that's the base of life, right there.
> Tells you everything you need to know,
> and once I had knowledge of self, I
> became very wise, my eyes was open a lot
> wider that they wasn't before that. With
> this right here, I can see things more
> clearly now, so I know how to use my
> mind, and things of that nature....

And here I sit - white-boy on the earth - wondering what the

hell its all about; Plato to Bartok, Bartok to LaoTze. The

trouble, I guess, is that I don't know Rakim and I ain't

black.(See enclosed for more Truth.)

Muslims and deconstructionist alike gorge themselves on

morality, They suck sick succor. Raising their staffs, they

parade as Moses' through our libraries and coffee-houses -

like the Priest on Potemkin. Cross-eyed and sweating - as the

good Christians of yore - they try to exorcise the absence of

good -

which, of course, is the Evil that is the West. All priests must deconstruct - to biblically reduce evil to non-existence, that is the only way Christians - and, apparently, Mulims - can philosophically understand and tolerate Evil.

We are back in the Dark Ages fighting the hair-shirts. Some struggles seem never to go away. Especially those between the bright and the stupid; those battered, but willing to live alone in the universe, and those battered, but needing a Daddy to tell them it is for their own good.

Enough!

Alone in this desert I dwell, a monk. I contemplate, meditate, ponder, day-dream, agnonize (without moving), and, in general, try to understand the world's truly greatest absence - me:

Deep in day-dream, with vacant eyes turned toward the reddening horizon, I flit my fingers over the grainy desert sand: arabesques and other strange figures appear. Looking down, I rub them out. I resume my former vacant gaze. They reappear. Again I look down, and again I rub them out again. But again my fingers move, and they reappear. I get annoyed. My fingers and the designs they etch are destroying my concentration. Again, my fingers trace these strange figures in the sand. And again I.... All my life I have been on this desert - and doing only these three things: pondering the world's greatest absence, drawing arabesques in the sand, and getting annoyed.

The other day - a day like all others - I discovered that

these arabesques and strange figures were my soul trying to communicate with me. Forming almost of themselves on the dirty sand, these strange signs are the hieroglphics of self. It is them I must ponder.

Imagine this:

T. wakes up one morning having dreamed his history away. Moreover, he is unaware of his loss.

Fortunately, he spys an empty cup, and smells coffee brewing. He calculates - helped perhaps by some now distant memory - that they are meant to go together. He is right, for when "X" walks into the kitchen, it also asks for a 'cup of coffee'. "Good", says T. to himself, "Coffee. Cup. Together." Slowly, throughout the breakfast, T picks up that "X" is different than he; 'X' seems to know how things go together, and what they are for. He speaks as though he is at home in the world. So when "X" combs his hair, so too does T, when "X" brushes his teeth, so too does T., etc..

For the next fifty years, and with moderate interest T. observes many patterns of human behaviour. He memorizes them, and mimicks them on appropriate ocassions. Themselves an object of intense memorization, "ocassions" prove more difficult to memorize. He also notices the traces of behavioral patterns left by others - how long couch stains are left unattendeed, how one leaves books when one is not quite done with them, etc.. He waits for others to leave scenes to be able to reconstruct absences.

Since the interiors of others are inacessible to him, T. surmizes that motivations for action - which some say precede and cause human behavior - do not really exists. Nonetheless, T. tries to imitate patterns of behavior that are universal and whose imputed motivations are above reproach or questioning. He leaves in sticky situations.

There are, of course, many patterns T fails to see - many, in fact, are purposely hidden from him. He is helplessly unaware of their existence. His range of activity therefore, is limited to the 'public' aspects of humanity; street scenes, parties, auditoriums - any thing involving more than two people.

Alone, he is not, strictly speaking, with himself. He is simply mute. Nature and reality cease to exist. For T, esse est pecipi only when seen through the eyes of others.

An alien among aliens, T conceals his parasitic existence. There is no traitorous motive. Indeed, there is no motive at all, other than, of course, to to conceal his existence as a parasitic.

Every morning when the alarm sounds, he is off and running. Patterns of behavior must be performed, expectations must be met.

All to no end of course - for ends or purposes of behavior, as motivations for action - are never revealed to him. But they must be done, and done exceedingly well, to aver suspicion of idiocy.

For ninety years T is positive that no one suspects. He

considers himself a success. He scoffs at the superficiality of humanity, and it's brutal stupidity in not recognizing an alien presence.

One day, cane in hand, grey hair flowing out from under his cap, a loose slab of mud fell from high on an ancient Indian dwelling and landed with a thud on his head. T died. His bones dry on the desert. Later they are discovered by an anthropologist. They are catalogued and buried on the spot. On a twisted pinon tombstone is carved: Bones of an Unknown Victim.

Moral: Don't dream away your history. Or: Pay Attention When Sand Moves, It May Be You Trying To Come Back.

Glad you liked the Herder — and yes, it is typical of his time: Faust walking on tip-toe through the unknown.

Like you, as I career around the mountain pass thinking I am finally on the right road and on my way down into the world, some one on the over-pass shouts down "Hey, didn't you see the sign? That road is the way back up!"

Oh well, certain things do seem to be changing. For instance: 1) words such as 'me', 'myself', 'my history', 'my past', and 'experience' are gaining new dimensions in my understanding; 2) the inexplicable gap, hiatus, void, universe between me now and me of a moment ago, is appearing more as the gap, the hiatus, the void, the universe between me of fifty years ago and the world today; 3) I begin to understand that the gap, hiatus, etc, is not an interior gap, hiatus, etc, at all, but rather a space-time warp between me and present reality. I am living in the universe of fifty years ago! It is as though I am trapped inside a de-railed train-car watching the world and time whizz by. For fifty years! Time/space is the veil between me and the world - and, as all know, there is no time travel. I am marooned in a universe which no longer exists. All that moves in my observation-car are phantoms, spirits, images, the dustless geometry of things that used to be, and me, a thirteen year old Dorian Grey. My hands, even my vision, can not really penetrate the time-space barrier of my observation window. Yet, this is where I live, caught behind a window upon whose outer surface I appear as in the present and as though real. All that has acreted upon me over the years - the dress, the mannerisms, the thoughts, the experiences, etc., however, are simply plastered all over the outer surface of the window, glued. Behind the glass, I can not move without revealing my surface as surface.

In the crucible of childhood, I forged the prison of my childhood. An Alcatraz of the spirit. I used bars of anger, locks of resentment, floors of contempt, the air of disappointment, and the rusted wheels of humilation to build it.

I apologize for this long excursion into the depths of what in the end must disappear as all neurosis disappear, without a trace of ever having existed. But, I do expose the anger to rawly, and without purpose. It is embarrasing.

But wait, I think I hear the porter coming to open the door.

There are a few things other than me that have occupied me of late - not many - but some.

1) audience - for whom does one write? Up to now my writings have been a monologue - "for my eyes only". Not designed to persuade anyone, nor to create anything, they have simply been adventures in a perambulator, or rather, in an osterizer that does not leak.

2) What does one make when one writes? a reality? But of what sort? The reality Chateaubriand creates with a wave of his magic wand is there for all to feel - where is mine? Do I have one? If not, where does fiction end and reality begin?

3) How do mountains, rocks, sunsets, cats, lamp-posts, people, etc., exist? By themselves? Or must they be perceived? Up till now, I thought only of themselves. But they do not. They must be perceived. How does one do that? I seem unable to perceive them.

4) Either rocks, mountains, people, cats, etc., speak to one or they do not. If they do not, how does one communicate with the world? If metaphor, analogy, and simile are the means by which one constitutes oneself as a being - i.e., by hearing the speech of oceans, books, trees, cats, lamp-posts, etc., - how can one have a being when one is deaf to the world?

Why is it that without a being one is full of oneself - endlessly repeating the plentitude of nothingness?

I remember telling you several times of my "fire-cracker" experience. Well, now I am sure that if an atomic explosion were to occur directly over my head - my head being ground-zero

- I would successfully manage to ignore it. If I can daily so
ignore the entire world, why not the A-Bomb? I would keep on
walking as though nothing happened. Others, at the moment of
their death, would look up in amazment at me. A slight smile
would curl my lip. See: I told you. That's what you get for
living.

A dictionary - the solipism of the intellect. The world -
the solipism of experience. The past - the solipism of the
self.

Hegel described the flora and fauna of America as too weak
to support more than scraggley, demented humans. Perhaps he was
right. The atmosphere over the continent _is_ vaporous, dank, and
geologically mysterious.

But must we also contend with the Rakims and
deconstructionist who daily rewrite the Malleus Malificarum?
They are out to destroy the reality that I am trying to
recapture. That I am crawling toward across the vast desert of
the past to reach - parched, dying, and out of my mind. They
literally want to expose the past by denying that the present
ever existed: Eden (a mosaic of observation-cars scattered over
the earth, each jammed with it's own tribe of people) is still
here, if only you could feel the wet grass between your toes
and the spear in your hand! They hit my neurosis where it
hurts. If Allah descends to create these observtion-cars, I
swear I'll shoot him before he raises his staff to dispell the
non-existence of Evil.

Ah, there is so much more to say....but it is late and

tomorrow I must depart early in the morning for Phoenix.

Stay in touch. I need your letters.

Dear Ted,   June 1, '99
Just took another look at this passage
in *Sky*. Do you remember Cendrars
talking about Churchill? Isn't this
Lukacs' portrait in a single stroke:
"- the living, prophetic word of
Churchill . . . announcing 'blood,
toil, tears and sweat,' gave renewed
life and hope to the millions of
listeners tuned in to the BBC, because
this dreamer, whose humor and
conviction shook the Jerries to the
core, derived his ideas from reality,
tragic and desperate though it was,
and this prophet, with his profound
good sense, his cynicism, his way of
calling things by their name without
sentimentality and without letting
himself be led astray by preconceived
theories or gulled by received ideas,
spoke from day to day as a good
fighter, without ever losing sight of
the Earth . . . " We certainly know
how to pick our historians and poets,
says I with pride.
                    Steve

Ted Sitea

Glendale

95

Jan. 21, '92

Dear Ted,

    The image of Maya Angelou was so frightening and her poem so awful
that I had to get the thing out of my system. It's a parody of sorts.
Doesn't she looks like a child's worst nightmare come to life?

A Hydrant, An Electric Train, A Microwave

Outdoor plumbing marks the spot where canines left tokens
Of their sojourn here.
You may open me in summertime,
But only if you face your abject brutishness,
On streets pulverized with greased machines
Spilling angry words.

High above the prison plates of poisoned air,
A window calls to you:
Give everything you own away,
And I will let you play with my electric trains.
I hear Vinnie Sica, Kenny Delson, Lenny Tash
Telling me that they're at one with everything.
They know.
They know plenty.
They can hear the choo-choos talking each to each.
I do not think that they will talk to me.

Up from Canarsie, Bensonhurst, Bay Ridge,
Out of the cradle endlessly rocking,
Lift up, lift up your coffee cups,
And place them all inside of me,
Me, microwave of plenitude,
I give you the three-ringed sign of purity, body, and flavor
And keep alive the dream of a multicultural communion,
A sacred rainbow menu of boiled Virginia ham on matzoh bread,
Warm fermented yak cheese on a bed of kelp,
And hot banana soup to build strong bodies eight ways.
In the restaurants of eternity
Chop suey destinies proclaim that you do not have to live
Yesterday tomorrow,
Although you may have to check from time to time
With the proper authorities.

As you climb on Plato's ladder
On the way from here to there,
Listen hard for clues.
Read poets who know everything
And have a song in their hearts.
Look upon the riddle of history
With moist eyes and parted lips,
And say,
Hello. How are you? Have a nice day.

From the heart of the Marquesas, I
steal a line from Paul Gauguin and

pinch your claws,

Steve

96

Dear Ted,

You haven't drunk the hemlock yet, have you? ("I have no self"). Apropos your (can we call it self-?) observation, I remembered Drummond's conversations with Ben Jonson:

> That he struck at Sir Hierome Bowe's breast, and asked him if he was within.

Kafka doubted the business of his own identity as well, ending one letter, "Yours (how shall I put it?), Franz Kafka."

Thank God for the morons of America. There's a Hemlock Society, did you know? The right to suicide! The <u>Hemlock</u> Society. There's Allan Bloom talking away on the finest, the highest points of Socratic courage, the model he holds up against those worms at Cornell, and all that America can do is read the <u>Apology</u> and come up with a slogan. I can see it now: Hamlet alone after the court has exited: "Oh that this too too solid flesh would melt,/ Thaw, and resolve itself into a dew,/ But that the Everlasting had not fixed his canon 'gainst self-slaughter./ How weary stale, flat, etc," and in walks a demonstrator with a placard, comes up to Hamlet, and yells in his ear: "Go ahead, man. Kill yourself! Fuck the church. Fuck your father's ghost. Kill yourself. Go with the flow." <u>Hamlet</u>, by the way, teaches us that murder hides behind platitudes.

But look at it this way: given the idiocy of the place, maybe there's something to be gleaned (or stolen) here for us to make our way. Len Jenkin used to get catalogues from a reprint house specializing in weird Americana and once showed me some material from a dentist up in Rhinebeck who developed a cosmology based on visions off laughing gas.

I was annoyed with CNN's slick "Gulf War" signs--you know, the ones that peel off to the left revealing images of military machines in the Gulf--and I thought, well, maybe that's the way of the place. The slickness is part of the machine. It's the way the country recognizes itself. I mean, sure, it's nauseating, but on the other hand, <u>The New Yorker</u> quoted one woman as saying how sick those CNN Gulf War computer graphics made her feel, and suddenly it seemed to me that it's so damn easy to feel disgusted with this place, so damn easy to criticize, to feel smarter than the boobs. But something makes me want to stick with them, or rather, feels a healthy respect for them. After all, they said Russia had slave labor camps when all the smart and right thinking people had this warm glow inside of them when they saw pictures of Uncle Joe. I remember how ignorant the <u>Daily News</u> sounded when it used the phrase "slave labor camps." My feeling is that the morons are right some of the time and at least good for a laugh at other times. The tragic mode is no good unless we're open to the comic one as well.

July 18,'92

Dear Steve.....

Let us fly, you and I, into art as we would fly in search
of exotic lands for they exists no more while vanished
gestures, preserved on a page in Flaubert's description of a
19th century Arab fart, in the chiseled hip of Marcantonino's
Eve, or in the recorded sound of a single bar of Mahler's
Nachtmusik, are all more invigorating and dangerous than a hunt
and slash adventure through the jungle to find the one and only
McDonald's in Timbuktu. These moments in time past are true
fountains of Ponce de Leon where we may sip at will and regain
our strength. Let us submerge ourselves in these arabesques of
the soul, and never surface undrenched. Where else is the the
present so real, so dark, but in the depths of an Breughel eye?

Fukuyama, a Washington intellectual, has written that
history has reached it's Hegelian end - the Spirit has been
realized - time is now only the world manifesting the details
of the Enlightenment. Wars, pestilence, and brutality will
continue but to one end; the eradication of excellence. The
unconditioned victory of the deformed, the blind, the stupid,
the petty, the unskilled, the shameless, of "men without
chests." And the price we pay for that historic struggle in
egalitarianism is the loss of history. The loss of a past built
on bravado, desire, want, and the struggle for excellence..
All that went into its making - the art - will no longer be
necessary. Not even to the memory.

Will the art of world-wide democracy be a folk-art? Things
shed of all standard, aesthetic, reason, and universal
humanity? So individualized that the making of them requires no
common, historic tradition (none beyond the blinking light at
Lake Huntington junction, and the famine of 'ought8), and the
relating to arouses no more than dumb curiosity (in Cotton
Plant,Alabama we don't paint the cruifix thata way)? Each piece
taken as it is; always, as it were, out of your context? Does

this mean that the 'art of the massses' is not Art, but unrealized gibberish? Or will there be an underlying substratum of culture - an aesthetic of a Weltgeist - that informs them all, but so immense that 10 thousand years would not suffice the understanding? (Like the Weltgeist that perhaps informed the paintings of Lascoux, yet would remain obscure to even those who worked within the same Spirit on the Oklahoma mounds? And passed before any of them could.)

But Oh, that Steel Town rag that rocks my soul! Those Sunday afternoon picnics in the Black Oak Forest below the Bethlehem foundry where black-shoed, mustachioed Romanians, drinking, sweating with ties undone, played their trumpets, clarinets, mouth-pipes, and saxophones and we danced the hora under the trees, babushkas flying, stomping our feet on the dusty ground, and afterwards in barbecue smoked filled air, ate mush and sausages. That too, is the past. (Medieval festivities that prefigured my destiny in America!) And in those moments lay unrealized sentences, paintings and choral works that would shake the world in only nine days. (What world?) If only I could put my hands on them.

In Norman Cohen's Pursuit of the Millenium, he mentions one Diodorus Siculus (2ADcirca) who wrote of a utopia on seven, distant islands. He called the inhabitants of this place "heliopolitans". Isn't that marvellous!

You must read Uncle Tom, especially chap.35 - a wonderful nocturnal phantasy; brutal as all get-out. She is wonderful - and right on the money. (J.C. Furnas, in '56, wrote a study of Stowe's book called Goodbye to Uncle Tom (awful) - some day soon I will to you of this and Wilson's study in Patriotic Gore . She deserves it - as do I.)

What is life all about?, is a question that has just now occured to me. At 5000 feet elevation I should have some perspective, no?

At any rate, enjoy the enclosed tape, AND HAVE A MARVELLOUS TIME IN FRANCE!!! It is Brooklyn rocking on the Atlantic that is vertiginous, not you! In case you miss him in the long halls, I am sending you a fancy reproduction of "Paysage". Give my love to Clover. (Len returns 7/30.)

WRITE!! BOTH OF YOU!!

Jed

Voodoo & Jazz on '78's

1. Moundongue Oh Ye Ye Ye (Rada Song) Damballa Wedo Singers
2. Erzulie Nainain Oh (Jenvalo Song)
3. Soleil Malade (Rada Song)
4. Jean Pierre Poungue (Congo Song)
   (All of the above are on the General Label, Consolidated
   Records Inc.,NYC. #5002-B(2651), undated)
5. T. Monk Sextet- <u>Suburban Eyes</u>. Idrees Suliman,trumpet; Danny
   Quebec West,alto sax; Billy Smith,tenor sax; T. Monk,piano;
   Eugene Ramey,bass; Art Blakey,drums.
6. T. Monk- <u>Thelonius</u>. Same sextet.
7. T. Monk- <u>Well You Needn't</u>. Trio of above.
8. T. Monk- <u>'Round About Midnight</u>. George Tait,trumpet; Edmund
   Gregory, alto sax; Robert Paioge,bass; Art Blakey,drums.
   (All the above are on the Blue Note Label; 542 & 543-B & A)
9. C. Parker Sextet- <u>Crazeology</u>. M. Davis,trumpet; J.J.
   Johnson,trombone; Duke Jordan,Piano; Tommy Potter,bass;
   Max Roach,drums,; Parker, sax.
10. <u>Crazeology II</u>. Sextet.
11. <u>Lover Man</u>. Howard McGhee, rumpet; Jimmy Bunn,piano; Bob
    Kesterson, bass; Roy Porter, drums. Parker, sax.
12. <u>Be-Bop</u>. Same as above.
13. Howard McGhee Sextet- <u>Midnight At Minton's.</u> Teddy Edwards,tenor;
    Dingbod,bass; Dodo Marmarosa,piano; Arv Garrison,guitar;
    Roy Porter, drums; McGhee,Trumpet.
14. <u>Dialated Pupils</u>. Same as above.
15. <u>Up In Dodo's Room</u>.   ''
16. <u>High Wind In Hollywood.</u>
17. <u>Dorothy</u>. James Moody,trumpet; Milt Jackson,tenor; Hank
    Jones, piano, Milt Jackson, vibraphone; Ray Brown,bass;
    J.C. Heard,drums; McGhee,trumpet.
18. <u>Night Mist</u>. Same as above.
    (All the above are the Dial Label)
19. Miles Davis- <u>Israel</u>. J.J.Jonson,trombone; Sanford

Siegelstein,french horn, Lee konitz,alto; Bill Barber,tuba;

G. Mulligan,baritone; John Lewis,piano; Nelson Boyd,bass;

L.A. Salaam, drums.

Boblicity. same as above.

20. Stan Kenton- The Peanut Vendor.

21.   Thermopolae

      (all the above are on the Capital Label)

22. Paul Robeson- Water Boy. Lawrence Brown,piano. Columbia Label.

                John Henry

                Joshua Fit'

                Nobody Knows...

                Go Down Moses

23. L.ARMSTRONG - I Double Dare You. Decca Label.

                Satchel Mouth Swing

24. Wagner- Lohengrin (Act 3) Karl Muck,conducting the Boston
Symphony. Victrola Records, 1909 (from 1903 recording).

It's you I'm concerned about. Your negativity spins off into little whirligigs of self-annihilation, but then I'm at a loss to square it with the way you actually handle things. I remember the first time I became aware of your sense of comfort and practicality. Yes, in that respect, you do hide your presence and do a disappearing act, but the acts remain, nevertheless. In fact, they grow and progress. I can see now how for you the results that you actually do achieve must give you a secret pleasure--not simply the results themselves, which you obviously enjoy--but the deeper satisfaction of playing the magician. "How does he do it? I haven't seen him move for years, but son of a bitch, he's off again doing something else. Does he send out a double to do his work? Where did it all come from? Amazing." To follow out your puppet metaphor, I'd have to conceive of you as a logically impossible, self-directed marionette, perhaps like Petrushka, the puppet who is suddenly imbued with love and will and comes to life, a puppet-saint, really. I remember the first time I saw Nureyev in the role on TV, I felt an identifi- cation with the love-sick marionette. He's really a kind of Christ figure, held up to ridicule, a mere bag of wood and cloth into which a magical spirit enters to animate the parts. I suppose you would say these parts write doctorates, buy and sell houses, raise children, struggle to understand themselves. Trieber spent a session with me finally getting me to admit that I actually had a doctorate from Columbia, I was that resistent to acknowledge my own achievements. I'm always ready at the drop of a hat to confess my sins but equally adamant in the other direction to avoid owning up to my accomplishments.

Strange that you should focus so keenly on the issue of my inordinate tendency to subservience. You understand, I don't necessarily have to do anything to act that way. It simply comes with the territory. I can experience my very presence as an unwelcome demand on the world around me. It's a kind of low-level living in fear, which is always ready to be activated into panic, a panic I express by being completely flustered, groping for words to express my needs, groping for the obvious. It's not that far between me and the kids who shoot someone for looking at them crosswise. Or let's put it this way, they're another example of how easily I can identify with the blind and the lame. When the steam blows, though, I know what I'm feeling and I know exactly what is going on, or rather, exactly up to a point. The hook is still in there or I wouldn't need to explode to do the job. Case in point: I had to stop by at Macy's for a 50% rebate on a stainless steel pot (I'm acquiring things!). I asked the service clerk (faggoty, black, 40ish, flower pinned to his sweater, graying hair, trim) how it worked. He shoots back, "Think about it logically. How could it work?" (verbatim). Low earthquake rumbling in my guts. "I don't know. That's why I'm asking you. Do I get a refund?" He says, "Think about it logically. Could you get cash for it?" "Oh," I say. "It was on Mastercard. No, no cash. So how does it work?" (I am feeling very uncomfortable. I've already given him too much). And again he throws it back at me (people standing in line behind--here I go. I'm about to become a public basket case): "CUT IT OUT! JUST TELL ME HOW IT WORKS!" Little faggoty moisture on his lips (do they use lip seal for that varnished effect?) "I'm trying to," he says. "NO!" I yell. "ALL YOU'RE DOING IS GIVING ME A HARD TIME." "No I'm not," he says, in a voice of hostile melodiousness. And that's when I flipped. "I DON'T NEED ANY LESSONS FROM YOU. JUST FILL THE DAMN THING OUT." And he did. And I got the point about the rebate as soon as the anger was expressed. But you see, it's still rankling in a way. I didn't get it in the first instant. Better than nothing, though, or I'd still be crazed. The residue that's left comes from the hook that's still inside, the dredges of guilt I still feel in reaction to the initial blow--still the sensation that I am responsible for the shit that's handed out to me. And of course, as long as I still feel the guilt, I am, in fact, still blind to some part of me, the part you put your finger on in describing that subservient side of me. If I doped things out better the first time, I'd meet these situations without these head-on confrontations coming on. Who knows? The whole thing is bewildering. But you see, I really did have the guy pegged correctly from the start. There was something naive in my expecting an answer in the first place, knowing, or at any rate, clearly sensing who he was. I pull back from my negative reactions to people and try to make up for them by playing nicey-nice or dumb, which is how my fog and naivete roll over me. Still replaying the old motif of trying to make my mother well, of being scared to see she's nuts.

Surviving who we are is quite a trick. The memory of my mirage came back on me in the form of a double ghost, as well I should have known it might. Last time I spoke with Pam since writing you was around the beginning of Jan. How much of a mess she was didn't come through till last week, however, but she just had to let me know. She was disappearing nicely from my mind except for some vague hallucinations flitting through the halls for me at school (I had work to do there over Jan.). Then a call from her about a week ago. I couldn't talk that evening. Could I call in the morning? Yes, she'd be there. I called. She wasn't and didn't call for a couple of days. When she did, the first thing I asked was why she did that sort of thing to me. I didn't like it. As far as I was concerned, it was over and done with, and her calls did nothing but revive feelings I would rather forget. Tough, eh? Not as tough as Pam, who just had to tell me that she had been seeing a guy all of last semester (???!!!***), which turned out terribly, and now she's swearing off men for good! I say to her she's one amazing act, to be able to lie half naked on my couch telling me she can't go through with it because she hasn't been with a man for years when in fact she was with someone the night before. Then she calls a few days later from work to tell me she doesn't feel up to going to her first day of class. I ask her why she called to tell me that. She says she doesn't know. I tell her she doesn't seem to know why she does anything she does, but she doesn't even understand what it means to know or not to know why one does something, so even those words of mine mean nothing to her. She tells me she's feeling miserable. I tell her no, she's not. Anyone who could put on the kind of act she did is in total, deliberate control. She tells me I called at the wrong time in October. I tell her no, I called at the right time. I called when I felt like it. I just called the wrong person. And therein lies a tale. Some adventure. I remember a line from "North by Northwest" that says it all. It's when the CIA people are discussing the odd situation of Mr. Thornton (Cary Grant) being mistaken for a man who doesn't exist, whom they've made up, and who is now being pursued by James Mason as an alleged spy. One of the spooks looks around the table and says, "It's all so terribly sad, so why is it that I want to laugh?"

Possible reason for Eliot's insanity in blowing into Nancy's office as he did: he met a woman about four months ago and married her!!! Nancy and a guy from the department went to his ceremony at City Hall. It seems that when the judge asked if anyone knew any legal reasons why they shouldn't marry, Dexter leaned over and whispered in Nancy's ear, "Not legal, but psychological." Proof positive: I come into his office a few days ago and ask him how is married life and he says, "I wouldn't know in general. I'm just married to this one woman" (!!!???). I met her last night, incidentally. They had a party for themselves (postal card invitation with little pink hearts dotting the i's). As I more than half suspected, knowing Elliot's politics, there were politically correct single women there (wearing buttons that said "US Out of the Middle East"). I find myself speechless to say anything else right now on the subject of "relationships."

Much moved to get your Maurois Chateaubriand. I cannot mention his name to anyone without getting a wisecrack about steak. The book is lovely, a great gift from Corrales indeed.

My second thoughts about Kimball were borne out somewhat in this week's Sunday Times Book R. He has a review on what seems to be an interesting collection of essays on modern trends in the humanities, The Philosopher on Dover Beach, by Roger Scruton, which apparently has "thoughtful" things to say about Spengler, among other goodies. But what rankled was Kimball's description of "that monumental paean to despondency, The Decline of the West." I hear remarks like that and then wonder about the rest of him. He is a journalist, after all. I think I told you that I saw him on CUNY cable TV and was bothered by his polemics. He's making a living off his points, and though I'm grateful that some people are talking about the disasters in the universities, I have to remember that for some, it's an ax to grind. Truth to tell, I feel mistrustful right now about anyone who has a clear conviction of any kind and am simply trying to keep my own head above water and find my voice.

Why can't we get used to feeling isolated in our culture? Our daddies, granddaddies, and grandmommies (spiritual) had better reserves than we do on this score. I think of people like Melville, Ryder, and O'Keefe living by their lights--just living--and not being blown by every gust of wind that came along. D. H. Lawrence calls it being "pinched by anxiety," the consequence of little boys having the life throttled out of them by mothers and schoolmarms. Better that we feel embattled, at least, and groping, comfortless, in the dark, than settle for the ease of an all-too-familiar despair.

I have to tell you (here I go serving my head up on a platter) that I mistrust your negativity. I didn't until now, and I'm not sure how much of it has to do with you or me, but ever since that last phone call from Pam, I have to wonder what people mean when they tell me (and when I tell myself) about global feelings of despair. You see, the whole time she was telling me that she's been betrayed by men, that she hasn't been with one for four years since her last terrible separation, etc. etc., she was seeing someone and, as I read it, taking great pleasure in stringing me along. Clover too has gone on remote control with me, all this after so many heart-to-hearts with me. I feel very mistrustful right now about my propensity to simply be an ear and not a mind and voice as well. I can even take your words and hear them as a powerful, steady, external flow, a solid individuality. I sometimes credit everything outside of me as having its own integrity, its own solidity, as Hamlet says about young Fortinbras leading his army from Norway to avenge his father's loss to Hamlet Sr, "How all occasions do inform against me." Clover has this problem in spades. Any sign of strength from the outside, in fact, almost any _experience_ that she has, somehow rattles her cage. I just wonder, that's all, and want to hear more about your actual circumstances that may be impinging on your consciousness, instead of just getting Ted as _ding_ _an_ _sich_.

Again, much pleased by the _Chateaubriand_. Flights to Alb. seem higher in price than the planes themselves actually fly, but I'm working on it. I do so want to see you and big sky country again. Sonya and I, by the way, are tentatively thinking about a trip out west in June to visit colleges. I have just wrestled an FAF form to the ground.

Much love,
Steve.

Dear Steve,

Sorry for the long silence. It's so hot here time evaporates like water on a grill. Even this will be a just a slip of a letter to say yes, I did receive the disks - and I send them off - and yes, I did receive your startling newspaper installation and its premature deconstructionist review by Ruth. Yours deserves to be glued to the prymamids of the Louvre. Ruth can glue her ruminations to the Arch de Triumphe. The entire event can be headlined as the "War of the Worlds." Yours was wonderful - dadaist or pataphysical. More on all this later - it did give rise in me to many thoughts.

Nothing on the homefront - except I'm tring to find a new audience I can write to. Have you seen any around with nothing to do? I'll tell you, reality can be a bitch; neurosis is cozy and comfortable and the audience is always guaranteed. It's just I'm getting so bored with them. "Get Real," is my personal motto.

Don't take any wooden nickels.

29. BOGOTA
Puerto aéreo de Techo.

Nov. 17 - Dear Ted: Just received *The Wilt Alternative* (I cannot even guess at the meaning, unless it be "Have You Thought of Impotence as an Alternative to Sex?"). I look forward to it as soon as I finish *A Life for the Stars*. Blish has a wonderful way of setting a scene and keeping the story moving along. *Cities in Flight* is conceived with Wagner's *Ring* and Spengler in mind. I came across a fine example of Spengler's analogy between Valhalla and the Elizabethan stage in *Shakespeare's Blackfriars Playhouse* (Irwin Smith, NYU, 1964), which I pulled off my shelves the other day. "Olympus rests on the homely Greek soil," writes Spengler, "but Valhalla is nowhere." Shakespeare's scenes take place "in the unbounded," "years fly past in minutes," and "the whole thing is merely *indicated*." According to Smith, act and scene divisions in most Elizabethan plays are arbitrary and only served as a bow to classical conventions. The action in the public theaters was continuous. There are no scene indications in Shakespeare's plays published in his lifetime. All of his 750 scenes were localized as stage notes by subsequent editors. The texts offer nothing more than hints, and often not even that. Smith notes that Shakespeare only indicates a setting when he needs it and that until we get to Brabantio's house in *Othello*, for example, there are no references to streets, to Venice, or even Italy. In Smith's words, the stage is "nowhere in particular." Iago and Roderigo are simply talking somewhere in space. It's only the notes that stick "A street in Venice" or "The Ramparts at Elsinore" firmly in our minds, which he calls a serious misrepresentation of Shakespeare's intent. I'm going to buy a Pelican *Hamlet* and white out every last act and scene reference and see what it's like to read it as one continuous flow, letting the play alone work on my imagination. Wagner hid the orchestra in Bayreuth and wished he could do away with the stage as well.

Ted Sitea

Dear Ted,

Yes, those F-15s are "a line of defense against the barbarians" (with pilots as knights--technology our magic and romance--and flight crews as squires), but all the same, I can't help remembering Pound's "Hugh Selwyn Mauberly", perhaps because I once heard a recording of him reading it, with <u>ferocity</u>:

These fought, in any case,
and some believing, pro domo, in any case . . .

Some quick to arm,
some for adventure,
some from fear of weakness,
some from fear of censure,
some for love of slaughter, in imagination,
learning later . . .

some in fear, learning love of slaughter;
Died some, pro patria,
        non "dulce" non "et decor" . . .*

walked eye-deep in hell
believing in old men's lies, then unbelieving
came home, home to a lie,
home to many deceits,
home to old lies and new infamy.

usury age-old and age-thick
and liars in public places.

Daring as never before, wastage as never before.
Young blood and high blood,
fair cheeks, and fine bodies;

fortitude as never before

frankness as never before,
disillusions as never told in the old days,
hysterias, trench confessions,
laughter out of dead bellies.

There died a myriad,
And of the best, among them,
For an old bitch gone in the teeth,
For a botched civilization,

Charm, smiling at the good mouth,
Quick eyes gone under earth's lid,
For two gross of broken statues,
For a few thousand battered books.

§ Horace: <u>Dulce et decorum est pro patria mori</u>--It is sweet and right to die for one's country. When Pound came to the line non "dulce" non "et decor," his voice went into a rage such as I've rarely heard before or since in anyone (even our current political angers--"Rage in Chicago," etc.--are cheapened versions of authentic passion--more like fulmination, and cries of self-willed helplessness than rage). I think it was Pound's voice, his voice and the line, that has given me pause ever since on the issue of war, or rather, added another turn of the screw in my feelings, which I share with you, over the need to defend against the barbarians. I remember someone saying, I think it may have been Golda Meir, that one of the hatreds Israelis felt toward Arabs was that they had forced their children to learn how to kill.

I have, by the way, a wonderful facsimile copy of Baedeker's guide to Jerusalem and environs, 1876, which I picked up in Israel in '82. I had totally forgotten about it until I read a review in <u>The New Criterion</u> of Melville's Middle East journals, recently edited. The reviewer was taking him to task for his "despondency" and "bellyaching" about conditions there in 1855: ("Whitish mildew pervading whole tracts of landscape--bleached--leprosy--encrustation of curses--old cheese--bones of rocks--crunched, knawed, & mumbled--mere refuse & rubbish of creation--the unleavened nakedness of desolation"). I had just read portions of the journal in some book or other and was pissed off at the review. Melville's prose is absolutely fantastic--actually sounds like James Joyce and Kerouac rolled into one--and so I sat down and wrote a letter to Kimball (he's the managing editor). I'm typing away, and suddenly my 1876 Baedeker pops into my head. I rummage around, find it stuck among my maps and travel books, and yes, the landscape is pretty bleak. Jerusalem is piled high with garbage and fanatic communities, the inn at Jericho is vermin-infested, the inn-keeper will fleece you if you don't watch out--best to sleep outside in a tent--ladies should not venture into certain areas, because conditions will simply make them faint, the bedouins on the way to the temples at Petra are perpetually at war and must be paid off, etc. etc. It's really quite marvellous. And this was Baedeker, the guidebook for the tourist trade. The engravings, by the way, are wonderful. Jerusalem, you understand, was simply what is now known as the Old City--a walled town among the Judean hills, piled high, as Melville says, with "rubbish & rottenness--encrustations of old curses" (so what else is new?). Somewhere I also have Chateaubriand's travels to the Middle East, but have not found it yet. At any rate, I sent the letter off to Kimball, with a final note on his remarks on Spengler's "monumental paean to despondency" in a recent issue of the <u>Times Book Review</u>.

I don't know what it is, but this letter-writing mania has to stop. Actually, I do know what it is. I want my voice to be heard, I want to get it out (I want to get that dick out of my pants as well), but I'm not all there as yet.

Apropos of Horace, I had a friend in Vermont, an ex-navy man from San Diego, whose motto for any typical winter crisis was to look at the scene (a car that had to be pulled out of a frozen ditch, etc), stand up ram-rod straight, head thrown back, and salute, "Morituri te salutant" (the cry of the gladiators before bouts at the Coliseum--"We who are about to die salute you"). It was always unexpected, and it always had the effect of jolting me into a good-humored frame of mind. Those were the days when I was living through the winter on Carpenter Hill--morituri te salutant indeed.

Larry Josephson (from WBAI and now on WNYC) had a two hour special last night on multiculturalism and political correctness, which I taped and will bring out with me. He had Searle on for the last hour, who came across pretty well, better than the others who spoke. Josephson said he called a few of the hot shots, like Gates and Stanley Fish, the enfant terrible of radical criticism, who brought us such towering penetrations as, "Let us suppose that I am reading Lycidas. What is it that I am doing?" Sounds like a Polish joke, doesn't it?--It's ten o'clock and you're reading Lycidas. What are you doing? As you might suppose, Fish says that, of course, he's not "simply reading," since it's "an activity in which I do not believe because it implies the possibility of pure (that is, disinterested) perception." In fact, he is not reading at all but making "interpretive decisions" (get ready for this), that 1) Lycidas is a pastoral poem, and 2) that it was written by Milton. Fish has a little trouble with the "fact" that "Milton" called it Lycidas, A Pastoral Monody, but he disposes of it rather quickly, or at least he thinks (he "thinks" he does). Anyway, these and a few other hot shots did not appear on the show--Josephson didn't explain why--and Searle had a field day, as you may get to hear. He comes across much better in life than in print, but even he does not get down to it in the end, though he's comical and lucid in a sort of Yankee-pragmatic way ("Do you want a deconstructionist car mechanic working on your carburator?"). In Josephson's interviews, by the way, there's a stunning moment when the first speaker, an obnoxious woman who runs graduate studies at Rutgers, suddenly mentions Spengler's name in the midst of her rhapsody on multiculturalism ("I don't go around moping, like Spengler").

This from The New York Times on "Elite Kenyan Women Avoid a Rite: Marriage." It too reads like a poem for our time:

> For generations, marriage in Africa has been a rite
> never questioned. Now, for more and more of the rela-
> tively small numbers of university-educated women like
> 27 year-old Kay Makuku, marriage is a custom to be
> avoided. . . . And simply put, the disdain toward
> marriage can be summed up in two words: African men.

Yes, I too have thought about Saddam as the Prince of Deconstructionists, and I too am hoping that the war will change the climate of the times. But Bush has to use the leverage that he has. Now that would take real finesse. On the other hand, just as recession is good for the environment, it may also be good for education and the intellectual character of the time (trust funds can buy up a lot of land for preservation now that prices have plummeted in Maine development land, for example, from $10,000 an acre, or whatever, to $199, and so too, the scene may shift away from celebrity consciousness. Perhaps we'll get to the point when we'll realize that we just can't afford these jokers any more. All these clowns like Saddam and Fish made their way in palmy times, when everything got deregulated. Trieber, my therapist, ~~his chair~~ calls Michael Milken the prince of deconstructionist investment bankers (high risk means security--junk bonds yield efficiency, etc.).

One of my remedial writings students last semester took some photographs of the class after the final exam (did I tell you that nearly all of them got through?), and at some point, it came to me that you would recognize the scene immediately. I am really proud of the work I did with them, and of the work I'm doing with Sonya too, by the way. Things have never been as tight as they are now between us. I'm getting everything I ever wanted out of her. Not that there aren't problems. You can bet your bippy there are. She had a bit of a car crash in College Smallville last week. Everything turned out OK, but I had a talking to with her about the need to drive defensively and that, one way or another, she's not yet got her mind focused on herself. Some distractions over Allison are in the way. Something about the way she blamed the other driver (not that it wasn't his fault) made me zero in on that issue once again. She really seems to hear me and understand. Of course it's all pretty delicate, touch and go, but there we are, talking at least once, if not twice a week on the phone. Gutsy kid, and she seems to have her head screwed on right. Called me last week to tell me she was moving out of her room. It seems she got stuck with a disgusting Lebanese kid, who tried to mau-mau her, and Sonya ended up wanting out. It seemed that she just couldn't do her work at all with that girl around (I'm thinking to ask her if she thinks that problem didn't have something to do with her not taking enough care over the blind driveway where the guy ran into her). At any rate, when I talk to Gerson about these things, he responds with his usual "Sonya was fucked up terribly by Allison. It'll take years to work it out, assuming she can." I finally called him on that one the other day, and try as he might, he couldn't get around what I had to say to him. It's just as you said, he's got an investment in sickness. But the thing of it was that I finally got myself squared away with him on that one, but of course, it's only because I'm squared way with that issue for myself. For the first time, I'm simply not afraid of Allison. Sold off my mother's jewelry the other day, as well. Nice consequence of my talk with Gerson. I'd been holding on to that box of coins and jewelry for years, and now it too is finally gone.

I'm making a little collection of things to bring out with me. Did you ever see "The Man with Two Brains"? I've got it on videotape, along with some other goodies to take along. About ten years ago, one of the late night film stations had a weekend series on grade F movies, the kind made in local Hollywood garages. The greatest of these, which I miss in my collection, was "I Stole Hitler's Brain," the great scene, of course, being the theft itself--two or three Nazis living in Argentina after the war and driving through Buenos Aires in a taxi cab with Hitler's head under a bell jar. The fiendish plan was to hook it up so that it could give speeches and capture a new generation of Hitler youth. I think, in fact, that they did hook it up and that there was a secret coven of new Nazi youth. You saw Hitler's head under the bell jar, mouth moving like a plasticene doll, with Hitler's voice connected to a loudpseaker blaring out old speeches. The whole thing came back to me when I saw "The Man with Two Brains" (written and co-directed by Carl Reiner, down to his playing an Austrian doctor at a medical convention in Vienna).

One of my students the other day wrote this sentence on a paper: "It's just like the old days in the Bible story, just like Saddam and Gommorah."

Nuff said. Regards to Len. Can't believe all you guys are out there. "The Corrales Home for Reviving New Yorkers." Something like that. Can't wait.

Uncle love,
Steve

Sun., March 9

PS Just got a phone call from the Community Bookstore up the block. I put in an order for a new book out called <u>Reinventing Shakespeare</u>, by one Gary Taylor, who teaches at Brandeis. I might have expected it, but now that I'm reading it (now that I'm looking at it and creating interpretive strategies), it's clear to me that it should be called <u>Trashing Shakespeare</u>. Ted, Ted, shall I simply close my eyes? Shall I move out to the desert too? This on Keats's "On sitting down to read King Lear once again," the sonnet that begins:

> O Golden-tongued Romance, with serene Lute!
>   Fair plumed Siren, Queen of far-away!
>   Leave melodizing on this wintry day
> Shut up thine olden Pages, and be mute.
> Adieu! for, once again, the fierce dispute
>   Betwixt Damnation and impassion'd clay
>   Must I burn through . . .

Prof. Gary Taylor: "It is not, to tell the truth, a very good poem." In fact, the best thing about it, the "most memorable

12

thing," more valuable than "the trail of words" from beginning to end, is its historical context (that is, the context that Taylor sees but which he mysteriously claims is solid truth, his assumptions about the impossibility of truth notwithstanding)--eg: "the poem's physical posture [??], its place and shape, its time and teller, the title above and the date below." Two more jewels: on A. C. Bradley, whose <u>Shakespearean Tragedy</u> (1904) is one of the most carefully thought out books on the bard I know, with that solid Victorian construction which marks it of its time, and which, beyond that, is filled with the ripest, subtlest observations on Shakespeare yet to come down the pike. Are these virtues for Taylor. No! They are signs of British imperialist hegemony: "The lectures were designed to serve, and can still serve, as a ritual of initiation; the experienced master carefully guides an innocent neophyte into the intricacies and intimacies of a restricted discipline." (He makes it sound terrible, doesn't he?): "The first paragraph of the first lecture of <u>Shakespearean Tragedy</u> illustrates Bradley's intellectual method throughout. He imposes a relentless clarity on his material; he defines by a steady aggregation of phrases, of examples, of arguments. Meaning piles up." And finally: "Like women, the lower and middle classes are systematically underrepresented by Shakespeare. . . . 'Merrie England' knew unemployment and economic exploitation, inflation and dislocation, in even crueler forms than our own; but if we want to see such realities dramatized we will have to look elsewhere. Shakespeare decided not to write about that misery around him." In the end, there is no Shakespeare, there is no "star." Only a "black hole," sucking up meanings, sucking up our energies, giving off no light but sucking it up, the vampire on our literary consciousness, like the British imperialist hegemony that turned him into a system of oppression: "In our society Shakespeare has become the subject, in most schools and universities, of 'required courses'; for almost a century now, students have been compelled to study him, as they were once compelled to study Greek and Latin. The badge of cultural elitism and the instrument of pedagogical oppression, Shakespeare now finds himself needing to be constantly justified against the determined boredom, the soaking resentment, of conscripts." And what is this oppression based upon? A fraud. There are five million interpretations, different editions, different Elizabethan texts with variants. Did he ever finish <u>King Lear</u>? He "may at some point have closed the book; but he could reopen it again whenever he wanted. There is no Last Judgment anymore. You can appeal your conviction; you can remarry your ex-wife. Even death is no longer final; we resuscitate the dead, we put them on life-support systems, we distinguish between heart death and brain death." In this magical universe, however, Shakespeare is dead and "no longer transmits visible light."

There it is, in all its gory nakedness. <u>King Lear</u>, by the way, the play without a heart for the victims of nascent British imperialism, is the one that Taylor chiefly trashes, the play that has two of the greatest passages on what Taylor supposedly believes is the truth of life, "unemployment and economic exploitation":

> Poor naked wretches, wheresoe'er you are,
> That bide the pelting of this pitiless storm,
> How shall your houseless heads and unfed sides,
> Your loop'd and window'd raggedness, defend you
> From seasons such as these? O, I have ta'en
> Too little care of this! Take physic, pomp;
> Expose thyself to feel what wretches feel,
> That thou mayst shake the superflux to them,
> And show the heavens more just.

And again,

> A man may see how this world goes without eyes. Look with thine ears: see how yond justice rails upon yond simple thief. Hark in thine ear; change places, and handy-dandy, which is the justice, which is the thief? Thou hast seen a farmer's dog bark at a beggar? And the creature run from the cur? There thou mightest behold the great image of authority: a dog's obeyed in office. Thou rascal beadle, hold thy bloody hand! Why dost thou lash that whore? Strip thine own back; thou hotly lust'st to use her in that kind for which thou whipp'st her. Through tatter'd clothes small vices do appear; robes and furr'd gowns hide all.

Incredible, no? I tell you, these people are all frauds. They couldn't give two shits about "misery and economic exploitation," as well you know yourself. But to see the things I love and know about, to see the truth trashed with all the accoutrements of "elitism and oppresive pedagogy" is more than I can bear. Sorry for this outburst. No, not sorry. I just wonder when I'll come to the end of it. How much more true and just my student who wrote, "It's just like the Bible story of Saddam and Gommorah."

Village Cigar Store
Sheridan Sq. New York City, NY.

Photo by Gail Greig
© 1990 All Rights Reserved.

2/18/97

Ted—

Here's the place I get my Gauloise tobacco when I don't stop at Barney's Cut Rate — and it's the stop on my underground route to and from Tribeca. Just got up. Letter today — a pleasure. Five ways from Sunday. Found a copy of the old D'Oyly Carte production of "The Mikado." Can't stop listening to it. What a relief after a long diet of the Germans. "And make each prisoner pent/ unwillingly represent/ A source of innocent merriment" — Utly delicious — every note — every word — "To be happy in an unhappy..." — What a wonderful awareness — More later,

Steve

post card

USA 20

Ted Sitea

Dear Ted,

My sails hang limp. Three weeks and not a stir. Most of CUNY is shut down. It was in doldrums like these that Queequeg called for the ship's carpenter to make him a coffin and then went into a death trance temporarily (the coffin later to become Ishmael's life preserver--oh those iron cages--if only the crew had taken arms against a sea of troubles). No iron cages here, man. Hi, ho, liberty. Ca, Ca, Caliban, has a new master, has a new man. (I quote from the "text," you should pardon the expression. They don't tell you this in liberation criticism, but Caliban, in fact, has such a desparate need to be controlled that he puts himself under the power of Stephano and Trinculo, court jesters and drunks!)

I came back to a disaster as one CUNY president after another folded, while "students" took over the buildings. There are schools still functioning, but as for the ones that are shut, nobody is willing to call in the police (I think NY Tech called them in briefly, but that was about it--I have not kept au courant and it would be too depressing to do so, given my experience at two faculty meetings). Unmitigated disaster, and not a teacher I spoke to registered any sense of anguish over the unfolding scene. My coordinator at the Writing Center, John Short,was about the only one who seemed to have a feeling for the work being missed. I'll try to speak to him tomorrow--I'd like to have at least one voice of recognition around me, though it's too depressing to make contact with them right now. My colleagues tell me that "I guess I don't see things as clearly as you do." Nancy says she's "not political," my chairman (a walking internal disaster in himself) tells me he can understand both sides of the issue, and some of the ladies are actually bringing food money to the takeover artists in our building. Did I tell you about the homicidal maniac in The Man Without Qualities? Christian Moosebrugger, a carpenter a la Jesus Christ, who walks through the Austrian countryside at the mercy of his psychotic fantasies, kills women in moments of extreme hallucination, is finally arrested, taken to Vienna, and gets to hear so many lawyers and psychiatrists that he ends up talking like them, not that he understands what they're saying, but he instinctively realizes that their words have magical properties, since they're spoken by his captors, who are free to move about. In court he's able to incorporate the latest political ideas into his psychosis and gives long, rambling speeches in which he claims he's a "theoretical anarchist" and a product of the times (brilliant, isn't it?). He becomes a cause celebre, and one of the heroines of the book, a woman who plays long Wagner duets with her husband at the piano, urges "the man without qualities" to break into prison and free Moosebrugger. "It would liberate you," she says hotly in his ear.

Well, that's our scene, on a petty scale. What's that famous Marxian remark on historical recurrence, "First time as tragedy, second time as farce"? But he has nothing to say about the modern tone--when things happen a third time, fourth time, fifth time through meaningless, inarticulate, ignorant rage. The "students," by the way, have no real demands, although they scream "No tuition raise." Revolt itself has been deconstructed. As soon as they took over the building, they insisted on one point only, that there be no disciplinary action taken against them, a circular process leading to nothing, signifying nothing, except that 16,000 students and 300 teachers, staff at our school alone are hostage to the situation (55,000 students CUNY-wide have been immobilized by a "strike committee," very "articulate," I'm told, and we know who they are).

Total breakdown, paralysis, and you can imagine the havoc the whole event is playing with my inner life: my mother flips out, dominates the scene, pervades the whole atmosphere with sensations of doom and collapse, and my father folds. What about the child? Where's the consideration for the 55,000 students in all of this, the ones who can least afford a shut down, the hundreds of thousands of dollars in work studies money lost, tutor wages lost, grant money down the tubes, the private catastrophes happening right here and now? And the city--shelling out millions in paychecks for work never done. What's really grotesque is that, in some ways, the situation is no different than what happens every day, only more so. Enclosed, the latest _Times_ piece on the situation. The point about the income status of the strike committee is truly disgusting but no surprise. Isn't it odd that I should have sought out an interview at another school a week before?

Apropos my love of eloquent prose, I am convinced that truth always carries an echo of the beautiful. My mind, like yours in that wonderful description you gave of your mental museum, is filled with the debris of a hundred thousand glinting truths--a rubbish pile of jewels. I got just enough of a taste of Latin to appreciate the firmness of understanding the historians convey: Desertam faecunt, pax appelunt ("They make a desert and they call it peace"). The Latin historians are resplendent with experience, and it's all down the tubes. Gerson tells me that mathematicians don't bother with Euclid at all. I wouldn't feel so bad if I had a way to teach what I know, but my crippling fears pulverize my dreams.

I cannot tell you how stunning my time in New Mexico was for me. It would have been, in any case, but with the school shut down, every act I perform carries a poignant memory of how clearly I moved inside myself out there. That sense of strength is being badly sapped by the city scene that's happening right now. I am in the doldrums, and that's a fact. Trieber, by the way, is on his spring break for the week, which is no help at all. The days seem to melt away, and I can't get a handle on anything. I am working on my apartment, though, cleaning things out, repainting (reframed the painting

I bought), getting money together from Schaeffer people to do the final fixing on the place before I try to sell, and calling a few people here and there. I continue not to date or seek women out, with no end in sight. As usual, in every moment of distress, I cannot tell if I am clinging to my mother or separating from her, if I am allowing myself to remain in her vise-like grip or holding on to myself. Either way, the relationship with her (and with one ear cocked to hear my father's voice) remains interminable. Everyone I know seems to be in a matrix of humanity of some kind, but I feel no sense of continuity for all the connections I make and have. Horrible sensation of feeling more valuable for others than myself. Every advance only raises the ante, hence my procrastination after every accomplishment. I thank you for the few words you gave me over the kitchen counter one morning about my 25 years at school, my pension, and all that I've achieved. I feel it has come to me as in a dream. I haven't worked for it, at least I have never consciously told myself that I was aiming for that goal. Achievements stick to me like thistles, simply because I walk through an untended field.

Cleaning out my clippings, I came across the Jan. 10, '85 article that I've enclosed. Please show it to Jenkin (I don't know why I don't have his address, but I think it may be because I felt so at home with you guys that I never considered the need for it.) The story about Kraus is positively brilliant. What an acting out of deepest lunacies of mine. How I'd love to get my hands on his manuscript.

Sent off a letter to the <u>American Educator</u> and another to <u>Harper's</u>. There has to be a better way to make the connection between childhood and present rage. Something, as usual, is running its course. Did you know that I sent a letter to <u>The Daily Worker</u> when I was in my teens? Mike Gold wrote something about "bourgeois pessimism" in Joyce et al, and I got pissed. <u>Actually</u>, it started a lot earlier, when I was ten years old in summer camp, Camp Wochica (Workers' Children's Camp). We used to have these indoctrination sessions on the lawn during the afternoon, and one day I asked the counselor if the Russians were so terrific, how come Vishinsky kept vetoing everything the Americans proposed? By the way (what an amazing flash), during that summer, I organized a theatrical around the story of Daniel Boone, and afterwards, I was called to account for my political incorrectness, because I narrated something bad about the "red men." They never sneaked up on Boone, I was told. <u>He</u> was the infiltrator. Can you believe it? This was in 1948. I <u>grew up</u> with "political correctness." Paul Robeson came to sing for us in camp. He had just come back from Russia, and he gave a speech to us about how wonderful it was. He really did. That was about the time that Stalin was preparing his "doctor's plot" against the insidious "cosmopolitans" (Jews) and, in fact, getting ready for a "cleaning," as the purges were called. This was known as the "correct approach."

On the other hand, I also grew up with what was laughably known as "criticism from below" (I knew all the catch-words by the time I was seven), since I knew from my father that Stalin had killed the Russian Jewish writers in '46 or so, right after the war. My father had a furious argument with an old friend of his in the CP over this issue in our living room. These writers, by the way, had come over to the US during the war to raise money for Russian War Relief and my father had seen, and for all I know had met them as a member of the Brownsville club at Madison Square Garden. Staggering, isn't it? And yet, in all these times, my overriding feeling was that I wasn't really with him in any way. He was in the driver's seat and I was simply there, looking on, with my life going on somewhere else, and I didn't know where. When Gargiulo started talking about my mother in my first sessions with him, I had the distinct feeling that he was talking about someone out in left field. "My mother? What does she have to do with any of this?" The moment came back to me last week, and for the first time I understood what was so mystifying for me about Gargiulo's words. The problem was its own answer, in fact. I simply didn't see my mother. I just didn't see her, and that, in a nutshell, is what he did for me, helped me to see her. Given all I knew as a child, and I really did know a hell of a lot, what else was possible for me except some sort of horrible prison experience, when I was exposed to a million and one books, facts, events, hobbies, different languages, etc. ad nauseam, and in all of that never saw my mother. I'm reminded of your story about sitting impassively with firecrackers exploding around you, and the other one about diving into the quarry pool, was it? and simply not seeing what was happening. I don't mean this in any mystical way. I simply mean not seeing what was happening. It's when the mother wants the child to be fused with her that there's no way for the poor kid to see anything, really, since it is not being seen.

So how in the world can I talk to people when what I have to say to them is, listen man, it's fucking hard. If you have no money for tuition, then you're just going to have to figure out a way to get it, if that's what you really want. The state has given all its got, and then some, and to begin with, that's not a very good way to go about getting what you need. And you know what, it'll take you years, it'll take you your whole fucking lifetime to make it out, if that's what you want. And that's what this country offers you, a chance, a chance of some kind. A study just came out saying, as if we didn't know, that the poor are enormously overcharged for groceries, in lousy conditions, and in poor quality, and I read that and thought, what in God's name are they doing flipping out against the Koreans, the only people who have anything decent to offer them? And now it hits me, very simply, that they can't see their condition at all. All that dependency makes it impossible for them to see, and the ones who struggle have about the only answer there is. My cousin Boris, by the way, who was washing cars on the Island, then got into a taxi service in B'klyn, so a few weeks ago I ask his wife if the hours are still hard on him, and she doesn't know what I mean. The car service, I say. Isn't he working weekend shifts as well? Oh, she says, he got himself a regular job as an electrician out in Jersey through a friend of his. You were absolutely right. These people have all their ducks lined up in a row.

I want to mail this off before it all becomes passe. Three weeks and the takeovers finally ended. The nursing students at our school barged in, actually had a long talk with the strikers at the school (I hate to use that word to describe them--they weren't strikers at all), and what with police coming into Bronx Community, I think it was, and other groups fading out, the whole experience evaporated. Today is Sunday, 4/28. I go back tomorrow. The semester will probably be extended into the middle of June, making it impossible for me to teach summer school if I wanted to. OK? That shutdown cost me over $3,500, and yet I saw people denying their own self-interest all over the place. So what else is new? I actually had some people from the department over to my house last night. I just wanted a get-together of some kind. Remember my chairman, Phil, the guy whose ex had a sex harrassment charge against him over the kids? He hasn't been able to see them at all for years, and part of his salary was taken over too. Well, it seems a woman who shared his office found out about his troubles, and though he was absolutely blind to what was happening, she was not. She nailed him at the worst possible time for him, and what his ex didn't accomplish, Jane finished off. This Jane, by the way, had an ex of her own, who recently died of AIDS. Sound familiar? These are walking disaster zones, known as teachers. Phil, by the way, looks the Harvard type, wrote a book on the Arthurian romances (!!), and looked befuddled when he told me the story about his ex and I replied, stop working, man. Don't make any money. Steal your kids. Go to jail. Do anything but what you're doing now (he became a member of some divine justice for fathers committee and they too nailed him to the wall with their legal advice, which ran him into the thousands). If I was the greatest Yiddish movie script writer, I couldn't come up with stories to match the ones I've even forgotten at my school. When Jenkin was still teaching at the school, he told me one day that he wondered how long Phil could keep up his act. And of course, he's a nice guy. It's Mel's story but raised to the 10th power.

I put my apartment through another transformation. Repainted, though not entirely finished, and lighter than before. I miss you all and look forward to the summer. Other events have gone on for me these past few weeks, much more interesting than the CUNY scene, but still need digesting and thinking through, and doing! I just bought a few art books from Hacker's, including a volume on Signorelli (c. 1470s), whose work I saw with Janet when we were in Italy. Those pictures, for some reason, never left my mind, and now I'm looking at those reproductions and craving time to meditate. It was something about going through all those northern museums, getting to know the religious traditions, seeing miles of Byzantine gold-background icons in a dozen churches and museums, the same subjects over and over again, learning a bit about the iconography, and realizing that I was seeing slow developments in the same material, and then Assissi and Giotto's frescoes, and for the first time having a sense of warmth about religious experience. _Seeing_ is deep business for me and goes right back to life with mother and her photographs. Two of my best teachers in college, by the way, used to pack up for France and Italy every summer, and the fact is that it can still be done and done well on the cheap. All these daydreams prompted by memories of your big skies, which I also crave to see again.

Love,
Steve

29. BOGOTA
Puerto aéreo de Techo.

Nov. 28 - Dear Ted: Many thanks for the all info
- I don't quite know how to read the web pages
but will call Amazon if they have an 800#. Read
The Wilt Alternative over Thanksgiving and was so
beside myself with laughter it was all I could do
to get from one page to the next. It's like a
"Condition of England" novel as seen through the
eyes of Inspector Clouseau. Carol has a friend in
England who fits the book to a T, right down to
her nettle soups and search for alternatives to
alternate therapy. Read *The Iron Heel* (almost in
Jack London country itself) for the second time
since high school, and it struck me almost
immediately as the best piece of pulp socialism
ever written. The stampede of "the people of the
abyss" is a truly amazing scene. I thought of
1984 more than once and was surprised to find
that London pays homage to Wells, just as Orwell
did. Have taken Berlioz's memoirs as my bedside
reader. In Chap. 18 he describes seeing the first
production of *Hamlet* in France (he married
Ophelia five years later - Harriet Constance,
from County Clare!). He says he was so entirely
blown away by Shakespeare that he wandered around
Paris for months and collapsed four times into a
"death-like sleep": twice in fields, once "on the
banks of the frozen Seine," and "lastly on a
table in the Café du Cardinal at the corner of
the Boulevard des Italiens and the Rue
Richelieu." Then came Beethoven, like "one
thunderclap" after another. I can believe it.

Ted Sitea

Dear Steve,

In Sir William Smith's, <u>Smaller Classical Dictionary</u>, it
is noted that Choerilus of Iasos was a "worthless epic poet in
the train of Alexander the Great." The West forgets nothing. It
is truly astonishing that a 'worthless epic poet' is remembered
for his worthlessness for 2300 years! To so doggedly hold on to
'details' is the mark of being alone in a very large universe
where one's humanity can be easily lost and forgotten. What
infinite regard, and patience we give to the maintance of
ourselves!

And speaking of Alexander, un-doer of the Gordian knot in
Phrygia to free Greece (while reading Choerilus, no doubt),
there is Gen. Schwartzkopf a little to the south, un-doing the
knotty myths of Sadamm to free America - while reading Gibran.
Leather booted atop a dune, over-seeing a desert crowded with
magian Cyclops, Circes, Lotophagi he, with armed reason,
managed to rout them all. They vanished, decapitated, on their
way to the horizon. He is Greek through and through. An
Odysseus in a far-distant, mythic world; Penelope at home
knitting flags. But, like Odysseus, he too has returned to a
city whose aged leaders can not complete the remaing epic
stanzas. The story ends. The rest is not worth telling?

Reread your piece on Spengler - both the '85 and the '86
versions. Very impressive! The second is superior to the first
in that it clarifies - by more examples - Spengler's context in
historiography. But your <u>einfuhlen</u> in both is teriffic. Your
sense of 'place' is strong. What you value emerges with rigour
and strength. Your <u>Queen Lear</u>, in this regard, is a precisely
coordinated geographic Spenglerian history of the self. An
<u>einfuhlen</u> of private, primal symbols. We thus try to

methodically relive our complex origins - the seed-time of a self/culture (apparently tantalizingly obscured in memories resembling those Dutch landscapes painted with single-hair brushes). And within the confines of our own heads, with the same 'monadic'(?) distance/perspective as had Spengler when he relived Breughel's Renaissance man dancing in fields of corn, codpiece swollen, in the confines of his nearly windowless apartment. For Marx, Freud, and Joyce this was the nightmare of the past!

A review in the Times literary section tipped me off to the recent publication of the letters of Mary Beard. Arguing against the feminist image of victimhood and brute subjection to the tryanny of men, she wrote in 1944. "The effect {of that image} has been to make woman a sex lost to history and to weaken a segment of society into infantile imitation, to the injury of all". What is really teriffic however, is her saying, "if women knew their own history down through time, they would realize their own historic leadership as they do not know it today....I believe their leadership to have been exerted always in every aspect of life." The reviewer, of course, then goes on to point out that Mary failed to notice the "many barriers that had prevented women from acting", and so wrongly and shamelessly blamed "women's lack of progress to their own failures of will". A "curiously misogynistic" position, the reviewer says, which shows no sympathy toward women who, as Mary said, "cringe before nasty husbands" or are "too indolent" and differential in the presence of men to assert themselves. The reviewer, of course, would kiss them all and send them off to the hospital - and the police to file a complaint. The reviewer however, does mention a book written by Mary in 1946, Women As Force in History, which I now want to read.

Ach, Steve, my barriers weary me. The wind rushes past, leaves rustle, the sun glows red on the Scandia's - yet I might as well be forty fathoms deep. I am like one of those horny-skinned prehistoric fish without eyes, clumsily searching the darkness for unknown things. Or, like a dumb-founded Marcel

Marceau, I press my finger tips against a pantomined box only to find I can not escape. History as mute idiocy in a zoo of lucite.

Have been as busy as a beaver - pulling out from my thesis text 475 references and entering them as legitimate footnotes has occupied me night and day for over two weeks! But it is now done, and I have sent the 330 page tome to my 'committee'. My printer drove me crazy. Not only the noise, but the roller is uneven and after a time pulls the paper on a diagonal - thus I had to constantly hover over the damm thing.

The story out of Len is a little confusing. He, Romona and Zoe came into the bookstore last week, ordered a few books for Zoe, and said that the university had indeed offered him the job but only for the Fall term. Thus he + family were returning to NY. in August. But the job he applied for was for an annual position - right? I simply nodded. I think Romona is going bonkers in the desert. And oh, at that same encounter, Len, holding a restless Zoe, wanted to know if the bookstore would stage a book-signing for his, New Jerusalem. Before I could respond, he immediately scotched the idea, saying the book was several years old. He then said it was a great book. (I later ordered a copy for myself.) Somehow I think he was giving me a coded message; I felt like Clint Eastwood in "Where Eagles Dare" - when Richard Burton, his friend, tells him to throw down his gun in the room full of nazis. Other than that brief, tangled encounter, we have seen neither hide nor hair of them since you left. We have yet to see your TV show. My 'gun' remains with him.

Did you see the latest issue of Lingua Franca? A joust between David Lehman and Walter Kendrick - but they are in different tournaments, and nothing happens.

Today on PBS they showed the people of Bangor, Maine filling the airport to greet returning GI's on their way to points further west. They lined the walk way hugging and kissing soldiers whom they did not know, and would never see again. All 'white' of course, kissing all who walked by. For days they have been doing this, and for days more they will continue. There is something surprisingly elemental about this country - a people cynical about politics, unemployed and desperate in an economy ruined by ungrateful fat cats, surrounded by crime, destructive city services, and an insane educational system, yet they come out Americans all, proud, loving, and giving. In Iraq the people knelt and kissed our soldier's hand, as though the evil of war and death were somehow unreal, a visitation of the supernatural. Here reality is celebrated. Bloom speaks of the wisdom of the Enlightenment thinkers, of their grasp of the need to sacrifice the illusion of commmunal man founding heaven on earth, and to instead build a civilization which recognizes our individual selfishness in a life that is brutish and short - they were right, and that is what we have done. But is it in the unconscious, guilty recognition of a civilization so built, that such a scene brings tears to our eyes; that our common humanity in such scenes both betrays and astounds us, as though we conceal it in order to live our inhuman life, and only cry when the deformity is exposed in public, or are they tears of the profoundest joy; a jubilant recognition that selfishness has been again sacrificed in order to preserve it for all? Thus, those who kiss and hug the returning soldiers in Bangor, rush to the airport to praise civilization, not the warriors. The Greeks have returned, let us shower them with gifts, for they have brought Greece back with them! Tomorrow, like us, they are on their own. And we cry only because the festivity expresses our primitive love of civilization, of ourselves, of our soul? As those who knew who they were - those not frightened to build monuments celebrating their greatness - we should erect a giantic arch festooned with wreaths to commemorate the victorious, inhumanity of sacrifice. (Should they have failed, self-destructive depresssion is the only response. Vietnam?) (I just tonight discovered that for the past twenty years or so my writing consisted in the stringing together of cliches, and trying my dammnest to animate them. The hope being to fashion a self that was at once real <u>and</u> communicable. I thus looked at everything for its cliche-value so to speak. The amazing thing is that this was possible! The nitty-gritty is yet to come.)

Just received your letter! So, your sails are limp, eh? Well, out here the winds are blowing rather vigorously (I just can't mange to turn mine the right way. They flap alright, but the ship doesn't move). Your colleagues are a sorry lot. Basket cases. Nancy's comment that she is "not political", and the other's comment 'guess you see things more clearly', are not only out of left field, they also smack of the parental message; 'take your self and shove it. I don't want or need it around'. They strip one naked, leaving one on the promontory of existence alone. (Like the photo's of those living before the death-camps, they secretly say, 'leave the village and you are dead'.)

Enough! Days have passed since I started this note.

Dear Steve,

> If we want to live and work, we
> must be very reasonable and look
> after ourselves. Cold water,
> fresh air, simple good food,
> decent clothes, a decent bed,
> and no women....
> VanGogh

Doggedly in pursuit - at the expense of boredom perhaps.
Hope not however.

> "America and South Africa, in the
> whole world, are probably more
> color-conscious than any other
> nation," he said. "But Americans
> don't want to realize that."

And:

> "... after me, what happens?"

These two remarks from the clippings you send, sum up the
philosophy of Relativism. Including Spengler. These few lines
capture the mystery, the sublimity, and the awe of relativism
that stops people dead in their tracks. Not the people who, as
Whitman says, "are ungrammatical, untidy, and their sins gaunt
and ill bred", but the "good", enfeebled by others. For them,
the "overthrow {of} syntax" would mean nothing, or, rather, it
would liberate them from reality. Man letting nature flow
through him in full realization of its powers, enjoying holding
it in rein while figuring out how to turn it productive, is
anathema to them. Each 'new age', from close observation,
<u>learns</u> from the past - we do not merely suffer another
theoretical twist in our mental screws (like passing

unconsciously from twenty to fifty, and then wondering why our
bones creak). Praxiteles, Grunewald, Braque; Homer, Aquinas,
Hemingway; Oswald Von Wolkenstein, Berlioz, Copeland; a chain
in the experience of reality, each learning from the other. As
VanGogh, again, so nicely put it:

> When old Corot said a few days before his
> death - 'Last night in a dream I saw
> landscapes all pink', well, haven't they
> come, those skies all pink, and yellow and
> green into the bargain, in the
> Impressionist landscapes? All of which
> means that these are things one feels
> coming, and they are coming in truth.
>   And as for us who are not, I am
> inclined to believe, nearly so close to
> death, we nevertheless feel that this
> thing is greater than we are, and that its
> life is of a longer duration than ours.
>   We do not feel we are dying, but we do
> feel the truth that we are of small
> account, and that we are paying a hard
> price to be a link in the chain of
> artists, in health, in youth, in liberty,
> none of which we enjoy, anymore than than
> the cab horse that hauls a coach full of
> people out to enjoy the spring.
>   VanGogh
>   Letters from Arles

   Some ages are dead, and can not feel the "link". The age
of Relativism, for instance - the age which thinks it looks
into the past as they would into a zoo of defunct, geoglogic
creatures. They pretend to gaze into glass cases - Rousseau,
DeSade, Braque, Newton - and see creatures swirling in their
own dreams, in their own nightmares - and thus feel nothing
coming.

   They are like Slim Pickens riding the Bomb, only they ride
a metaphor, the destructive metaphor of 'culture'. And so, of
course, "...after me, then what?" The answer can only be -
nothing.

   My spleen at myself has been pricked. Duped by the siren
call of Relativism and its promises of total knowledge and

power, my neurosis grew in intellectual, if isolated, splendor. I, destroyer of reality, lived in my own waste. Shit-yard of the world, my soul stinks of disgorged things, and over it all hangs the odor of putrefied anger. My kingdom for a breath of fresh air! But who will trade such a deal?

Am presently reading Len's New Jerusalem. Shocked, I find it is a diatribe against Western imperialism. It begins with Kurtz living in London hamstrung, then he goes to the colonies. The man has unbearble disdain for the urbanite - seen as human vacuities creating an unredeeming, unrelenting, de-sexed materialism. Without the saving grace of a Whitman. Len seems to agree with Whitman in saying: "Confess that to severe eyes, using the moral microscope upon humanity, a sort of dry and flat Sahara appears, these cities, crowed with petty grotesques, malformations, phantoms, playing meaningless antics. Confess that everywhere, in shop, street, church, theatre, barroom, offical chair, are pervading flippancy and vulgarity, low cunning, infidelity, ... everywhere an abnormal libidinousness, unhealthy forms, male, female, painted, paddded, dyed, chignoned, muddy complexions, bad blood,...shallow notions of beauty, with a range of manners, or rather lack of manners ... probably the meanest in the world." But he does not go on to "... but I know nothing more rare, even in this country, than a fit scientific estimate and reverent appreciation of the People - of their measureless wealth of latent power and capacity, their vast artisitic contrasts of light and shade - with, in America, their entire reliability in emergencies, and a certain breath of historic grandeur, of peace or war, far surpassing all the vaunted samples of book-heroes, or any haut ton coteries, in all the records of the world."

With Len cast as the lonesome cowboy Faber, who owes nothing to nobody - in fact, everybody owes him for making him ridiculous and useless in a world that is inexplicably ridculous and useless - the novel begins. In New Jerusalem, the colony, populated as it is with civilization's cripples and

131

indigious ignoramusus however, he meets himself for real - the deformity of his life springs to life as he is surrounded by the oppressed Komoro - a 'fanatic' group of Calibans who live the Truth of oppression. These are his people - victims. He has found Utopia disguised as a prison of the insane. In the end He, Eve and a Christ-child, in the after-glow of utter destruction by fire, begin to re-build Eden, and the "Black Bastard", the "the ship, the black freighter" (of Brecht fame), the Engola Gay, glides on undulating, evil waves of Reason back into the gloom of civilization.

   Spleen. Spleen. Spleen. Probably, in this case, caused by Len's pretending - my only surmize - not to know what I was referring to when - before reading his book, and in a causal conversation about the book which he initiated - I wondered if the name of the hero, Faber, was a play on homo faber. Especially: "To 'make up'; to frame or invent (a legend, lie, etc.); to forge (a document)." He denied all such knowledge, and I felt the fool for having wondered about such a forced, overly-intellectual symbolic referrent when the book, he made clear, was not 'intellectual', but real. Made me feel, need I say, like an intellectual in falsetto. The world slid out from under my feet. I am prone to such feelings, i.e. feeling that I don't know what the hell is going on of course, so I may be projecting overly. But spleen gushes forth nonetheless. Was Len 'playing' with me as he had the woman with bargain-basement shoes in Price Club, telling her how wonderful they looked? And going on and on about them, embarrassing Romona and Ruby, who finally pulled him away?

   Beside, his style is too harsh. There is no softness to it. It glints like rough stone. All angles and corners. No contours, shadow, or resonant depth. True, he writes as the journalist hero Faber is, but what Faber writes is not for the Press, it is Faber writing as a human for posterity. Mayakovsky:

                    Agitprop
                         sticks

Dear Steve:

Thanks for the serious annotations of the manuscript. I had the pleasant experience of not objecting at all to your suggestions for improving the essay. In fact, I incorporated every one of your criticisms and the result, I'm certain, is a much stronger essay. I've shipped the revision off to Sanford Pinsker this morning and I'll enclose a copy with this note.

Thanks also for "The End of Correctness." You're right: I don't know whether to laugh or cry - maybe a little of both. May I offer a brief story? When my buddy Matt Schneider and I were in graduate school together, we both got the assignment to teach English 101 at the same time, and had to attend the same preparatory seminar. One of the things that struck us was - I'm sorry to have to put it this way - the school-girlishness of the instructors who were, of course, the local composition experts, most of them women. It wasn't just the content of their presentation but its style that provoked us to react against it as against something unhealthy. I'd call it a combination of sentimentality and viciousness. If you do this and obey these "suggestions" then you'll be a nice sweet friend-to-students like us, but if you don't, have a nice time in Lefortovo!

I find the same repulsive combination in "The End of Correctness," with it's "aren't I clever" style and propagandistic earnestness. *Apparatchik* is written all over the piece.

· Every sentence in this... whatever it is... is simply diametrically out of phase with the truth. Take the last paragraph, where whoever the writer is claims that students don't want to learn to distinguish between true and false or to "fill in the blanks" (i.e., acquire knowledge), but want, instead, to engage in "metadiscourse" (gesundheit!): wrong, wrong, absolutely wrong. Students quickly understand that they're lacking in knowledge and then want knowledge badly. They also want to know the difference between true and false, if not precisely at first, then when their eyes have been opened a bit. Eric Gans might be amused to know that his theory of linguistic origins has now been surpassed.

Thanks again. One thousand thanks!

Tom

Dear Ted,

Or should I say, dear <u>someone</u>, to whom I address this invitation to perform interpretive strategies. Yes, I've seen the Trudeau commencement speech. I think it came out several years ago, also at graduation time. It's priceless. He has it down pat: "Moreover, a faculty of deconstructionists have reconfigured the rhetorical components within a post-structuralist framework, so as to expunge any offensive elements of western rationalism and linear logic" !!! And then to make the disclaimers the content of the speech by ending it after the politically correct apologies. It's brilliant.

Speaking of which, Mel passed me another novel by David Lodge called <u>Nice Work</u>. A minor gem. This one is based on 19th-century "Condition of England novels" and features a woman, a professor of English, whose specialty is 19th-century condition of England novels. She becomes involved with Vic Wilcox, factory manager, and at one moment toward the end, when he asks her if she's ever been in love, she says, "Yes, I was once constructed by the rhetoric of romantic love."

I await the story of how you got the tape. I await any story you have to tell. Sorry I cannot help you with your spasm, though come to think of it (and I haven't thought about it for years), my copy of Burton's <u>Anatomy of Melancholy</u> probably has a listing for something in your range.

(I just pulled it down from the shelf). It has the flavor of your book on witchcraft:

> The First Partition: Section I: Member 1, Subsection 4: Dotage, Phrenzy, Madness, Hydrophobia, Lycanthropia, Chorus Sancti Viti, Extasis, 5. Melancholy in Dispostion, improperly so called. . . . Sect. 2, Memb. 1, Subs. 3. Of Witches and Magicians, how they Cause Melancholy. . . . 6. Parents a Cause by Propagation.

Aha!--Memb. 3, Subs. 15. Love of Learning, or over-much Study, With a Digression of the Misery of Scholars, and Why the Muses are Melancholy:

> How much time did Thebet Benchorat employ, to find out the motion of the eighth sphere! forty years and more, some write. How many poor scholars have lost their wits, or become dizzards, neglecting all worldly affairs and their own health, wealth, being & well being, to gain knowledge! for which, after all their pains, in the world's esteem they are accounted ridiculous and silly fools, idiots, asses, and (as oft they are) rejected, contemned, derided, doting, and mad! Look for examples in Hildesheim, read Trincavellius, Montanus, Garceus, Mercurialis, Prosper Calenus, in his Book On Black Bile. Go to Bedlam and ask.

Part. 2, Sect. 2, Memb. 6, Subs. 1, Passions Rectified:

> Friends' confabulations are comfortable at all times, as
> fire in Winter, shade in Summer, as sleep on the grass to
> them that are weary, meat and drink to him that is hungry
> or athirst; Democritus' Collyrium is not so sovereign to
> the eyes as this is to the heart. . . . Tully, as I remem-
> ber, in an Epistle to his dear friend Atticus, much con-
> doles the defect of such a friend. *I live here* (saith he)
> *in a great City, where I have a multitude of acquaintance,*
> *but not a man of all that company with whom I dare famil-*
> *iarly breathe, or freely jest. Wherefore I expect thee,*
> *I desire thee, I send for thee; for there be many things*
> *which trouble and molest me, which, had I but thee in*
> *presence, I could quickly disburden myself of in a*
> *walking discourse.*

"Friends' confabulations" apart, I've been using Collyrium
ever since my dizziness came on and David recommended it (for
I'd never heard of it before). The first time I used it was
thrilling. I'd been using Visine up till then, and it was
useless. Suddenly the itching stopped and everything came into
focus. It was one of my little discoveries during vertigo. So
I'm standing there, blinking my eyes and thinking, isn't
modern medicine wonderful. And a year and a half later (two
minutes ago), I thumb through my Burton, excited at seeing
that marvellous scholastic precision in him that you showed me
in <u>Malleus Malificarum</u> (almost as good, in its own way, as the
Basho you read that moisture-filled evening in Hortonville
years ago)--and bingo! delightful discovery that Collyrium
goes back to Democritus (assuming it's the Greek he means and
not some medieval alchemist, though that might be better yet).
Burton, by the way, was a 17th-century reverend of some sort,
and his <u>Anatomy</u>, like Montaigne's <u>Essays</u>, was bedside reading
for the next two centuries--a man who lived somewhat
cloistered and, like my mother and all those recluses that I
love, traveled through the world without ever having to go
anywhere. Melville loved his prose for the density of it all--
the density and energy.

I enclose for your amusement some examples from Lodge's
anthology--each one a comic moment in itself (around which he
constructs many a plot). I quote <u>Nice Work</u> from memory:

Robin: Couldn't I just give you a massage? Touching,
      rubbing, non-penetrative sex?
Vic: No, it's not enough. I'm a phallic sort of a
      guy.

<u>Nice Work</u>, by the way, picks up some time after <u>Small World</u>.
Phillip Swallow, who had that intense but self-aborted affair,
is back with his wife in Rummidge, and when the novel begins,
he's dithering into mental vacancy as chairman of the English
department. Morris Zapp makes a brief appearance, smoking

cigars "the size of small zeppelins," and Robin is a radical feminist deconstructionist literary critic, a la Lily Pabst, but without her driving lunacy. Come to think of it, I actually read it in black and white images, sort of like looking at those early 50s British films--gritty Burmingham realism ("Condition of England"), which is exactly what Rummidge looks like in the book. It's quite brilliant, as a matter of fact. Robin becomes Vic's "Shadow" as part of a university outreach program, and later feels herself to be going to the shadow side of town and the shadow side of herself when she drives through Rummidge to his factory.

There's a delicacy in all these things that needs to be observed, which is why I like the way Lodge does it in his books. I followed Paglia till she said Madonna was the first intelligent-sexy woman "in history"!! I had a similar feeling watching Kimball on TV and suddenly hearing the journalist in him. It occurs to me that for the first time I see what Kafka means when he says that even in someone like Goethe, he can feel the disappointing flaw, the little tail wagging. But it's always that way, isn't it? At least for me there are times when I can suddenly feel arrested in my delights and need to bring my thrill back down to earth. It's a very tricky line, which is why I prefer Braque to Picasso, for example. I have trouble when the experience is too defined, too fixed, too complete, the way Picasso is so damned perfect in his execution and the immediacy of his imagery. At some point, as you once said, his works would be perfectly at home in a corporate office. A Braque on the same wall would look uncomfortably out of place, because it would be busting out with the intimacy of art--in that quiet way of his. But still and all, it's all so damned delicate, since there is for me an inner moment where Picasso has his place.

I am done in two weeks with school, two weeks beyond the original end of the semester, and therefore cannot teach summer session because of that damned three week takeover. My timing remains as it was, to head out after the first week in July. The paperwork for Sonya's schools never ends. Every time we send in one form, three come back with new requirements. Perhaps this is done in order to justify the need for 800 numbers. If it weren't for them, my phone bills would be through the roof. Or perhaps they're generated by the sheer existence of computers and printers, which allows people to zap out forms at the touch of a switch.

When I was with Sonya up in Beverly, Mass. for her graduation last weekend, we spent an afternoon wandering up toward Cape Anne and found a little town, Essex, near Gloucester, both along water, both of which were once centers of ship-building in the days of schooners (last one built in '27). In Essex, I found a restaurant on the docks above a canal that Lutece couldn't touch, and a small (tiny) museum of shipping lore, filled with old photographs, maps, tools, bits of naval bric-a-brac, and a twenty-sixish year old guy, Huck Finn on Sunday, straight out of 1840 in voice, speech, and music was wonderful, and then when the symphony began, thought it all sounded like military marching music--and another one Spengler notes about people who listen to Russian folk music, thinking how sad it is, and being told by Russians that it's actually quite joyful and uplifting to them. So there you are.

Clover and I had a good day hanging out and gabbing away. It is a shame that our difficulties have to be so major, but I am actually doing just fine with her and the rest will just have to be the rest.

One final weirdness: Allison's husband's father wrapped a hose from his exhaust into his car and gassed himself to death a few days ago (in the version Sonya told me). It seems he left $500 for everyone to get drunk over his corpse, and that's just what his son did. How's that for a grimoire of craziness? Any time would have been the right time, but somehow it all fits that I got Sonya away from those people when I did.

There is actually a fireworks show going on over the East River right now with a violent thunder and lightening storm happening at the same time--I am turning this into a portent in the skies to end my letter.

Regards to Ruby. We look back fondly on our trip to N. M. and think of how good our two weeks really were.

As ever,

Steve

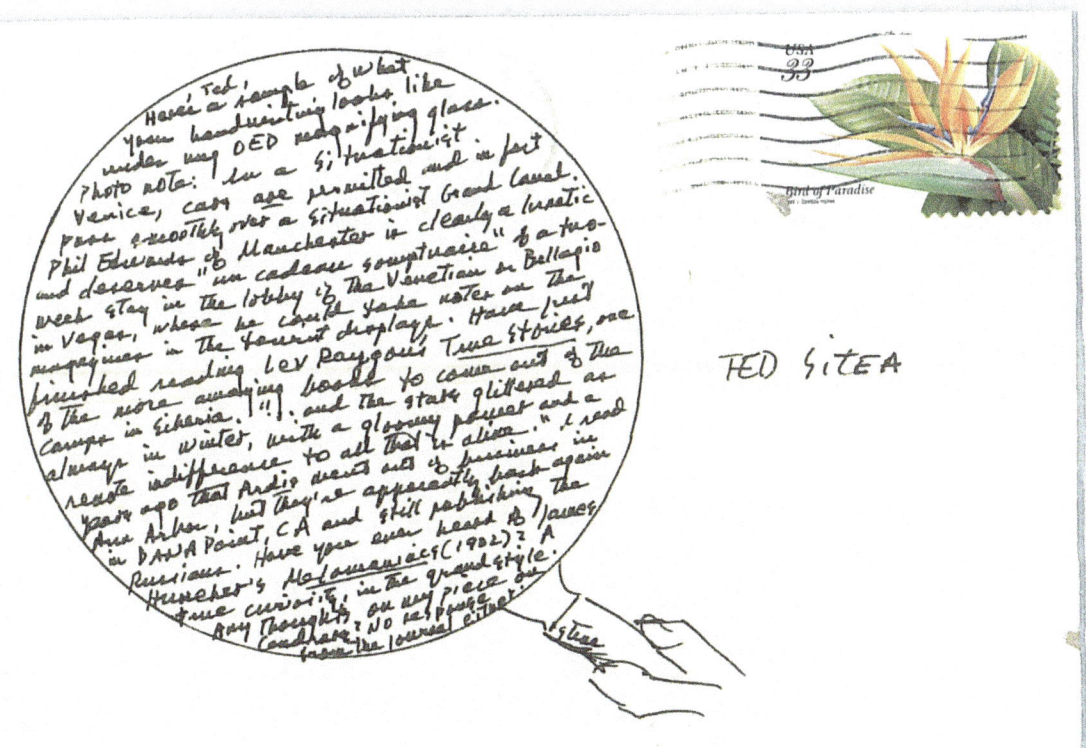

may,'91

Dear Steve,

I must admit that your last letter - one of your shortest
- fell upon me like a ton of bricks. It sent me reeling for
days! Well, you ask, what in such a tiny letter could wreck
such enormous psychic turmoil? Why, nothing more than the wee
phrase: "still pulling my punches". My instant, peculiar
understanding of that phrase opened vistas as wide as G.E.
Moore's sudden clap before a philosophy class proving to them
the existence of reality. Strange! Weird that such a little
phrase, such a punch-drunk metaphor, should be - an epiphany of
sorts.

True, my mind has been in a 'poetic state' for a while:
images of the past - a frame from a 40's movie, an unnamed face
of twenty years ago with pursued lips, the open grave of my
father, etc., are being triggered by present perceptions,
gestures, thoughts, etc., and then the two merge in a startling
psychological unity; myself welling up from the deeps and
bestowing symbolic force onto the present, the present then jumping
alive within my heart: Reality born afresh. It is as though I
am trying to merge with myself, as insane as that may sound.
But it is poetry. Yet, like so much poetry nowadays, I don't
quite 'get it'. I surface within myself as a Mallarme poem -
one word printed in the right hand corner of the page, another
to the right three lines down, another, five lines down, in the
center, and at the bottom, surounded by vast, white space, a
lone question mark - trying to tell me something. At any rate,
your phrase entered into my poem somewhat as a title. To write
'without punch' for me is to write without communicating - a
travesty of words, a subversion of their existence. It is to
write in secret code. Writer as Jack the Ripper - words so

razor-sharp the reader is unaware of being slashed to death -
from the inside. And Jack, as always, thinks he gets away with
murder. But he doesn't, for no one reads him seriously - they
are hip to his dock-side, Mack-the-knife behavior. Words
deprived of purpose, motive, of their revelatory power of
self-expression but used instead to blanket them, to conceal
them under guise of 'simple' reminder, 'obvious', truth,
statement of 'interest', 'curious' observation, etc., are the
most devious of all. They are delivered 'without punch', even
prefaced with disclaimers to possessing 'punch'; humbled before
their reader like the head of Mantegna's St. Sebastian lying
limp on his right shoulder while tormenting arrows pierce his
chest, they enter others like whispering sucubi and incubi, into
the heart of the onlooking tormenters they go, destroying their
power from within ('without punch'). I do not place such a
burden upon your use of the phrase "without punch", merely upon
mine. Talk about writers block! I have it in spades. I dance
about my father's grave frozen in time. A DeSade in Periclean
robes, yet also a Pericles hiding under DeSade's cape.

The philosophy of Relativism is not unacquainted with the
sorrow of repression. As does neurosis, it too puts a spell
between self and reality. The former the spell of the past, the
latter the spell of culture (the world as image / intellection/
urphanomene beheld in the mind). Relativism enters the world
claiming to disturb nothing, yet in its wake the world lies as
in the left panel of the Garden of Delights. To the extent that
one confuses the past of one's culture (history) with one's
psychological past (nightmare), to that extent do the spells
merge and one's self become the microcosm of the macrocosm;
Gothic arches, Grecian temples, Druidic stone become the new
facades of the nightmare. The self is every where, in
everything, crawling about in undisturbed glee. It becomes the
laughing, universal overseer of mankind's inevitable delusions
of being Real. The nightmare is rationalized; 'culture' is its
metaphor. Clothed now in handsome bridges, fauvist colors,
etc., one's nightmare enters 'culture' like a dove-wreathed Ceasar

swordlessly reaping its hollow glories - if not the adulation of the ignorant populace who see only Reality and do not notice the entry. Ceasar enters into humanity on condition of its being unreal, and once landed transforms himself into St. Sebastian, martyr to the undisturbed universe. The nightmare freely grows, glutting itself on culture like Goya's monster in the Nightmare of Reason, scarcely disturbed by the nonplussed onlookers who see nothing going on.

Relativism is neurosis writ large. It is reality without REALITY, power without POWER, Knowledge without KNOWLEDGE, Morality without MORALITY, truth without TRUTH, self without SELF. In its hands oppression is freedom, conformity is individuality, hate is love, empowerment is deprivation of power, diversity is without difference, art is without artistry, war is peace, sex is masturbation, nature is convention, and men are women. At least that is what it is to me. DeTocqueville and Chateaubriand would only scoff at such ideas. Relativism is only for those defeated by their own experience, who can not stand the mud bottom in their hearts.

Ach, I yell at my self too much. The man doth protest too much! Yet the difference between Degler in In Search of Human Nature, as well as Camille Paglia in Sexual Personae and the Relativists is revealing! Their topic is the same -NATURE- yet between them only Degler and Paglia believe in The "Ancient of Days". The differences between Degler and Paglia are even more interesting than those between them and the relativists. Degler likes to account for the differences between man and women - women's lack of aggression, poor visual-spatial ability, interiority etc. - by pointing to differences in our biology. So too does Paglia. But whereas Degler lets it go at that Paglia waxes evermore poetic: She likes how the West has mythologized that difference, how it has twisted its psychology and produced our array of sexual personae: homosexuals, lesbians, sadists, straight-men,etc.. Woman, she says, is chthonian: the vegetative, Dionysian swamp; man, the Appollonian penis of dominance, ejaculating order out of chaos. And never the twain shall meet - except in pain and conflict.For Degler it is all a matter of 'levels of testestrone', for Paglia that is the least interesting thing about it. It is really the nineteenth century all over again. However, the feminist of today are like West-bank Palestinians who now want the Israelis to migrate - but to leave the forms of their civilization behind them.

Degler (approvingly): "Maccoby and Jacklin set forth three general reasons for seeing aggressiveness as rooted in biology: "(1) the sex differences manifests itself in similar ways in man and subhuman primates; (2) it is cross-culturally universal; and (3) levels of aggression are responsive to sex hormones." He later adds: "It is worth noting that, though the identification of sex differences has an ancient history, these more recent identifications, unlike many of those in the past, lack any implication that the differences justify confining women's place or opportunities in society."(pp.289-303)

Paglia (at her tamest): "The chthonian superflux of emotion is a male problem. A man must do battle with that enormity, which resides in woman and nature. He can attain selfhood only by beating back the daemonic cloud that would swallow him up: mother-love, mother-hate, for her or from her, one huge conglomerate of natural power. Political equality for women will make very little difference in this emotional turmoil that is going on above and below politics... Sex is metaphysical for men, as it is not for women." (p.19)

The relativist claim that all is culturally induced, is like a damp, dirty dishrag suddenly thrown on an erection. Who needs it? Puritans all!

Reading this stuff - thought grounded in nature and biology - curiously, is taking me back to the world I knew as a child, where men were men and women, women and where all my fears and nightmares thus make sense. Reading them makes me feel comfortable, at home in the world again. I grew up in a naive world when people knew they were humans, grounded in nature, and not "theoretically sophisticated". My neurosis requires that world to make sense - otherwise it is the uncaused cause.

Which again bring me back to myself - how did Valery put it - 'I get back to myself by detour of the universe'? I wander the earth a period in search of the final sentence.

Revamp your Spengler paper if you must - I still think it stands as it is. But say it: was Spengler (for you) right or wrong, not simply a good pedalogical tool? And _that_ is the question. (For me, Spengler is 'moral' because he does not 'disturb' the world, he reads it as a novel to be 'lived into'. Just as one can not disturb the "full rose of dawn" in the sorrowful pupils of Billy Budd, so too one can not disturb the course of history in different cultures; they are delicate perceptions that one must enter on tip-toe, as one would surreptiously enter the dreams of another. One must einfulen and anschauung them - silent processes that gently move among their contents without knocking them over and awakening them: otherwise there is nothing. Puff! Spengler, first purveyor of dreams, then inserts himself back into his dream culture on beat, and no one is awakened. While Melville, Whitman, and Orwell noisely go about expressing themselves, Spengler, in his grim flat, mirrors the grand illusions of others. I imagine that the likes of Whitman and Melville imagined the self a tornado. A tornado flying through the world with a silent center through which all must pass but for a moment. To hang out only in the center - as I imagine, again, Spengler to have done - is to neglect the distruptive power of one's presence. To speak from within the center, over the noise of one's presence, to shout it down, merely wearies the other who feels the wind rushing past. In the center there is nothing - ghostly images of things that have flown through, perhaps - only the purposeful energy which sustains the tornado. Art is one of the results of tempests passing through the world. Do not speak from the center or, like me, you too shall go unheard through the din of yourself.

Do I become too preachy? Or, more importantly, do I make

sense? I have not yet torn the mountains, trees, oceans, Europe, philosophy, people, etc., sufficiently out of me so that I can experience them, so I often incorporate reality into my nightmare and merely analogize my neurosis - rather than present an actual experience of things in their Teddyized roundness and fullness. My coma is deep. Sometimes I think I threw my self into my father's coffin. Buried in Potter's Field, no one remembers exactly where. (One of the most embarrassing things about me, and rarely revealed, is that when I write I seldom know, (consciously feel my motives and purposes) why I write. What I write is clear enough, but why I am writing it remains a mystery to me. I do not grasp what I wish to accomplish, or why I wish to accomplish it. The finished work, in some sense, stasnds before the world naked waiting for final judgment I stand back holding my breath. I will accept anything said about it as gospel - my elation or depression hangs on their assesment of its intent. Although I see myelf as having no counter-arguments, I, of course, do, but these are offered naked as well, awaiting judgment. So I never approach my motive or purpose. What deep, drk purposes do I have in mind? What so terrible a wish do I have that I scare the shit out of myself? The answer to that question would unlock the Pandora's Box within, and all the petty demons would fly out embarrassed now themselves by their impotence in real time and space. A clever Indian who brushes away his horses hoofprints so that others can not tell where he went nor from where he will come. But then he gets lost - not so clever an Indian after all.*)

Ach, the struggle is long and hard!

"Your Show of Shows" - sorry for the delay. Len had promised to premiere it at his house - so we waited. Then, sometime later, he changed his mind. A day or two after that Ruby and I left for Phoenix for an extended visit. And then.... well, another week passed.... I felt I had to get it off to you before anymore time lapsed. I viewed it, enjoyed it, enjoyed seeing you again, and got it off. Unfortunately, my brain was fried, and this -though not quite the ten pages as promised - is the letter that should have accompanied it, restarted four

Marty has since called. His daughter is making her way here sometime in the summer, so he wanted to know if I knew anything about health service for Indians out here. I didn't. She has not called me, so I do not know when she plans on being here. Olivia told me of your ill-fated date with her - she will contact you when she returns to renew the time and place.

Romona - perhaps Len as well - is truly frightened out here. She feels here the way I felt on Bond St, a moment away from sudden violence. She locks her doors and windows, and feels at the whim of marauding strangers. Clockwork Orange type, I think. Fear of the unknown is terrific. Reminds me of Clover. They will definitely be back in August, safe in the known violence of New York. Len is warming-up quite a bit, the more he does the more I like him. I think, I hope, he likes us. He seems too. He is comfortable with himself, much more than I can be with myself. He openly likes himself, and moves reality about like a pro. Neurosis bores him. Feelings in things and people fascinate him. Not symbolically either, but as they are. He is a good tonic for beached whales like me.

At any rate, I am looking forward to spending afternoons with you in Santa Fe. We will sip our coffee, discuss Paglia and other current fads, and listen to chamber music rehearsals. Were it in Rome it would be better, but... we will make do.

I write to you because your are one of the rare few to whom when I write I can also speak to myself without overwhelming fear and trepitation. I thank you for that - you are a window onto the universe for me - and would do nothing to jeopardize it. I hope I have not done so now.

Love
Ted

* What kind of letter for instance, is this? Begining in the wilds of thought it outlines the abyss of Relativism as a warning to all who thread into its make-believe castles of knowledge. But it is essentially a warning to myself - and a word of presumptious caution to you (for I feel a hidden force in your phrase "without punch"). But at the same time I can not

put that purpose into the writing - so I express not myself, but loose thoughts, bits and pieces of the world that fly through me, and which I think I throw back unspoiled by my desire thoughts held together by logic not feeling, thoughts "without punch". Yet write I must. Someday, I will come into myself.

Steve —

yes, I am familiar with "Au Coeur du
Monde" — Imagine Cendrars walking beneath
that window and the infant bouncing across his
feet. "Knock my fucking childhood to the ground
My family and my habits
Put a train station in its place
or leave an empty lot —

Ted

147

June 7, 1991

Dear Ted,

Wonderful. I get your letter before last, feel nervous as usual about responding when the mood strikes me in a timely way, and bingo! You brush my nerves aside and simply send me another ! Wonderful.

I feel the divine afflatus coming on. This writing to you is taking on a life of its own. I want to use it for all it's worth. There's something about the issue of writing itself that's important for me in our correspondence, a thought that's been revolving in me for a while. It's an adventure every time, a roller coaster of excitement, involvement, self-blame, and excitement all over again. I cannot help it, as I'm sure you cannot when the fit comes on--the feeling is lodged in my genes--apologies, doubts, and apprehensions for the rambling nature of my thoughts--exhausting, self-indulgent, importuning--more material with which to beat myself up. My sheer existence, putting one foot before the other, can sometimes be grounds enough. When it comes to myself, now there I don't pull any punches--if anything, I pulverize with hidden strength.

Kogan's laws of pulled punches:

1) Every pulled punch has a fixed and precise quantity of undischarged energy.
2) The undischarged energy of every pulled punch recoils upon the puncher, like Milton's Satan, whose evil "back recoils upon itself."
3) There are people whose psychic lives would make Joe Louis look like Dickens' Tiny Tim.

Your citations of Van Gogh (speaking of writing letters) were a surprise. How beautifully he writes, how clearly, and movingly. I hadn't heard his voice in years. In high school, he was for me a holy man. The Van Gogh museum in a state park (I believe) in Holland felt for all the world like a shrine when I was there (once) with Danielle (that marriage is on my mind these days).

This relativity business, I'm afraid, calls for many martinis and manhattans. Very simply, I have not thought it through but need and want to hear your words. I take my cue from Montaigne, by the way, who struck a chord in me from the very first time I laid eyes on him, which was in Freshman Humanities. It's that sense of life I love in him--that clear-headed sense, a la Heraclitus (on whom Spengler wrote his dissertation, and perhaps Marx and Kiekegaard did as well!), that all things are changing, that it's all a shifting, cloudy, mercurial experience, including our forms of thought themselves, which take on the color of our humanity--the endless panorama, the insane contradictions, the endless catalogues of philosophical points of view, the vast humor and tragedy of it all, in which we cannot see things absolutely, "as they are," but only by hints, indirections, in "cloudy poesie," in veils of meaning, symbol, metaphor. Read "An Apology for Raymond Sebond," if you have not. It's a wonder. Actually, any of his essays is a feast. Now there's a man who swims in life. It's as Spengler says of Goethe, by way of comparison to modern "thinkers": science, technology, Russia, the decline of parliaments, the question of feminism, folklore, the environment--is there anyone today who can make sense of it, who seems equal to the world? "I look in vain for a thinker, and find none. Goethe would have relished it." Ditto Montaigne, ditto Chateaubriand. And that's how I feel about Spengler. I relish him. I don't even want to bother with the question of right or wrong (a bit overdone but true enough for now). Is Dante right or wrong? Is any half-way serious metaphor right or wrong? It's either "deep or shallow," as he says. It's either filled with life and sensitivity or not. Reading him is like being thrilled by Olivier, like eating steak, like a good run down a ski slope (I used to envy you and the kids doing flying cannonballs into the pool at Lake H). Everything, says Montaigne, is transitory. That's the theme around which the essays flow, develop, gather moments of experience, of thought. And it is all filled with self,

Montaigne in every line ("warts and all"--that's his phrase in the preface about how he will describe himself). And that's what Spengler means by culture--the world imbued with self, with identity. And it's all a flowing, changing thing, moments of depth, of infinite depth, in which "we see imperfectly, by indirection," whether you want to call it hieroglyphics or Platonic veils or metaphor. "Everything transitory is only a metaphor." Of what? Of whatever we bring to experience and whatever experience brings to us. None of it is iron-clad. The real metaphors are living, limited, imperfect things. It is this sense of life, of depth of meaning that Spengler says is being destroyed by our modern world of "hard cold facts," brute facts, power, and in the end, formlessness. I mention, by the way, in my essay (all versions, I believe), that Spengler even regards nature figuratively. How does the opening of Vol. 2 begin: "Regard the flowers at evening," etc. Now this business about metaphor is itself a touchy thing. It does not mean rhetorical trope, as the scholars would have it, but exactly what Nietzche means when he says that

> For a genuine poet, metaphor is not a rhetorical
> figure but a vicarious image that he actually
> beholds in place of a concept.
> (The Birth of Tragedy, 8)

Spengler subjects everything to this point of view. It's not that stars aren't real for him. It's simply that stars are infinite, like everything else, and therefore, whatever we see, we pick and choose and define out of our limitations, out of who we are, what we are predisposed to see; and even our transformations of perception carry the marks of who we are, metaphors of ourselves. Our very discoveries are expressive of ourselves, which does not make them any the less discoveries for that. My readings in 17th-century garden poetry actually helped me to see flowers more deeply than I ever had before. His book is but another way of seeing, of being in the world. To use relativism to confirm what is in one's head is to confound the very meaning of the word. That is what the ideologues of relativism do not understand, because at bottom, they are only a reflex of the times, the shallowest reflex at that. I cannot go on without having that drink with you in Santa Fe.

Apropos the close of your last letter and to heighten the Rome/Santa Fe nexus on both sides of that lovely itinerary: were we to have our cup of coffee in Rome, it would be magnificent--but to have it with you in Santa Fe will not only do but do grandly.

Pulling my punches: ultimately a torture. I suppose if I weren't punching at all I'd be a zombie (the wish to be a zombie--the idea fascinates me--note that African sound--Zombie--"make it weird," said Thelonius, so bop titles came out like "African zonga sounds," according to Kerouac--Zombie, which is how a lot of us are feeling at BMCC right now).

OK, so I'm not a cripple (thank you, Dad). My punching, such as it is, means two things: I am punching, and (of course), I am not really punching (this is where my stories seem to live, in twilight zone). Example: one summer when Danielle and I were in Paris, we spent about a month at the Bibliothèque Nationale doing research on our doctorates. She was actually doing it. I was looking at some 17th-century theatrical material, mostly engravings, but generally feeling that I wasn't working on my doctorate at all, simply acting as if I were doing it. I literally spent the time hoping that I would look like someone doing research. What I really wanted to do was travel (three or four times, to her discomfort, I punched us out of her godfather's apartment, with Dani each time making the remark that, well, after all, Steve was a bit of a bohemian!). We lived with her godfather and his wife in Paris every summer for three years (summers of 60-63). I was, as you can appreciate, desparately trying to look like I was married. For the most part, I lived in silence. I learned French in silence as well. Except for some lessons with her mother, no one for a minute thought that I was working on the language, since I never spoke about it, never told them anything about my struggles, difficulties, resentments, interests, etc. and silently continued to read my newspapers on my own and listen (silently) to everyone around me speaking a language I did not understand (I even took a semester of French in General Studies at Columbia, but if I mentioned it at all it was silently--the pulled punch. The third summer it all came to me one day in a flash when Dani's godfather had the morning news on the radio, and I understood it all. And even then, even then, and for the rest of the marriage, I never once showed them that I understood, never once spoke a word in French to them (I have the feeling I may have recounted some of this to you before).

One evening, there was a dinner given by a couple who were Dani's parents' friends (we simply revolved around her family). The people were actually quite charming and apparently very courageous during the war. They were Jewish. He was the head of the Paris-Mutuel--the gambling or horse racing syndicate. Their apartment was somewhere off the Arch of Triumph. It was a large banquet dinner. Most of the men had little red pin dots (signifying, if I remember right, the Croix de Guerre--or was it an emblem for the medal of the Resistance?) placed, oh so discreetly, in their lapels. Warm summer wind blew through the fifteen foot windows, slightly open, from across the Bois de Boulogne. Footmen in livery stood behind every third or fifth person, and I was there, silent as a post, except for a single moment, in which I turned to a woman sitting next to me in a black, semi-bare at the shoulders evening dress. Had I not spoken, I don't think I would have remembered that scene at all. How I did it, I don't know, but I simply punched as best I could. I said one sentence to her, something like, "I don't speak French very well," only it came out, "I speak French very bad." I heard the grammatical error instantly and went back into my dream, staggered that I could not let myself speak as well as I actually could, staggered that I should have said to her, of

152

all things, that I could not speak _correctly_. She, by the way, did not reply but looked at me and turned away. And there you have the history of a punch that I pulled. I have so configured the events of my life that when I describe them, it's as if it took sheer guts simply to exist, to live through the weird existence that I lived. "Make it weird." And I did. _C'est à pleurer_. It's enough to make one weep.

When I came back to teaching in 69-70 at BMCC, I remember going into a Woolworth's and buying a briefcase for $5.95. I didn't know anything else at the time except that teachers had briefcases, so I got one. That's how out of it I was, and yet, I knew that much. Jenkin told me before my doctoral defense to be sure to have a tie. He wasn't interested in my problems, or perhaps didn't think I'd really have any (which turned out to be mainly true). But he knew me well enough to know that I needed to hold on to reality. That's how it was with the briefcase. I could hardly speak a word in those days, for I was mainly coming off acid in 69-70. The briefcase really kept me intact. Ditto all my pulled punches. They mean sheer survival. I get nowhere but I remain in the ring. When I was a kid, I went through a similar experience as you did with the firecrackers at your feet. Some guys tried to pick a fight with me one day on Herzl Street, and I simply disappeared right in front of them. I believe you when you say that if Napoleon had met you before Borodino, he could have ended up not knowing who or where he was. And yet, and yet, if I only call them signs of a neurosis, I rob them of a piece of life, a piece of the unnameable.

Your letter: I feel I want to reply to everything. "To hang out only in the center--as I imagine, again, Spengler to have done--is to neglect the disruptive power of one's presence." For Spengler, though, everything, including his point of view, is filled with _character_. It is no mere theory he presents, as he says over and over again. To be at the center of things (that is to say, the free movement of the mind everywhere, equally) is for him, as you said of the western spirit holding on to Alexander's tenth-rate epic poet, to be a spirit that finds its foothold in infinity--and the center is thus not simply in the material, the ideas, but in the man himself. It is a full-blooded personality that speaks on every page. For me the almost inhuman quality about him is the absolute centering that he works upon himself. He's _made_ himself into a human being, a historian, a voice. Personality regarded in this sense is truly metaphysical and has nothing to do with what we normally take it to mean, which is eccentricity. Perhaps that is what you meant by Spengler neglecting the disruptive power of his presence--the fact that he lives inside his amazingly severe character--his "Roman" character, that is to say, Gothic Roman character--although, as you see, his presence is enormously disquieting--not so much his presence as what it represents. "A spectre is haunting Europe," said Marx, "the spectre of communism." It sounds like journalism compared to Spengler, who didn't have to trumpet himself. He is truly like the novelist--Flaubert's and Joyce's novelist--standing apart from his work paring his finger nails. He is there like a mist, a deeply held intuition, a steady, silent witness to our profound unease. How does he put it? We live in extraordinary times, perhaps the most extraordinary ever lived, and yet, as part of the strangeness of it all, people simply do not perceive the enormities we're passing through, have an incorrigible inability to face the facts, the "cold, hard facts." I don't know if he's right or wrong. I simply haven't come to terms with the issues he represents for me, but on his own terms, and so far as I can see, hardly anyone else has the guts to be honest to the issues of relativism. These ideologues who want to make timeless truths out of "multi-culturalism" are not simply frauds but diseased. When you say that "Relativism is neurosis writ large," I want to say, "Neurosis is neurosis writ large." Imagine what it must have been like in Germany when National Socialism actually sounded believable, sounded _right_. Spengler's is a living center--a free personality in the infinite--moving, directional--so incredibly open that the only possible life is sheer solitude, like the village idiot in "Boris Godunov," a voice of clarity in the insanity all around, "uncontaminated by the hatred peculiar to those years," as Borges says of him. That other center you speak of is a false one, I know all too well ("power without Power, diversity without difference," as you so deftly nail it to the wall). The idealogues of relativity (relativity without Relativity) are simply the grotesque mirror image of "scientific" humanism. I cannot imagine how I would make it through their courses, having hated their precursors down to my core, though I thank the gods for having spared me the illusion of doing battle with my graduate professors and becoming even worse than them. I simply fled. In some utterly bizarre, mysterious way, our real battles have spared us the false ones--not always in the details, but on the whole--so we end up in the strange situation of feeling drained of self and yet amazingly substantial and intact. Our ghosts keep us alive! "Wealth beyond measure in the regions of the dead."

Just saw "Pepe Le Moko" on CUNY-cable. They have a weekly French film festival. It's amazing what dreadful prints they use. That's CUNY for you. After each showing, they trot out various critics from CUNY--French professors, the head of the Alliance Francaise, film mayvens, etc. Tonight while listening to them for about 5 minutes before putting on "Das Rheingold" again, I realized just how hard, how insensitive and cruel all that critical language really is. While Spengler walks delicately, patiently, carefully through the museum, a conservator in every best sense of the word, these guys crash into walls, knock down shelves, break vases no amount of translucent protective covers could guard them from. These fucks, these deadly, stinking, successful, destructive fucks. They make their way by destroying life every minute of their lives. It's how they live. It's how they teach and how they write. I saw something about myself tonight listening to that troika of experts on TV, and I hope I can hold on to it.

I think we can have poetic strength. Didn't you write something in one of your letters about trying to get at the poetic power in yourself? It's just that strength, that "punch" of thought and feeling which makes one line of Neitzche, one line of O'Keefe or Ryder or Valery or Constable "outweigh a whole theater of others," one living line a whole generation of dark, stupid burdens, noise without end. Your letters crackle with energy: "De Tocqueville and Chateaubriand would only scoff at such ideas" Thank God for that line. It grounded me for the other parts of your discussion on neurosis and relativism.

Why do they detest Spengler so? Claudio Arrau died yesterday, and in the papers they noted that his teacher, Kraus, was one of Liszt's last pupils. Aha, says I. That generation of Horowitz and Arrau, as I generally understood, were the last connections to the 19th century. So I come home, feeling his death all day long, and go to my videotapes, since I remembered I had taped an Arrau/Beethoven program off 13 some time ago and never heard it. I put it on, and after the recital, there's a brief biography of Arrau. Here's the whole connection, as I heard the narrator tell it (I nearly went off my chair): Kraus was a pupil of Liszt. Liszt was a pupil of Czerny, and Czerny of Beethoven. Now that is exactly what Spengler means by a tradition, by "keeping in form." I feel this sense of lineal heritage too (an aristocratic notion, isn't it?) in my own helpless way, because my schooling goes all the way back into the 19th century as well--Chiappe from Van Doren--back a few people to A. C. Bradley and from Bradley no doubt to the romantics. Same for the beats, by the way, as I once heard Ginsberg tell it--the line reaches back via Burroughs to Beckett to Joyce to Eliot to Pound to Yeats (they actually read for each other in lineal descent). And the little I have of that consciousness in me seems to drop dead right at my feet. All the writers that I love have that smell of mortality, which is where I have to be careful and not spread my neurosis around. Do you remember Chateaubriand tracing a village plowman back to nobility? It's a theme of his: the decline of noble families. Every last person I've mentioned Chateaubriand to responded with a joke about steak. So what else is new?

> Diodorus tells about a deposed Egyptian king who was reduced to living in one of those wretched upper-floor tenaments [of Rome].

Here's another possibility: what the "professionals" despise in Spengler is precisely his cleaving to the idea of tradition (in his "Capsule Biography," by the way, Borges sees him as the last of the German line from Meister Ekhart through Leibniz, Kant, and Hegel--better should have said Herder and Neitzche as his 19th-century predecessors). It's like Jack Lemon says in "Save the Tiger" when he tells his partner that the banks don't care about the 15 years of work and credit their company built up. "Nobody care about history any more." That movie is haunted by the past, our past. Walking home on Court Street today, I came across a guy selling ices. A real block of ice, with the bottles of syrup and a scrapper. I hadn't seen real ices in I don't know how long. It's an old, old complaint. Fezziwig, for example, in A Christmas Carol, represents a happier time of English business, before the coming of the new, "vested interests." Marx and Engels also pin-point the issue of the death of rural, "merrie England," as did every sober thinker of those times. Constable lamented that the picturesque was disappearing from the English countryside--the canals, the tow barges, the mills, and weirs. One of my guidebooks, however, tells me that the Stour Valley in East Anglia where he lived and worked has been bypassed by industrialism and that there's a lot still intact. How I'd love to see those places once in my life (my East Anglia/ across the Channel/ medieval Holland fantasy trip--the Norwich Museum, the ferry ride, and the museums in Haarlem and the Hague).

I know only too well how I spread my mother across the universe. That's the nub of what frightens me in taking to Spengler as I do, the decline business. How to extricate--that's really what it's all about for me--every day. I mean really extricate. We must take from our past, pick and choose. "He has his yes, he has his no." It's the only way to leave the past behind. Seen in this light, Hamlet is stunning, almost beyond belief. He will not be his father's puppet, not even the puppet of a ghost:

> The spirit I have seen
> May be a devil, and the devil hath power
> T'assume a pleasing shape, yea, and perhaps
> Out of my weakness and my melancholy,
> As he is very potent with such spirits,
> Abuses me to damn me. I'll have grounds
> More relative than this. The play's the thing
> Wherein I'll catch the conscience of the king.

Isn't this passage astonishing? He comes to know every last fiber of himself. And they call this a play about "a man who could not make up his mind"! They turn everything into the drivel that they are. I've been playing my videotapes of the Ring. One day I remembered the cliche about Wagner being "bombastic," you know, the way Anna Russell makes a joke out of him. What's astonishing, though, is the economy of it all. There are hardly ever more than two people in any given scene. Three figures on stage are already a lot, and choruses are very rare. What bombast? It's all quite intimate, in fact, deeply, deeply intimate.

Taking from the past--perhaps that's what drives my feeling for history. Did you know that Constable's artistic problem was how to reconcile the old masters (Ruisdael, Hobemma, and Claude Lorraine) with his immediate sense impressions? Ditto for Cezanne. He said he wanted to redo Poussin from nature. The Louvre was his landscape before Mont St. Victoire. God knows what my landscape is--some mental picture of junkyards on Ditmas Avenue.

My Ms. keeps being rejected with an iron regularity.

Why do you think that your letter doesn't make sense? Is it perhaps a case of, "The devil . . .Out of my weakness and my melancholy . . . Abuses me to damn me"? The deep belief to hold on to is that <u>something</u> is working itself through. That's the razor's edge, isn't it? For me, a piece of clarity is worth everything, because then I can act. But each time it's shovelling shit against the tide. Hercules cleaning the Augean stables--what a perfect paradigm. You must understand, there are ways in which I think that you too move reality about like a pro. "Not symbolically, either." There's many a dead shark in New York would have given his rows of teeth to be a whale in Corrales. Are you really beached or is it that you need more room than a children's aquarium, swimming round and round? You do not "jeopardize" things for me, since we have a history of telling each other what we feel when a hurt comes up, and that's about the best that one can do in the damaged goods department. What does it matter what "kind" of letter you write? The only issue of concern to me is, what are you going through? If it's any help, I have my own version of what you feel. I get worried that I'm becoming burdensome with my stories and my references, the way I seem to live so much in the culture that I love. I think it's a case of anxiety coming to us precisely where we're strong (easier said than believed).

You ran into Jenkin's nasty streak. I have also felt small and worthless when he has run the game of hard-boiled reality genius on me. If we could affirm ourselves in the presence of that withering voice, a voice we carry all too powerfully inside ourselves, his response would not be nasty, though. He used to be much worse, biting people's heads off if they went against his grain. It's an issue that he's recognized himself. So let's say, for argument's sake (since I'm not entirely convinced), that he didn't know about <u>homo faber</u>. Look at his epigraphs, his allusions. Sometimes he plays the Rambo/Rimbaud, but it would be OK if we only had our voice.

Many thanks for the videotape. I can't believe I really did it, it seems so far away. I really wanted to do that program, but the thing that amazes me is that I let myself do it. You must understand, I don't believe I did it, and there's the rub, although I had an incredible sensation of being released the whole time I was there. The guys, by the way, all said that your face looked wonderfully open and relaxed (I took two *photos* of you--one in Mah-drid and the other in Santa Fe).

Will call as soon as I see my way clear to making final plans. Photograph enclosed of the Verrochio. I send it so that you can practice till it loses its sting. Be a peasant at its base. That's perfectly OK. Look at those TV aerials! It's too bad we have to approach things from the negative side, because with a slight turn of feeling, there's real clarity and understanding in the negativity. Your picture of yourself as the dark rider in Daumier's railway carriage is superb. Far better to feel like a peasant beneath a Verrochio than to be like a nice guy, socialist professor I know at school, who's torn between wanting his son to feel comfortable in the world, entitled to live, and guilty that this sense of security should come at the expense of the victims of the world; although if it's worth it, perhaps no real desire can come without our being up against a barrier, like Chateaubriand's 16th-century lovers having to make their tryst in the dark, outside the city walls.

Much love,
Steve

Now this one is a bozo, but it will have to make its way as best it can.

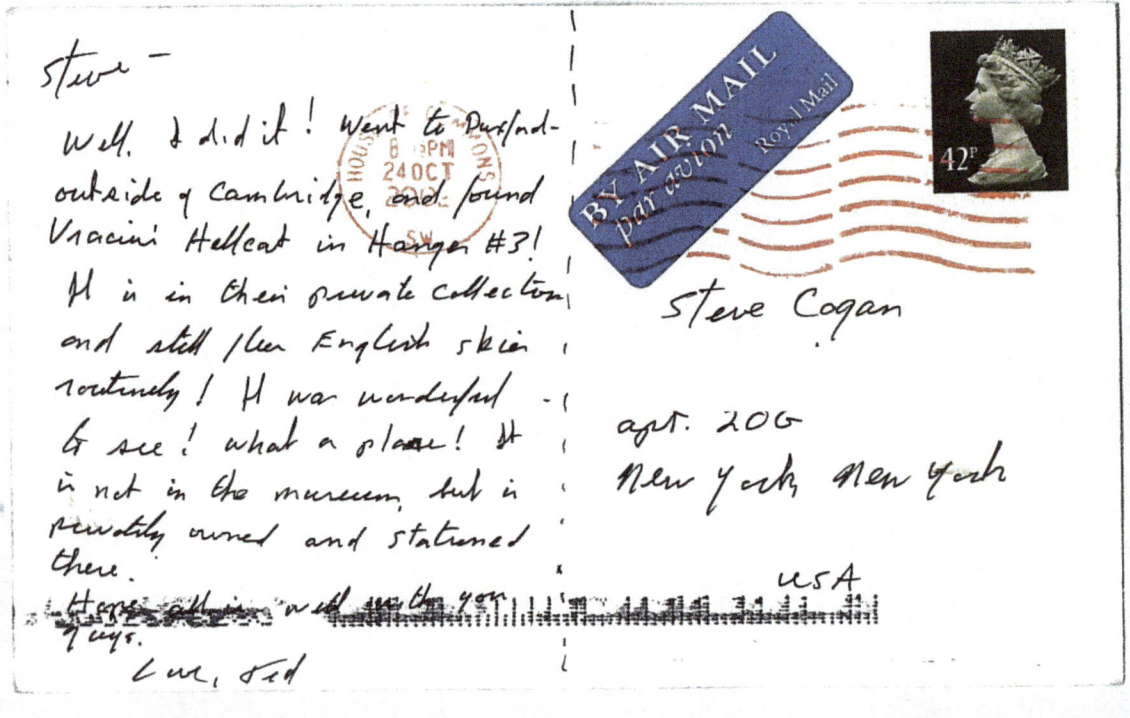

Dear Steve,

Hooray! Received your letter. Loved it - especially your
evening spent across from the Bois de Boulogne - soft breezes
over bare-shouldered women dressed in black and you with the
mile-long-stare (in Paris!) - and the digression on Spengler.
Our letters are not at all like the correspondence between Gide
and Valery which often seem, in comparison, so laconic. You and
I reach out to each other not only across a continent, but
across time as well, from those miserable years spent in
bone-crunching Siberia. We share our exile like recently
landed, weather-beaten immigrants swopping stories of village
pogroms - in desperate attempt to shed them and become
American. Do you think that one day - in utter forgetfullness -
we shall don flesh-fitting, electric-blue jogging outfits and
run through Central Park wearing ear-phones? Ha! Fat chance!
Even the thought of wearing a muted Hawaiian shirt causes me
nightmares.

Spengler, I swear, takes the words right out of my mouth!
For instance, in the course of the past several weeks I have
been writing you a letter, now reaching over fifteen pages in
length. In it I spoke of the Kritios Boy and his startling walk
out of Egyptian myth into reality; of St. Thomas' smashing of
Albert the Great's mechanical device - a sound emitting device
of thirty years work which proved, to the horor of St. Thomas,
the existence of the real distance between 'here' and 'there',
one which did not depend upon interpretation; of O'Keefe's and
Marin's conquest of the perspectiveless space of the New
Mexican desert, a landscape dissolving background and
foreground into pure dimensionlessness, pure, materialized
myth, leaving 'no room' on its surface for the artist to paint
anything real. Marin did it by collapsing multiple, fragmentary

pectives of the desert within a small frame, recreating in that
way the feeling of being on a crowded street: all perspectives
converging upon a single point, the point where reality bursts
out of the depthless distance. He, unlike O'Keefe who painted
'things' above a ghostly desert but not in its foreground or
background, refused to paint the unpaintable. (An experience
similar to your experience of being both in and out of
Albuquerque at the same time - how do you paint where you are?
Where do you precisely paint a you in the city? In what
'space'?), and the similarity of all this to my psychic state
wherein I apparently experienced myself as living in such a
desert (trapped in a dimensionless past), without the use of
arms and legs. i.e., unable to take my body for a walk
into reality let alone into the presence of others. I walked
everywhere flat as a pancake, slipping between the H2O
molecules of reality, and: the consequent necessity of my
'breaking out', like the Kritios Boy, from the depthlessness of
my past, from a halted psychology. I was in the middle of this
now defunct letter, as I said, enjoying the liberating curves
of the Kritios Boy, the revealing anger of St. Thomas, the
fully rounded presence of O'Keefe's flowers, when I read
Spengler's open-coffin meditation on death:

> The child suddenly grasps the
> lifeless corpse for what it is,
> something that has become wholly
> matter, wholly space, and at the
> same moment it feels itself as an
> individual being in an alien
> extended world. "From the child of
> five to myself is but a step. But
> from the new-born baby to the child
> of five is an appalling distance,"
> said Tolstoi once. ...Here, in the
> decisive moments of existence, when
> man first becomes man and realizes
> his immense loneliness in the
> universal, the world fear-fear
> reveals itself for the first time as
> the essentially human fear in the
> presence of death, the limit of the
> light-world, rigid space.... The
> experience of depth (through the

recognition of death}...is an act,
as entirely involuntary and
necessary as it is creative whereby
the ego keeps its world, so to say,
in subordination."

And there it was, all spelled out for me - my father's death when I was five, my "sudden" refusal to see "depth", to 'subordinate' the world to a realized ego, and my preference to hang-out in dimensionless dream, a desert without foreground or background, where 'distance' is interpretation, and the world of the Kritios Boy is on the other side of myth - all in matter of sentences! As Tolstoi said, form 'there' to 'here', from five to manhood, from myth to reality, is but a step - a tantalizing close step, from psychology into the "immense loneliness of the universal". What it is I 'refused'- my ego - is what I must come to grips with. Until then, in an essentially creative way, I am but an increasingly astute five-year old trapped in a crib, That is my being 'without punch'. (I still often reel in the presence of others, before a decision, or on the corners of intersections, indeed anywhere where 'depth' must be realized, where my own 'dimensionality' in the universe, my own 'subordinating, volitional ego must be realized. It can take me days to recover from 'close encounters' of the human kind.) This letter is somehow a 'step' toward that more momentous "step". Inch by inch I approach that abyss (of joy?) I feel like an itch beneath my skin.

As of late, I am intrigued by the roundness of human bodies. I actually stare at the bare arms of men, or, more often, the exposed thighs of women (wearing 'shorts') half expecting human reality to reveal itself through the dimensionality of their limbs. The sensation is one of trying to slip on to the other side of my fears; my fear of others, as well as my fear of experiencing myself. Escape from the defunct Eygyptian into a Faustian universe. It is people in reality that I am trying to experience, not the ghosts who occupy the dream-childhood world that I presently live in, where everyone is only a reincarnation of either my mother, my father, my stepfather, Oliver, June, Jim, Bud, or Margaret living in the long dead time and space in which they existed.

Living often alone and going no where, I have the options of either reading, going crazy, or exploring the ins and outs of my soul (the latter two are sometimes indistinguishable). The other day I walked a large circle - library through living-room through kitchen - at least five hundred times. I walked them briskly at first with head hung low, later with head erect. The whole time I felt myself the Kritios Boy, and was walking myself back into the third dimension, back into reality. Exhilarated but exhausted when done, I slipped into a minor depression. Today, I feel terrific. The walk did me good.

But, as I said, those fifteen pages are now in the trash-bin, and I have worn myself out.

I take back some of the severity of my judgment of Len. The other night we all went to Santa Fe for dinner and a Rodeo. The entire evening Len was apologetic. He repeatedly apologied for the presence of Zoe, later for "being tired" and not up to social snuff. Ruby finally had to say to him: "Stop apologizing, just be Len". Of course, such directness took me aback, but her remark made me acutely aware of Len's presence in a way I had not been before. He was self-conscious, receeding from view, apologetic somehow for having a self - in much the same way I would before I start to reel. I felt an essential loneliness in him. Or do you want to say: "Stop him, the man doth project to much." In any case, I feel closer to him once again.

Read today a passage in a new book on Paul Bowles and friends (Burroughs, Ginsberg, Corso, Copeland, etc.) in Tangier. (Author unkown to me. A journalist - what else?) Reading between the lines (widely spaced) the only reason I could figure out why so many 'exiled' themselves there was because ten year old boys were legal, plentiful, cheap, and their pederasty would be easily exotic rather than struggled for. All other 'reasons' - dope, the desert, the Arab soul -

came after this. (In the 70s, when the laws changed, and the natives could get even, they fled for their mundane lives!) Years earlier, in another country, Gide, who was a sensible man, could write (to a friend) in his Journals: "The pederasts, of whom I am one (why I can not say this quite simply, without your immediately claiming to see a brag in my confession?), are much rarer, and the sodomites much more numerous, than I first thought", was so much more sensible about it. (Although he also wrote: "Had Socrates and Plato no loved young men, what a pity for Greece, what a pity for the whole world!" - not so sensible after all.) I suppose, in some way, I envy the 'expatriots' their concentration upon desire, upon need, and their willingness to have life conform to it (subordinate the immense loneliness), but lust is easy to give in to - providing that one has given up hope of anything else. (Are homosexuals so fearful of sex (with a women), that they fuck boys thinking they are free of the 'sin' of sex? Somehow remain pure though they feel the sweat and warp of desire everytime they enter a men's bathroom? Was Tangier exotic to them because the forgiving 'grace' they gave themselves was also offered by the society - a heaven on earth?) What really strightened my back at the time of reading this book was the thought that at the time - the late 50s and 60s - I considered these 'beach boys', these next-door devotees of Brahms, American wanderers like myself, when actually they were internationalists high on dope and screwing dreamy-eyed ten year old Arabs in never-never land - boy, was I a 'naif'. My dementia was local, the kind induced by kicking stones along the Burlington railroad tracks, not the Orient Express. Chicago style.

Well, hope to see you soon. This will probably be the last letter for some time. But the last letter of this season of the soul will have to be a letter in which I tell you all that these letters have meant to me. I feel almost up to the task - the end has come just minutes before the right time.

Am sending you some tit-bits. Mostly about the awful things in life and the dreadful state literature in this country seems to be in. Not to mention its pop music, movies, and etc. - experience counts for nothing. Winter is in decline.

Before the 24th is here, I rush to the post office.

Decadent co-conspirator
of Stevoeski Koganovich,
Fyodor Stenhieski.
NKVD ARCHIVE 3.2.42.8

> (this is an interpretation, and does not
> take into account orthodox Jewish and
> Islamic beliefs, nor Mayan, Chaldaean,
> Chinese, and Hindu calendars, cultures
> whose feelings I do not wish to offend
> ((this too is merely an interpretation)))

And now, armored in Complete Truth,

Dear Ted,

First of all, something to nosh on--this from Henry Beard and Christopher Cerf in the NY Times (7/14). They are the authors of The Official Politically Correct Dictionary and Handbook, which Mel could not resist buying, and showed to me--a giggle--anyway, this:

The aging: chronologically gifted persons.

Adultery: Consensual nonmonogamy.

Drug addicts and alcoholics: The sobriety deprived; people of stupor.

Homeless: Underhoused; involuntarily undomiciled. A long Island teacher, quoted in US News & World Report, prefers "house-less" because, as she informed a group of local street people, "home is wherever you are."

Sadomasochists: The differently pleasured.

It's just like your old high school, isn't it? Everybody gets a medal. Actually, how different is satire from the real thing? This, from a book review in the 7/19 Times:

In what becomes the central (oft repeated) operation of her collection, Ms. Williams conjures what is missing simply by noting its absence. The stories force us back to their own failure, the failure to contain something more than a motley of words and devices. It is a reminder that for all their ambitions and conceits, writers can only offer words, and words are inevitably empty; words are markers for what is not there. Ms. Williams's fiction dwells on this radical absence by her persistent mention of what she has failed to include.

And there are so many things which are not there! Remember the art critic "Faith Bradshaw" on a Peter Sellers' radio skit? Delicious jabbering about the paintings of "Augustus Streptaconipus Bonstadt" and how he "habitually used angular fragmentation of pigment in order to consumate his all-prevading theme of hermetic anarchy."

Also this, from a lovely profile of the pianist Richard Goode in _The New Yorker_ (6/29/92):

> "I love Schubert's modesty. But, you know, once when he had been drinking he was approached by two musicians from the Vienna Opera who wanted to commission a composition from him, and he rudely refused them. They protested that they were artists, and he shouted, 'Artists! Artists? Musical hacks are what you are! Crawling, gnawing worms that ought to be crushed under my foot--the foot of a man who is reaching to the stars!'"

And, apparently, when Goode was studying with the pros at the Marlboro music festival in his teens, he kept a copy of Flaubert's letters in his pocket "as a sort of talisman. 'I felt alienated from the world around me,' he says. 'This was a secret I kept largely to myself [obviously]. . . . There was something beautiful but grim in his outlook. He was enmeshed in his surroundings, and had a great deal of hate and spleen. These letters were a consolation to me--an outlet for my dissatisfaction as well as for the deep feelings I had about art.'" His remarks on Schubert are right on the money and much better than Brendel's in an old _New York Review of Books_ article.

A beautifully written elegy on Eric Sevareid by Russell Baker, also in the 7/14 _Times_.

Did you ever hear of Nicholas Chamfort (_Maxims, Characters, and Anecdotes_)? An article on him appeared in the 6/25 NYR:

> The rareness of genuine feeling sometimes makes me stop in the street to watch a dog gnawing a bone.
>
> It has to be admitted: to be happy, living in the world, there are sides of the soul one must entirely paralyze.

Chateaubriand wrote with great passion on his wisdom in his _Essai sur les revolutions_ but thirty years later "exploded in a footnote":

> Let alone the impertinence of comparing certain witty maxims of Chamfort with the maxims of the Sages of Greece, there is a total error in the judgment that I bring here on Chamfort himself. I retract, in all the maturity of my age, what I said about this man in my youth.

There isn't a word that comes out of Chateaubriand's mouth that doesn't stop me in my tracks. On to the isle of Grand Bre and his "lonely tomb" facing the North Atlantic. A 20 minute walk through tidal shallows to get to it. The Baedeker description itself is enough to send my mind spinning and sounds like something right out of his work. After reading his chapter on Napoleon and that incredible description of St. Helena, I had the strange feeling that he was Napoleon's double in some way--and it's Poe all over again in those lines I love--"in her tomb by the side of the sea."

Right in the middle of <u>Cousin Pons</u>, at the end of a bit of
dialogue, Balzac suddenly writes:

> And herewith begins the tragedy, or, if you like to have it so, a
> terrible comedy--the death of an old bachelor delivered over by
> circumstances too strong for him to the rapacity and greed that
> gathered about his bed. And other forces came to the support of
> rapacity and greed; there was the picture collector's mania, that
> most intense of all passions; there was the cupidity of the Sieur
> Frasier, whom you shall presently behold in his den, a sight to
> make you shudder; and lastly, there was the Auvergnat thirsting
> for money, ready for anything--even for a crime--that should
> bring him the capital he wanted. The first part of the story
> serves in some sort as a prelude to this comedy in which all the
> actors who have hitherto occupied the stage will reappear.

Balzac's Grand Guignol--drum roll--the curtains part--step right up
ladies and gentlemen and see avarice unchained, Monsieur Frasier,
whom you shall presently behold in his den, a sight to make you
shudder. (And it did!) The "Sieur Frasier" is a lawyer--a Napoleonic
genius in a slum, working as a petty advocate in a seedy district in
Paris--biding his time. Pons' art collection sets his wheels in
motion. The spirit of the thing is just like the story of Lacenaire
in "Children of Paradise"--"I have in mind something altogether
prodigious," which strikes me now as something right out of Balzac
himself. And the dates for the Parisian setting are right as well,
along with a chunk of the plot devoted to behind the scenes at a
theater (Pons is a conductor for one such variety stage). But the
lawyer Frasier in his "den"!

> Arrived on the second floor above the entre-sol, La Cibot [Pons'
> concierge] beheld a door of the most villanous description. The
> doubtful red paint was coated for seven or eight inches round the
> keyhole with a filthy glaze, a grimy deposit from which the
> modern house-decorator endeavours to protect the doors of more
> elegant apartments by glass "finger-plates." A grating, almost
> stopped up with some compound similar to the deposit with which a
> restaurant-keeper gives an air of cellar-bound antiquity to a
> merely middle-aged bottle, only served to heighten the general
> resemblance to a prison door; a resemblance further heightened by
> the trefoil-shaped iron-work, the formidable hinges, the clumsy
> nail-heads. A miser, or a pamphleteer at strife with with the
> world at large, must surely have invented these fortifications.
> A leaden sink, which received the waste of the household, con-
> tributed its quota to the fetid atmosphere of the staircase, and
> the ceiling was covered with fantastic arabesques traced by
> candle-smoke--such arabesques! On pulling a greasy acorn tassel
> attached to the bell-rope, a little bell jangled somewhere
> within, complaining of the fissure in its metal side . . .
>   "Mme. Cibot, I believe?" queried he, in dulcet tones.
>   "Yes, sir," answered the portress. She had lost her habitual
> assurance.

Something in the tones of a voice which strongly resembled the sounds of the little door-bell, something in a glance   even sharper than the sharp green eyes of her future legal adviser, scared Mme. Cibot. Frasier's presence so pervaded the room, that anyone might have thought there was a pestilence in the air; and in a flash Mme. Cibot understood why Mme. Florimond had not become Mme. Frasier.

She thinks that she is bringing news he doesn't know, but Pons' doctor is Frasier's friend (real complications of character here), and he knows all too well how to set her up for the scheme he already has in mind from the night before:

He had set himself to frighten and quell La Cibot till she was completely in his power, bound hand and foot. She had walked into his study as a fly walks into a spider's web; there she was doomed to remain, entangled in the toils of the little lawyer who meant to feed upon her. Out of this bit of business, indeed, Frasier meant to gain the living of old days; comfort, competence, and consideration. He and his friend Dr. Poulain had spent the whole previous evening in a microscopic investigation of the case; they had made mature deliberations.

This novel is without a doubt the most staggeringly complicated 19th-century work I've ever read. I read it as if I were a babe in the woods. I mean complicated just on the sheer surface level of the intrigue involving character and circumstances. And there's a mystique to the whole thing too. Mme. Cibot goes to a fortune teller in the neighborhood, who goes into some kind of trance and lays out what will be the actual outcome for the concierge (completely favorable, after walking on the razor's edge)--plus Balzac comments on the new invention of photography (the previous generation, he says, would have thought you were a lunatic if you would have told it that objects have their spectres that can be captured on paper). And this, of course, in contrast to the Watteaus, etc. that Pons has in his collection, including four staggering masterpieces: a Durer, a Sebastian del Piombo, a Fra Bartolommeo della Porta ("which many connoisseurs might have taken for a Raphael"), and a Hobbemma. I cannot tell you how strange the sensation was that I was actually in Paris at that moment--spectres indeed, since the work was actually written at that time and is so completely of its world, everything delicately lifted from life, almost like a surgeon's operation, and placed into words. And here I thought that "naturalism" came in with Turgenev, Flaubert, and Zola. There's no ism for Balzac. I don't know what he is. Balzac talks about Mme. Cibot's torrents of conversation as a "tornado of words," which is a good description of how Balzac writes, if you also include monstrous complications of character, volcanic eruptions of feelings, and the whole thing swirling in the midst of historical change. I think we once commented on this strangeness of French literature, how little it seems to fit the cliches about the French. Chateaubriand, Balzac, Flaubert, Rimbaud, Cendrars all seem to have this incredible wildness about them--like Rabelais, in fact, and from the little that I've seen, in Racine and Corneille as well--I think Rimbaud

talks about the madness of his Gallic ancestors at the beginning of
"A Season in Hell." Torrents of words--the desire to exhaust
everything. Montaigne talks in one essay about his frenzies of
digging into his library while writing--looking up quotations,
locking himself up from his family, turning pages like a madman,
books piled everywhere.

July 17 & 18 (these dates are real)

 Ah, these last two days, a great event in my life--the Sullivan
County Air Show at the Int'l. Airport outside White Lake--
staggering, Ted, truly wonderful, and here are some photos to prove
it. I mean, I mean--to see a P-51 Mustang and P47 Republic
Thunderbolt come in from the skies at 10:00am, "Flying in from
Virginia," the guy on the PA said. The Thunderbolt moves at over 400
mph! A monster, really big. The P51 much more delicate and with much
greater range. You can imagine--I'm standing there like a kid as
this lanky (yes, lanky) young pilot steps out from the P47 and
deftly, as you please, stands there answering all these questions.
Terrible weather the 17th. There was hardly any ceiling or
visibility range at all, so all I could do was photograph a few of
the planes they had there already--a Heinkel 111, a C46 jumbo cargo
transport (the one that went over the Himalayas, along with the DC3,
renamed the C47--the C46 the largest twin engine plane ever built--a
real mastodon), a PBY--the air-sea rescue plane, much larger than I
thought it would be, a TBM Avenger, another hulking single engine
plane--torpedo bomber, I believe--and the glory of the show, a B25
(it's the B25 that made thirty seconds over Tokyo). I caught a local
news announcement on my way back to Schaeffer House (I painted the
interior of the porch--the place looks superb--Kathy F. again did
not show up--I will call Freda tomorrow)--the announcement saying
that some planes might be flying in the next day if the weather
cleared. I jumped in my seat and knew I'd be there again. Saturday,
9:00am--sunlight! I get to the airport just in time to hear the guy
announcing the imminent arrival of the two pursuit planes. Yes,
forgot to mention--the day before, not many people, but a nice
feeling all the same--German Kielbasa stands, air force souvenir
displays, some old guys in army fatigues moving things around,
actually handling a lot of the show, all kinds of old timers, one
with an "Air Force Pilots' Association" windbreaker, nice looking
old men, talking all kinds of details about magnetos, landing gear
assemblies, intimacies all their own--sturdy looking too, and me
staring at their age and trying to imagine the young men that they
once had been--a very strange sensation. And how odd that two weeks
before I should have gotten a cab ride to the 3 Columbus ships by
the Intrepid from another old timer, Joe Finkler--you hardly ever
see an old time Jewish cabbie any more--and it turns out he flew on
Liberators in the last two years of the war. And, Ted, the natural
solemnity of the thing--no flags but a whole history show coming
over the PA system--old recordings of the time, music, radio events,
speeches, all in chronological order, interrupted now and then when
the announcer mentioned another event about to come on, and
apologizing about the weather (since it cost 6 bucks and there was
no air show, and some planes missing, including a Flying Fortress

5

that had to cancel due to mechanical difficulties, plus the weather). But what love he had, and he communicated it pretty directly--announcing at one point that we ought to get ready over by the B25, because they were going to run the engines to get the dampness out of them, and these two grey haired guys climb in. And the announcer was right when he asked us to listen carefully-- "There's nothing like the sound of a 14 cylinder, 1,700 horsepower radial engine--it'll rumble right through the runway into you, and the prop wash and smell of the gasoline--if you like that sort of thing, nothing can beat the B25. These guys rebuilt these planes all on their own, and you can feel the dedication and the love," and he was absolutely right. "We made 11,000 B25s and there aren't but three around" (or so, minimal numbers, in any case for all the planes--there's an air museum in Midlands, Texas, and some at this show from another museum in Geneseo, NY). So you can imagine what it was like for me today when those planes flew in--and about an hour later! . . . the B25 taxis out to the runway and takes off! making several fly bys, an absolutely beautiful sight. I was almost out of my skin. Pure industrial America--heavy looking but clean, long lines, the combination of bulk and grace enchanting--and all absolutely simple. I stepped into a world that shares my feeling for that kind of design simplicity and robustness--the bomb bays, wheel wells, and radial engines themselves literally nuts and bolts--you could see the pure mechanism of the thing. I don't know what I expected. Those black and white films and photos and the aura of the time make for a certain unreality. I'm always amazed when I come upon the thing itself. It's always so damned physical and simple, so limited to its own sheer materiality, like the time I saw one of Van Gogh's palettes on display at the Louvre. I don't know what I expected these planes to be made of--magic, I think. But you touch them, knock them with your finger joints, and feel the sheet metal of the thing--just metal, bolts, and rivets, simple mechanisms--the PBY really battered around a bit. Most of them were salvaged from scrap or literally off battlefields. Some battered exhaust manifolds, the cockpit of the Heinkel a mass of old black rods, thin tubes carrying wires and hydraulic systems, dents all around the fuselage--and they fly! They fly beautifully. The B25 was simply stunning coming in forty feet over the runway in a pass, and then lifting, wings tilted against the clouds, and it seemed, almost in an instant, a dot in the sky. You see what I mean. I discovered in a moment that there's a world of people out there who share this love of mine. And every once in a while, the announcer saying that this was a piece of our heritage--they put it together on a shoestring-- all on their own. You can feel the ordinariness of it all. Some wealthy backers too, but there was no getting away from the hands on feeling of the show. And a real air show--grassy fields, the hills in the distance, the same sense of original experience that was there in the barnstorming days, because that's how these planes were put together again--people just going on their love of these machines and their history. I felt whole and complete every minute I was there.

Hope it goes as well in France. Clover and I are talking a good deal about the trip, getting maps and interesting research material together (stuff out of Bannister Fletcher's mammoth textbook on architecture, Henry Adams' "Mont St Michel," and the Guide Michelin books, which are fairly detailed. Do I know what Romanesque means? I do not), plus some good talking about ourselves, what we want and what we don't want. It's an adventure all the way around, and on the cheap! Round trip tix for $480 apiece, free apartment, and a one week car rental for $170, unlimited mileage--c'est extraordinaire. Our motto is "On to Poitiers!" She did a gutsy thing for herself by extending her trip a few more days so that we get a full 2 weeks on the ground--gutsy because it means she's giving up 2 weekends of work, which is a lot for her.

My place at Schaeffer House is all painted--the porch too. It looks as good as it can without being renovated. Really clear and bright. I just called Freda--a woman who works as an agent there, and she says she'll let me know what she thinks as soon as Harry shows it to her. She sounded serious in the questions she asked. I found Kathy F's cancelling of her appointment almost intolerable, because of what I went through on my mother's apartment, meaning my own propensity to stick with what does not work for me. Trieber tells me that I seem to find it acceptable to live with things that do not really function well. A clarifying statement, that one.

A tape for you--I was having some wake up coffee listening to Steve Post on WNYC one morning last week, when he said that for the next few days he'd be playing selections from a newly issued CD of Paul Robeson, some of which we had on an album of 10" 78s, which I listened to a hundred times over when I was a kid. You can imagine how powerful and complex the feelings are for me listening to those recordings now. And when I was 10 years old, in '48, I heard him sing "Joe Hill" for us at the Workers' Children's Camp--stunning, isn't it? On some of the songs I just managed to get the tape started right after Steve Post began. The quality of the tape itself is not very good, but it's all I had and did not want to delay the letter any longer. On the other side a bit of experimentation with the higher technology. I managed to get one channel off the VCR into my receiver and put on my Channel 13 recording of the opening minutes of Von Karajan's Don Giovanni (he only deserves several minutes on one channel), followed by Fúrtwängler's recording of the same (he gets both channels and the entire overture, as well as Leonora #1 of Fidelio and the introduction and first aria of Act II, Florestan in prison). I find the differences with Von K glaring, even with the poor recording off the VCR (actually a favor to him-- he sounds even worse on the original). And a sheaf of odds and ends, since I probably will not be writing for some time. I figured I'd wait to talk to Sal once you know what you'll be doing in the fall.

Would love to hang out on the back patio and talk with you as the evening settles into dark. This will happen at some point if you don't come back east.

Regards to Ruby,

Love,

Gene

Shadow magic indeed —
    We all loved your card,
and Zoe could read it. (being 6,
        after all)
    Actually, the winter here is
mild — and we're doing O.K. —
    Be in New Mexico in April,
and sorry you're not still in
the neighborhood — — — saw
Mr. Sabbatical — its making him
younger — — — Our love to — both
            Cheers

Ted & Ruby Sitea

Dear Steve

Shortly after we spoke on the afternoon of Aug.5th, I
went to my Painter biography of Chateaubriand and gazed upon an
engraving of his grave majestically poised on the tip of the
islet of the Grand-Be off Saint-Malo. The perspective of the
engraving is from thirty or so yards further up the cliff wall,
and so includes the jagged shoreline below, a distant castle,
and the sea stretching out into a murky, grey horizon. The
grave itself, occupying the entire rocky point, is surrounded
by a low, wrought-iron fence, and the large, tubular cross
marking it seems to be made of black granite. It is massive,
lonely, and above all, mute, inarticulate - like an ancient,
mysterious ruin which, had it lips, would reveal the Beyond,
but now can not. I imagined you threading your way down the
steep cliff walls, into the engravings perspective, vaulting
the wrought-iron gate, stretching your arms along the
horizontal axis of the cross while laying your head upon the
vertical, and your hair cushioning your brow against the
salt-damp granite. And as you so stood, the sea became history,
wave after wave of the grand moments of the past rolled up; the
seige of Troy, the battle of Actium, the face of Homer, the hip
of the Kritios Boy, a page of Ovid, of Alcuin, the coronation
of Charlemagne, the glow of the Primavera, one of Flaubert's
great farts, prisoners stumbling out of the gulag, all rolling
up and dissolving in to the wet sand. Releasing yourself from
your humble pose you push away from the cross, and walk away
purified, whole and at peace with yourself. Suddenly however,
the engraving positioned itself on the page, and it is I that
push myself out from this somber scene, back into this world,
as though from a dream.

In 1520, Aug.27, in Brussels, Durer wrote in his
diary: "I saw the things which have been brought to the King

from the new land of gold {Mexico}, a sun all of gold a whole fathom broad, and a moon all of silver of the same size, also two rooms full of the armour of the people there, and all manner of wonderous weapons of theirs, harness and darts, very strange clothing, beds, and all kinds of wonderful objects of human use, much better worth seeing than prodigies. These things were all so precious that they are valued at 100,000 florins. All the days of my life I have seen nothing that rejoiced my heart so much as these things, for I saw amongst them wonderful works of art, and I marvelled at the subtle Ingenia of men in foreign lands. Indeed I cannot express all that I thought there." From a man who could smell salvation and populate his engravings with phantasmagoric creatures flying from Hell, surely such a grasp of the beauty of Mayan gold should leave contemporary mouths open in multicultural shock!

I sit in my patio looking at the distant mountains and wonder what it would be like to be sitting in my patio looking at the distant mountains. I don't know. I think I lost myself somewhere about fifty years ago. Probably in a dime-store.

Historicism - as a way of thinking - drives me mad. It crept into my being unnoticed. It somehow justified my emotional defeat in that dime-store I mentioned above. Its claim to omnipotentence, to an Olympian vision of all forms of life (from rock-scrawls to the Met, from bound feet to lesbians fornicating on subways), and its therefore implied contempt for any one of them as snares of the emotions, appealed to my sense of reality as pointless bullshit. Beneath contempt really, reality, for me, was merely the arena (latin: sand & blood) where only fools and charlatans waged their violent contests for power over ILLUSION. Imagine the stupidity of that! True Reality was lodged in the mind. The true Caesar of humanity was impotent and without hands.

Imagine my surprize then when I read the following: "What is man? And how did he come to be man? ¶ The answer is - through the genesis of the hand. Here is a weapon unparalleled

in the world of free-moving life. ... the activity of living is
gathered into it so completley that the whole bearing and
allure of the body has - simultaneously - taken shape in
accordance with it. There is nothing in the whole world that
can be set beside this member... To the eye of the beast of
prey which regards the world 'theoretically' is added the hand
of man which commands it practically." (Spengler: Man and
Technics)

  I must capture my hands as they moves before my eyes!
I must learn to see them. That, and that alone, will bring me
back into reality. But what a sight I must perform. It must
traverse a dimension. Cross from one world in to another. Spengler
speaks of man's realization of the hand as weapon as sudden,
epoch making, and the result of a genetic mutation. Wow! And do
I know it.

  You must read H.B. Stowe - Uncle Tom's Cabin. She
creates a world in which man reels in pain because he is in
control of the life and death of others. Slavery for her is a
curse as deadly to the slave owner as it is to the slave. It
saps every fibre of the owners intelligence and heart, and
renders him - kind-hearted or brutal to his slaves, it makes no
difference - feeble, impotent, tainted, corrupt, sadistic,
masochistic, and incapable of love - simultaneously! It is a
dark world she creates, full of crippled mind, destroyed women,
and wanton torture. But the slaves, destroyed as humans,
physically and emotionally brutalized, have the saving grace of
intellectually recognizing the malaise slavery causes, and of
spiritually recognizing God - racial features which one day
will result in their creating a better world. It is the owning
of people that, for Stowe, destroys people. It must be
abolished to save not only the slave, but America as well.
Simon Legree is only an example of what is latent in all
notherners , in all of humanity, if slavery is permitted or
even simply tolerated. Because this is reality only a god can
save humanity, human nature alone is not enough. The South
proved that. And Uncle Tom is a magnificient character! He is a

black Jesus who bears the slings and arrows of misfortune with a courage and strength that must suffer a martyr's death – while his counter-part goes off to Liberia to found a rational, Just Society. She writes as she feels reality to be, and uses every trick in the trade to convince the reader that what she says actually happened.

But enough! You must be full of your trip; overflowing with sensations, feelings, confused reflections upon your life - as lived heretofore. Let me know of all of them. As of yet, and it is already Aug.17th, I have received nothing from you - or Clover. I often think of you both as I sit looking up in to my blue, blank sky. Up there, there are no Gothic cathedrals, Ruisdael's, pieces of delicious French bread, museums redolent with Renassiance whores and Fragonart petticoats, no Rue de Valery's, no streets upon which Chateaubriand darted, dodging revolutionary bullets, no over-stuffed Tahitian beautys lounging on yellow shores. No, in a word, CULTURE. I feel, in short, so provincial watching Indians peddling their routinely mystical wares. Ten trinkets for a buck – each revealing the sacred words of the Seven Ancient Grandmothers – who now apparently, in addition to having woven the weave of history - support AID's victims. (There is more spirituality in Flaubert's description of fucking Arabs then there is in all of Indian lore.)

I tell you, when I do find my hands (they are somewhere in real space moving things around), I will be quite myself! In the meantime, I must put up with this charlatan (this "shadow", as Clover would put it), who can't bear the thought of strutting out on to the stage in high, white silk turbin, garish purple robes, and curled, golden slippers - a person! (merely a naked infant hiding under the dining-room table.)

And oh, by the way.... Things out here look rather dismal, job-wise. So, with ever decreasing doubt, I will be back in New York come Sept. I know I have asked you several times, and each time you respond positively but, I can not help myself, if you have any hesitations as to my coming to live with you - at least for a while - please let me know. (ah, and then there is the question of Sol!)

Oliver and Elly arrive here tomorrow and will remain a week. (Ruby's parents left just a few days ago.) I suspect I shall be busy showing them around - and then my time here will be almost up.

I called Marty. Left my condolences on his machine. Will try to make a real call and send off a 'sympathy card'.

I truly hope that you and Clover had a wonderful time. That your trip to Europe, as Len and Romona's, wasn't a grind - something that should have been done at another time, in another country.

This letter, of course, as all my (our) letters, has been spread out over a number of days, moods, and cycles of the moon, and only comes to an end because if I don't mail it tomorrow I'll probably see you before you receive it, and that would be anti-climatic. I want this letter to be on your doorstep the moment you arrive home - god knows why. (Or does he?)

I have written nothing that I will show, thought deeply about nothing (except myself - if that is possible). I live as unproductive a life as I possibly can without becoming a vegetable. One of the 'boched and bungled' that Jack Lucas spoke so eloquently about. I would be a Walt Disney, of course - if only I could see my hands!

Love
T

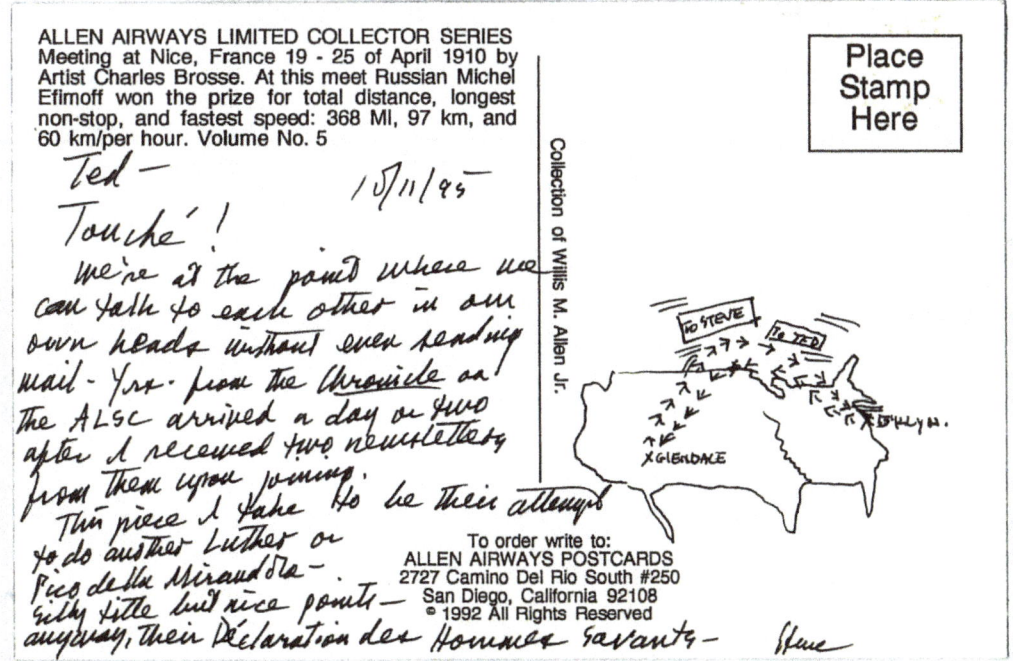

ALLEN AIRWAYS LIMITED COLLECTOR SERIES
Meeting at Nice, France 19 - 25 of April 1910 by
Artist Charles Brosse. At this meet Russian Michel
Efimoff won the prize for total distance, longest
non-stop, and fastest speed: 368 Ml, 97 km, and
60 km/per hour. Volume No. 5

Ted —

Touché!

We're at the point where we
can talk to each other in our
own heads without even sending
mail - Yxx. from the Chronicle on
The ALSC arrived a day or two
after I received two newsletters
from them upon joining.
This piece I take to be their attempt
to do another Luther or
Pico della Mirandola —
silly little but nice points —
anyway, their Déclaration des Hommes Savants —

10/11/95

To order write to:
ALLEN AIRWAYS POSTCARDS
2727 Camino Del Rio South #250
San Diego, California 92108
© 1992 All Rights Reserved

Collection of Willis M. Allen Jr.

TO STEVE   TO TED

X GLENDALE   X BKLYN.

Steve

Place
Stamp
Here

182

Dear Steve

For me, the central problem is how to disentangle reality
from my dream of the world. Appearing as those 'apparitions'
Pound spoke of in the Metro (a lousy haiku), the world and
all its contents are insensible to me; I touch, see, and hear
only my dream-things. My arms extend in to a fog so thick
they are invisible from the shoulders down, my eyes seek the
vanishing points of all scenes, my tongue tastes only what it
remembers, my ears censor all sounds other than those of the
past, and my thoughts are ruled by a great, ancient King who
sits in the center of my head transforming all who enter in
to a dream. So, given that for openers, how do I get to
Benjamin, Musil, LaFarge, or those Tahitian beauties with
brown breasts, black nipples, and fat arms? How shall I get
them to pop out of my dream and materialize in the real world
where I can really see them? It is all a matter of ontology:
not exactly and classically - 'Why something rather than
nothing?', but 'why nothing rather than something?
It is amazing how the entire world can fit in to such a small
dream-space. Artistic giants shrink in to one dimensional
phantoms, the pyramids of Egypt barely graze the top of my
inner skull, and the entire length of history only reaches
from ear to ear! Nobody seems to mind hwever; the world is
so dreadfully nonchalant about losing so much weight!.

Between Gaugin, Scholem, and LaFarge, Gaugin emerges the most fruitful. In clarity of feeling both Scholem and LaFarge are his pupils - inattentive to themselves as they may be.

Compare these descriptions of friendship from Scholem:

-After our return to Germany our relationship became very harmonious,...Was it the physical distance that guarded the rising curve of our friendship against disturbances and made the much more infrequent days we spent together so positive? Was it (as it sometimes seems to me in retrospect) that three young passionate, gifted people {Scholem, Benjamin, and Dora, Benjamin's wife} who were almost completely dependent on one another and were seeking the road to maturity had to use one another as release mechanisms in the private sphere? Were there in this "triangle", of which we were unaware, unconscious emotional inclinations and defenses that had to be discharged but which we were not able to recognize in our "naiveté", that is, owing to our lack of psychological experience?

Or: *-The conflict I found myself in was a moral one. For me Benjamin's ideas had a radiant moral aura about them; to the extent that I could intellectually empathize with them, they had a morality of their own, which was bound up with their relationship to the religious sphere that at that time was quite clearly and openly at the vanishing point of his thought. Juxtaposed with this, however, in Benjamin's relationship to things of daily life there existed a strictly amoral element that I could not come to terms with, although he attempted to justify it by his contempt for the bourgeois. ... Benjamin's life did not have that enormous measure of purity that distinguished his thought.*

As if that were not looney enough, Scholem later incredulously remarks: ...*-Dora {Benjamin's wife} was still greatly attached to Walter, and yet she started speaking of him in a new tone. Not that she doubted his gifts and his genius that meant so much to her, but she began to speak about features that had never before been voiced between us, including her experiences in marriage. She labeled Walter a person suffering from an obsessive-compulsive neurosis, and this came as* *a surprise to me, for both of them had great reservations about psychiatric terminology.... Later I spoke with several other women who personally knew Walter very well, including one to whom he proposed marriage in 1923. They all emphasized that Benjamin was not attractive to them as a man, no matter how impressed or even enchanted they were with his intellect and his conversation. One of his close acquaintances told me that for her and her female friends he had not even existed as a man, that it had never even occurred to them that he had that dimension as well. Walter was, so to speak, incorporeal. Was the reason for this some lack of vitality,... or was it a convolution of his vitality...with his altogether metaphysical orientation that gained him the reputation of being a withdrawn person?*

The simplicity of Scholem is stupefying. His writing has the effect of reducing one to being the bull just before the moment of its death; total bewilderment. Simply put, he leaves one cross-eyed.

Scholem himself says that military doctors *"had diagnosed my case as mentia praecox"* (but finds no humor in the fact that upon that diagnosis he was *"given permission to wear civilian clothes."*) In what world did they live that they could be so blind to each other, so unfeeling of each other, so ignorant - and hence, uncaring - of each other? Can what they had properly be called a "friendship"? What the hell would one call it?: 'harmonious enchantment'? the 'convergence of variant metaphysical orientations'? 'Defective affinities'?

It occurs to me that Scholem's output - as well as Benjamin', probably - could only have been used not for finding or expressing reality, but an unconscious compulsion to deny themselves and reality to boot. Writing was their tool for accomplishing these secret goals; the annihilation of self and the world. Some mysterious way in which the real world,for them, is destroyed in the act of writing. As each word is written another object beyond the page vanishes. (But again, the world does not notice.) I remember Sartre once writing that each time one lights a cigarette, one places between one's vision and the world a flame in which the world is consumed.(Never mind that across the table there may be a black-haired, red-lipped beauty with out-stretched hand.) The same may hold true for writing as well.(Never mind that theremay be hot blond lying on your white sheeets, panting!) Especially certain kinds of writing - moral writing, critical writing(of the Marxist variety, but maybe not only.).

How refreshing then, are the letters of Gaugin! In each word he establishes the existence of the world once and for all. He is the unwobbling pivot which radiates meaning upon all he sees. How wonderfully lucid is: *-I know M.F. He is stingy, and there is more vanity than emotion in his pictorial taste. M- is enthusiastic about Cézanne, and he is right. But it's always the same thing, now that his pictures are expensive, now that it is good taste to understand Cézanne, now that Cézanne is a millionaire.* Neither Scholem or Benjamin are capable of such clarity! For both of these myopic idiots such directness is impossible; they could not experience M.F.other than as a painful, amoral blur on the horizon. He would be the occasion for a *"metaphysical* *laugh"*, and his existence would be wiped off the face of the earth.

How masculine, how robust Gaugin is: - *I seem condemned to live when I have lost all moral reason for living.... There is no glory but that of one's own conscience. What does it matter whether the others recognize or acclaim it? There is no true satisfaction outside of one's self and just now I am disgusted.* Or; {to create a work of art is} - *Very easy if one thinks only of nature, very difficult if one wishes to express oneself a bit mysteriously - in parables - to search for forms.* Which leads to: - *It* {Nevermore} *is painted badly.... But it doesn't matter, I think it is a good thing.* And: - *If any cracks are still visible (in a repaired Van Gogh) what does it matter?* And: - *But I finally found a panel in two pieces, about a metre in all and 4 centimeters in width. I shall have to work in relief, and the figures will be a bit small on that account. It makes no difference.* And; - *Perhaps they* {my paintings} *are good. In them is so much of agony, that perhaps the awkwardness of the execution may be overlooked.* All of which 'culminates' in the sentences: *Before death I put in it (* Where do we come from?-What are we?-Where are are we going?*) all my energy, a passion so dolorous, amid circumstances so terrible, and so clear was my vision that the haste of execution is lost and life surges up....So I have finished a philosophical work on a theme comparable to that of the Gospel. I think it is good; if I have the strength I will copy it and send it to you.*

How strengthing then to read Gaugin! He is all sense. There is no non-sense about him, no head. More precisely, there is no childhood about him. His ghosts are dead. Completely. He enjoys being himself. He finds strength there, a strength which isolates him, drives him away from Europe in to the jungle where all is exotic - and there is no one there to ask him "Where is your head?" Could it be that as early as the turn of the century "it was {only} here on the last boundaries of civilization, at the uttermost verge of all known things", that a man of concentrated feeling could be free? Was the Western Weltgeist already neurotic? Of course, it is now psychotic, and there are no more edges near the abyss. (Just where is the abyss now that civilization has no end?)

Which bring me to LaFarge, the American artist who left Tahiti just two weeks before Gaugin arrived, but who could never write (as did Gaugin) - *My life is now that of a savage: my body naked except for the essential thing women do not like to see - so they say.* As LaFarge's son later put it, J. L. would rather neglect dressing {properly} for dinner at his home in Newport than show up without starched collar for diner in a grasshut in Tahiti. No Cendrars character him! No up-the-river wild pagan! Yet, his vision is a tempered relativism. After discussing some generous acts on the part of the Tahitians and who would now like the U.S. to repay them in kind, LaFarge says: *All this is politics, and you are probably, like the United States, more or less indifferent to anything that has not the name you are accustomed to. To me, on the contrary, my real and absorbing delight is the sense of looking at the world in a little*

nutshell, and of seeing everything reduced to such a small scale, and to

so few people, that I can take, as it were, my first lesson in history.

I don't know that i should put it all in the form that Mr. Stevenson

uses{Robert Louis}, in which I don't quite agree with him: that here, at

length, we were free from the pressure of Roman civilization. I own of

course, that all comes to us through Rome, and that the dago has had the

making of us. The words which I use of course imply that. I can't talk

of politics, of civilization, of culture, of education, of chivalry, of

any of the aspirations of the western world without using the words

implanted with the ideas in our barbarous ancestors; but before the

culture and development of Rome was a something which had some analogies

to what i see here. I am continually thinking how it may have been with

my most remote ancestry, whenever I understand any better the ideas and

habits of our good people here. As also they have passed from some still

earlier or more remote stages, their ideas are easier to understand than

those for instance of the Australian or even the Fijian. A tendency to

the commonplace, to a certain evening of ideas, seems to belong to them,

and makes them easier to understand because in so far they are not

unlike us. They dislike excesses in thinking, and too logical extensions

of what might be called political ideas.... I am troubled also at

writing about things and ideas, and using words which have grown out of

things and ideas extremely different and often contradictory. As the

Christian terminology, the very language of the Gospels, was perforce

made up of pagan forms and terms, so to-day, I shall have to describe

what might be called pagan forms and ideas in a terminology now influenced by Christianity, and saturated with problems connected with it, so that probably Greek or Latin would be more natural, though even they, you know, are read by us with a bias that their authors never dreamed of.~ But as long as I do not write, it is pleasant to see the ideas without words, and perhaps descriptions may not have been the worst way to give them.

The 'progression' in thought here is interesting: *For a thousand years, probably two thousand, perhaps three - for an indefinite period - these people of the smallest island have lived here and modified nature, while its agencies have as steadily and gently covered again their work. So that everything is natural, and everywhere one is vaguely conscious of man. Hence, of any place that I have seen, this is the nearest to the idyllic pastoral; it is not so beautiful as it is complete.* To: *...we have saved these people from a hell of slavery under the Germans. ~ I am impressed here, as I have been before, by the force that America could have for good, and by the careful calculation on the part of those who know us best, the Germans and English, upon our weakness of action and irresponsibility, and our not knowing our enormous power. ~ The Pacific should be ours, and it must be.*

He also is quite perceptive. For example: *You know from all that I have told you of Samoa that in Polynesia descent is the only real absolute aristocracy; there is no ruling except through blood. Hence the absurdity of the kingships that we have fostered or established, which in our own minds seemed quite legitimate, because they embodied the European ideas which belong to our ancestry. Hence the general discomfort and trouble that we have helped to foster. Hence also - and far worse - the breaking down, in reality, of all the bases upon which these old societies rested, the saving of which in part was the only hope remaining for the gradual education of the brown man for his keeping to ideas of order different from our own, it is true, but still involving the same original foundations. hence the demoralization, the arbitrary "white laws", always misunderstood, always bring on the vices which they were meant to control; hence the end of the "brown" man by himself.*

A tit-bit: *We try to find, by the little river that ends our walk, on this side of the old French fort, the calaboose where Melville was shut up. There is no one to help us in our search; no one remembers anything. Buildings occupy the spaces of woodland that Melville saw about him. Nothing remains but the charm of light and air which he, like all others, has tried to describe and to bring back home in words.*

Ah, so short is the memory of the unexceptional. Who was Melville after all, but another sailor looking for a good time? (And as such, when he was such, also an elect member of 'those without voice, of 'those without history'.) But we can resent their loss of their being memorized! (If not of every slave who built the great Wall.) At any rate, the book is chock-full of interesting asides, cultural reflections, America, and what are, in general, very different pictures of Gaugin's languid paradise. They are almost anthropological, and in the spirit of Catlin. The way one might imagine an artistic Herodotus might have painted. And yet, here too there is a struggle to capture the alluring grace, ardor, and

physical beauty of a people who have the innocence they have
lost. A sinful peep onto the playground of themselves in the
Garden? Objectivity is a strange thing. Subjectivity too!
(One can imagine *No te aha oe riri* a reformulation of Seurat's
Sunday Afternoon on the Island of La Grande Jatte, *Nevermore* as a
resighting of Manet's *Olympia,* etc. Is this a sighting of the
Garden behind the appearance of the reality? Is France really
Paradise in disguise? Or is France a nation whose essence is
in, and revealed in, the Marquesas? In brief: is the truly
seen *Olympia* reclining in the South Pacific, and is she,
appearance not withstanding, French? Or is she, objectively,
at this particular time on this particular island in the
South Pacific in the last remaining piece of the Garden which
is to be seen no where else, and is doomed to extinction?)
But enough of prologue. It's reality I set out to find - the
real Gaugin, Schloem, LaFarge, Musil, and I have not yet
truly sen them. (But before I try to set foot out side the
dream, what do you think of this: "There is a good possibility
that Gaugin never attempted suicide and that virtually everything he
said about the shortness of the period of work on the painting {*Where Do
We Come From,* etc.} is open to question. ...{there is evidence to
suggest} that Gaugin worked extensively on the painting throughout the
first held of 1898, in spite of the 1897 date on the canvass.... In view
of his later musing about the suicide of van Gogh, one wonders about his
motivation for forging so strong a link." From *The Art of Paul
Gaugin*)

I look for entrances in to reality via the thoughts, actions, and productions of others. What world did they live in, how did they conceive it? How did others respond to them? I actually look at a Gaugin painting for answers to the questions of life. And my book shelf of letters, journals, and autobiography swells. Like Namier, I watch as a stranger the strange consort of humanity in its off-moments, panting for a peep of reality. But then again, one must question what a strange voyeur such as I means by the word "reality" - what strange hopes, expectations, and fears does the very thought of "reality" precipitate in a mind such as mine? Where do the beads of sweat gather, and why? To answer that, of course, would end the quest. I have no choice, reality is dragging its heels like a reluctant bitch and won't appear until.... Musil speaks of the need of precision in matters of the soul. And that is probably the answer. The dream (my dream) needs a little precision to wake it up, to dispel its demonic spell. The dream must be taken to account. To be asked precisely how it makes sense of this or that thought in my head, this unrealized, unhappy response, that devastating encounter, this inexplicable life-style, this avoidance of mirrors, this grimace gliding across the face, that peculiar flick of the finger. Just what do they mean, Really?! Where do they come from? Why do they seem remote, as though I were seeing them through a long telescope but neither hearing, smelling, or tasting the world in which they occur? But can this be? Is this at all a precise observation? Perhaps the telescope itself is part of the dream, and what I already see is reality, since to see the world without actually sensing it freshly impinging on my nose, ears, tongue, and heart, is impossible. Logically impossible and realistically impossible. I can not look at the world through a long telescope somehow stretched out under my balding skull. This is precisely where my dream looses all precision, and becomes an eternity of nightmare. It can answer none of these questions satisfactorily. My dream can not handle logic - it can not place me in the world where I actually am whether I recognize it or not. I try waking up, but I only awake in another dream. The question remains: why nothing rather than something?

Musil, with his bright optimism, has convinced me that 'relativism' is an articulated dream similar to mine (unarticulated and feeble) - no matter whose it is, Spenglers or Foucault's. At the heart of all 'relativisms' lays a great lack of precision of soul; a dream of greatness, of having conquered the Faustian illusion of possessing it all: the source of all knowledge, all knowledge, and everyday Life. There is no one so cock-sure of knowing something than a relativist. Most others speak of 'probablity', a 'working hypothesis', 'until further evidence comes in', of the 'finitude of man', of (and get this), of 'different ways of seeing things'! It is only the relativist who knows something

- everything - absolutely! God (or the Devil, take your
pick) on earth! They all crawl up their own ass, and speak
with great farting at the mouth. Truth-seekers, as Musil
points out, is much softer, unsure of themselves, and have
difficulty making generalizations about anything. They have
to touch, smell, hear, taste, and see each thing a thousand
times - and even then, like Gaugin, they say: "oh, well, it
may not be perfect, I was in a rush, but it will have to do
for now. Besides, today I saw my vahine lift a bowl to her
lips in just the same way I have seen Orientals, so I must
rethink the entire business."

I will spare you my choice quotes from Musil, since I assume
you too will buy his book, and find plenty of your own.
(ut I can not resist one quote from Musil for it seems to
'sum-up' your "ABC" article. I would be absolutely sure of
this if understood completely what Musil is saying - but, as
you know by now, one can never understand Musil completely!
Here goes:

*It is not to be assumed that people really have as much to talk
about and tell as people do in literature, and if one examines the
content of what is imparted, it is mostly not by any means so original
as to explain the compulsion to express it. Looking at the matter this
way one recognizes, rather, in general little else than a constantly
stirred-up subjective rearrangement of an old inventory. The imagination
does not fly or rove (an idea of long ago!), but writing appears, as
when a minor religious functionary comes home and is the head of a*

family: power, capricious order, subjection of the world in effigy. My
book is my castle [in English in original-trans.]; the writer is always
right! This explains why there is really no longer any audience for this
literature, but only authors, who move toward or away from one another.
The reader is not looking for the leader, but the person who shares his
point of view; he is himself the author of a weltanschauung and an
anonymous aesthetics, and - based on the error that every judgment about
art is, after all, merely subjective - he is in the other only a kind of
executive authority, someone who displays the arrangement of his mind.
The consequence of this is the extraordinary lack of influence of this
literature on the society and its debasement to an empty self-
affirmation on the part of the authors. If one see this self-affirmation
practiced daily by innumerable otherwise amiable Europeans as a harmless
habit, painlessly and among their daily tasks, the idea burgeons to that
of an ugly mania, a belated schoolboy vice practiced by bearded men.
{From "Literary Chronicle" p.53.)

Forgive the length of the quote, but heavens isn't it
something? Here, in this brief space, somehow, is the "death
of the author", the "deconstruction of sense from reality",
"the loss of self(as presence in the world)", and all the
other nonsense associated with the word "intelligence" today
said so non-polemically. It also brought to mind Mr. Graff,
whom you mention in your article, and his desperate attempt
to find a release from his 'harmless habit' by claiming his
writing is not "intrinsically incapable" of being read by

someone real - the common man! (The atempt to find reality through the back door.)

True, Musil does not explain why "something must be wrong with the living of life if its migration to paper is so extensive", but he does capture the essence of a neurotic crawling up his own ass quite beautifully - as I tried to do so badly in your room a few days ago. When ideas are healthy, and people read to experience something they don't already know, the ideas must "fly or rove"!

Well, I did say only one quote but I have already given two. I will stop. Besides, I still have not worked my way in to reality! (Perhaps you'd rather read quotes from Musil!) My hands still seem to protrude from my shoulders, and the faces of others remain 'apparitions'. The notion of forcing life to give me what I want because I want it, still brings sweat to my brow. Panic. Musil, Gaugin, Lafarge speak to me! Tell me the secret of finding as much meaning in my own writings as I find in yours! As much of myself as you do in yours! Of not having to use you to find out what I mean! You look in to yourselves and see your selves, I look in to mine and see you! This is not the point of reading. At the end of one of your pages, I should not run out of self, or in to darkness! And yet I do. I want more so I should not have to pick up the thread of my own which vanishes the moment I look at it. Joyce somewhere spoke of forging in the 'smithy of his soul', but first the self must be a hammer - otherwise the forge merely blazes but makes nothing. And I am so old to have a blazing soul but too not yet be an adult!

From **Splengeriana**: *An act of faith, an act of imagination, is required in order to form a hypothesis even in the purely rational sphere.(But we should not distort this familiar fact the way Sp[engler] did.)* <Musil;p.158.>

Emphasize that the theor[em] of shapelessness is a vulgar philosophy. Against false phil[osophical] pathos, greatness, sublimity! Spengler appears sublime! (as sublime as a canary). These people's primary demand is that every conception must be sublime. < Musil;p.170>

A severe Musil meditation: *By characterizing a person's profession and adding a bit more, we can say today what is most important about a person. When we learn that a man is a judge or a businessman, and hear in addition that he is good at his work or not, perhaps also that he is a 'nice' fellow or a 'clever' one, we know most of what can be known about a person living today. The consciousness of being a ... consoles us is the empty hours; ...~ There are also some leisure-hour professions. All of them really are professions, which then appear with the modifier amateur: for instance, stamp collecting, tennis, record setting on the mount of Venus.~ Outside these bonds the individual can not raise an arm or lift a finger. He collapses like a deflated balloon or, if inflated by an impulse, he deforms himself immediately in some single, random direction. He has (aside from this) no shaping or guiding ideas."* <pp.158-59. "~" signifies a paragraph break.> (I am sure we have been so described by countless others to countless others, and each has walked away feeling they know us! Are we so simple that we refuse to recognize this description of ourselves as accurate? What more is there - the abyss? What is it that rebels? That 'deforms' us by leaping in some 'random direction' which turns out to be the opposite from that which we thought we were leaping? The self as abyss.)

I am tired of quoting others! Enough of coming to myself by way of detour through the universe (from Valéry).

What would it mean if Michelangelo had taken up golf near the end of his days saying "Art, so much hogwash!, now it is time to live!". Or if St. Thomas Aquinas, walking out of Chartres, had grabbed a tennis racket in a similar spirit: "Enough of God and salvation!, says he. Would it have the same force as Einstein taking to watching Oprah? How would Foucault interpret any of these possibilities?

Those words of self reference, "I", "myself", "me", etc., give me such a headache! To what do they refer? I am afraid I can not see the forest for the trees. I am always asking myself the wrong question. It is always - What should I do - never - What do I want to do? The latter question is so unfamiliar to me, and when I do ask ask it - perforce, abstractly - I do not know how to answer it! It is as though the center of my inner eye has been burnt out, leaving me with only peripheral vision of myself. The more intently I look the less is visible.The self as deceptive abyss.

All it takes is a few notes from Mahler however, and I am right back in the cradle of my soul, rocking majestically in timpani of despair, horns of courage, and strings of soaring lyricism. The self as articulated triumph. The abyss can sing! (Even if it is not mine.) Which leads me to believe that the residue, what is left of the self after Musil's deft description, remains unknown even to the self. It is what becomes art - if it is articulated. The abyss in human form. My abyss however, is due to a myopic psychology. It is not a true abyss. A mock abyss. Merely a blind spot. It can not sing. It can not do anything - my wristless hands still protrude from my shoulders because I can not see even my own body. I mock this. I mock that. Because I should! But the point of writing is not to write in defense of the old verities or to join in the attack upon them. Rather, the point is to be oneself - to express the abyss. That which is beyond 'good and evil', reality and dream, subjective and objective, but combines them all in one big, chocolate malt. The difference between health and neurosis: Gaugin had to go ten thousand miles to leave art behind, I can do it in the middle of the art world. One can't have everything, right? Reality and the comfort of home?

Well, my attempt to reach Reality by the end of this letter happenmed, but not quite the way I thought - isn't that the way of reality!! The other day I had a dream in which rooms actually had depth, perspective. I realized that in my waking

states I do not see things so clearly. Rooms, like street
scenes, tend to be flat surfaces in to which I do not walk,
but float across. (So my hands won't seem so out of place, I
suppose.) I am an unconscious reality. ,
Today, the sun rose then set. All is well. The End.

Steve

#19 was the plane that
alex flew. the painting
is of the battle of
Tenk when his
wing Commander was
Butch O'Hare.

Seeing you both will
be a great pleasure

Love Sag

Steve Cogan

752 West End

New York, NY
10025

Dear Ted,

It is on Easter morning that Goethe's Faust goes out to the countryside, where he remembers that

> Once heaven's love came to me with a kiss
> In the deep silence of a Sabbath day,
> The deep tones of the bells, it seemed,
> Had much to say,
> And every prayer brought impassioned bliss;
> An unbelievably sweet yearning
> Drove me to wander through woods and meadows,
> And with a thousand tears burning in my eyes,
> I felt a world arise and grow for me.

OK? That about say it?

I'm writing so as not to leave my blanket judgement of Count Immaneul Wallerstein's "looniness" unspecified. My daily trips to the bathroom reveal page after page of C- thinking. Apart from his mind-numbing catalogue of theories and statistics and counter statistics, the ideas themselves just don't add up, even phrases, like "the long seventeenth century" (intro) and a little further down, "the long sixteenth and seventeenth centuries." He states that a "convincing proof" of major changes in the map of "core, semiperipheral, and peripheral" world areas would require "economic indicators" that are "intrinsically difficult and extrinsically perhaps impossible" to construct, since overall data, _in particular_, are lacking, so that all we can do is "sketch out what seems more and less solid, review explanatory models that encompass the data, suggest a theoretical view, and arrive at some notion of our empirical lacunae and theoretical conundrums" (I'll say). Sounds tentative, right? Yet sandwiched in between he tells us in detail what such a world map "should" look like between 1500 and 1650. So here I am on the john reading what might be fascinating material on medieval agriculture but is totally dead, leaden prose, with its "agronomic shifts" of barley, oats, forage crops, madder, buckwheat, hemp, pastels (?), plus fertilizer "(both humus and marl)," more statistics, more theories and counter theories, all of which has a strangely peristaltic effect on me as I plow on through Vallerstein and he plows on through me. Names:

Slicher von Bath, K. Glamann, G. N. Clark, Wilhelm Abel, Gaston Imbert, Pierre Chaunu, Jean Meuvret, Pierre Vilar, Ivo Schöffer, René Baehrel, Carlo Cipolla, D. C. Coleman, Francois Crouzet, E. J. Hobsbawm, (I can't believe this), Francois Simiand, Ferdinand Braudel, Murdo MacLeod, J. V. Polisensky, Gilles Postel-Vinay, Etienne Balibar, Dona Torr, Maurice Dobb, E. M. Zhukov, Paul Sweezy, Domenico Sella, Perry Anderson, Douglas Garman, "see also Le Roy Laudrie," Christopher Hill, Spooner, Duby, Jacquart, De Maddalena, Lèon, Mauro, Mousnier, Topolski, Reinhard and Armengaud, J. de Vries, Ralph Davis, Ruggiero Romano, Geremek, Friederich Lutge, Carsten, Kamen, Roger Mols, Jeannin, Vajnshtejn, Elliott, Wilson, Minchinton, Fanfani, Bouwsma, Bouwsma, Bouwsma

Remember Lucky's hymn to the public works of Puncher and Wattman, Fartov and Belcher?

> Given the existence of a personal God, Who, from his divine athambia, his divine aphasia, loves us dearly with some exceptions, but time will tell qua qua qua

And what does he emerge with, this genius, this thinker on the cutting edge of new frontiers? Marxist cliches par exellence to the effect that the rise and equalization of income among the "lower strata" represents "the real crisis" of feudal nobility. And what is wealth? You guessed it, "surplus value" and "surplus appropriation." And why the development of the modern world system? Why the transformation from feudalism to capitalism? Answer: THERE IS NO TRANSITION! This deep thinker, he who is so careful to qualify every statistic with ten more, every theory with a dozen more, who hunts down every last nuance of "nomenclature" so as not to fall into the pitfall of ahistorical categories, now gives us the iron law of modern western history: Capitalism is feudalism in another mask! The spirit of expropriation lives on in a new set of clothes. History doesn't happen!!!

> There was no way out of it [the "crisis" of the Renaissance] without drastic social change. This way, as I have previously argued, was the creation of a capitalist world-system, a new form of surplus appropriation. The replacement of the feudal mode by the capitalist mode was what constituted the seignorial reaction; it was a great sociopolitical effort by the ruling strata to retain their collective privileges, even if they had to accept a fundamental reorganization of the economy and all the resulting threats to familiar modes of stratification. There would be some families, it was clear, who would lose out by such a shift; but many would not. Additionally, and most importantly, the principle of stratification was not merely preserved; it was to be reinforced as well [through ascetic ideals, which supposedly didn't exist in the late middle ages, and through the absolute state].

He also has maddening contradictory statements along the way, such as "Since losers are many and manifold, strange alliances are made, and the process is drawn out and unclear." What he means, I think, is that feudal power is held onto by most families. The many losers are . . .? Yes, the lower classes, the eternally shat upon:

> For Anderson, "absolutism was essentially . . a redeployed and recharged apparatus of feudal domination, designed to clamp the peasant masses back into their traditional social position . . .

So: "This makes the seventeenth century not a 'crisis' but a needed change of pace, not a disaster but an essential element in furthering the interests of those who benefitted most from a capitalist system."

Do you believe it? I don't. Notice that there are no people on any of his pages, no real situations, no stories, no narratives, nothing happens "in the course of human events." Wallerstein grinds on, but nothing happens. Not in his prose, which is dead to human experience, and not in his thoughts. He's so, so careful not to carry the idea of "transition" too far, lest everything become transition, yet there he is at the end of Chapter 1: absolutism is the oppressor's "transition" to capitalism. End of Chapter 1.

So nothing means anything in itself. Nothing has a self. No period is different from any other. They're all a series of additions to an infinite tapeworm spinning out to nowhere, as Spengler says of mechanistic histories. For a touch of color, you can make the tapeworm progressive, reactionary, whatever you like. The only thing that really matters is to look busy and keep your job. God, when Huizinga writes, when Burckhardt writes, when Spengler takes off, or half a dozen literary scholars I've read on medieval tragedy or the Jacobean temper, then you start to learn something about what went on. You see what drool the Count's "system" really is. The truth is that we could master his "apparatus" in a month. And then my eternal question arises: Why is my mother the way she is and Why does my father let her get away with it? How did this stuff get by people? Do they really not know anything? Didn't they have to study Hobbes? Didn't they have to read Trevelyan on the 17th century at <u>some</u> point in their career? Or the constitutional historians? Cultural history? The Wars of Religion? What a pointless profession if Wallertsein is a landmark nowadays.

Well, Parsifal sings on (he's just rejected Kundry). My late Shakespeare papers wait to be graded, and I will be hungry soon.

Love,

Heve

Dear Ted,

After you left I started fooling around with my pages on Cendrars and found the following in L'Homme Foudroyé. I aim the passages at the dark regions in our hearts, where Bernals and Wallersteins and other Bosch-like characters have found hosts to feed their gnawing torments. Isn't it interesting, by the way, that all these radical paranoids keep referring to their enemy as the devil? I was struck by something you said apropos radical teachers tearing apart education and then attacking it for not working, which I immediately twinged at as another hopeless craziness happening today. All these excrutiating torments find fertile soil in our feelings and imaginations. We zero in on them faster than the speed of light, like anti-Supermen, the way Clover zeros in and clings to people who reject her, "like a magnet," she said. Maybe that process itself is part of the devil's work (as Hamlet says it is). One cannot zero in like a magnet on something good, because it does not permit it. Maybe the path to heaven has to be "steep and thorny" by necessity, because separateness and psychic health are the very opposite of seductive pain. Yes, the whole gamut from complaining to outright depression is compelling when the fertile ground is there. Just to hear about a torment is tormenting to me--and millions of others also zero in on catastrophe. It's a thriving enterprise:

> The spirit that I have seen
> May be the devil; and the devil hath power
> To assume a pleasing shape; yea, and perhaps
> Out of my weakness and melancholy,
> As he is very potent with such spirits,
> Abuses me to damn me.

O to leave it all behind and feed myself with good things only.

This, for example, from something I found in Cendrars' L'Homme Foudroyé (1945) after you left. The book, by the way, has been translated twice with the following titles: "The Astonished Man" and "The Detonated Man," both of which sound faggoty to me. "The Man Who Was Blown Away" gets the two senses of foudroyé exactly). And look at the way Cendrars does it. He just says what he thinks, flat out:

> There are courageous people all along National Highway 10,
> from one end to the other; I hear poor people, the truly
> poor, those who are ashamed and haven't lost their hope,
> poor people like those of whom the Gospels speak, and not
> those nouveaux poor, more arrogant still than the nouveaux
> riche, full of demands and who know their rights, who have
> no other word but this one on their tongue, who intrigue,
> who come together, who insinuate themselves into all the
> commissions, victims of this, victims of that, of the War,
> of Floods, etc., etc., and for twenty years in France have
> perked up and gone into politics. They are humbugs, but not
> as much as the idle intellectuals, ugh! who are professional
> opportunists, hypocrites, and pharisees, who knock while
> waiting patiently behind all doors.

206

And again:

> I am surprised that no contemporary novelist has yet dedicated a work to the automobile, to the modern highway, to motor inns along the way, to the excitement of the road, the way Casanova did in his *Memoirs* for the coaches and inns of polite society at the end of the 18th century. . . . I am surprised that no contemporary poet has sung the automobile, as I sang the railroad in the "Trans-siberian" on the eve of the other war (it's fortunate that aviators, taken by their new and dangerous profession, are sitting down to write and that the airplane is entering poetry and prose completely naturally and not as a theme . . . What are all these artists doing, my contemporaries? My God, one would think that they hadn't lived! . . . . My rupture with Paris and its "intelligentsia" sometimes frightened me, because I am not a despiser of the world--of stupidity, at most--and yet, sometimes I rejoice in it!

> [And a footnote on his contemporaries: To speak only of those of whom one speaks today (the middle of October, 1944): Picasso, for example, this painter, who for 40 years and although guided, counselled, and surrounded for years by his friends the poets, Max Jacob and Guillaume Apollinaire, is unable to extricate himself from the dated and sterile aesthetics of Mallarmé.]

There's something <u>thrilling</u> about a real point of view. It's alive, that's what it is. And we were given precious little permission to live. As a further act of disobedience, I'm going to drop into the Gotham Book Mart soon to see what they have of Cendrars in translation. His French is really dense.

FACTORY B

"In the very earliest Times,
when both people and animals lived on earth,
a person could become an animal if he wanted to
and an animal could become a human being...
That was the time when words were like magic.
The human mind had mysterious powers.
A word spoken by chance
might have strange consequences.
It would suddenly come alive
and what people wanted to happen
        could happen —
all you had to do was say it.
Nobody could explain this:
That's the way it was."

        a Netsilik Eskimo

Can this mesa be a word? a left
over from the old, true dictionary?

POST CARD

Sinclair Lewis

USA
14

Steve Cogan
386 Henry street
Brooklyn, New York
11201

PUBLISHED BY HELIOS SOUTHWEST, P. O. BOX 6035, SANTA FE, NEW MEXICO, 87502.

Dear Steve

. Much has been going on, most of it in my mind but in
reality as well. I have been lifted from one life and
dropped in to another - just like that. Things have kept me
preoccupied. I am driving all about town seeing new sights,
and traveling to all points of Indian interest -if there are
such things - to fulfill my sabbatical obligations.
Disoriented, confused, feeling, as usual, a novice at life, I
wander from daybreak till moon rise as though I were a
disfigured blind man begging for revelation to be dropped in
my cup. I assume you are doing well and have nothing to do
but to sit down and read another long letter addressed to the
gods. Well, you'd better be!

When Mahler descends from a mighty, agonized crescendo
to a whisper of wounded pianissimo, or Wagner trumpets
paroxysms of brutality beneath shimmering rivers what are we
to make of them? Why do they do it? (And why would they do
it with "a degree of knowledge and perception that cuts
through the soul like a knife," as Neitzsche says they do?)
Why, renting a great hall, would they enlist 50 violinist,
twenty French and English trumpeters twenty clarinet, flute,
oboe, bassoonist and drum players, three over-weight
sopranos, two fat tenors and a slender bass to blow, rub,
bang, and yell out every flutter of their heart to thousands
of strangers? (Or Len Jenkin for that matter. Does he not
provide a script to others, schedule rehearsals, have sets
painted, refine the make-up on his pretty heroine - all in
order to express every flirtation of his amorous eyes, and
expect us to stampede in for a view - though seven seconds of
an overheard Mahler oboe across the hall would be enough to
draw one away. Or am I comparing apples to oranges?) Why
indeed?

Nietzsche is a very careful writer. Everywhere he
meticulously contrasts the botched and bungled to the clear-
headed and strong in most lucid ways. Yet, he always speaks
intimately. But in whom is he confiding? Why? (Nietzsche
himself wrote: *In picturing the perfect reader, I always
imagine a monster of courage and curiosity, as well of
suppleness, cunning, and prudence - a born adventurer and
explorer.*)

Hegel invented a most abstract history promising the
world paradise, and Spengler another that would end in icy
ignorance - while most of humanity did the night's dishes
and checked their pocket watches in the morning.

Why did Constable and Ruisdael paint such startlingly
detailed landscapes when all one had to do was stroll down a
country lane and lift one's eyes?

It is clear why reformers do these things - they have a
vested interest. They wish to change the world in gratuitous
ways. They work from their heads, not as a friend or equal.

It is strange that after all these years, I never once
thought about art as a sharing of oneself with a world that

quite possibly doesn't give a damm - just because there is nothing else to do!

The 19th century - whata century! When you think of all the music, literature, paintings, journeys in to the Orient, Africa, Central & South America, China, the South Seas, and the consequent journals and letters of adventure, war, and conquest which followed, and the eccentric genius' in their laboratories pricking bacteria under hand-polished lenses, the Morgans, the Rhodes, the Rothchilds digging at the earth, littering it with the nuts and bolts of civilization, or creating financial empires by throwing gold across continents, etc., and all of it alone, not sitting on committees, teams, or writing pleading letters of grant, etc.. The energy of them is astounding. It was the Age of Sharing. The age when people gave of themselves unstintingly (how many died in the jungle, the desert, on mountain tops, in the pots of cannibals, or ruined their health with malaria, dysentery, exotic bacterial infections, or broken bones, or lost their minds in the backwaters of Patagonia, the Congo, or on the banks of the Snake River?) - selfishly, to be sure, but always for humanity as well. How else can one share oneself and with whom? Thus, Mahler, Wagner, Goethe, and the whole heped-up crew.

Nietzsche called all those who could not so give of themselves 'decadent,' self-absorbed sickies who either remained silent all their lives, or joined crusades to change the nature of humanity for its own sake. I think I am one of those decadents. But for my own reasons. It is not as though I don't love myself, but I do find it despicable, in the way a good Christian would, i.e., as better than the slime around me. I have no wish to communicate with humanity. Why, I wouldn't even hire a trio! But, I did join protest marches....

Why? Because....Well, to tell the truth, I don't know. Somehow I didn't conceive of the world as good enough for me as it was. It was not as though I didn't talk (i.e., ostensibily communicate), its that I didn't talk to anyone in particular.. Or rather, it never occurred to me that talking (writing, for that matter) was anything more than lifting my sewer lid and letting those near.me hear the gurgle for a few moments.. It was like letting the world eavesdrop on sprayed up bits of interior excrement, nothing more. This, of course, meant that I didn't listen to anybody, for I was always to busy listening to myself, or, with great impatience, momentarily lifting my lid. The continuous moving of tons of shit from one side of the brain to the other was a prodigious activity of neuronic engineering requiring vast amounts of unconscious, uninterrupted energy.

So you see, I spend most of my time desperately avoiding communication, while in the dome of my head I constructed viaducts as great as those of Rome, irrigation canals as intricate as those of the ancient Inca, and drainage systems rivaling those of the Renaissance Dutch - all to keep the shit flowing. In comparison, communication to me was as the fly which annoyed Napoleon on his way to Moscow. Ah, greatness!

Enough of this! The self must be sublimated in to life or it is nothing. Only such a merging can illumine it and the world, can give birth to it and the world. Everything is for naught unless this be accomplished, for without it art (communication) is impossible. (With these very words I open Albricht's shackles holding me in the land of Mu. Now, to rise. Help, I cry.)

It seems all I wish to write about is myself. However, when I do, I write the most absurd things: "I don't know why I write." It is clear I am not in this world. In some profound way, I do not understand what I write. I can be like that character Wilde once described as taking a half a day to enter a coma and the other half removing it. Looking, that is, for the sentence to tell me what it means, rather than my expressing myself. I want the unwritten paragraph to write itself, revealing to me its content for my judgment. I wish only to correct it for its accuracy, but I have no idea what it is being accurate about. It is as though in deciding which adjective I should use in describing a morning, whether bright or drizzly, I would hope the day would tell me, then I judge its accuracy. The process is insane!

And there you have it - when I write about myself, as I said, I write the most absurd things. But not only that, I seem to write about this absurdity over and over again, in precisely the same way, complaining about my inability to express myself, to know myself, to separate myself from the unconscious, to have a self, to feel myself, etc., etc., and etc... I have filled letter after letter, journal entry after journal entry with this quackery. For years! Jesus!! I am stuck, like a needle on a cracked record. How many metaphors, similes, analogies can one invent to pin an illness aganist the wall? Perhaps one day one of them will be accurate enough to actually conjure up the real thing.

Degas once said that the cubist do something much more difficult than paint. Such distain is precious.

Picked-up another wonderful curio: *Paris Salons, Cafés, Studios* by Sisley Huddleston (Blue Ribbon Books, 1928). At least it is a delight to me - she seems to have been known by all who one cares to know: Valery, Gide, Proust, France, Matisse, Manet, Pound, Joyce, Mme. Curie, A. Monnier, Cendrars, etc.. I am sure she served as the source for countless anectodal tit-bits for many a know-it-all who quote the illustrious with such aplomb - such as myself. Her concern is to record the differences between pre and post war Paris, a difference she does not, on the whole, like. With precise insight in to the sensibilities of the artist she writes:

Sometimes I regret that I have ever known another Paris - not because I am delighted with the meretricious mixture [of the classes], but because I find myself continually comparing it to a much better Paris which has vanished. . . . the former Paris satisfied one's sense of

*order . . . somehow I have kept an old-fashioned predilection
for sharply defined categories of people. I like all the
classes, but I do not want them shaken together - orange
juice and gin, butter merchants and nobles, actresses and
princes, cabaret-keepers and diplomatists.**

Quite nice, uh? But when she adds:

*Later came the Surrealists. . . . Marx, Lenin,
Freud, and Rimbaud, make a particular appeal to them. They
are aggressive. They are as ready to express their dislikes
with fists as with words. . . . At the Studio des Ursulines,
an advanced cinema, where Man Ray's amazing photographs were
shown, there was a[n] . . . outbreak. Then Maurice Martin du
Gard, . . . was a victim. They told him they would not
allow their names to be mentioned in his paper. In spite of
this injunction they were mentioned. Therefore, the
Surrealists armed themselves and burst into his office. In
the* bagarre *the office furniture was broken. . . . It is
dangerous to offend the Surrealists. [Andre Breton wrote]
...*"We accept absolutely nothing. We believe that we are
capable of reducing reason and the faux bon sens. We feel
sympathetic towards revolutionary parties. We want to
support all movements of opposition - violently, at the peril
of our lives. . . .Time does not exist. I would rather
destroy than construct. We insist on a complete revision of
artistic values. We exclude all literary talent, and
literary quality we consider of secondary importance. We are
wrathful against present reality." *. . . The Dalai Lama was
informed that the Surrealists are his faithful servants.
There was a demand for the erection a the guillotine and a
new reign of terror.*

And then adds that *A book like Theophile Gautier's
"Mlle. de Maupin" or Pierre Loüys "Chansons de Bilitis,"
beautifully written, would make its appearance; but it could
be taken as a piece of art, not as a revelation of morals.
Now all that is changed.. . . A whole literature has lately
sprung up which is tainted with homosexuality.. . . A great
deal has been done to drag what has hitherto been an obscure
practice, confined to an occult group, into the public
domain. Just as the proud mother, watching the young recruit
marching with his regiment, cried, "My Jimmy is the only one
who eeps in step," so the abnormalists are decalring that
they are the normal part of humanity - or at least the better
part of humanity. It is deplorable. Let them, if they
please, behave in their fashion among their fellows - that,
it can be argued, is their affair. But do not let them preen
themselves in public, and loudly boast of their superiority,*

---

* Of course Chateaubriand was the first to notice this, then Flaubert as
in writing:"Speaking of politics, in Geneva I saw something very
curious: the restaurant run by old Gaillard, the shoemaker and ex-
general of the Commune. ...It's a world in itself, the world democracy
dreams of and that I'll never see, thank God. The things that will hold
the center of the stage during the next two or three hundred years are
enough to make a man of taste vomit. It's time to disappear."

and call for converts, and mock the rest of the world. (She places the "blame' for this change in Paris onto the shoulders of first Proust then Gide.) The blueprint of **our** world, as it were, can be seen. World War 1 was indeed, a great calamity, unleashing the formlessness of humanity when not reigned in by controlling governments. We fall to pieces, not knowing or selves or our ass from another man's.

Do not let my exerpts from this book put you off - she is not at all as didatic as I may make her seem. She really is quite free of all this, and delights in great descriptions of Parisian life. Great stories of Valéry, Proust, Anderson, Stein, etc..

Like me, she asks the right questions (I paraphrase freely): Where are the Boulevardiers, where are the hurdy-gurdy organs, where are the Tziganes, where are the former, charming rotundities in women, the square-shouldered, heavy-moustached men, where is the clarity between the sexes, the café concerts, the wines, coffee and lunch for 1 franc, 25 centimes? Was it worth losing these to have underground railways instead of the horse-omnibus, to have cubism instead of painting? Was losing the pre-war world worth being given typewriters, Bolshevism, football, boxing, tennis, one way streets, gramophones, coloured photograhy, cinemas, illuminated skysigns, cocaine, silk stockings, safety razors, monkey glands for rejuvenation, painless divorces, egalitarianism, and the unatural vices of golf, wireless telegraphy, telephony, motorcars, aeroplanes, and cocktails? (You may stumble on cocktails, but give it some thought.)

But back to the obscure question of this letter: what is art and life all about? (Coming from the depths of Steel Town I suppose I have little right to ask these questions for who am I but one miserable, out of order, creature given an half-assed education and pretensions because of an egalitarianism which smells of decadance?) Was not the "audience" of the nineteenth century lost after the war? I mean, Hemingway and socialist realism do have one thing in common, they are for *the masses* - that ideological group-think which has no basis in reality. It only did, if it did, in the age of nobles, princess, aristocracy and then *the rest*. But even among *the rest* there were clear value and cultural divisions, say, between the artisans, the inn-keepers, etc..With whom then does one communicate today, i.e., make art? Art for arts sake was no accident - its audience had disappeared with the collapse of Europe. For whom would Mahler or Wagner compose today? With whom could Neitzsche be so intimate - a few scragglers, the botched, the bumblers he despised? Hence, no Mahlers, Wagners, or Neitzsches. This is to objectify my psychological collapse for I was born, it seems, with the inability to want to communicate - you see, I do start at the beginning - the desire! (I write despite myself.)

Avempace (d.1138) wrote a book called *The Rule of the Solitary*. He thought the ideal state would be one best modeled on the solitary man's discipline. Now, what would that nation be like? Off hand, it seems to be what I would want - all are beyond good and evil, merely, perhaps, gazing quickly and suspiciously at one another, each vying to possess the greatest solitude. Each one, of course, is crazy as a loon. The great thing about this nation, however, because art is impossible, is no one could possibly know he is crazed, and quite possibly believe all others are silent because they are either hostile, stupid, or not true solitaries depending on his mood of the day! But that is not it, that is not it at all. Although that is the nation I act as though I live in. Sometimes!

If I knew what I wanted to communicate, I would write long letters. All Cretans are liars. I am a Cretan. As a Cretan, I have a difficult time believing myself. Art, under these conditions, is impossible.

Mahler too was always personal, but by then the audience was disappearing and he knew he was whistling in the wind - hence the cow-bells to assure him that *things*, at least, were still there. Things without people are pontless, however, hence, again, the cow-bells. Neitzsche, I think, would call his music decadent.

So you see, not only do I not know (feel) what it is I want to communicate, I wouldn't know who to tell it to if I could. But does all this matter? Probably not. Hemingway did not, after all, write for the masses, the social realists did.

It was Barrés, apparently, who coined the phrase *Le Culte do Moi*. In it he included Valéry, Claudel,Fargue, Romains, Mallarme, Gauguin, and a whole host of other 19th century born early 20th century luminaries. These were defiant artists, they talked only to Art, and were socially silent. Orderless society left them confused, without rudder, without an audience. Hemingway established a new meaning to *Le Culte de Moi* - he created an audience while in the process of creating his art, a stupendous achievment! By then the masses needed some cohesion, someone to give them a sense of identity. But now, today, they have fallen apart again, and think they are self-sufficient. One can not even create one's own audience any more. We are back to the feisty Surrealists (the PC's of today). Is it back to art for arts sake, again? A retreat?

What does it matter? As Valéry once said: I reach the universe by detour of myself. If only. I am always on the detour! The universe is out there somewhere, but where? Where is the map? I lost it, I lost it, and on the way I lost it, a green and yellow -what? - bruise?

One of these days, I'll look in to a mirror and actually see something. Then, maybe, I'll find my way back into the universe. But what, oh, what, shall I see? Well, at least a body, I hope.

If only I could stand on a corner and see the passing parade instead of the usual nightmare right behind my eyes. I never see the sights this way. The problem is I love myself too much and can't bear to be away from it for one instant. Greece, Rome, the Seven Wonders of the World can't hold a candle to it. The trouble is I want to keep it all to myself and want the world to know they can't have it. Go figure.

Is it a: Love me for who I am or I'll kill you? A daring of you to love anyone else in the face of this St. Sebastion who fashions his own arrows and plunges them into his own flesh - so exhalted that ordinary mortals are not good enough to do the job? Does resentment know no bounds? You see, I confuse this with humility! How <u>does</u> the world work? Do not my feet stink?

In *The Free Spirit* Neitzsche wrote: *..and he who perpetually tears and lacerates himself with his own teeth (or, in place of himself, the world, God, or society), may indeed, morally speaking, stand higher than the laughing and self-satisfied satyr, but in every other sense he is the more ordinary, more indifferent, and less instructive. And no one is such a liar....*

You see, in this letter I am trying to find something, anything, a Rapheal nude, Mt. Everest, Schindler's list, to interest me, something other than myself. This can be either like clearing the air of motes or trying to move the Grand Canyon over an inch. Sometimes I feel like a Dostoyevski who carves catus roots on the Pecos is writing my life.

It is amazing how the world does not interest me. Yet, I am very attentive to it. Generally, I am aware of every cloud, the texture of the wind, a tangle of tree branches, the posture of this or that stranger across the street, whether a waitress has pulled up her socks, the weight of flatware, the disintegration of dust in my jacket pockets, etc., but only *after* they have impinged upon me, *after* I have made them mine, shrouded them under my magical cape. An atomic bomb could fall on all of them once I have so enchanted them - I wouldn't give a fig. (Have I offended Muhammed here?) I have all the ear marks of interest: rapt attention, an observing eye, a certain obsequiousness that seems respectful of the right of plants and other helpless things, but these merely hide my profound haughtiness. Its me I want to fondle - like some filthy necromancer rubbing the breasts of beautiful maidens.

Bear with me, I do so want to communicate, not ruminate.

On the cover of Paul Johnson's *The Birth of the Modern* is a reproduction of "The Wanderer," a painting by Caspar David Friedrich. In the foreground, it shows the back of a well-build young man standing bravely on a large, black boulder. In the far distance are misty mountains upon which, leaning upon a chic cane, he gazes. It is an adventure painting, a calling to new worlds. I am afraid that if the young man were me, I would be interested only in how manly my backside looked, the thought of climbing over the new world would only fatigue me. I would, however, soon scamper down, run to a near-by desk and begin writing of my fatigue and the metaphysical inexplicablness of my legthargy - as though that should interest the world far more.

I am pure bathos. I have yet to write one real sentence! In English, not Libido - the Esparanto.of those "always five feet from the hospital."

I come to the edge of myself, then turn back in fear. What an abyss is out there. I find it much more comfortable to think I don't exist (or is it the world?). This way no one can see me, and I am free to do as I please. I can out dance Astaire, walk through walls, write unwritten great novels, paint unpainted masterpieces, never age, smoke ten cartons of cigarettes a day and not once cough. Of course, the price I pay is I am not allowed in to reality. I do not have the ticket.

There, I've gotten it out of my system! I shall change my diaper, and walk out into the world as though nothing has happened.

Now the question is: if not of myself, what else is there to write about? The all to glib answer is: anything in the World. The less glib answer is : whatever interests me. The most important answer is: whatever will bring me money and fame. The most crucial answer is: whatever I can bring enough 'knowledge and perception to as to cut through the souls of men.' The most obvious answer is: just write.

The most fundamental questions are: do I want to communicate (make art), and, if so, to whom and why? I am afraid I can't even begin a real sentence until I answer these questions - in some fashion or another, consciously or unconsciously..

Of course, there are other ways of communicating. I can paint, draw, carve, sail, look for sunken treasure, piss golden arches on ghetto walls, plunder Indian burial grounds, invent new ways of serving broccoli, even blow half inch glass figurines of Degas dancers. Since I can remember however, I have thought of myself as a writer, in much the same way, by the way, as a primitive might believe himself the descendant of the crocodile that happened to stumble over his camp fire one night on his way to the swamps. Like a snifling follower of the gods, in other words. Forty years of this would drive any man in to self deception! Yet, all arts are the same and it only depends (if one has talent) upon which one feels at home in, whether it it be in the Pantheon of the Crocodile or the Kilns of Pottery. I certainly feel comfortable in the Castle of Words. (Although I do deplore my lack of knowledge of grammer, style, spelling, and punctuation. I blame this on my other-worldly attitude since emerging from the womb, and Mrs. Anderson, my forth grade art teacher, may she rot in Hell.

When Neitzsche writes: *All questions of politics, of the social order, of education, have been falsified from top to bottom, because the most harmful men have been taken for great men, and because people were taught to despise the "detail," more properly, the fundamentals of life,* and that he considers these men as *the excrement of mankind, the products of disease and the instinct of revenge: they are so many monsters, rotten, utterly incurable, avenging themselves on life*, he is certainly saying - especially if for us today one adds to his list public women and the mass media - that things were and are not at all like what we read, indeed, that they are quite the opposite..(Musil, some years later, also noticed this lack of knowledge of 'details,' of an appreciation of the 'fundamentals of life.') If what he writes is true, as I believe it to be - today more so than ever - it goes a long way in explaining why I feel I live in such a fantasy world, two actually, my own and the one waiting for me in newspapers, journals, TV, Indian scholarship, and assorted rags of the Liberal press when, on occasion, I do leave my head. Like Stendhal, I suppose, Nietzsche, perforce, wrote only for "The Happy Few."

I bet you've never heard of the Italian Capt. Theodore Canot, one of the last smuggling African slave traders on the high seas. Well, Malcolm Cowley did and published his *True Account of the Life of...Trader In Gold, Ivory & Slaves on the Coast of Guinea: His Own Story Told in 1854*, in 1928. (I can't seem to getaway from these damm twenties.) Early on, when still a young man, Canot recounts an adventure aboard a British ship: *The Capt. and his wife, who accompanied him, were both stout, handsome Irish people, of equal age, but addicted to fondness for strong and flavored drinks.* Betaking himself to a *hammock which was slung on the main boom*, he was roused by a prelude to their drunken "opera" between them: *Madame gave her lord the direct lie. A loaf of bread, discharged against her head across the table was his reply. Not content with this harmless demonstration of rage, he seized the four corners of the table-cloth, and gathering the tea-things and food in the sack, threw the whole overboard into the bay. In a flash, the tigress fastened on his scanty locks with one hand, while, with the other, she pummelled his eyes and nose. Badly used as he was, . . . I am much mistaken if the sound spanking she received did not leave marks of physical vigour that would have been creditable to a pugilist.* Afterwards, Canot could hear them kissing madly. Nietzsche, who miles away on some narrow medieval street, had just written: *The perfect women tears you to pieces.. . . What a dangerous, creeping, subterranean little beast of prey! And so agreeable at the same time! . . . A little woman bent on revenge, would annihilate Destiny itself*, would have loved it. Wagner without timpani, and on the High Seas!.

And now the News: FLASH: A. Dworkin grafts on a long dick to prove women can fuck themselves....Indians take over gambling in US, use profits to restore natural harmony....Gays prove heterosexuality is abnormal, give demonstrations.....people are throwing away their condoms, marrying cows and horses claiming spiritual peace.....The Pentagon goes nude under MTV ownership.... Reno burns law books. denys rights she says....Scientist discover Europe was an accident.....humanity declared illegal....

The world zooms by but only because I am standing still. (You see, I can prove the theory of relativity, too.) Novels, essays, paintings, concerti (well, maybe not concerti) are being produced by the droves everyday, and not only by such fools as Angelou, Cisneros, and Glass but by ordinary people, you know, artists.

Time in Arizona is strange. It is like the immense sky ending on the four horizons: big, real, but empty. It passes, yet is non-linear. When I think of myself in time it is as though I were standing at the center of a circumferenceless desert, all directions, past, present and future are one. I am free of having to go forward. There is no having breakfast then going to work, lunch, home, dinner, bed - each day a cannon ball shot in the morning and landing at night. Nor, it seems, are there the usual obligations: appointments, salons, chores, you know, all the odds and ends that one also uses to sparse out time - give it content and direction. Sometimes I can feel claustrophobic, trapped in a two dimensional world. I must now make time, it is no longer being made for me. This is a new wilderness for me, untamed time, and I don't have to kill any natives to civilize it - that should make by fellow western historians happy! - simply experience desire. Though the situation is bracing for me, I suspect that most people have felt this way in time for most of their adult lives. It is not as though I relied on the kindness of strangers as most, but upon their telling me what to do and when.*

Why did I move to Phoenix? Well, Neitzsche says it best: *Enumerate the places in which men of great intellect have been and still are found; where wit, subtlety, and malice are part of happiness; where genius is almost necessarily at home: all of them have an unusally dry atmosphere. . . . genius is dependent on dry air, on clear skies -...* (You see, I learned this when I was but 15. Perhaps now I can properly age.)

It's time to disappear as Flaubert would say; let you get back to work. I think I'll sit on the couch and think some more, for I have barely touched upon serious matters....

---

* Have you noticed how all my letters have a certain rhythm - they have notes of progress, as though I am going to become whole for the first time right before your very eyes. I seem to ask the reader to bear with me saying the effort will bear fruit on the next page, as though dreck will become gold. I begin by saying: excuse me while I disappear, but I'll be right back. In the meantime, I allow you overhear me yelling at the wall in the next room. When I return, however, the letter ends. I go away to be with you. Go figure. Does this answer the question about art and communication? I guess so. Ugh.

Several days later and after.....

Joy, joy, joy, - a letter in response to mine sent from beyond the moat, or thrown from atop the sinking mast, or slid from behind the hand deflecting despair, as you so well put it. I can't tell you what a profound effect it had upon me. A squeak from the bedroom is finally heard by someone having coffee in the kitchen. Reality rears its head. Steve 'responds' to my letters, of course, but once written he merely casts them into the air and I must run to pick them up not knowing which is for me. But yours hits the spot. I love your sentence: "Not in the sense of Valéry's 'no one thinks,' but in the day to day intellectual sense of being able to put into words, spoken or writeen, the events of the day, the reading of the day, of the appearance of the day, the sense or even the lack of sense of the day, of days past and of days to come, all based on an active memory, 'at my fingertips' sort of memory that operates mostly unbidden, involuntarily brings the sort of order that a lifetime of reading, sporadic and undisciplined, a lifetime of being alive with moments of awareness, a walking encyclopedia of quotations carried in no particular order, very few of which are original, that enables one to speak out as if out of a continual stream of words, or write letters say as if out of a continuous flow of substantive prose, phrases from the building of a coherent edifice, the monument of oneself as an ongoing project, something that people can *recognize* and relate to their ongoing project meaningfully." This I understand to mean: one should be able "to separate what should not be brought to the dinner," and present a self. A tall order. I don't know about Eleanor, but I certainly can't make such a separation. I think she planted that idea in your head. In fact, in point of fact, as Jennifer Jones would put it, I am of all whom I know the least able to accomplish this unremarkable feat of humanity. Like you, I always begin my letters with the provisio "I can't write" meaning by that, 1) my education was so poor I literally don't know how, and 2) I don't have anything I know how to communicate or, rather, I have never felt the necessity to communicate anything to anybody so why should I now, or rather, I didn't know people could communicate - is that why they write and speak? Gee, I always thought it was to conceal. The difference is that I go on to explain why I can't write or have nothing to communicate. And this I take it is what you mean when you say, unlike me, that you are "unfocused, to say the least, and get no pleasure in saying it, indeed I feel guilty for whining, berating myself for not being able to separate"..... Unlike you, that is I figure that this is all I am capable of, and rather than keeping my contradictory self abberations a matter of silent rumination why not put them out in the air, try to force myself to make sense of them in the real world, as it were, and see what happens. For they are, of course, in you as well as in me, frauds, illusions brought about by the fever of illness. They must be communicated - but seriously, as a doctor would report each change in a critically wounded patient. Just as one can not logically write "I can not write," so too can one not logically berate oneself. It is important to know why we believe we can (No one else believes us, you know, when we say it unless, of course, they are ill as well). What illness makes such an illogical belief possible? Makes us into clowns or things of wonder in the eyes of others (auto-mechanics, the girl behind the counter, the garbage man, one's own wife, etc.)? The belief is tantamount to believing 2+2 equals 5, and insisting upon it in public. What can the world do with such creatures? Yet, we demand reverence - as a San Diego among the stupid Indians (who really knew better)..

When I sit down to write a letter it is as though I am entering a wrestling match on rotting dilapidated warf wet with fog. . My sleazy opponent is who I think I am, he is dressed as Plastic Man and grins a lot. In the ring, using every ounce of my strength, I bend and twist his body; I bring his shoulders to his belly-button, his head to his arse, then, standing back, laugh, saying "you are an impossible being. No one in their right mind could do that!" But my opponent is sly and devious, as you can imagine. Sometimes he bends me just as hard and roars with glee. Only a few are invited to these vaguely pornographic matches (not nearly as much as your movies would be!), but as I make friends quickly they are multiplying: Nietszche, Sisley, Benjamin, Johnson, Kemp, Capt. Canot, Flaubert, etc.. Sometimes I even send them into the ring for relief. The rules are always the same: the ring must always be well-lit and every bend and twist held for at least two minutes for accurate description in the blow by blow accounts published in my sports column. Winning is passé. I have been in the ring only a couple of years now, though I have seen my opponent warping about the piers for a long time. A new friendship is developing as I introduce him to my friends. It is the only game in town that really interests me. Unlike Don Jose, I have not got around to hanging over the ropes and asking Micaela "when are you leaving?" Hopefully, she is still there (that is why your letter is so important to me). I don't know how many rounds are left to this match, but, fifty years later, I feel like Rocky.

So this letter won't be a complete bust I send you some spare tapes of a program I took off the air in New York. The recording is pretty lousy at times, better at others - I had a very cheap radio.

My view of World History: If all the anthropological evidence points to any conclusion it is to the fact that for for the first forty thousand years of human existence women were the drudges and were so if men performed three basic functions: 1) got erections, got food, and gave protection to the hearth. This made them happy as all get-out. Once the men got the bright idea of inventing labor saving devices for the women to distract their eternal gaze for a moment, they snuck off and invented civilization. Before they knew it, women were living with many labor saving devices but also in cities with many winding streets and shaded windows where men could hide. They have resented this cunning for the past eight thousand years. Nor have they ever forgiven.

Keep the letters flying. They spur only health and good-cheer. Mount your camel, don your turbin and head for Petra. Look for treasure, under moonlit skies, on the desert floor of the self. Leave your graffitti etched on ancient, perhaps sacred, walls. As Pat Riley would say: *Leave footprints!* (I will carry a flashlight.)

TWENTY stories above the snow-swathed construction beehive ground zero has become, the very veteran landscape architect Peter Walker contemplates a view he was recently commissioned, with the greatest of fanfare, at the 11th hour of the World Trade Center memorial competition, to change for the better.

Michael Kamber for The New

artistic problem here is h
et people to see nothing a
something."

PETER WALKER

USA 37

FIRST FLIGHT

Ted /itea

March 23, 1994

Dear Ted,

   After getting your letter, it suddenly seemed all wrong for me to
use a computer and _process_ my thoughts to you. One can't call it
typing, because there's no type, and it's certainly not writing but
more like conjuring millions of invisible witches who can instantly
turn into words. I bet there's a sub-category of "alphabetical
apparitions" in your Dover book on _The Hammer of Witchcraft_ or
whatever it's called (See also Rabelais' new listings from the
Bibliothéque Saint Victoir: _The Mumbling Devotion of the Celestine
Friars_, _The Paring-Shovel of the Theologues_, _The Push-Forward of the
Alchemists_, _The Niddy-Noddy of the Satchel-Loaded Seekers_, _Ars
Honeste Fartandi in Societate_, _The Cobbled Shoe of Humility_, _The
Crucible of Contemplation_, etc.)

   And March 23 will soon be laughable as well, because I'm going to
go back and forth adding and subtracting words in hyperspace. I could
mark off the separate sections, but that wouldn't be accurate either.
Just take the date as the time I received your letter, plunked myself
into my easy chair, and brought myself back to one of those places I
belong, namely, hearing your voice. I belong in school as well, but
it does its best to make me think otherwise. Nancy and I compare the
hearts written on our sleeves--you know that conversation, I'm sure.

   As for dating _your_ letter, I would place it c. 1855, not Paris,
though, but more like St. Petersburg. Apropos of Wagner and the
"little French decadents," Nietzche says that "in St. Petersburg they
have thoughts the French haven't even dreamed of yet." Everything
about your letter made me feel at odds with my "Mac Plus." Mac. The
name alone is drek. An article in the _Times_ talks about the instant
expectations we now have because of computer chips. According to
Steve Mann, nobody likes busy signals any more. Everybody expects
answering machines, voice mail, E mail, faxes...Big Fax. As I read
him, I thought, No, I really dislike answering machines. A busy
signal tells me someone's there, and a call waiting intrusion drives
me to distraction. Russell Baker says that nowadays telephones
actually _keep_ us from speaking to someone. The other night I caught
John Corry on the Charlie Rose show. Corry worked for 30 years or so
on the _Times_ (he wrote a book about it, which just came out, along
with Edwin Diamond's _Behind the Times_). One day Corry found a room at
the Times filled with 1940s upright Remingtons, the big square ones
with a deep inset for the keys, which he says he prefers to anything
else. The day after the Hasidic kids were shot on the Brooklyn
Bridge, _The Post_ had almost immediate photographs of the aftermath,
with an inset photo of some old timer with a press card in his hat.
For a minute, I was thrown back to 1935, that's how powerful the
image was. It turns out that he was an old press photographer who had
been laid off at _The Post_ but was still driving around with his
equipment and was right there on the scene--best photos of the whole
affair, and he was hired back. Oh yes, and he wrote the lead article
as well, with real punch to it, like you just don't see any more--the
genuine article. He could have been James Gleason in "Meet John Doe."

Huddleston has it right, and even in the early 60s, Paris was very different from what came afterwards. Hemingway has a wonderful description of the Rue Mouffetard in "Kilimanjaro," but it's just a schlock street now, full of fake watches and pathetic shops. By the time I saw Paris again after 23 years, all the street life had disappeared, including the oyster shuckers and crepe makers, with their homemade stoves and frying pans. Now they have "creperies"-- whole restaurants devoted to sitting down and getting fat. You end up feeling more and more like a child that has to stay in place: buckle up, don't smoke, don't say nasty words, don't burn leaves, eat this, do that. It's really stunning how invaded we've become. Paris still had something in the early 60s, which was probably the tail end of what Huddleston experienced. And the traffic I saw! I still remember the sheer variety of things that moved--little minicars welded together from motorcycles and small pick-ups, motorized bicycles and "mobilettes," which were motorized bikes in the shape of motorcycles, along with puppet theaters, magic shows, circus dancers, and the chalk painters doing imitation Raphaels on the sidewalks--all this was still on the streets in '61. Now it feels like a combination of tidiness and EuroMafia real estate. No, it's not the 19th century, but they saw it coming. Perhaps Chateaubriand would have loved it. More meat to chew upon. I don't know. In his introduction, Spengler lists a half a dozen things from physics to empire building that "Goethe would have revelled in." Cendrars certainly did. But when the Germans invaded, he retreated to a house in south-central France (where they had stolen nearly all of his books) and came out of three-years' solitude with 1,500 pages of autobiography. It's nice to know that EuroDisney is on the skids in France.

Public events seem more freaky and dwarf-like than ever before. Newsweek mentions a Serbian commander target practicing from an encampment in a Jewish cemetary overlooking Sarajevo. His unit operates under a black and white skull-and-crossbones flag, and he reads Soldier of Fortune magazines for the latest fashions. A lot of Arab terrorist commanders apparently do as well, from what I've read of hotel lobbies in Damascus. It all seems insane, murderous and comic all at once. The hottest item right now is whether or not Bill and Hillary's legal actions were really legal. "We want to know," says one Yale law professor, "if Hillary Clinton's avoidance of the appearance of impropriety was sufficiently ethical." Or: "As far as we can tell, there is nothing wrong in making a legal business speculation." This is said in all seriousness, as if these mayvens were not only talking to morons but were also morons themselves. I send you a few gleanings from the public looney bin.

I loved your thumb-nail historical scenes. It's the kind of thing that can't come out in talk. We should be writing history books together, or something (writing, not buying them--we could make our own Book of the Month Club if we could harness all that neurotic energy). Your descriptions of the 19th century are so true, and they confirmed my feelings about Cendrars as well. He has that same sense of global discovery, exile in distant places, and aesthetic wonder and invention you describe, right down to making poetry out of the Trans-Siberian and icebergs off Patagonia. This is near the beginning of his "Panama, or the Adventures of My Seven Uncles" (1918):

Books
There are books that speak of the Panama Canal
I don't know what the library catalogues say
And I don't listen to the financial journals
Even though our daily prayers come from the bulletins of the Bourse

The Panama Canal is entwined with my infancy
I played under the table
I dissected flies
My mother told me the adventures of her seven brothers
Of my seven uncles
And when she received those dazzling letters!
Those letters with their beautiful, exotic stamps and
        epigraphs from Rimbaud
She didn't tell me anything that day
And I remained sad under my table

It's also around that time that I read the history of the
    earthquake of Lisbon
But I really think
That the crash of Panama is of more universal significance
Because it completely upset my infancy.

. . . I had a beautiful picture book
A large greyhound called Dourak
An English maid
Banker
My father lost 3/4 of his fortune
Like many honest people who lost their money in the crash,
My father
Less stupid
Lost other people's money,
Pistol shots.
My mother cried.
And that night they sent me to sleep with the English maid.

. . . It's the Panama crash that made me a poet!
It's amazing
Everyone in my generation is like that
Young people
Who suffered strange ricochets
One doesn't play any longer with furniture
One doesn't play any longer with antiques
One breaks dishes always and everywhere
One embarks
One chases whales
One kills walruses
One is always afraid of tse-tse flies
Because we don't like to sleep.

... My uncle said
I am a butcher in Galveston
The slaughter houses are 24 kilometers from the city
It's I who gather the bloody animals, in the evening, all
    along the sea
And when I pass the octopuses rise in the air
Setting sun . . .
And there was something else
Sadness
And homesickness.

The original is wonderful. Parts of <u>Mahagonny</u> sound like "Panama" but 15 years later and a lot less healthy, though a brilliant thing.

As for "who or what is it all for?"--Melville writes in his middle east journals that he stood on a bridge in Istanbul one day over-looking thousands of people moving about, when all of a sudden his mind started to reel and he felt completely nauseated to see that swarming ant hill down below. I had that same life-sickness in front of Karnak and certain Roman ruins. There was something utterly <u>creepy</u> about facing all that oblivion. To stand in front of the Saqara pyramid and to think that it was ancient when Plato was there was just too weird. No Napoleon complex for me, who apparently told his men before the Battle of the Nile: "Soldiers of France, four hundred centuries are looking down at you!" Ha! 4,000 year-old necropoli, the walls and columns filled with hieroglyphics, all speaking to an empty, baking desert. In high school, I loved "Ozymandias." You know that one? It's the same picture--a busted monument in the desert proclaiming the eternal might of the king, and nothing else remains: "The lone and level sands stretch far away." That's one way I hear your questions: "What point is there speaking into the void?" Our ancestors had no trouble, though, because they <u>knew</u> that history goes that way, and they were filled with the excitement of studying it all over again. Napoleon brought over 100 scholars with him, and Champollion taught us how to read those hieroglyphs (if I could have read them, I would not have been Karnak-sick). That's how Gibbon began--by sitting at the Roman Forum. This used to be called the historical sense, and it was the common property of the educated.

> When I see by Time's fell hand defaced
> The outward pomp of buried age . . .

Something like that. That's what Shakespeare was for--to give one a sense of place in the life of things. I saw a wonderful exhibit last year at the Pierpont Morgan of Hubert Robert, Piranesi, and other 18th-century painters and engravers--wonderful scenes of tourists and antiquarians walking in small groups through the Roman ruins and pointing to the sights. Constable has the same image in one of those Salisbury Cathedral paintings of his at the Frick or Met--a man and woman on a tree-lined path, the cathedral before them across the meadow, the man (Bishop Fischer?) pointing with his cane. (Did I write this to you once before? It's still on my mind.)

Alright, so Constable and Fischer lived with that cathedral and spoke to it, and maybe we're just looking into nothingness, as Spengler says we are, but I can't make a theory out of it, and anyway it's a living thought for him as well. Van Gogh says that we still have a flat-earth conception of life and death, but "Life is also round. We take a railway to Paris and a stage coach to Tarascon. We take life to travel to a star." When I'm in front of a Ruisdael, I'm in 1652. Why not? A piece of the living past is right in front of me, and the passing of the moment too--clouds, sun-swept fields, two villagers walking on a sandy road, windmill in the distance, Ruisdael's hand everywhere--and all of it saturated with that mystery of drawing and oil painting which still holds the experts in awe. Some Polish poet recently wrote a book about Dutch painting and said that when he was in Holland, he kept looking for that 17th-century landscape and couldn't find it anywhere; but in fact it was changing for Ruisdael as well. He simply understood the metaphysics of it all. It's amazing how _alive_ a Ruisdael is compared to most Dutch landscapes, which are very beautiful but always remain pictures, whereas for Ruisdael, painting was just his starting point (Constable actually disliked the idea of making pictures, which he contrasted with "the Art"). When Rembrandt went on sketching tours around Amsterdam, he only drew things that were old and out of date-- medieval forts, ancient trees, old-fashioned cottages, and even the tearing down of the old town hall in Amsterdam, while others waited to paint the new one after it was built. That poet was looking in the wrong place to find those 17th-century fields. Of course they're not in Holland any more. They're in the Ruisdaels now. He _knew_ that everything changes. That's what his landscapes are all about. We're so irreligious that we don't have any way of understanding life any more. But if I can stand in front of "Entrance to a Village" and immerse myself in every thought and feeling that goes through me at the time, well... there it is and there I am. I've had these moments before, with Balzac especially. I'm right there in Paris in 1842 walking up that flight of stairs in _Père Goriot_; yet I spend so little time "living myself into" those experiences and so much time with drek. I guess that's the other way I understand your questions: why am I not more present to myself? When I see those exhibits or go into any artist's work, I can eat myself alive in feeling so completely _fitful_, so unfocused and unselfsustained. Time was when art rendered life with a sense of permanence, you know, lifting it into something rich, focused, and complete (after a few recent conversations with Len J., I decided that what bothered me, both in his work and in himself, is that he is so _unsatisfying_. It's the best way I have to sum up his effect on me). And speaking of art and the Jenkin issue all at once, two years ago in Paris I spent an afternoon in a wonderful museum of French folklore and found myself relating the exhibits to the art of the time, to Watteau, Mozart, and Balzac, and feeling that without those larger visions, the pieces themselves had a kind of narrowness and cramped beauty that needed more air and light to reveal their richness. I remember going through a whole exhibit of 19th-century French board games, truly wonderful-- ecclesiastical games (see who gets to faith, hope, and charity first --watch that sin!)--military games (pick a card and see if you get a French division or an attack by wild savages), and I realized that I could never see them any other way but through everything else that had filtered through me--Daumier lithographs, scenes out of Balzac, Rimbaud's _Season in Hell_ ("I loved old signboards, naive rhythms, tales from the days of our grandmothers, old-fashioned Latin poems," etc.) I love what I've acquired and I loved reading your evocations, but it seems so impossible to hold onto such moments of "entering into" life and history, let alone sustaining them. Kafka says that a writer should sink his teeth into his writing desk and not let go.

The sickness flows in and out of us. It too is part of the world. It's hard to wrap one's mind around the fact that _everything_ that means anything, meaning itself, is being buried in shit or getting blown to hell. What George Sand mentioned to Flaubert about revolutionaries is becoming true of everything today: "I have lived with these people and looked into their souls and found one thing underneath: no principles." That's what nihilism means. At bottom, there's nothing there. I just picked up a copy of Paul Johnson's Intellectuals (along with his history of the Jews and The Birth of the Modern). It's totally depressing. The fact that I'm devouring these sick biographies doesn't make it any the less dismal. So here I am, having dates with women fitfully, the latest, several times, with an Argentinian lady of interesting dimensions though not for me--and then I go to Intellectuals and what do I find? Looney ideas, women by the truck load, money rolling in. Intellectuals. I'm writing it with a Jewish sneer--intellektchuvals, as in:

> So you know, Sam, I meet dis intellektchuval and he tells me he's shtupping six, seven goils a veek. So I says, oh yeah? Yeah, he sez, and vat's more, I got dis vuman vat teaches philosophy and writes books like you vouldn't believe. I ken vipe de floor vit her and she luffs it. Dese Barnard goils come vit dese taperecorders, but right avay I'm shtupping them. Ya vant philosophy? Put dat stoopid machine avay. Shtupping foist. Den ve tink. And boy can I write, maybe five-six hunded pages a veek. And lectures, shemctures, God knows vat. So how's by you?

Put a French, German, or British accent on it and it comes out smelling roses. Karl Marx. I'll tell you what I think about him now that I've read Johnson. Remember your point that Marxism, in the end, offered the only modern critique of western life? Something like that. And I said to you that there were other critiques, and more interesting ones than his. But now I go back to my rule of thumb: no matter what they say, the opposite is true. In other words, Marx may be the only modern thinker who doesn't offer a critique. Every once in a while, Johnson says something like, "And here we come to an irony that is typical of what one finds in the lives of these intellectuals," at which point, he mentions something completely loopy about these guys, something that contradicts what they said they stood for a minute ago. In fact, the more they yell from the rooftops, the more it's guaranteed that the opposite is the way they actually act. And never mind their actions. The chaos is right there in the writings themselves. It's all the same thing--their ideas are completely at war with each other without the author's consciousness. Derrida says flatly that language is indeterminate, and Marx says that history is built on "material" class struggles that will lead to something for which history has no material precedent. How? By the magic of "scientific socialism"! And all the time he's arguing on behalf of "materialism" he never makes any money himself, never sets foot in a factory, has no connections with the working class, and is blind to the sheer pace of economic development happening right before his eyes. Instead, he takes out-of-date figures on problems in the English economy to attack the system through which they've been gathered for the sake of correcting them! Some critique. Spengler makes the observation that radicals actually don't like to work. And as for "the iron laws" of class struggle, Johnson says in The Birth of the Modern that the very idea of classes was a fiction to Coleridge, who believed that economic and political life was simply too permeable to justify the concept. The New Left likes to say that "phony" communism is dead, but Marxism is dead by virtue of its own ideas and by the way it came about: Biblical prophecy in clothing borrowed from the anti-clerical side of the Enlightenment. This from the ideology that made "inherent contradictions" a principle of thought when it came to everything but itself. I was surprised to learn from Johnson's A History of the Jews that many radicals came from old rabbinical families--not just Marx. Rosa Luxemburg's went back to the 12th century! In The Hour of Decision, Spengler notes that disaffected religious types were prominent in the French Revolution and that their utopias represent a watered-down version of medieval Christian social consciousness (which was always very strong in English literature). When I was in France with Clover two years ago, I appreciated for the first time the degree of anti-clerical hatred in the Revolution. Throughout Normandy, we saw monasteries, including Mont. St. Michel, which had been in existence for six hundred years or more, only to be closed by order of revolutionary tribunals. Johnson says that Chateaubriand's Genius of Christianity was a major response to these attacks.

Apropos of Intellectuals, I found a piece by F. Scott Fitzgerald called "Pasting it Together" (1938), which was reprinted in the 1973, 40th anniversary issue of Esquire. I think it's part of The Crack-Up now. It's only two pages long but wonderful. His disillusionment, he says, involved "the usual horses shot from under me--Punctured Pride, Thwarted Expectations, Faithless, Show-off, Hard Hit, Never Again. And after a while I wasn't twenty-five, then not even thirty-five, and nothing was quite as good." Then it dawned on him that he'd fallen apart in a similar way once before in college:

> Only gradually did a certain family resemblance come through--an overextension of the flank, a burning of the candle at both ends; a call upon physical resources that I did not command, like a man overdrawing at his bank . . . a feeling that I was standing at twilight on a deserted range, with an empty rifle in my hands and the targets down. No problem set --simply a silence with only the sound of my own breathing.

> In this silence there was a vast irresponsibility toward every obligation, a deflation of all my values. A passionate belief in order, a disregard of motives or consequences in favor of guesswork and prophecy, a feeling that craft and industry would have a place in any world--one by one, these and other convictions were swept away. I saw that the novel, which at my maturity was the strongest and supplest medium for conveying thought and emotion from one human being to another, was becoming subordinated to a mechanical and communal art that, whether in the hands of Hollywood merchants or Russian idealists, was capable of reflecting only the tritest thought, the most obvious emotion. It was an art in which words were subordinate to images, where personality was worn down to the inevitable low gear of collaboration . . . there was a rankling indignity, that to me had become almost an obsession, in seeing the power of the written word subordinated to another power, a more glittering, a grosser power.

> I set that down as an example of what haunted me during the long night-- this was something I could neither accept nor struggle against, something which tended to make my efforts obsolescent, as the chain stores have crippled the small merchant, an exterior force, unbeatable--

> (I have the sense of lecturing now, looking at a watch on the desk before me and seeing how many more minutes--)

In another article in the issue, Arnold Gingrich, the publisher, compares Fitzgerald and Hemingway on the subject of crack-ups and says that "They were both changing when I knew them, but I felt that Scott was changing for the better, while Ernest was changing for the worse. . . . Aside from two major lapses . . . Scott hadn't had a drink in three years before he died. On the other hand, Ernest, from all I heard after that, was in the process of crossing the great divide between great drinkers and great drunks." He also says that Fitzgerald's taste in clothes never left him:

> In contrast, a mental snapshot of Ernest at about the same time, pulled at random from memory's file, showing a hulking creature looking as if he were about to burst the seams of a blue tweed suit (cut by O'Rossen in the Place Vendôme--a ladies' tailor, for god sake) with the sleeves and the pant legs both too short, an oatmeal flannel shirt with the collar unevenly turned down and a russet wool tie askew, with pebbly-grained thick-soled shoes of a wrong shade of liverish brown. The general effect is that of items left over from a rummage sale.

Fitzgerald came in for a lot of abuse by Hemingway (though Gingrich says that his pages on Scott in A Moveable Feast are excellent--which fits with Johnson's assessment that when it came to literature, Hemingway still had his integrity). Gingrich also notes that when Fitzgerald was at his height, he brought the relatively unknown Hemingway to the attention of Scribner's, and he makes it clear that if Fitzgerald had wanted to, he could have put down Hemingway far more effectively than Hemingway did him, as in: "Ernest was always ready to lend a helping hand to those on the rung above him." But instead he apparently never stopped insisting on Hemingway's greatness as a writer. As for his drinking, Gingrich doesn't think of him as a drunk but more in line with O. Henry's quip that "I was born eight drinks under par." Fitzgerald comes across a lot cleaner than Hemingway. It would be interesting to do another kind of Intellectuals, with people like Scott, Cendrars, and Nadezhda Mandelstam. Fitzgerald, by the way, says that "For twenty years a certain man had been my intellectual conscience. That was Edmund Wilson." And he ends the piece this way:

> (The watch is past the hour and I have barely reached my thesis. I have some doubts as to whether this is of general interest but if anyone wants more, there is plenty left, and your editor will tell you. If you've had enough, say so--but not too loud, because I have the feeling that someone, I'm not sure who, is sound asleep--someone who could have helped me to keep my shop open. It wasn't Lenin, and it wasn't God.)

Your letter has that same Fitzgerald ring to it, problems and all, and open, clean, and sharp. It gives me a wonderful sense of permission to keep thinking for myself. Breton sounds like a complete idiot by comparison: "We are wrathful against present reality." Cendrars couldn't stomach any of them. His descriptions of modernist housing projects in Paris should be nailed to the door of every school of architecture. And speaking of what was lost in the First World War, if I didn't already mention it, Cendrars says that it killed off a whole generation of uncorrupted workers, turn-of-the-century kids he grew up with whose type he never saw in France again.

I'm looking forward to NM. I don't think I want to wait till August and just may tell Trieber that I'd rather go off in June and make up the sessions in July. I'm tired of being there in the same old month, when everything is baking hot, and it would be great to see Sonya right after my classes and tromp around with you as soon as I can. I'm itching to see her now that her college days are over and she's living in Albuquerque, which she really likes. She seems to be in line for a job editing photos on Channel 13 (?) news out there. She made some changes with amazing speed the moment she got back to Santa Fe after Xmas. I should be so sane, or rather, I should be as sane for myself as I was for her.

From one he who's gotta be he to another,

Steve

PS It's gratifying to see that the advanced state of social awareness among the sun people in Central and South Africa has finally made front-page news.

But the sun people at all costs! According to a <u>Times</u> article on Special Ed, "Studies show teachers refer kids who bother them, and we've been able to demonstrate that specifically African-American males demonstrate behavior that bothers teachers." So, my friend, you were "bothered" by disturbed sun people, were you? There's a stunning conclusion to be drawn: black students and parents who are similarly "bothered" are not children of Helios but dark ice people!

Steve & Carol

May your holidays be free
of pain —
Come, join the dance of life

Love,
Ruby & Ted

April 29, '94

Dear Ted,

Boil my brains but they must be as thick as whale omelettes at TRS, or don't they have your address? And another thing, Black Adder. It's not enough that they don't have your address, but they don't have my name either. They must be a bunch of thickos over there. I mean, what would it take for them to get it right? Either way? A book the size of Samuel Johnson's dictionary with our addresses written a hundred thousand times? Address Book II? The Return of Killer Address Book? Anyway, I found the letter under a pile of royal papers and am sending it to Sarabande Circle, where it will do some good, or maybe won't.

Is there a Gavotte Lane?

Hornpipe Avenue?

Everyone lets me know you've written to them--Len, David, Clover, and now Nancy. If you keep it up, I'm guaranteed at least once a month to hear someone say "Ted just wrote to me." In time, I will understand my feelings about these little moments and develop a mechanical response instead of searching for a fresh reply each time I hear that "Ted wrote to me" (right now it depends on who tells me, how they tell me, what time of the day they tell me, what the weather was like that morning, etc.) Nancy was pleased by your invite and continues to be one of the few people (and the only woman) in the department who doesn't stop my mind two minutes into a conversation.

I am reading a collection of F. Scott Fitzgerald's college writings, together with interviews and assorted essays by and about him from 1915 to the 1930s, which I found among the paperbacks of that woman on Court Street. Yes, I wrote you about Fitzgerald, didn't I? And a few weeks later this odd collection comes my way. The Princeton pieces sounds like this:

> Ethel had her shot of brandy while she powdered for the ball,
> If a quart of wine was handy she was sure to drink it all;
> People thought she was a dandy--called her Ethyl Alcohol.

By twenty-two he's writing stories all the time (rejected) and a novel (rejected) and trying to get a newspaper job in New York (rejected)--In 1919 he's got nearly 20 stories and 122 rejection slips "pinned in a frieze about my room." Goes back home to St. Paul disgusted and writes This Side of Paradise.

He made a list in '27 of the most influential books in his life from 14 to 30, among them The Picture of Dorian Gray (at 18), Sinister Street, by Compton MacKenzie (20), Tono Bungay (22), The Genealogy of Morals (24), Karamazov (26), Ludendorf's Memoirs (28), and, yes, The Decline of the West (30), which one interviewer around that time calls "his favorite book":

233

There is now no mind of the race, there is now no great old man of the tribe, there are no longer any feet to sit at. People have to stage sham battles in their own minds.

Interviewer: Why isn't it any fun to be an American?

Because it's too big to get your hands on. Because it's a woman's country. Because its very nice and its various local necessities have made it impossible for an American to have a real credo. After all, an American is condemned to saying, "I don't like this." He has never had time--and I mean time, the kind of inspired hush that people make for themselves in which to want to be or to do on the scale and with all the arrogant assumptions with which great races make great dreams.

And he was correct, almost to the year, when he said in '27 that "The next fifteen years will show how much resistance there is in the American race. The only thing that can make it worth while to be an American is a life and death struggle, a national testing. After that it may be possible for a man to say 'I'm an American' as a man might say 'I'm a Frenchman.'"

Yet we, whose families came through that test, came of age right at the time that the nation began to fall through the bottom and we as well. First there's an incredible outpouring of books, films, plays, paintings, highways, homes, and education in the 50s, and then it all snaps back to Fitzgerald's USA in '27, only grosser still:

Everything in New York [after 3 years in Paris] seems mouldy, rotten. We went to the night clubs. It was like going to a big mining camp in the boom days. I got a sensation of horror. There were these fat men smoking fat cigars and big butter and egg men and half nude women. There was nothing fine about it all. It was vulgarity without the faintest trace of redeeming wit. Coming from Paris to New York was like plunging from a moral world to a state of moral anarchy. It gave me a fear that everyone had gone crazy--that everything was being done for nothing; that human lives were being exploited for nothing.

He is all meat and potatoes, even when he borders on the commonplace. He has a tone that I find wonderful and which I haven't heard in any modern American with any pretense of talking about what is going on. And there's something clarifying and reassuring about him. He has the same effect that Flaubert's letters had on me. And he's amazingly consistent. I can open him up anywhere and be satisfied. From the little I know, he seems to have had the most articulate crack-up of any American writer after Melville.

Found in Spengler the other day: "Equal rights: the right to be equally vulgar."

Two items enclosed from the last few days. You might be interested to know that Pacific made the _Times_'s most wanted list. It's up there with James Monroe for closing, or something.

I am talking it up, passing out copies of my _Academic Questions_ article right and left, including folks at other schools, as well as making some contacts, getting calls from Kingsboro C.C. about how I run our Writing Center and deal with budgets, etc. The other day I gave a talk to about 25 teachers in the department about how to make things run better. I'm a regular tornado. Something I realized after that talk (others were quite casual, in other words, unprepared) is that I actually work harder than most, maybe more than anyone there (not to mention _smarter_--that one finally came through as well). Most are lazy, even when they're bright--no, not bright, just cunning. But you know what Hamlet says to Gertrude when he tells her he's being packed off to England with Rozencrantz and Guildenstern and that he knows something's afoot: "It shall go hard/ But I will delve one yard below their mines/ And blow them at the moon." My presentation tunneled right down, and they loved it. All this is strategic, as I see the multiculties gnawing away at this and that, while everything at school gets worse. But the thing that amazes me most is how easily I took the opportunity last week when I told the remedial writing coordinator that I wanted to give a presentation at our day-long "retreat." I spent some serious time thinking it out and talking to Nancy (talk about powerful race qualities), was the first to speak, and fairly blew people away with everything I covered in 15 minutes--all written out, clear as a bell, so much so that the chairman (Phil of problematic fatherhood) asked me to put a copy of it in everyone's mailbox in the dep't (all voices agreeing). There is some _merde_, I believe, that will hit the fan, though it may be that I've unplugged the machine, so that the shit will simply stick to it, _because_ . . . I'm on Personnel and Budget, together with Nancy (one other woman, also a friend, is a hitter, though not as heavy as Nancy, and a former P&B person, with personal access to Phil). Plus . . . I run the Writing Center, am part of the remedial writing committee, and am active in our new committee to consider changes in our writing program. The marvellous thing is that it hasn't taken anything out of me. It all seems to be happening quite easily, and at times I feel I'm barely doing it. So much for the challenge of the academy. It's the stuff of which Marty made tempests in teapots, but truly, it's all happening like water running downhill. This too is no accident. Marty had no allies, and certainly no one like Nancy. I even work well with Ruth of the Marxist Compassion. I'm also noticing that in some cases, I've not seen things as clearly as Nance. I need to talk to her about that one, and to Trieber too.

And another thing--remember that old high school friend in Beverley Hills I've been corresponding with? She's in town and coming over for dinner on Thursday--flew in for a wedding. So things are revolving a bit.

I think our mothers sang, "You Gotta Be Me."

May 3, 94 etc.

Dear Ted,

One out, one in. I mailed my last letter to you this morning on Chambers St on my way to my 8 o'clock, got back home at 4, and there it was, a nice, hefty envelope. You are Nietzchean, aren't you? down to 19th-century Spain. N. has interesting things to say about "Carmen" as an antidote to the clammy grayness of Wagner's operas. But northern art in general is wet and dark, and "not of woods only." Ruisdael is saturated with the climate of the North Atlantic; landscapes from the Dutch through Turner, Constable, and the impressionists are never far from water; and the sea appears in every one of Shakespeare's plays, many of which also try to get to midnight as soon as possible. "Midsummer" is all moonlight and water, with contagious vapors thrown in. "Romeo" has blinding sunlight, but only to accentuate the dark. High noon is the moment when Mercutio and Tybalt are killed, the great love scenes take places at night, and the whole romance ends in a tomb. As for painting, intelligent connoisseurs say that the new craze for restoration damages certain original varnishes and dark color shades, turning Poussins and even the impressionists into flat color cartoons. I've seen reproductions of the new Sistine that look garish and grotesque. If that's Michelangelo, I'm Howdy-Doody. When Nietzche talks about sun and dryness, he means the <u>Mediterannean</u> in a classical sense, which is essentially Latin Europe, and mostly the region from Florence to Rome, with Spain and the north African coast thrown in. As for the Renaissance, the Gothic stands between the Italians and the ancient Greeks. Northern Italy manages to look brilliantly clear yet feel somehow dark at the same time, because of the northern influence. I've never been below Rome and actually have never seen a pure classical setting, such as the Greek temple at Paestum. The Roman Forum comes close, but it's overblown classicism and not at all like the photos I've seen of Delphi or the Acropolis, though the landscape itself is brilliantly blue and dazzling (so is Jerusalem, for that matter, but it's not classical at all, and I can't imagine Nietzche going for the Judean hills). In the summer, Tuscany is dry as a bone, if you can imagine a lush landscape in a desert atmosphere. The only thing that saves one in Rome in the summer is the fabulous drinking water in thousands of fountains and old stone troughs. In August, everyone is indoors between 1 and 4, and you live on cold white wine and stay a little drunk all day long.

Ah, for a year to taste the climates from England to Greece! Sounds like Keats' "Nightingale": "O for a beaker of the warm south, the blushful Hippocrene, with beaded bubbles winking at the brim," something like that. Two literary spots moved me in Italy-- one on the main square just off the Uffizi Gallery, where I came upon a house with a plaque that said Dostoevsky finished <u>The Idiot</u> there, and the other a house (oh marvel of unconscious sympathies) at the top of the Spanish Steps in Rome where Keats died. I have a head for these things. When I was there, at 11 one August morning in 1986, the sun already hot, and having come upon it by chance, I was stopped dead in my tracks to realize how close I was to touching the man himself. It was Keats who gave me eyes to see when I opened "Endymion" and read the first line, "A thing of beauty is a joy forever." That was early in the fall semester of '59, and it changed my life on the spot. You know, they all ran south and stopped at various points between Provence and north Africa, Poussin, Corot, Delacroix, Van Gogh, Matisse, Klee, etc. I think Chateaubriand opened the way in the early 1800s with his travels from Paris to Jerusalem--or rather brought northern Europe up to date with its past. His whole sense of the trip was a following of the medieval and renaissance travelers, and his historical extracts go right back to the Crusaders. You can stand inside Mont St Michel on the edge of the Atlantic and <u>feel</u> the urge to Rome, Athens, and Jerusalem. Or you can come upon a house in northern Italy and discover not only that Boccaccio was born there but that the town itself (Certaldo) was on the pilgrim's route. In fact, the town hall has a map of the route from England, France, and Germany right down to Rome. The superhighways only bypass the old road on a direct parallel. All you have to do is get off them and you're as close as you can get to 1325. What a way to live! Fly to London and head south. Europe's like Mexico that way. You can disappear so completely that you wouldn't create enough shards to fill a thimble. My friend Marsha from LA tells me she's met elderly women who've arranged to receive their social security checks in such a way that they can spend all their time traveling between Nepal and Indonesia, rotating with the seasons like birds. She was in the city this week and came over for dinner last night. We talked for hours. She's a Cendrars' woman down to the ground, with a body like Gertrude Stein's and a personality like a well-read Gravel Gerty. She tells me she loves the chaos of India and thrives in places where things go round and around senselessly, hence her life of riches and poverty, investment and debacle, crime and sanity, and on and on. She seems born to get embroiled and come up dancing on her toes, and she knows a million and one people and things. She got on the trolley in the aftermath of the beats and never got off, or rather, hopped one ride after another and convinced every conductor that she had a new transfer slip, even though it was the same one she started out with in the Bronx forty years before.

Farley Mowatt--I haven't read him in years but have a few of his books and had a thing for him in the 70s, though he never took hold the way others did. Two places in Mowatt give an indication of who he is, but there may be others, since I too had no idea he wrote so much. One is the first chapter of <u>People of the Deer</u>, in which he describes a train trip with an uncle into the hinterlands of Canada when he was a boy and saw a giant deer migration stop the train for several hours, which left a permanent mark on his inner life. The other is a battle scene on the march through Italy in the second war (<u>And No Birds Sang</u>--a phrase either from <u>The Web and the Rock</u> or <u>You Can't Go Home Again</u>, though it may go back to scripture). Mowatt was with the Canadian forces in the Italian campaign, and his anguish was such that when he returned, all he wanted to do was disappear and make his way back to the region of the deer. I thought his writing wonderful at the time but there was something too pat to sustain me for long. Thomas Wolfe's passage on Brooklyn on a Sunday morning in March has lasted much longer for me. In fact, Wolfe is always good. Whatever else he is, Mowatt isn't a writer, at least not for me, but this north business is a big thing in Canada, and Glenn Gould got into it as well. As for me, I have my doubts about this love of wilderness. I just bought Charles Bronson's "Chino" at PathMark ($3.49, how can you go wrong?). It was probably set in the middle of Spain, which looks exactly like New Mexico (a Dino DeLaurentis Hispano-Italo-Franco production-- very horsey and a nice flick). At some point, the barren land and absolute crudeness of the corrals, adobes, teepees, and mission church got to me, and I thought of the <u>comfort</u> of culture and history. In this respect, the stoney hills of Israel have a different feel altogether from the west. It's not so much a matter of climate, because I had the same trouble in the Caribbean, which is physically delicious but a kind of exile in paradise. Two weeks seem to be my limit there. I was about to say that I was never there on a sex binge--isolated and deprived as I always see myself --but, in fact, it's not true. Lee and I played house in Jamaica for several weeks, and I still got bored with sun and sand and waving palms. I don't know how the Europeans did it, but then again I don't know how the Vikings managed it away from all their fjords and mist when they headed to Sicily, the middle east, and India.

Enough for now (5/14). I'm about to open the floodgates of final papers and exams and will never send this off if I don't do it now. I still have to make some complicated arrangements juggling trains and planes, but I just don't want to bypass the country every time I come out. I even thought of flying to London in August and wandering from there. Tourists won't be anywhere I want to go.

Good news on your new house! I'm looking forward to the trip but also staving off my summer thoughts because of this brick wall of school work facing me. Maybe when I get my tickets it will all become real to me. Meanwhile there is still some <u>merde</u> to wade through on my way to May 26. My travel plans still begin on 6/10, but I like the idea of staying as long as possible in June, and it's OK as far as Trieber is concerned. I'll simply tack on another session a week in July. That scene goes well too, by the way.

Yes, your tank is bigger than mine, but mine's in color! I have a great 1940s Popeye in the tank corps, in which all he wants to do is get back to Olive Oyl - America's answer to Odysseus and Penelope!

A bientôt,

Steve

Dear Steve,

Rilke opens a letter to a dear friend with a brief inquiry, then starts the third sentence with the world "I". In the following pargraph - after a moments reflection - he writes: "You see that I am, as always, in a hurry to get to myself; I always assume that this theme is of interest - would you like to find your way in again?" Ah, so too is it with me, often without even the false start. In comparison to my letters, however, his are as milked tea to my burnt coffee. But do not think that I receive pleasure from this display of bitter tasting egoism. Far from it! It is a compulsion I inflict upon myself. Ha! That's a fat one!

In your most recent letter you write that the "challenge of the academy" is as easy for you as "water running down hill," but then add that it is also true that, "in some cases," you have "not seen things as clearly as Nance." Although I am glad to hear good news (and especially news about the hit you made in the dept's 'retreat'), I zero in on the dark things. Where, precisely, does that last remark lead?

And yes, one day, in a fit of communicationites, I sent off postcards to a number of people. I don't know why they feel it necessary to tell you that fact. I suppose confirming with you the possibility of receiving postcards from me makes me more real to them - then they can return home, fall in to an oversized armchair, and say with conviction, "I got a postcard from Ted.". I think that if I received a postcard from myself, I too would call to tell you - just to make sure I existed, and it wasn't bogus. (Ever walk by a mirror, and notice with indifferent surprise that you, of all people, have a reflection?)

Mathilde Vollmoeller once said of Cézanne that before Nature he sat "like a dog ... and simply looked" I am much different; I sniff everything, return it home in my mouth, then, raising a leg, piss on it.

Rilke, quoting Fräulein Vollmoeller again: "Here," she said, pointing to the spot [on an unfinished painting of Cézanne], "he knew what he wanted and said it (part of an apple); but there it is still open, because he didn't yet know. He only did what he knew, nothing else." To achieve this clarity of soul in writing is also extremely difficult.

Did I tell you we bought a house? A modest one, in the very heart of suburban Glendale. But it has a wonderful diving pool surrounded by lush greenery. The privacy is immaculate. There was some pressure to buy now, before I go in to offical retirement and, as far as the banks are concerned, lose my salary. We will not move in - if the mortgage application goes well - until after June 16th.

When are you arriving in the west? We will be in the Albuquerque area toward the end of this month, May 20th or so. Let me know. Soon!

Spengler, Fitzgerald, and mothers, what a mix! Some how one thinks immediately of anger, violence, and late-night moroseness in the kitchen. But that's Oedipal me, unable to reconcile father and mother, strength and weakness, reality and desire, indeed, all the yins and yangs of life..The refrain "I gotta be me" (the flip side of "You gotta be me"), can take on the air of struggling to <u>realize</u> a nightmare.

I am not a creature of thought, but of instinct. I feel my way through the universe like a mole. Reality has always seemed evil to me. A place where the rough toss coins, and prostitutes stroll. Down the block I kneel at a pew, hands clasped, praying none discover my sanctuary. When I do leave, as periodically I must, I am armed as Percival and in search of the Grail. I look neither to the left, nor to the right - onward intellectual soldier! Living in reality is hard!

Rostopchin - the man responsible for the burning of Moscow before Napoleon's entance - is described by Count Philippe-Paul deSégur as one who "combined the civilization of modern times with the energy of the ancients." How should deSégur describe me? As one who combines the crass bravado of post-modern times with the sulkiness of the primitive?

The card you sent, "Breaking Up Camp at Sunrise" by Jacob Miller, is truly wonderful. I keep looking at it. The entire history of the settlement of the west is all there - in all its brash "diversity". The vast expanse of sunlit, untilled prairie, the animal drawn migration on to it of thousands of self-hewn, married people and children who place their fate in the hands of wild men riding gun-shot to their caravans of life, and the Indians, in the foreground illumined by fire, dressed in the outlandish reglia of primitve hunters, nonchalantly looking on - says it all (the cradled papoose, also in the foreground, is a sign of their fertile strength). The perspective offers an intimate view of what Fitzgerald called people who had the time "to want to be or do on the scale and with all the arrogant assumptions with which great races make great dreams." The Indians are there to draw the dream to scale, and to remind us of what we leave behind. Is the "dream" worth it?, the Indian scratching her head seems to ask as she looks towards us as we gaze beyond her. Or is it the scratch of the non-comprehension of history? Perhaps both.

Well, this letter does not convey an iota of what I had hoped it would, but let me get it off to you anyway. I do want to know when you are arriving.

Dear Mr. Fish,

My name is Babatunda Olantunjii and I hail from the
Yoruba tribe of famous *maqam*, song and fabulous deeds. I
write to tell you that above all others of the white race I
love you the most. I want to share my hospitality with you.
As my spiritual guide (my *Oni*) I want to invite you to live
in Sun City with me and other heliopolitians and share
freedom like the animals that roamed on top of leaves and
between bushes in my long ago stupendous Yorubaland paradise.
We can eat mock bannanas together, and drink nonchantly of
the fruit of the imported palm. You see, I agree with all
you say. I worship your words (*Shango*) above those of any
other white man. They are, how do you say it, senile. They
would give me great repose to hear their wisdom (*Eshu*)
emanated by you, disembodied of western notions of beauty,
sense, and skin. They are truly the *ur* words before
civilization and are from *Yemanja*, free of western capitalist
arrogance, Oriental yellowness, Polynesian browness, Indian
redness, and Australian demons with blond hair. They are of
the original language of Africa! Truly, you are as black in
soul as me. As we say in Yorubaland of our famous poets,
your pecker must be 18 inches long (*caramba*!) for you write
so well with it! Come. Share it with us. We will, as we do
in my country, put it in a boiling pot and eat it to gain
your wisdom. Then we will stuff it with rosemary, sage, and
thyme, and hang it on the village pole for all Africans to
feel with awe stiffened fingers! I know you will not be
shocked by these things, for you are a man of Africa and know
our wise, hidden ways even before you think; you are as one
with us. There is only one other living white man man who
writes with so much senility, it is the one you call I.
Wallerstein, but truly his name must be 'the man born before
knowledge.' I extend this invitation to him too. If you see
him walking about in this country ask him to visit you. My
emmisarries will arrive soon to abduct you for first you must
be cleansed of all your skin and returned to me freshly
referigerated. I know you shall not mind speaking without
your lips and mind, for you do already. I shall open the icy
door and call upon you every evening, then I can eat in
silence and you shall later speak as an emanating burp
floating out of African lungs, or a spurting fart resounding
as a Tempest in my Toilet Bowl. Ahhh. Yoruba aesthetics are
no where matched in this world, for in the passing of my wind
you will become metaphysically of the *Original Race*, and
terrifically smelled by all!

                              Black Like Me,

                              Prof. Emeritus of Truth
                              Univ. of the Universe
                              Heliopolis, Az

I send you a copy of my latest, Rablesian, communication with the academic world. I do not know how else to respond. How can one speak as a rational human? As Feyerabend has written, it is *Beyond Reason*. So why even try on that score? How else can one reach the New Academic? To engage them in debate is foolish, one would do better to tea with the Cheshire Cat. I figure it might drive Fish to say: "Why, I've never been spoken to like this in my entire life!" You know, like Monty Wolly gruffing at Shirley Temple. Something!

Key to Yoruba glossary: *maqam* = hummed introductions; *Oni* = spiritual overlord; *Sango* = lord of thunder; *Yemanja* = goddess of the sea; *Zungo* = percussion?, *caramba* = great bigness. (Except for *caramba*, all terms are gleaned from the back of a 1960 CBS record called *Zungo!* - the blurb of which says that the music of Babatunde Olatunji was so rhythmic that even the recluse Kerouac at the Village Gate was moved to dance.)

Ted,

Your letter to Fish is delish. And what marvels of Africana scholarship! I had no idea. And you say you got it by deep research into a blurb on a 1960 album cover. . . . Heavy. I feel humbled in the presence of sun scholarship and can barely understand the wisdom embodied in the:

CBS RECORD PLATTER OF WORLD KNOWLEDGE

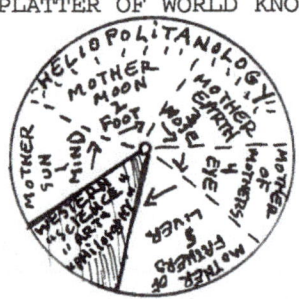

According to Devin, who sat in on a grad. class with Dr. Fish and the Minnows, he just about spoke without lips or voice. I think it's done with Vulcan mind-meld.

I submit the marginalia of an abject novice into <u>Das Grosse Wissenschaft des Sonnes Aufklarungheit</u>, a.k.a. <u>La Haute Connaissance de l'Eclairissement du Soleil</u> (Berlin-Paris-Mombassa 1925)

Alternative High Schools Do a Heroic Job 5/13

To the Editor:

As the superintendent responsible for six of the New York City "low performing schools" cited in an April 30 news article, I object to their linkage with "principals who have presided lazily over failing schools" (editorial, May 3). In each of the schools with which I am associated, the faculty and principals, along with students, are making Herculean efforts to move youngsters toward diplomas, college and gainful employment.

In the 1980's, the State Education Department and Schools Chancellor Nathan Quinones realized the six alternative schools were different from mainstream schools. They were then exempted from the list of "schools under registration review" and the Chancellor's minimum standards.

The six alternative high schools do not accept zoned populations: in five, having dropped out from one, two or three previous schools is an entrance requirement, which means that youngsters are enrolled on any day of the year, bringing with them whatever skills they have into any grade level. By board mandate, these schools also accept large percentages of students suspended from other schools. The median age for entrance is 17.5 years — a full two years above normal entrance into high school. Yet these schools graduate a higher per-

centage of their total registers each year than many regular schools in the city. Last year, they granted 707 diplomas — all to students meeting full state and city requirements.

The Chancellor is correct to demand that all schools and students be held to standards and that high expectations need to be set. But to assume that performance standards of students in our schools are the result of "lazy" professionals borders on slander.   STEPHEN E. PHILLIPS
Superintendent, Alternative
High Schools and Programs
New York, May 3, 1994

Handwritten marginalia:

DIPLOMA

A "HERCULEAN EFFORTS"

IN THE CUTTING EDGE OF ACADEME →

in TELEVISION VIEWING HANGING OUT 101 BEEPER CONSCIOUSNESS →

↑ How could you leave him in the lurch, Dr. T? At least send him a Fish-note, or a prayer to the Sun.

AND PARENT-TEACHER DINNERS ARE FILLED TO OVERFLOWING —

RAISE THE REQUIREMENT TO 10 DROPOUTS FROM 10 PREVIOUS SCHOOLS

← WHEN SO MANY ARE BUSY FUCKING IN EMPTY CLASSROOMS OR DRAWING CIRCLES OF OPPRESSION 5 TIMES A DAY!

Yours for a bigger and better theory,

Dr. Will To Live (a genius)

Ted--I thought you might enjoy this letter. I was flipping the channels Thursday night and hit a C-SPAN tape of "The Trial of Hamlet"--a real giggle, with Justice Kennedy as judge, Ruth Bader-Ginzberg in the jury, lawyers from previous administrations, and assorted "expert" witnesses in forensic psychology from Harvard--debating whether Hamlet was guilty of murdering Polonius or innocent by reason of insanity (the jury found him guilty, since that's the way the issue was stacked--sanity = guilt). I taped the last 1 1/2 hours--an interesting glimpse into the play and our legal-academic elite--at times truly funny, though Ginzberg never laughed and looked like a Charles Adams witch in a Charlie Chaplin film. It was great talking with you (Chinese elegies of separation in the background, etc.)

Steve

The Shakespeare Theater
301 East Capitol Street NE
Washington, D.C. 20003

3/19/94

To the Shakespeare Theater:

   I recently finished teaching Hamlet in my Shakespeare class, so "The Trial of Hamlet" on C-SPAN was a delicious coincidence for me. To my surprise, it was both educational and wonderfully quirky at the same time, a marvellous combination of emotions, as one could see by the audience's serious attention and laughter.

   On the educational side, I wish that more attention had been paid to the historical context. The expert witness for the defence did indeed acknowledge that he was not trained "in the law of Danish royal succession"--a comic-accurate touch that nevertheless avoided the key question of revenge in Renaissance thought. My copy of Elizabethan Revenge Tragedy by Fredson Bowers notes that "The Elizabethan audience would instantly recognize Hamlet's revenge as just, for a revenge for murder either by legal or extra-legal means was still felt as a bounden duty" (90). Dr. Stone came closest to this contextual awareness, but I often felt that the trial was reading present concepts into the past and neglecting well-charted ground.

   This point brings up the only troubling feature in an otherwise delightful event, namely, the jury's recommendation that Ophelia's madness be added to the charge of Hamlet's killing of Polonius, which for me reflected an element of "political correctness" through a feminist sensibility. In all fairness, the jury should have added the other tragedies that occur, since Hamlet's actions are directly or indirectly reponsible for every death in the play except his father's. The jury's added charge recalls a body of feminist literary criticism which claims that Gertrude is wise, that Ophelia is denied her full humanity as a woman, etc. Yes, Hamlet is a misogynist, but when he says "Woman delights not me," he adds "nor man neither," and he attacks both sexes throughout the play. Moreover, although he "speaks daggers" to Gertrude and Ophelia, he reserves real ones for the men. Should he have been an equally opportunity revenger and killed the women as well so as not to show "patriarchal" condescension to them?

   As I said, the "trial" was both educational and delightfully off center and a real treat to watch. I wonder how my students will react when I tell them about it.

                                        Sincerely,

What is dismaying is the sophomoric truth of Stanley Fish's assertion that "Deconstruction is dead in the same way that Freudianism is dead. It is everwhere." (I think he read that article on Freud by T. Nagel in the NY Review of Books a while back: post-modern writers never have their own ideas and mangle those of others.) But are people really committing psychological suicide all around us - by the droves? Is the West self-destructing in self redemptive loathing? Nah! I do everyday, but Sam the butcher doesn't. Or does he?

> Here we go round the Western world,
> The Western world, the Western world
> Here we go round the Western world
> forgetting who we are.
> The West is here, the West is gone,
> And we all fall down.

Self-love after the death of God is really difficult. There is no one to approve of it. O, the stars shine bright deep in the heart of Phoenix - but they are Pascal stars; reminders of the Big Loneliness out there. The Great Father is no longer watching and handing out pats on the back - and mothers only spank. (God as Reality Principle [Descartes' proof], woman as Swamp Principle.) "At bottom, man has lost the faith in his own value when no infinitely valuable whole works through him; i.e., he conceived such a whole in order *TO BE ABLE TO BELIVE IN HIS OWN VALUE*." (Nietsche, *The Will To Power*.)

And what about God? I was told 'God was dead' when I was about 12 or 13 by my friend Paul in a corn field in Berwyn. He said it maliciously, but the point was made. Few childhood experiences match the one I had when Paul spoke those words. The utter novelty of them convinced me that they must be true, and I think it was then, while smoking cornsilk wrapped in newspaper and blowing blue rings into the fly infested mid-West air, that I knew all my ties to the outer world had to be severed. My belief in God humliated me! The world could poke fun at me - once again prove I was a fool. (Blow 299 out of a possible 400.) I think I believed Paul to spite him, to show I was strong enough to accept anything without flinching - like firecrackers thrown at my feet. I gave no indication that I was thunderstruck, but, in that instant, I revised all my thinking, and made myself the unmoved mover. But what a silly experience to base a life-long rejection of God upon! It's time to rethink the issue. From Moses till now the heartfelt struggle to find or abandon God went right over my head. The agonies of St. Augustine, Anselm, Ockham, Aquinas, Pascal, Bach, Dostoyevsky, Tolstoy, and Kierkegaard, now put me to shame. I am still in kindergarten, drawing angel wings in yellow crayon.

And how goes your paper on Nietzsche? Are you convinced that "you have a right to exist"? If so, let me know.

A hundred years ago Ernest Renan wrote: "A century from now, humanity will know pretty much everything that it can know about its past, and then it will be time to stop; for the nature of these studies is that, as soon as they have attained their relative perfection, they begin to demolish themselves." I think we failed to stop.

Under separate cover I send you a new set of Microsoft Word. It took a while - and a few unsoft words.

A hiatus.......

Bric-a-brac I forgot to send. Was not sure if I should include a Jan.'94 NY Times Magazine article on Derrida (do you have it? Have you read it?) - an awful thing written by - in my imagination - a gay ignoramus, one Mitchell Stephens. He idles on women who idolize the way Derrida dresses, who are awed by his elegant, commanding demeanor, who swoon over the romantic, Berstein quality of his white, flowing hair, who marvel at how the color of his swarthy skin plays off his "soft-blue suit and a patterned gray tie that carries on a complicated dialogue with his hair", and are entranced by his involuted yet "piercing eyes." Then, of course, there is Heidegger, DeMan, Nazism, the impossibility of knowing anything, and Derrida's profoundly infantile infatuation with death - "If I have one goal, it is to accept death and dying," he is quoted as saying while wearing his soft-blue suit. Were Derrida not an Algerian Jew with brown eyes, the image Stephens conjures up is one of a debonair Aryan; a sado-mashocistic-handsome-storm-trooper-questing-for-mind-bending-orgies - whom Stephens is simply in love with. It's a dream of Tristan and Izzy ecstatically butt fucking in the heat of the fires of Hell. The essay is a sex letter.

If you recall, in the envelope prededing this, I wrote of the suicides of Benjamin and Foucault, and the transference of this impulse on to the audience by their progeny, well, in the Stephens essay, Derrida, to my muted surprise, is quoted as saying (during a NYC seminar on "Bartleby the Scrivener") that: "What is at stake in this seminar is the death of the other or my own death." (He could just as well have written this as the preface to all his publications.) Precisely! And since we know that Derrida is not about to sacrifice his life on the alter of the intellect, it is his audience's death he expects. Not their physical death, but their psychological death. His is a narcissism so complete that in order for him to survive we must, as egos, die. The Humble Anti-Christ. (Apropos your dropping out of graduate school, my dropping out of graduate school, so too did Derrida: ..."there were scenes of failed or uncompleted examinations and even nervous collapse . . . he preferred not to defend a doctoral disseration until 1980 - when he was 50," reports Stephens. Derrida blames it all on his mother: He remembers himself as "a child about whom people said 'he cries for nothing.'" He was born in 1930. Ten months before, his brother died in infancy. Ten years later an ill, younger brother died. Derrida says that his mother, "whose anxiety I perceived each time I was ill," usurped his precious life. He lived so she could live. Now he lives by assuming others will do the same for him.)

A number of years ago Louis Borges published a story called "Three Versions of Judas." In this story Nils Runeberg, theologian and member of the National Evangelical Union, published *Kristus och Judas* in 1909 and *Dem hemlige Fralsaren* in 1909. Both works attempt to prove that "the treachery of Judas was not accidental; it was a predestined deed which has its mysterious place in the economy of the

Redemption." A man whom God has distinguished from all others deserves from us the best of interpretations of his deeds, Nils argues: "In adultry, there is usally tenderness and self-scarifice; in murder, courage; in profanation and blasphemy, a cerain satanic splendor. Judas elected those offences unvisited by any virtues: abuse of confidence (John 12:6) and informing. He labored with great humility; he thought himself unworthy to be good. Paul has written; *Whoever glorifieth himself, let him glorify himself in God* (1st Corinthians 1:31); Judas sought Hell because the felicity of the Lord sufficed him. He thought that happiness, like good, is a divine attribute and not to be usurped by men." God, argues Runeberg, "lowered himself to be a man for the redemption of the human race; it is reasonable to assume that the sacrifice offered by him was perfect, not invalidated or attenuated by any omission. To limit all that happened to the agony of one afternoon on the cross is blasphemous. To affirm that he was a man and he was incapable of sin contains a contradiction; the attributes of *impeccabilitas* and of *humanitas* are not compatible. Kemnitz admits that the Redeemer could feel fatigue, cold, confusion, hunger and thirst; it is reasonable to admit that he could also sin and be dammed. The famous text *He will sprout like a root in a dry soil; there is no good mien to him, nor beauty; despised of men and the least of them; a man of sorrow, and experienced in heartbreaks* (Isaiah 53:2-3) is for many people a forecast of the Crucified in the hour of his death; for some (as for instance, Hans Lassen Martensen), it is a refutation of the beauty which the vulgar consensus attributes to Christ; for Runeberg, it is a precise prophecy, not of one moment, but of all the atrocious future, in time and eternity, of the Word made flesh. God became a man completely, a man to point of infamy, a man to the point of being reprehensible - all the way to the abyss. In order to save us, He could have chosen *any* of the destinies which together weave the uncertain web of history; He could have been Alexander, or Pythagoras, or Rurik, or Jesus; He chose an infamous destiny: He was Judas."

Such a Redeemer ask nothing less than that we recognize our utter reprehensibility and denounce our self-love - for His greater glory. Does Derrida (or post- modern writers generally) ask anything less of us? How else could Judas write? Is this not absolute nihilism, where the mere flicker of a desire, an aspiration to knowledge, an enjoyment one's grip on reality, is enough for God to send down a bolt of lighting? We should deconstruct ourselves, beg for Hell, and ask forgiveness for even thinking we deserved more - from whom? Why, Derrida, of course! For in reading him one does indeed write one's self out of existence - willingly. (It all amounts to a Nietzschian understanding of Christianity and a reveling in it. Ruby says that Christ died so that we should all feel "survivors guilt" - with, of course, the attendent anger and resentment of having been put in that position.)

Dear Ted,

   I can't help it. I have this craving to have contact with you.
Remember I wrote you once that I felt nervous about feeling free and
easy in writing to you? It's right there, all over again. So I say
to myself, Good. The risk means it's for real. But it's a fact. I
need the connection--and I don't seem to feel it anywhere else in my
life outside of myself. Which is not to say that I'm on Mars. I'm
right here on the ground and better than ever. But no one seems to
grow in any connected way with me--no one except Sonya, and one's
child is always one's child. Is this what's called "individuation"?
The better you get, the more alone you feel? Connection certainly
isn't happening for me in the ladies' department. I seem to be an
unbelievably picky eater--you know, like Kafka's hunger artist, who
said that his fasting had nothing to do with religious convictions.
It was just that he never could find any food he liked. I've been at
that issue nearly a year now, in very real and serious ways, but
it's a lot like my work at school: the better I teach, the more
painful it is to see what the school is like. My getting clearer and
stronger only seems to make my position all the more backwards--in
the same way that I achieved mastery over my dissertation and
professional academic work just at the moment when the field was
going down the tubes. That's exactly how my dates and get-togethers
with women have been. The clearer I get, the less they seem to have.
And all I mean is brains and heart--apparently in short supply on
either side, and impossible as far as a combination is concerned.
But then again, I'm told that I'm only scratching the surface. My
gut feeling is that I'm not living right--not living right with
myself. If I could follow my nose, I'd be okay. And speaking of
noses, did you have the same situation that I had at home of not
being allowed to go to the refrigerator? I literally was not allowed
to open it, the way kids come home and automatically open it to get
a snack. There's a woman in our department, extremely tight, upset,
unhappy, controlling, and holds up her heart as if she were Saint
Catherine bequeathing it to Jesus Christ. Her husband just died, but
you'd never know the difference. The only thing is that now she has
a major loss to corroborate how she's always felt. My mother in
spades. I always feel I'm losing it when Jane crosses my path.She
makes a lot of people uncomfortable, but with me it goes nearly all
the way--what's that you once said--that we're too sensitive?
Whenever I talk to her, my train seems ready to derail. I got about
ten of us together last night at Phil's and we started talking about
the very things Phil should have been taking care of three years
ago. He confessed to being glad to slough things off on the
administration because he was just so swamped as it was. But I know
what that means. It's the Clinton syndrome. Stay swamped and never
take the lead. Anyway, Jane . . . We're talking at one point about
this and that and I can feel every atom in me wants to rush over to
the couch, wrap my arms around her, and make it all OK. I literally
could feel myself ready to go off the tracks. Kundry. Hysterical
women in need of a sexy, militant monk. But I held a steady course,
talked, listened, and came out clean and clear on the other side.
And Jane runs the Comp 1 program, which is a thorn in everybody's
side, so the finesse is to bring her into the planning while making
sure that everyone stays in one piece. It went pretty well, but the

larger picture is a mess. There is now what is becoming known as "the school in a school": Writing for unwed mothers on welfare. Math for ex-cons. Data processing for people who can't speak English. All funded by the city and state. Programs for everyone. I told them about school as life mall (malls are turning into life malls). Everyone laughed, but they aren't ready to do anything. Reality just turns into words for them. I don't know about Nancy either. And Phil has to set the pace, which will never happen, even if he tries. Maybe I'm wrong, but that's how it looks to me.

Just saw some CNN footage of those old-timers parachutting out of C47s in the Normandy celebrations. But the thing that impressed me the most was the refrain "piece of cake" because no one was shooting at them.

The reportage, the whole journalistic world surrounding the commemoration, seemed pitiful to me. At one event, French public school kids were singing away in a chorus, and some CNN woman was gassing away to her male counterpart. "Yes. This is the town where blah blah." "Do you know what the children are singing, Pamela?" "Um . . . oh, yes. It's 'When Johnny Comes Marching Home Again." "Right, Pamela, and on our left . . ." Ted--I couldn't catch the words of the song, but it was "The Battle Hymn of the Republic." Honest to God. Not one TV reporter I heard seemed to know anything. I remember the last commemoration and the sense of awe surrounding it. It's all gone. I don't know where Clinton stands in all of this, but he's part of that diminished stature. There's something inorganic about the whole business--as though he and the reporters had primed themselves for the event but were missing the basics--weren't even connected to them. The whole business seemed empty or shallow, except for those veterans--the only ones who spoke like human beings. The others all seemed incredibly remote. Imagine asking combat paratroopers if they were "scared" to jump--from 2,500 feet, slow as you please, not 500, on a peaceful, sunny day, without any gear. It would be like asking an old infantryman if he was afraid to fire an M-1 on a rifle range. Utterly senseless. But it sells television. I doubt that reporters are allowed to talk like human beings. They're primed for sensation: "Were you scared?" And when ordinary people respond, the answers don't matter any more. You would think that after one or two big smiles, they'd get the idea. But no, they had to keep it up, so that you ended up with one man after another saying exactly the same thing. "Piece of cake." God forbid someone should be normal and actually know what he was doing. "It's amazing, Pamela. He's 71, and he still knows how to speak!"

But the press has it in for Clinton. They just seem to have him and Hillary by the throat, and they won't let go--all those European papers beating up on her by making something out of nothing. The London Sunday Times had "a withering report" that "suggests" Hillary sees herself etc. etc. Her entire bearing, the "motive" for her kissing children, going around with Bill to the sights, "seems clear": to dispel rumors that she's after the presidency. And her clothing? Forget it. Some Italian designer gives her the crushing blow, "no style." Her hats--impossible. Her face, "a goofy-looking smile and bug eyes." I saw those pictures of her. Seemed normal, sort of nice, in fact. But does reality matter any more when you can "reread/rewrite" literature through "reader-response theory"? When there's something out there in cyberspace called "virtual reality"? a.k.a. "infotainment" and "guestimates"? Reality as junk bond salesmanship. And the business about Clinton saluting. Apparently Reagan started that. Some of Clinton's "top advisers were fretting that he should not be saluting at all. They pointed out that, until President Reagan made it a practice, protocol dictated that the troops salute Presidents, but that Presidents not salute back. Dwight D. Eisenhower, they said, never saluted back, and he should have known." It's pathetic. Instead, Clinton "perfects" his salute to get the snap correct, as though a "snap" is correct. Why does he work on it? Because the media attacked his salutes two days before. I'm telling you, they've got him by the throat. In a ceremony at the American cemetary near Anzio on the 4th (not called a ceremony, however, but "a photo opportunity arranged by the White House"), he was greeted by a 73-year old army nurse, "with a saucy smile and the crisp salute of a professional." I'm looking at the picture. She's smiling, but "saucy"? She looks as if she's so proud that she's going to pop all her buttons, but even her smile and salute are turned into a stab at her president. "Mr. Clinton returned the salute slowly, tentatively, a self-conscious gesture that reflected his ambivalence about using the fraternal greeting of a military he once said he 'loathed.'" Did he really say that? I don't believe it for a minute. I bet what he said was that he respected the military as much as anyone but couldn't go along with the war in Vietnam. Wasn't that it? One D-Day veteran called in to CNN to say that he did everything he could to keep his son out of the army in '68, and so did thousands of others, and as far as he was concerned, Vietnam was altogether different than WWII. That's what Clinton comes out of--America tearing itself apart. People voted him in to help put it back together again, but he's like Dinkins. Impossible. And he seems incapable of understanding that Vietnam nearly wrecked us and that we beat the Russians and won (I agree with you, with provisos). But it's an incredible secret, isn't it? And Nixon's demise, which installed the media to first rank, tore apart the success--or maybe he succeeded by nearly ripping the ground out from under us. What was that line, "We had to destroy the village in order to save it"? Yes, OK. We won, but it's almost impossible for anyone to see it, because our perceptions have been torn apart. There was Nixon, a man who made a career out of destroying commie-pinko sympathizers, and what does he offer in Vietnam? The same old Johnson crap about winning "the hearts and minds" of the Vietnamese. What was that all about? Bible Belt missionary work among the little yellow people? As far as I know, they didn't even call it a war. "Conflict" was the legal term. And it's all come back to haunt us with Clinton, but the media beats him up, and then people are either for or against. It's pathetic. The old-timers are the only ones to get it right:

> "It bothers me a little, his activities during the war protests and so forth," Mr. Bender said [a 71-year old veteran]. "But he grew up. Maybe he's changed. I hope so. He should be aware of things. There's too much at stake."

> Even the sweet Mrs. Wandrey looked down and paused for a long moment when asked if it was time to let the president move beyond his problems with the military. "Well, each to his own," she said, finally. "You have to look in your own heart and see what you can forgive."

I think that Wandrey was talking directly to the reporter, who completely avoided what she said. Instead of Dowd writing a response of some kind (since she editorializes whenever she feels like it), she went on to quote some republican senator who was "more tart" in his antagonism to Clinton, as though the vets had been as well but didn't have the courage to speak, plebes that they were (only shnooks still believe in the flag). It's dreadful. Right now, we're deconstructing our values. Everybody knows that federal holidays are all about three-day weekends and weekend sales. Pretty soon we'll laugh at what we used to believe--after the old-timers are gone, I suppose. Either that, or we'll find our way back to who we are.

The other day I was listening for the 10th time to a tape I took off a country western hour--new music from Austin, Texas--one trucker's song I like a lot, mostly for the instrumental sound and steady beat, but then I started listening to the words (two stanzas and choruses repr. below, as best as I could make out), and I got an Idea that reminded me of that mountaineer's passage in your letter, the one about their political rhetoric getting more and more expansive the higher they felt themselves on the Divide--<u>superb</u>. My idea was that there actually is an American genius and that, if we go against it, we lose ourselves. Somehow, in all the changes coming down, that "high rollin', dust bowlin'" spirit has got to be there for us, because we aren't anything without it. We aren't going to be much without any brains, either, but I don't see the problem. Poe, Melville, and all the others show us just how far we can go in the brains department and still be American. And it's somehow tied to the land, underneath it all, even in <u>Call it Sleep</u>. Right? It's all there in the scene on the Hudson at the beginning when they pass the Statue of Liberty. Williams called it "In the American Grain," and it's interesting that he puts Poe right up there with Daniel Boone and suggests that the only socialism we need is the Abe Lincoln kind--with his beard and gangly frame, wrapped in an old black shawl--the mother of our country. It all seemed pretty clear to me.

Well I don't have no stetson, but I'm willin' to bet some,
That I'm as big a Texan . . . as you are,
And this girl in her bare feet, sleeps on the back seat,
And the trunk's full of Pearl . . . and Lonestar.

I'm a panhandlin', manhandlin', postholin',
highrollin', dustblowin' Dead Head,
And I ain't got no blood veins, just got them four lanes
Of the hard Amaril . . . lo Highway.

So gonna hop outta bed, pop a pill in my head, got a busted hub,
Bought a golden spread . . . under blue skies,
Go stuff my hide behind some power glide and get some
southern fries back o' . . . my eyes.

I'm a panhandlin', manhandlin', postholin',
highrollin', dustblowin' Dead Head,
And the closest I'll ever get to heaven is making speed up on old 87
Of the hard Amaril . . lo Highway.

On the __other__ hand:

"If you don't have an E-mail address you're not worth talking to," said Robin Saxby, president of Advanced RISC Machines Ltd., a computer chip maker in Cambridge, England.

I can just hear these high-techers giving the insult supreme, in the old French bourgois way:

    [glove across the opponent's face]:

    Aha, monsieur! Vous ne savez-pas avec qui vous avez à faire!

Trans. If you don't have an E-mail address, you're a nobody!
    (Monsieur! You do not know with whom you are dealing!)

Well, as Old Fezziwig said in __A Christmas Carol__, I'll just have to stand by the old traditions, even if they do go down before the vested interests.

("Native Americans" have it both ways at once. Their traditions are ancient, the best and ancientest, yet they're perfect for a society that operates off microchips. Not only that, but the traditions have been killed off yet are totally alive as well. Mel Brooks was right. They must be Jewish. Ya gotta believe.)

Furtwängler's piano concerto comes to me by way of that guy in Michigan who started a correspondence with me over my article in __Academic Questions__. He's a gas. I'll show you his stuff. Plus, I included Furt's recording of Strauss' Tod und Verklärung--some banging around but it settles down.

Steve

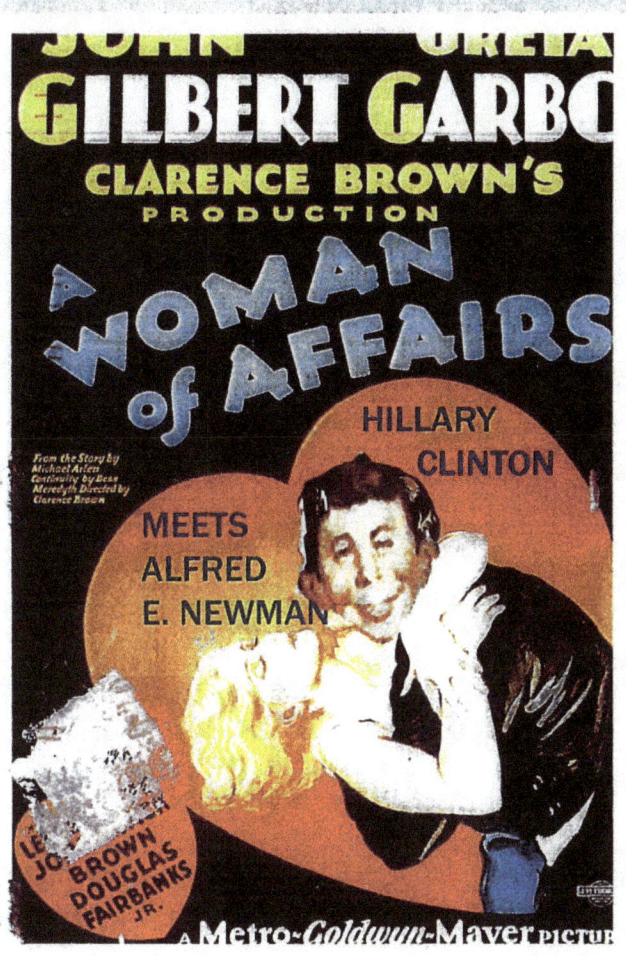

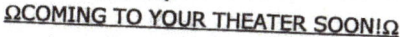
♣
ΩCOMING TO YOUR THEATER SOON!Ω

→A NEW SPEILBURGER PRODUCTION!
→WATCH HILLARY STOP GLOBAL WARMING
  WITH A WAVE OF HER HAND!
→SEE HER MAKE THE POOR RICH AND THE RICH POOR!
→WATCH HILLARY & NEWMAN CREATE A
  TSUNAMI TO WASH AWAY CAPITALISM!
→SEE HOLLYWOOD GO GAGA
→WATCH HILLARY LAUGH AS NEVER BEFORE!
→EBERT GIVES SPECIAL EFFECTS TWO THUMBS &
  TWO BIG TOES UP.
        ♥♥♥♥♥♥♥

Steve Cogan

Venice, CA

4/10/94

In order to keep you posted regarding my every feeling, the nuance of neurosis, I send you some paragraphs (with deletions) from my recent correspondence with Oliver - with whom I have tried to start a dialogue. I am afraid the wordly content is nil; no obejective comments on the nature of humanity, life, A. Dworkin, recent Beethoven recordings, or the quality of roads in Arizona. Simply musing on a desert mountain aire long since dissipated in old Bois de Baloney.

Here goes

At the moment I am rollicking through Italy with Harold. But wait, the tape has moved on and I am now a captive of Rodrigo's *Concerto Para Una Fiesta*. It is a sensual, nocturnal fiesta. In a fragrant garden, young men and women stroll, the men's saber's glint in moonlight, the black mantilla's of the women brush against the bougainvilla as red as their mouths. They circle each other with the elegance of flamenco movements. The music does not so much accompany them as it is produced by the heat of their passions. (Of all the music in the world - ancient, primitive or modern - the dark, swirling sensuality of 19th century Spanish music most stirs my soul. Happiness in this music is not expressed in military time orginating as it does in the folk not the state, in rhythms of cocksure bravado strutting itself before barefoot women poised before adobe walls. No wars rage in their music, nor do they rock themselves in alienated pain consumed as they are by jealous or loving glances. DeFalla's version of the Ring takes place in a corral stylishly called *El Sombrero con tres Picos*. It is the world sublimated by lovers, not Kings.) (By the way, if you can find a copy of this for me in any form, CD or record, I would mightly appreciate it. What I possess is a dub off a cheap radio.)

As I sit here, late at night, in my room I return to that question which has haunted me since I arrived in Phoenix, or should I say, since my life as a 'wage slave' on the streets of Brooklyn as ended, namely; why did Rodrigo do it? Why did he want to share his amorous feelings with humanity? What's in it for him? (Lets us set aside for the moment Benjamin's "No poem is intended for the reader, no picture for the beholder, no symphony for the listener," which if meangingful is nonsene and if nonsensical is meangingful. You notice he did not include <u>his</u> 'essays'in the discussion. But why not? Did he mean to imply that only the transmission of knowledge can be *intended* for a reader, beholder, listener, not sensual reality?) Or did Benjamin humbly "reduce" his essays to ruminations in a social vacuum without telling us? And if so, was it by an declared act of undeclared egoism, was it imposed by "capitalist, historical conditions," or was it by him stoically "facing the truth" about all human communication, i.e., it can not be done, so why not do it?   No matter which it was, his writing his essays proves him a man who thought himself into a hole (literally), i.e., a man who wants others to perpetually marvel over the way he eats, shits, thinks, ties his shoes, etc. but never because he asked them to - like me. (Or do I 'reduce' him to my measure?)

I guess what bothers me most is that sometimes I think the question I am trying to ask is really, at bottom, the question: Why can't I feel myself?. It is, in a word, a symbolic manisfestation of unresolved angers, humilations, rejections, and ultimately childhood insanity. The question is a fog I throw over my 'audience' to give myself legitimacy (in my own eyes). Sometimes I don't even know if I am at all interested in the question: Why did Rodrigo write the *Concerto para una Fiesta*? Perhaps I only want an excuse for you to look at me in love with myself - without asking.... (You see, I have this hang-up. I can't write letters, only journal entries to myself which I later put a stamp on.) Have I answered my question? Namely, am I saying that my audience is myself? World War 1 and Freud had minimal influence upon me. I partake of humanity the way a miser partakes in the world economy in his hidden bags of gold. The last thing one should expect from the pitiable is humility. Of course the world had something to do with me!!

A day or two later.....Another in the series of:

Letters from a Monad

If it weren't so expensive I should not write letters at all but send packages containing bits of my toe-nails, segments of my hair follicles, photos of me sitting looking at walls, eating, listening to music, as well as newspaper clippings or pieces of broken pottery which interested me, samples of dust from my book collection, an old wallet, a sound recording of my farts, grunts, and pensive sighs. Each month, of course, I would update the assortment. (In fifty years who could estimate the value of such a collection? I suspect, however, that each box would contain the same material, and not be like opening one box and hearing Mozart, and in another Debussy.) These packages would better accomplish what my words so feebly attempt to convey. Imagine, you could actually hold in your hand things that I once possessed, touched! You would see no phoney-baloney glimpses of me performing my daily routines! They would certainly more closely re-create the relation I have with myself - as curious washed up things on a beach; things mysterious, having no history or known origin, but demanding aesthetic judgment. Of course, in the end, they are simply 'things' washed up, subject to a thousand interpretations each as valid as the other, hence with endless possibilities. Yet, as I say, this intimacy could run into quite a bit of

money, though they would certainly raise eye-brows sent UPS..
Instead of "Letters from a Monad" these would be:

Debris from a Flying Monad

You see, my brain, unlike most, has a Mobius twist in
it. Each day I stroll along it looking for where the devious
twist begins, but as soon as I find it I flip over and am at
the beginning again.

But at least I answered my question: My audience is
myself, and that is why there is no point to my writing; it
can not transcend rumination.

It all boils down to being trapped behind a few lousy
childhood experiences which I don't understand; a forgoten
child pounding the sides of an imaginary bell-jar. Though
now, more like an impatient, crazed gorilla.

Sometimes I feel my writing has all the intellectual
force, grace, and novelty of Cliff Keuter's description of
his new dance work *Island*: "I am using two of Ravel's
Chansons madecasses to depict first the sweetness of the
island of Madagasgar, then the horror that visits the island
after the white man comes there." Or is as absolutely fresh,
dynamic, exciting, and revealing as María Irene-Fornes' new
play *The Conduct of Life* wherein the hero tortures people by
day, hides a kidnapped adolescent in his basement by night,
and teases his schizophrenic maid - all while his ignorant
wife, in the living-room pours tea. That is to say, is as
dull as a renaisance (pronounced as the English would) in
mutton-chops and beaver hats.

But don't get me wrong. The energy behind this letter
is happy, healthy, and strong. I just can't figure out where
it's coming from. It has a lot to do with the sky and
atmoshperic dryness - Nietzsche had it right there(as in most
other places) - but there is more to it as well..I also can't
figure out what to do with it - aside, of course, from being
driven to pounding against glass walls.

Of course, I could take an interest in something
else....Writing about some _thing_, for example.
Instantly,however, the legarthy sets in. A fog descends and
I want to run to my couch and think darkly for several years.
Yet I notice that planes fly overhead, car swoosh down the
street, bicyclers peddle past my window, and I hear the
panting of joggers - are they all rushing to the bleachers in
the hope of hearing what topical topic I have finally
selected? Yes, I think so. Will I dissapoint them?
Probably...

Someone just published Farley Mowat's *Born Naked* - the
title alone is a morally cleansing revelation for most I
should think - and it is only now that I discover he has
already authored 34 books which have been translated into 52
languages, and has sold 14 million copies of this stuff, all
before I have read a single word! I guess the world has
interests other than in me. He seems to be a learned man. He

says: "I'm a bit like somebody who lived in one of the Greek city-states watching Rome grow bigger and bigger and more and more ominous, more and more imperial, more and more careless of other people in the world." I guess back then a Greek could sit at an ocean front cafe table, turn his head west, and watch Rome go through its thing. Of course, he is joking, what he really means to say is that he can sit at a similar cafe in Labrador and watch the USA do those very things today. He likes to look he says, because people who value private property "terrify" him. "I admire people of the north'" he says, because they are not 'contaminated by our concepts of what is good and what is right and what we should have, and they are suffering mightly from it." More clearly; he admires non-white victims including the animal variety, you know, whales, geese, worms, that sort of thing.. I guess it sells for he has, three homes a secretary, and a few radios and televisions (not too many, I'm sure). Assuming the best about Mowat, namely that he captures that audience which likes first to be told that evil deeds are being done in the world, and that they, because they are reading the book, are not evil, and further, that by buying the book they have not only proven themselves to be Elected and loved by even the most hard to please Indian and other assorted victims, they will have also done more to save the world and the lives of more furred, dammed rascals than any imperialist president like T. Roosevelt, and uses this formula to make his big bucks while actually giving less than two, extinct owl hoots for the over-all health of Mother Nature. If so, then at least he knows himself and knows that a depressed audience is his ticket to happiness. Assuming the worst about Mowat, he believes what he writes, manipulates himself into thinking he is on the eternally right side of the eternal Angels, and he and God are his own best audience and only selflessly (without greed or ego, but passionately) writes to save the world from itself. He would not write if the world were perfect. Silent communion with God and Mother Nature would satisfy him. If this is so, then the houses, money, secretary, etc.,which he possess he would explain away as evils which he must endure but cannot enjoy. But has not Nietzsche proven that anyone who writes *because* the world is not perfect is a fraud?

     Oh, well, he's rich and I'm not.

     There are probably more humanitarians in America than in any other nation on earth. When one adds up all the people in organizations such as the Red Cross, Act-Up, the Retarded for World Peace, UNICEF, The Maimed for a Rubberized World, the NAACP, the Right to Life and Right to Non-life groups, Green Peace, AIDS for the Rich Coalition, DARE, Tibetan Hornist for a Multicultural Salvation Army Band, MADD, Cadre Against Cliterectomy and Male Erections, the New York Times, the Alliance of the Agressive Deaf for World Silence, the NEH, Indians for Peyote Chants in Elevator Music, Community Action for the Inclusion of the Brain-Dead, CARE, League of Minorities to Make the Majority a Minority, the CP, etc., it

is a wonder that there any selfish people left in America.
It's true that many of these organizations do not have the
whole of humanity at heart, but face it, they all have
interests in liberating humanity from inhumanity. I do wish,
however, that some huamitarian would start a Humanitarians
against Humanitarism Club on behalf of selfish people like my
self who can't remember signing the Social Contract.

Did you know that early in life Gauguin boasted "...I
tell you that on the maternal side I'm descended from a
Borgia of Aragon, Viceroy of Peru," as well as claiming that
through his veins passed Inca and Polynesian blood(due to the
Viceroy of Peru having sent an expedition to the Marquesas in
the 1700s)? Until he was eight he lived in Lima. Assigned a
little Negress to care for him, she was always naked to the
waist and slept with him. In the last year of his life he
was to write about this Negress: "Oh, that penetrating animal
scent, that tropical savor!" Is it not all clear now, his
disgust of France, of Paris, his "flthy Europe"? - his was a
search for childhood, himself as he used to know it, to feel
his original relation to the world! Tahiti was his Proustian
cookie. (Between Steel Town and Berwyn, between shoveling
coal in the basement of the Roxie and pushed off a cliff in
to the quarrys of Lyons, between the horror of 3232
Wisconsin Ave. and the pot-bellied stove on snowy nights in
the old train station, between Dostoyevski in my back-pocket
and my studded motorcycle boots, between burglarizing houses
and sobbing uncontrollably during *The Al Jolson Story*,
between my incestous love of June and my aesthetic martyrdom,
somewhere between these emotional black-holes swirls the
asteroid with my cookie on it. Oh, Why isn't it in the
animal scent of a little Lima Negress?) (Factual knowledge
culled from the pages of *Noble Savage: The Life of Paul
Gauguin* by Lawrence & Eliz. Hanson, 1955, 2nd.ed.)

Of what is Phoenix to me? Between what lizard and
rotting cactus shall I look for Tahiti? Or is it in the sky?
The big, beautiful, blue sky? Somehow the sky always saves
me.

I finally have some momentous, if pedestrian, local
gossip (i.e., Real Event kind of stuff) to relate, but I'll
save that for another soujourn into the abyss. Tomorrow
morning Ruby and I taking off for Indian Country - the sandy
land of hog-wash and noble poses(have you ever noticed that
where Indians live there seems to a great deal of garbage and
TV sets - just as in urban "ghettos"?).

Must leave now, though I don't want to.....

                    A week or so later

I approach you from the land of the botched and bungled,
feet heavy with clay, arms swollen with jaundice, knotted
hair, and eyes aflame with illness. So old to reach the
river - and on the wrong bank!

*First they were served with birds and green sauce in
plates of red clay relieved by drawings in black, then every
kind of shell fish that is gathered on the Punic coasts,
wheaten porridge, beans and barley, and snails dressed with
cumin on dishes of yellow amber. Afterwards the tables were
covered with meats: antelopes with their horns, peacocks with
their feathers, whole sheep cooked in sweet wine, haunches of
she-camels and buffaloes, hedgehogs with garum, fried grass
hoppers, and preserved dormice. Latge pieces of fat floated
in the midst of saffron in bowls of Tamrapanni wood.
Everything was running over with wine, truffles, and
asafœtida. Pyramids of fruit were crumbling upon honeycombs,
and they had not forgotten a few of those plump little dogs
with pink silky hair and fattened on olive trees -.....*

Flaubert sweated weeks over this passage* , but William
Thomas Hamilton, (in his *My Sixty Years on the Plains*), a
mountain man in the 1830s and 40s may have spend five minutes
on this:

*Pemmican is manufactured in the following manner. The
choicest cuts of meat are selected and cut into flakes and
dried. Then all the marrow is collected and the best of the
tallow, which are dissolved together over a slow fire to
prevent burning. Many tribes use berries in their pemmican.
Mountaineers always do unless they have sugar. The meat is
now pulverized to the consistency of mince meat; the squaws
generally doing this on a flat rock, using a pestle, many
specimens of which may be seen on exhibition in museums. A
layer of meat is spread, about two inches thick, the squaws
using a woooden dipper, a buffalo horn, or a claw for this
work. On this meat is spread a certain amount of the
ingredients made from the marrow and tallow....Buffalo
tongues are split the long way and dried for future use, and
thus prepared are a delicacy fit for a prince.*
*Another important article of food, the equal of which is
not to be had except from the buffalo, is "depuyer"
(dépouille). It is a fat substance that lies along the
backbone, nect to the hide, running from should-blade to the
last rib, and is about as thick as one's hand or finger. It
is from seven to eleven inches broad, tapering to a feather
edge on the lower side. It will weigh from about five to
eleven pounds, according to the size and condition of the
animal. this substance is taken off and dipped in hot grease
for a minute, then is hung up to inside of a lodge to dry and
smoke for twelve hours. It will keep indefinetly, and is
used as a subsitute for bread, but is superior to any bread
that was ever made. It is eaten with the lean and dried*

---

* Would you believe that the copy of Salambo from which I drew this
quote was one which I had apparently stolen from the Berwyn library when
I was fifteen or younger! I had not realized it till now. I kept it
for forty years - through thick and thin. I do no think I ever read it
all the way through. Yet.

meat, and is tender and sweet and very nourshing,...When going on the war path the Indians would take some dried meat and some depuyer to live on, and nothing else, not even if they were to be gone for months.

Hamilton has no art, though it is clear that he loves himself. But not as a "self" in a tradition of selves. He is historically alone. The artist isolated from his artistic past. He loves the way of the mountains, the Indian, the bear, the buffalo, the beaver as though for the first time in history. He loves watching them, noting how they live, wonderous of their beauty as though no one before him had, nor had recorded, painted, or made music to them. Killing, skinning and preparing an animal for feast is, for him, a most unique intricacy. It does not smell of Salammbô Nor does he hesitate to learn scalping from Big Jack as a novice learning human anatomy at the feet of Rodin. Of course, he scalps only those Indians who have scalped fellow mountain men, but he does use them in trade with their enemy tribes who greatly value them and use them for ocassion to yelp, hoot, and dance into the night. Another miracle sight which for him does not reverberate through Tacitus. But, like all artists, he has no need of a Great Father for he is in ample company with himself.

Art, I suppose, is an infatuation and celebration of self in the world (the more of both one can squeeze in, the better) of which Chateaubriand was the most exquisite and learned, (as the first of anything usually are), in Flaubert it is already tortured because of near societal meanginglessness, while in Kafka, the last of the lot, the celebration of self in the world is completely without point for the world no longer comprehends them - the War and Freud having first questioned the usefulness of those who do, then relegating them to corners of near lunacy. In a democracy who needs people in love with themselves, who have no mass-needs, and who do not need mass-rights bestowed upon them (and will not struggle for them)? Democracy depends upon depressed, uneducated people wanting a Great Father. When Flaubert wrote: "It is time to disappear," he didn't mean only himself, he tucked Art under his arm before closing the door. It is amazing that Kafka had the balls to appear even if it was as a non-entity. For whom does Hamilton write?

In acounting for himself he has this to say:

On the river Till, in Cheviot Hills, Scotland, in the year 1825, twenty-five men formed a company for the purpose of emigrating.

These men built themselves a bark, and when ready to sail held a council to determine whether their destination would be India or America. A vote was taken, which resulted in a tie, thus forcing the captain to cast his ballot. He voted for America, and by so doing destined me to fight Indians instead of hunting Bengal tigers in India. ......

*I was considered fairly good-looking, with smooth face,
agile, and quick in movements. I was the youngest child and
my parents had allowed me every indulgence [including five
years of education]. They owned a farm just outside St
Louis, and I always claimed I was a country raised boy.
Foxes, deer, and coons were in abundance, and it followed
that every boy would own a pony,providing, of course, that
the parents could afford it. At all events, I possessed one
of the best mustangs in Missouri - a little devil, which
would kick at everything and everybody which approached him
except myself. My brothers would say that we were a well-
matched pair, both little devils. At home we indulged in all
kinds of athletic excercises, such as dumb-bells, boxing,
trapeeze, and single-stick; and then we had constant practice
with rifle and pistol, in all of which I became very
proficient. It is productive of longevity, all things being
physically equal. I am at this writing past eighty-one,
straight as an arrow, supple and quick. I have had no use
for glasses. Almost every day some one asks me what I
attribute my suppleness and eyesight, and I answer that
"common sense philosophy conforms to the teachings of hygiene
[just as did Nietszche].".....*
*In the meantime [as a young man] chills and fevers were
undermining my constitution, and the doctor ordered a change
in climate. My father made arrangements with a party of
hunters and trappers,...to allow me to accompany them on
their next trip, which would last a year."*

He never returned. But even so, he does not answer my
question."I have often been asked," he writes instead, "why
we exposed ourselves to such danger [and there were many, not
least of which were Indians of whom he killed many] ? My
answer has always been that there was a charm in the life of
a free mountaineer from which one cannot free himself, after
he once has fallen under its spell....Give me the man who has
been raised among the grand things of nature! He cultivates
truth, independence, and self-reliance. He has lofty thoughts
and generous impulses. He is true to his friends"....Nor
were they dunces: "I found the Scotchman and the Kentuckian
[two mountain he met in Shoshone country] well educated. The
latter presented me with a copy of Shakespeare and an ancient
and modern history which he had in his pack. ... old mountain
men were all great readers. It was always amusing to me to
hear people from the East speak of old mountaineers as semi-
barbarians, when as a general rule they were the peers of the
Easterners in general knowledge."
Perhaps there is an answer somewhere in there.

According to Spengler the West will suffer rigor mortis
for another two hundred years before offically dying. Two
hundred more years of spastic twitching!! The thought itself
is enough to cause nervous ticks to appear about the eyes,
sudden, inexplicable leaps of one's fist into another's face.
We have three choices: One, we can stand watch as white-robed

clinicians over the opened-chest corpse, bitterely pointing now to the secreting spleen, then to the heart slowly turning green; two, assume, silently, the burden of the old masters in the hope that the body will someday be resurrected; three, sink into a stupor and watch AMC. It is clear that as of 3/26/94 all artistic audiences are dead - except perhaps for those still wishing to know something, the essay audience. But they make for a rapacious, unforgiving, and, in the end, dull audience.

No, the only audience today is the New Age audience. Those wishing their music, literature, sculpture, architecture,and painting to create for them the sensation they get when putting on a pair of those electronic glass which cause fuzzes of floating pastel light to appear before their eyes. All art should only throw them back into undisturbed, libidinal reverie. Free, Free at last! Free from desire, want, need, assertion, love, pain, having a self. Video Buddhism! (If its not this its agit prop.)

Do you realize it was painting that brought the house of Art down? It was the modern artists, but especially Picasso, etc., i.e. those who did "something more difficult than paint," who not only proved that anyone could do it, but that it could be done without history. What a hay-day Life magazine and Hollywood had with them. Remember the experiments which proved if a thousand monkeys were left in a room....

I feel as though my life were spend as a blind man pushed from an endlessly high cliff. Knotting my shoes, eating, going to the movies, writing, etc, must be done quickly - before I hit bottom.

In fact, in point of fact, as Jennifer Jones would put it, I am of all whom I know the least able to accomplish this unremarkable feat called humanity. I always begin my letters with the provisio "I can't write" meaning by that, 1) my education was so poor I literally don't know how, and 2) I don't have anything I know how to communicate or, rather, I have never felt the necessity to communicate anything to anybody so why should I now, or rather, I didn't know people could communicate - is that why they write and speak? Gee, I always thought it was to conceal. The difference is that I go on to explain why I can't write or have nothing to communicate. When I sit down to write a letter it is as though I am entering a wrestling match on a rotting dilapidated warf wet with fog. . My sleazy opponent is who I think I am, he is dressed as Plastic Man and grins a lot. In the ring, using every ounce of my strength, I bend and twist his body; I bring his shoulders to his belly-button, his head to his arse, then, standing back, laugh, saying "you are an impossible being. No one in their right mind could do that!" But my opponent is sly and devious, as you can imagine. Sometimes he bends me just as hard and roars with glee. Only a few are invited to these vaguely pornographic matches but as I make friends quickly they are multiplying: Nietszche, Sisley, Benjamin, Johnson, Kemp, Capt. Canot, Flaubert, etc..

Sometimes I even send them into the ring for relief. The rules are always the same: the ring must always be well-lit and every bend and twist held for at least two minutes for accurate description in the blow by blow accounts published in my sports column. Winning is passé. I have been in the ring only a couple of years now, though I have seen my opponent warping about the piers for a long time. A new friendship is developing as I introduce him to my friends. It is the only game in town that really interests me. Unlike Don Jose, I have not got around to hanging over the ropes and asking Micaela "when are you leaving?" Hopefully, she is still there (that is why your letter is so important to me). I don't know how many rounds are left to this match, but, fifty years later, I feel like Rocky.

My view of World History: If all the anthropological evidence points to any conclusion it is to the fact that for for the first forty thousand years of human existence women were the drudges and agreed to remain so if men performed three basic functions: 1) got erections, 2) got food, and 3) gave protection to the hearth. This made women happy as all get-out. Once men got the bright idea of inventing labor saving devices and enthralled women with fire, matate's, bowls, and eventually irons, gas ranges, dust-mops, etc., and finally got them to take their suspicious eyes off of them, they lopped off and invented the rest of civilization. Before they knew it, women were living with many labor saving devices but without men. Then the cursing began. They have resented men's cunning for the past eight thousand years. Nor have they ever forgiven.

Keep the letters flying. They spur only health and good-cheer. Mount your camel, don your turbin and head for Petra. Look for treasure on the desert floor of the self. Leave your graffitti etched on ancient, perhaps sacred, walls. As Pat Riley would say: *Leave footprints!*

The end

I take back everything I have written in my letters. What I wrote has been, and is, sane. It is I who am crazy. I'll tell what makes me believe this. I recently started reading in the letters of Rilke and what do I find?, a thousand sentences which begin with the word "I". Just as I do in my own! What's the difference? he is a smooth, silken tiger prowling his cage (though sometimes a bit boring), I, a beached duck with a broken quack. You see how far I am from understanding myself?

He paraphrases Rodin (in speaking of his wife) as having said: *non, c'est vrai, il n'est pas bien de faire des groupes, les amis s'empêchent. Il est mieux d'être seul. Peut-être avoir une femme, - parce qu'il faut avoir une femme.* This visionary old man with pieces of dusty, marble hands and breasts lying all around him, shards on his shoulders, chips lost in his beard, what else could he say?. Who else would take care of him; i.e., buy the toilet paper

June 14, '94

___Goddamn Masked Man, you can sure talk yer ass off! Now let's take that picture so's we can haul ass and ride.

___So vat you tink? It's just "Voop, voop, voop, und hi-o Silver"?

___"So vat you tink?" Goddamn, the Masked Man's a Jew.

___ [voice of little boy] Thank you, Masked Man.

___ What's that you said, sonny?

___Thank you, Masked Man.

___"Thank you, Masked Man." Is that what I've been running away from all these years? It's beautiful. I'm going to get a whole goddamn book of Thank You Masked Mans and put them in a scrapbook. And maybe when I'm old and gray, I'll exchange them for a bridge lamp. See that? I bet you didn't know. "Thank you Masked Man." I've led a very flamboyant existence. I've pissed them all away. Has the Thank You Masked Man Man been here today? [fading] The heroes are gone. There are no more Thank you Masked Mans.

Dear Ted,

I'm reading your last letter when Lenny Bruce's voice creeps into my head. It's that mountain trapper element that brought it on, plus references to Charlie Russell and Bierce in Mexico getting mixed up in my mind with Spengler's "West" and your moments of self-annihilation when the very coins seem placed all wrong as you leave a tip. Now if you were Picasso and David Douglas Duncan were walking around photographing you blowing your nose or choosing colored pens, all your moves would come out looking brilliant. Duncan went so far as to say that when Picasso threw his shoes in the corner, they ended up looking like a work of art. So humanity is forced to live with ugly coin patterns on diner table tops. Did I ever tell you of Clover's experiment one day while at a Mondrian exhibit, in which she fantasized that she had painted all those works she loves, and suddenly they all turned into shit?

Theory: our minds function just the way our pre-literate students seem at the mercy of the moment. All formless and void. I've been going to sleep this week looking at prints of Bosch's demons, pretty hideous, some of them. I'll check to see which one is responsible for ugly coin patterns--I bet he's got one.

Second Theory: the same round of self-annihiliation we perform on ourselves is happening in places like Rwanda and Bosnia, only there people do it unto others. If I could sublimate myself into fiction, or even pour myself into a garden or a set of Lionel trains, I'd feel a whole lot better than I do. Trieber calls it a failure to symbolize the self--to make a connection with the world.

I resonate altogether with your feelings about not knowing what to do with yourself. It's all there, yet I can't seem to get a handle on what I want to do. I feel at the mercy of the outside world and the mother-father configurations that seem to function like a cookie-cutter stamped into every experience I go through. I can be walking down the street and all of a sudden have Cendrar's life come crashing down on me. It's always something quite precise, like his first breakfast in Marseilles after returning from filming elephants in Africa with Jicky, that great ace of documentaries, he says, no less great than the breakfast itself, or the beautiful young woman they met in the jungles, the mysterious Lady of the Auto Breakdown, gorgeous, svelte, Anglo-French aristocrat. Every fucking moment of C's life comes crashing down on me. Or another time it's Spengler, who sits in public libraries for years, absorbing the German catastrophe of WWI into his morphological panoramas of history-- sitting still, staying put, perfect meditations and transumations of Nietzche and Goethe--just the opposite of Cendrars. It doesn't matter what these people do. If they have a voice, if there's sweep and clarity, they come crashing down on me and I screw myself into the ground, which makes for difficult walking down Henry Street.

It's all a replication of "the old time entombed." I was in 6th grade looking at Marty Maisel making perfect drawings and perfect model planes, not a pin out of place or a speck of glue where it didn't belong, and I remember feeling lost and small. I could build planes and draw till I was blue in the face. I could never have that grace or clarity, or so I believed. In my senior year in college, I fell apart when I read Keith's <u>King Lear</u> paper and walked around feeling that everything I wrote and would ever write was and would be shit. I ended up sitting in the children's section of the Flatlands library in B'klyn writing my overdue final paper in philosophy on St. Paul's concept of Christ crucified, can you believe it? When I talk to Trieber, he says that with a slight shift of perspective, it's all wonderful, rich, and strange and the stuff of which Cendrars are made. And yet I feel just as drained as the "exhausted soul" of the West before its own creations. The "new historicists" cannot forgive Melville for trudging over twenty years to his custom's job on East 23rd and emerging with <u>Billy Budd</u> in the end, every bit as profound as the greatest 19th-century European works, though no American in their eyes was supposed to have the brains or creativity. Why can't we rise to the occasion? Why impotence in every self-critique? Why not take the measure of the scene (we already have, a thousand times) and make our own way to being "equal to the world"? It's strange. We're pulled, as if by electro-magnetic force, to everything that's vivid and real in arts and letters, and tear ourselves down even as we rise. Perfect anti-heroes living anti-organic lives--miserable Penelopes, weaving and unweaving our tapestries while waiting for Odysseus to come and slay the marxists, gangstas, and academic village idiots who riot in our minds and eat our spirits out of house and home.

A few weeks ago I remembered when I left home for good. It was my sophomore year at Columbia. I took a furnished room in a mile-long upper West Side apartment run by a Mrs. Pick, Frau Emmy Pick. In the room diagonally from mine I could hear a typewriter humming away at over 60 words per minute. Dark hallway--Emmy Pick's list of

rules pinned to my door--unseen typewriter clicking endlessly--and
me wondering if this was what it meant to leave home for real. One
day I asked Frau Pick what the typing was all about (Kafka's got
nothing on me). She said I could see for myself. Then she knocked on
the door and introduced me to an arty-looking old lady, who turned
out to be a novelist for a literary market that was nearly two
thousand years out of date (only five hundred, if you consider the
Renaissance), writing Alexandrine novels and short stories in
perfect classical Latin. I can still remember the old lady handing
me a copy of a page she had just typed and me staring at the words
in complete bewilderment. Soon after I found myself alone during
Christmas break, with my friends gone for the holidays. I decided to
stay put instead of returning home (I never did go home again except
for that month in the summer of my senior year at the Flatland's
library). I spent a lonely but delicious week at Emmy Pick's curled
up with my next Humanities assignment, reading not just the three or
four assigned chapters but the complete text of Malory's <u>Morte
d'Arthur</u>. I never made the connection between that old lady and
myself (or that lady and my mother, for that matter, who might as
well have been teaching me to read, write, and speak classical Latin
instead of Russian), but I remember that she colored my feelings
about academics in upper West Side apartments from then on. I can
just hear Chateaubriand or Spengler if I were ever to end up like
her, absorbed in Bosch, Melville, and my Ruisdael prints. "Well,
that's the European race-instinct in him, fading away like the last
surviving son of the Duke d'_____'s family, who's working these days
on some Godforsaken farm behind a plow. Might as well be a ghetto
Jew living in Shanghai, Bolivia, or Chernovitz." Pretty grim. I have
several such landscapes, including No Man's Land, à la Remarque,
with a dead hand outstretched beneath barbed wire, though an antique
ruin will do as well. I am, by the way, playing with my Melville
essay again and am reading him with enormous pleasure:

ETYMOLOGY

(Supplied by a Late Consumptive Usher to a Grammar School.)

The pale Usher--threadbare in coat, heart, body, and brain; I
see him now. He was ever dusting his old lexicons and
grammars, with a queer handkerchief, mockingly embellished
with all the gay flags of all the known nations of the world.
He loved to dust his old grammars; it somehow reminded him of
his mortality. . . .

EXTRACTS

(SUPPLIED by a Sub-Sub-Librarian.)

It will be seen that this mere painstaking burrower and
grubworm of a poor devil of a Sub-Sub appears to have gone
through the long Vaticans and street stalls of the earth,
picking up whatever random allusion to whales he could anyways
find in any book whatsoever, sacred or profane.

I enclose two clippings from the newsstands of Manhattan, *plus a
additional comment on the idea of intellectuals* Yes, you are dead-

center right. Public dialogue on TV is an empty thing. So it strikes me that when I hear you or myself flail away, I remember how many times I've talked to Sonya about her own desparate moments, generally with women in authority, in which I keep telling her that there's just no point in it. Fire burns. Either put it out or walk away. The last time I spoke to her on this issue, a nice observation came to mind, to the effect that anyone who's grown up with a self-absorbed mother is in for trouble if they try to change a person like that, because self-absorbed is self-absorbed. At least that old lady had her Alexandrine romances--there's something in Longinus yet--but we keep being staggered by the likes of Fish--what was it that Clover said? "I'm attracted like a magnet to anyone who rejects me." Fish-heads not only stink but they also invent theories to repel any sane mind. The ideal way to read these people is not to read them. All the people with Mao's little red book, the millions with their Hitler salutes or the ones on Red Square watching the tanks roll by were all lost somewhere deep inside themselves--and one day the real world hit them over the head, _precisely_ where they had laid their projections over it: the Chinese killed off their Mandarins and became completely crippled and stupid, Hitler thought he could have all of Europe, so it attacked him from every side, and the Russians can't run a supermarket after claiming they had an economic theory to beat the band. I don't know about the Japanese. There's something weird with them. But my Cousin Adrian at Xerox tells me not to worry and that America will knock them over the head as well. He believes without a doubt that the world wants what we have and that, ultimately, the Japanese are still cranking out paper toys. We stand there gaping and beating our fists in the air--"But don't you see?" Steve Brandon up in Vermont warned me years ago that he and I could end up wearing sandwich boards on 42nd Street proclaiming the end of the world was at hand. It seems so clear to me when I think of our dilemma as being sucked into a self-absorbed mother. It's as though we still can't see that we can just walk away. It probably seems as if it would be a negation of our entire lives, when in fact it would be an affirmation of all the escapes we've managed to have so far. The opening of _M-D_ is superb:

> Call me Ishmael. Some years ago . . . I thought I would sail about a little and see the watery part of the world. It is a way I have of driving off the spleen and regulating the circulation. Whenever I find myself growing grim about the mouth; whenever it is a damp, drizzly November in my soul . . . I account it high time to get to sea as soon as I can. This is my substitute for pistol and ball. With a philosophical flourish Cato throws himself upon his sword; I quietly take to the ship.

"The watery part of the world." It's the unconscious as well. I'm not making it up. It's right there in the book. The new historicists are all little Ahabs hunting down any words that fit their iron grooves. Yes, Ishmael survives by a miracle. It's truly an incredible book. How does Pound open the second or third canto? "And Sordello/ But my Sordello?" Something like that. It always impressed me, and I always felt the same. "But my Ishmael?"

I _thrive_ on your gleanings.

Again its Bloom's Day 6/16 !

Steve

I read the Williamson
and the Vickers - interesting
but either dull or obtuse.
The Orwell was terrific.

© J. TROMBETTA PHOTO

Steve Cogan

Brooklyn, N.Y.

USA
20
1995

Published by FREELANCE PRODUCTS CO., Phoenix, Arizona

Dear Ted,

Be not dismayed by Greg Dening. I have a proposal for the both of us. And I made it up all by myself while reading an essay on Nietzche by one Sander Gilman, written in the Dening mode. It goes like this: If you don't like the surface, don't bother looking any further, because all you'll be doing is plummeting the depths of why you didn't like the surface in the first place. Do you remember a conversation between two Jewish scholars in Germany in the 1930s that Johnson cites in <u>Modern Times</u>? I may have mentioned it to you, because it made a strong impression on me at the time. The story is that one of them was writing a book exposing the lies of anti-semitism, to which his friend replied that it was a waste of time, because in the end all he'd be left with was an overwhelming confirmation of the fact that Nazis hate Jews. (It would have been better yet if they had taken the next train out of Germany.)

Apropos not doubting one's senses, Resa von Schirnhofer writes in 1884 that "nothing seemed to repel [Nietzche] more than bad manners and slovenliness" (you can imagine), which I think came from this same respect for surfaces. "Do not go behind the phenomena," says Goethe. "They themselves are the answer." (But how does one get there? and stay there?) Walter Kaufmann cites a passage by Heine on the appeal of nationalism to the worst instincts in the German character and how "educated Germans" have always seen themselves as belonging to European culture. It was the phrase "educated Germans" that stuck in my mind. They're the people whose portraits appear in my biography of Beethoven, the same types of men and women who appear in a collection of reminiscences of Nietzche that Gilman collected (more about that later). N's acquaintances all had first-class educations, many were from the nobility, and he apparently attended the best secondary school in Germany. Nietzche was gifted in the classics, just like Rimbaud at that age, and he was already writing better compositions in German than any of the other students. He says that his old teacher Ritschl thought that even his essays on classical philology sounded as though they were written by a Parisian novelist. Kaufmann, by the way, discounts all of Nietzche's remarks about women as needless distractions from his "ideas" - "philosophically irrelevant," he says - and nothing more than quotations from Rouchefoucauld, Chamfort, and other French writers. At least the objective scholars are honest in their sexless stupidities. Kaufmann reminds me of the ghosts we saw at that meeting of the Ntl. Assn. of Scholars. Paul Nizan describes the same atmosphere in the École Normale and the Sorbonne in the 1930s, in which "I listened to important men who spoke in the name of the Mind. . . . They join learned societies and convene congresses to determine what progress the Mind has made in the course of a year, and what remains to be accomplished."

As for Greg Dening (sounds like a Scotch single-malt), I was struck by the following: "And you, the reader are in any case a figment of my imagination." N. would say that Dening was not only an idiot but also speaking in poor taste (as you observe yourself in noting the absence of "Dear" before "reader"). It's boorish of him to engulf others in his abstractions, and, of course, he has no idea that he's behaving badly. In fact, the idea of behavior never enters his mind. N. would dismiss him as just another case of "bad company." He says that in the French definition of esprit, it was even considered "bad form" to speak from a strictly logical point of view, which is why, he says, that the French enjoy a touch of the irrational in their conversations. (The level of finesse, as opposed to academic hair-splitting, is truly striking in his work.) N. had difficulty with the best of scholars, those "objective mirrors without a self," and said that Goethe was the last of the old Germans he "revered." As for the living, Burckhardt stood out from all the rest. Nietzche, Burckhardt, Heine - they all go back to Goethe for nourishment. A lonely joy after 1848. At one point, Nietzche wonders why it is that all the academic followers of Goethe turn out just the opposite of him and end up as "abortions" and "fragments of humanity." And he's talking about the 1840s-1880s, when there was still an elite worth paying attention to.

It's all so depressing when I remember that I had trouble in graduate school right from the start. All the men but one seemed cut off from the neck down, and they could just as well have been talking about insect anatomy as Renaissance literature. In fact, Donne and Pascal talk about fleas and mites better than they ever could. I was truly, truly confused and when I eventually returned I remember telling Gargiulo how mystified I felt, because it just couldn't be that a straight-A Columbia English major couldn't make through all that insanity. The only belief I had at the time was that I had to exist too. I couldn't just drop dead, could I? There had to be a place in graduate school for someone who loved literature, pure and simple, and it didn't have to be wrapped up in my mother's distortions and my father's surrender. Time and again, Nietzche says that scholars kill the mind by complicating the simplest facts ("where, above all [above all], one is not permitted to live.")

The "Nietzche field" is particularly grotesque - in fact, all the new studies are particularly grotesque when viewed in light of their material. And what they all come down to is a question of belief. Ya gotta believe, or it doesn't work. Yes, I agree that it is idiotic to try to "prove" reality. All you can do is be real yourself. Spengler says that his book "is intuitive and depictive through and through . . . It addresses itself solely to readers who are capable of living themselves into the word-sounds and pictures as they read." That too is marvellous, the self-possession of a man who accepts the fact, accepts it as a fact, that some people are just plain incapable. Of course, the Greg Denings of academe would claim that this too is mere subterfuge, which is why one has to hold one's ground with them (assuming that one wants to deal with them), because, in the end, or rather from beginning to end, what they require is not reason and life (which they divorce) but submission to belief - in nothing. You don't even get another world for your pains. ("transcendence" is a bugaboo.) Here's Sander Gilman, the editor of Conversations with Nietzche: A Life in the Words of His Contemporaries (Oxford, '87):

The tradition of collecting the spoken discourse of important thinkers is one which reaches back to classical antiquity. What indeed are the Socratic dialogues but Plato's reports of Socrates' conversations? In the nineteenth century this tradition reaches some type of height in Germany with the publication of J. P. Eckermann's conversations with Goethe [Nietzche says it's the best book in German ever written]. Eckermann's conversations with Goethe share one feature with Plato's reports of Socrates' dialogues - <u>they were perceived as reliable reports of actual conversations, at least until the underlying structures of the texts as texts were examined</u>. Once this was done, it became evident that such "conversations" were elaborate fictions which used the device of the report to create the aura of reality. The report, with its basic structure of the "talking head," the recreation of a first-person representation speaking direct discourse (or reported indirect discourse), mimics our daily experiences of conversing. In this mimetic structure is embedded the possibility of a range of ideological messages, all of which acquire some believability as they are literally "put into the mouth" of a "real" individual. What makes this figure real to us, however, is not merely that the recreation meets our idealized expectations of the nature of discourse (for who ever spoke like Plato's Socrates or Eckermann's Goethe?) but that it confirms an image of a figure who has acquired some more general or mythic quality. Thus we expect Eckermann's Goethe to speak in quotable bon mots because the archetypal image which Eckermann employs is that of a wise old man, Odin-like, who speaks in gnomic utterances. <u>This is not to deny that the content of the conversation may have stemmed, at perhaps some remove, from the historical figure to whom it is attributed</u>. There is, however, little doubt that the structuring of the literary conversation provides the form and the context even for the material which could be successfully attributed to the actual speaker. <u>Until the introduction of acoustic recordings of speech in the late nineteenth century, however, no literary conversation was set down which is not suspect</u>.

So there you have it. We are asked to believe that 1) Goethe's reputation is based on the idea that he spoke "quotable bon mots," not real thoughts about real things, so that people like Burckhardt and Nietzche supposedly admired him for acting like "Odin" and not for what they said they revered in him, namely, the fullness of his humanity, 2) that everyone saw Goethe in the same way, "Odin-like" (otherwise how could there be a hegemonic picture?), 3) that people were fundamentally dishonest throughout history and that every last diary entry by people who heard Beethoven play and saw Turner paint is "suspect" in its admiration for their gifts (diaries are also "forms"), in fact, that all recorded history is false until the arrival of phonographs, cameras, and camcorders, 4) that modern instruments of recording somehow escape the net of human falsification, even though people in the field are supremely conscious of their technical limits and the inherent partiality of every context, and 5) that until now, humanity had no idea of its limitations and, instead of trying to do its best, was doing its worst. That's a lot to ask. Fucking slave-drivers, that's what Sweeney, Gilmore, Dening and all the others are.

I'll give you Eckermann's opener, p. 1 (Ottilia was Goethe's daughter-in law):

Weimar, June 10 [1823]

I arrived here a few days ago, but did not see Goethe till to-day. He received me with great cordiality, and made me feel this day as one of the happiest in my life.

Yesterday, when I called to inquire, he fixed to-day at twelve o'clock to see me. I went at that hour, and found a servant waiting to take me to him.

The interior of the house impressed me pleasantly: every-thing was extremely simple and noble; even the casts from antique statues, placed upon the stairs, indicated Goethe's partiality for plastic art, and for Grecian antiquity. I saw several ladies moving busily about in the lower part of the house, and one of Ottilia's beautiful boys, who came familiarly up to me, and looked me fixidly in the face.

This is what's called "elaborate fictions to create the aura of reality." And Gilman asks us to believe his drivel rather than "I saw several ladies moving busily about in the lower part of the house." Goethe never says anything "Odin-like" that contradicts the atmosphere which Eckermann felt the minute he arrived.

Moreover (to plummet the depths of an ugly surface - they all smear beauty, don't they?), since Gilman has to preserve his territory as an editor, he can't afford to deconstruct his own principles, and certainly not with the easy conviction with which he accuses Eckermann of "mythmaking" (just as Sweeney edits a book whose appeal lies in gorgeous color-plates of paintings he describes as vicious lies). But after all, isn't Gilman writing in the "convention" of editorial accuracy? and aren't his ideas new "constructions" in criticism? There's no end to the regress once you start thinking along those lines. So I ask again, why go to the depths when the surface says it all? The first "Huh?" or ""Aaargh" should be enough to make one put away the book. But I know. We're tough. They can blow up firecrackers all around you and you won't hear a thing, and a kid can punch me down Hegeman Avenue until I disappear in front of his eyes. By the way, Gilman makes no small claims for his project, which he says can lead to an understanding not only of Nietzche's conversations but also of "the importance, meaning, and function of conversations in general." OK?

It gets worse the more you think about it (which just goes to show you how absolutely accurate the surface is). When Gilman says that the recorded "literary conversation" is a "form," he includes everything, down to the simplest fact of the author telling us whom he spoke to, i.e., to a celebrated myth: "Who ever spoke like Plato's Socrates or Eckermann's Goethe"? Answer: everybody. Nietzche, for one; all the Sophists; and a hundred contemporaries of Goethe's, all of whom have fascinating things to say in similar recorded conversations. It has to be that way, in fact, doesn't it? or else there isn't a "form"??!! And as for conventions being fictions, doesn't everyone from Lao Tzu to Nietzche say that life is a dream and that the art consists in living in it well? It's Ishmael vs. Ahab. That's what all these thinkers are, academic Ahabs out to "Strike beneath the mask" and possess giants who have been to "the earth's foundations" but won't tell us their secret (see chapter 70, "The Sphinx"). Nietzche is right. These "abortions" are interesting only in the way that everything else is, as aesthetic phenomena. It all boils down to where one wants to take one's pleasures, of if one believes one has a right to live in the first place - "demon judges who know I am unworthy of even thinking I can defend myself." You remind me again of just how wonderful Poe is in "The Pit and the Pendulum." Sublimation forever. <u>Semper Fi</u>.

I read a marvellous review in <u>Renaissance Quarterly</u> of yet another left-wing study of the period, in this case a new historicist treatment of Queen Elizabeth, in which the reviewer refers to radical criticism as "Gottcha! scholarship." I never read anything like it before in <u>RQ</u>. Things are looking up. His name is Michael McCanles, from Wisconsin, and he's right on the mark:

> It seems to take being a member of a university humanities department to be continually surprised (and, of course, morally outraged) by the discovery that political power clothes itself in various rhetorical guises. Plato had said as much. And it takes the particularly skewed vision of a new historicist to believe that someone as canny as Elizabeth I "mirecognized" what she was doing in her speeches to Parliament on the subject of the Scots Queen.

McCanles is Nietzchean in all the right ways:

> But it takes an unusually naive parochialism to believe, as Gallagher asserts throughout this book, that people like Queen Elizabeth are driven to use evasive rhetoric mainly because they feel the need "to be in the right." That particular assertion, a common one implicit in much new historicist scholarship, is also unsurprising, because new historicism has labored long and mightily to make the Renaissance the repository of its own bad conscience.

That man deserves a letter of applause, and I think I'll send him one. So there you are, apropos your remark that "It's pointless to defend reality." Yes, if you think of defense in deconstructionist terms, of course it's pointless. It's like playing Go: which construction will swallow which? (damned clever, those Buddhists). But no, you have another sense of it yourself, and it shows up in your praise of Sowell as a "scholar in the trenches." Absolutely. I think that's what I was doing in responding to Ruth's voice in my head and maybe what we're doing in all these struggles with the demons, learning to stand up and pulverize them without becoming just like them, which is one way that demons reproduce themselves. And it's perfectly alright to make mistakes, the way Horowitz says he plays Mozart, with mistakes, "But always in good taste."

Beautiful epigraph you have there from Burckhardt on Rubens - "on his eagle's pinions." Goethe, Burckhardt, Flaubert, Nietzche, Spengler - they all talk about soaring. And how do they do it? By getting right down there and looking at the smallest blade of grass.

As for audience, Garguilo once said that I talked about myself as if no one were there. And I said "Yes, it all feels like an unreality." And he said, "But there is someone there. It's you." Dr. K says that nowadays everyone experiences themselves as a problem.

You'll be pleased to know that you're in tune with Jimmie Stewart. I saw a documentary on him on Channel 13, in which someone asked him why he thought that westerns are so popular. He said it right off the bat: because they're all about the settling of the west, and people around the world are interested in the American frontier. No doubt about it. There's more intellect in Hollywood than academe. Probably more anywhere than in school.

One more glance at your letter before I go. Yes, indeedee. I can see some readers getting all worked up over "The Last Manifesto." How dare you make a cruel system the goal of exploited humanity? And those Native Americans making money hand over fist. How cruel can you be mocking the false consciousness of America's victims? Yes, Virginia! There is a Santa Claus. But he's not in Macy's. That part was wrong. Yes, Santa has a beard. But his real name is Karl Marx.

Chico: Ah, gawaan. Dere ain't no Sanity Clause.

******

I've heard that one before about captains as theatrical props. I don't know how these things started, but they get repeated everywhere. Not the way everybody used to use Aristotle, like the Encyclopedia Britannica, but literally mouthing the exact same words. Maybe that's the whole point of these "ideas": they're easy to repeat. They're deliberately constructed to block out reality. The opiates of academe. As for Melville and the realpolitik of violent behavior in the navy . . . God, they write so hideously: "In the end, Melville recognized." Dening knows. It's too dreadful for words. First they tell you it's all a mental construction, and then they say, "In the end, he recognized that blah blah was nothing more than blah blah." I'll tell you what Melville knew. He says it in Billy Budd. On the cannon of the old men-of-war they put this motto: Ultima Ratio Regio - "The Ultimate Reason of State."

Yes, I remembered. It's Greenblatt who got up the idea. From Foucault, I guess. Art as the manipulation of symbols of constraint: English colonial settlers on board their imperialist ships. Captain manipulates royal symbols of constraint. Ship is wrecked in the Caribbean on the way to Jamestown. Reports get written. Shakespeare reads one of them (we conjecture, from certain parallels). Then he writes The Tempest. Which has a shipwreck. And a Caliban (who is a Native American, but also African). Prospero has a magic book and controls everybody. Shakespeare makes money through stock company. English ship also financed by a stock company. Ergo, ships are little theaters, and plays little ships. I kid you not.

On Colonialism:

Groucho: And Columbus made this big circle route across the sea.
Chico: Yeah, I know dat. Dat'sa Columbuses Circle.

I had trouble with the bit about the Tahitian woman not being "the mutual goal of our knowledge but the vehicle for our joined understanding. Her exemplarity is surely our shared invention." Who ha? Critic and reader can never hope to share knowledge but they can have a joint understanding and even "invent" the same idea??? (Marsha tells me her mantra is "Whaaa?")

Last paragraph by Alexander Nehamas in his bog (a slip, but yes, bog book) on Nietzche: "Just as Nietzche's texts are ever at their readers' mercy, so too is this one. The reading suggested here has aimed to show that N. was right to take this risk. And of course in so doing it has taken the same risk, though on a lesser scale, itself. But if this reading even provokes a refutation, then N. will have acquired one more reader, and one more reading. And, so long as N's writing is being read, the question whether truth is created or discovered will continue to receive the essentially equivocal answer presupposed, as I have argued here, by his very effort to turn his life into literature."

Back cover: "This is the best and most important book on Nietzsche in English." (TLS)

"This unusually engaging book demands our attention." (NY Times)

I open it at random and hit a line from The Genealogy of Morals:

"We can see nothing today that wants to grow greater, we suspect that things will continue to go down, to become thinner, more good-natured, more prudent, more comfortable, more mediocre, more indifferent, more Chinese, more Christian - there is no doubt that human beings are getting 'better' all the time." Recent history shows that Nietzche's view is most certainly false.

Thumbing through again, six pages later:

Nietzche's psychological hypothesis is that honesty is sublimated cruelty. It is not easy to decide whether this hypothesis is correct.

This can be translated in many ways, all of them idiotic:

Spengler's hypothesis is that Caesarism is advancing with inescapable force. It is not easy to decide whether this hypothesis is correct.

Keats opens Endymion with the lines, "A thing of beauty is a joy forever, / Its loveliness never fades." It is not easy to decide whether this hypothesis is correct.

Or, in the immortal words of Dr. K, I remain

Yours, how shall I put it?

Steve

August 12, 1994

Dear Ted,

   As I was putting the finishing touches on "Sun People," Ruth's
voice went off in my head and stopped me in my tracks: "Come on,
Steve. It's dishonest to attack the left through a lunatic like
Jeffries. That's not criticism. I don't know what it is. I can't
believe that you would do a thing like that. You're starting to
sound like Hilton Kramer."

   Priceless, isn't it? I know that she's an idiot (Nancy hopes she
never volunteers another idea to her), but that voice gets to me
every time, and I often run through whole monologues in order to
shut it up: "Dear Critical Inner Voice Disguised Today as Ruth:
Would you feel better if I dropped sun and ice and went to 'social
being determines consciousness'? Or perhaps something a little less
nineteenth century, a bit more chic? Perhaps Madame prefers 'dynamic
networks of material practices' or 'the circulation of social
energies'? Sounds like sun and ice to me. Come to think of it, if
you're so upset by my lack of subtlety, why do people in work
clothes and serapes seem more real and truthful to you than anyone
else? Why all those posters of African dancers, Guatemalan weavers,
and Indian cliff dwellings around your desk, or 'Hands Off Cuba' on
our office door? They look like pretty heavy sun worlds to me.
Jeffries may have something, after all. Look at the prints on my
side of the room: Durham Cathedral under stormy clouds, a bridge in
Yedo in the rain, a Russian church in snow, and even the French
chateaux have something damp and English about them--all those dark
green garden hedges and north Atlantic clouds. No, Ruth. I don't
agree with you. I think that Jeffries has his finger on the pulse,
whether you call it the north-south division or western hegemony vs.
people of color. So why not sun and ice? I could just as well say
'sunlight' instead of 'socialism.' Remember that 1917 political
cartoon in New Masses, the one with a muscular worker breaking his
chains at the dawn of a new day? So why be snobbish and use elevated
words like 'collective struggle' and 'capitalist accummulation' when
you can sum it up with sun and ice? Don't get me wrong. I'm snobbish
too. Your words sound as mythical to me as Jeffries' do to you. I
just happen to prefer Nietzche's definition of social determinism,
that's all: 'the theory of the milieu, a real neurotic's theory.'
That's not fair either, you say? It's just as flip as what I said
before? I don't know, Ruth. Why is it that every time I disagree
with you, my otherwise subtle thinking suddenly becomes pointless
and hostile? P.S. Did you ever wonder why the best jokes about
communism come from eastern Europe?"

   Apropos academic types, Nietzche says that "if one desires to
reflect peacefully on serious matters, he must not be disturbed by
disgusting sights." There's a man who knew the value of contempt:

   The only attraction of studying the quasi-philosophers who
   follow [Schopenhauer] is to see how they land at once in a
   situation in which scholarly pros and cons, brooding and
   disputation are permitted, but nothing else is--where, above
   all, one is not permitted to live.

And again: "I am unable to imagine Schopenhauer at a university. The students would run away from him and he himself would run away from his colleagues."

Two book reviews for your amusement (henceforth abb. as FYA), in case you didn't see them. Yerushalmi seems entranced by Gershom Scholem, so I'm grateful that you read to me from Scholem's book on Benjamin, which bore out my own feeling that there was something dense about the man - a case of the blind commemorating the mad. I think I told you that Jenkin and I found his studies on the Kabbalah incredibly dull. It's quite a feat to neutralize middle-eastern mysticism, but he managed to do it. His work reminds me of a book I have on English priories and monasteries, in which otherwise excellent information ends up sounding detached and meaningless.

(I'm thumbing through Scholem's _From Berlin to Jerusalem_. He's exactly like Danielle's father, high-quality name-dropping on every page. He sounds as if he wants to be thorough and get the record right, but it's amazing how quickly one forgets what he says from one page to the next. There's just no way to fix it in the mind. I open at random to pp. 50-51 and find half a dozen names thrown about as if they were on everybody's reading list: Jean Paul, Georg Christoph Lichtenberg, Paul Scheerbart, Eduard Mörike, Stefan George, von Hippe, Johann Caspar Lavater, Moses Mendelssohn, etc., and then, on the bottom of p. 51: "On a historical plane, the First World War was naturally the most important event of my youth." It's a strange and ghostly remark, isn't it? The very thought cancels itself out by the time it gets to the period.)

Was Benjamin some sort of _enfant terrible_ or "poetic" type to Scholem and the others? Am I missing something? I never read a line of his that seemed worthwhile to think about. Scholem even cites a letter to him from Benjamin that is almost unintelligible. Yet there they are - Arendt, Steiner, Kermode, and Yerushalmi himself, the Columbia Salo Wittmayer Baron Professor of Jewish History, Culture, etc. - all putting their energy into Benjamin. (On professional titles, by the way, Joyce has a great one in _Ulysses_, something like "Herr Doktorprofessorprivadocentwhorehousepresident.") Why do they bother with Benjamin if he had an "inner vision that could not itself be articulated." Say, what? An inarticulate inner vision? Then how do you know he had one? And why compare him with Kafka, who is always whole, _especially_ in the details? As for their lives and personalities, it doesn't take a genius to see how different they were from each other. I'd be surprised if Benjamin laughed even once in his life, about anything. Kafka's _postal cards_ are more interesting.

And then there's Louise Colet, that ever-popular companion portrait to Walter Benjamin, Super _Femme_ herself: "Able to leap high mansards in a single bound! It's a pioneer feminist! a literary star! it's FLAUBERT'S MUSE!" Some muse - he used to run away when he heard that she was coming. Did I send you du Plessix Gray's auto-biographical sketch? She talks incessantly about the horrors of a French education and a tyrant father who cared about what she learned in school. Nietzsche is a real connoisseur of her type:

Formerly the new generation wanted . . . to <u>found</u> itself on the older, and it began to <u>feel</u> secure in itself when it did not merely adopt the views of its fathers but where possible took them more <u>strictly</u>. Criticism of the fathers was then considered wicked: nowadays our younger idealists <u>begin</u> with it.

I bet you'd find the same observation in the Roman historians, whose main subject seems to be the republic's decline. It's curious but true that, in many ways, Nietzche has more in common with Ben Jonson than with Kant - the same fascination with the old, tough virtues, and the same blunt speech and love of epigram. It's amazing how much "the fathers" are part of Nietzche's work, the mothers too, in fact, who are always French and always upper-class (of Colet and du Plessix Gray, it may also be said, as Nathalie Babel once said to me of Danielle, "<u>elle a l'âme d'une concierge</u>"- they're cutting, these classy Frenchies - "she has the soul of a concierge").

How different from the professional philosophy that turned Nietzche's guts, for which he had the following suggested epitaph: "It never hurt anybody." Has anything changed? There's a popular idea among academics today concerning "the great Conversation," the big dialogue in the sky, but the fact is that real voices distress them (surprise). I've read half a dozen recent essays on Nietzche, and not one has anything to say about the man who's there on every page. That's a lot of reality to repress. I can appreciate a scholastic approach to the Kabbalah - maybe - but Nietzche? I've noticed, by the way, that he's not only intimate in his own voice but also gravitates toward other writers who speak from themselves. He says that Goethe's <u>Conversations with Eckermann</u> is the best book ever written in German, and that same sense of living speech comes through in his work as well. In fact, it's also there in Jonson's <u>Conversations with Drummond</u>, a work that basically means nothing to Jonson scholars except for its documentary value. When will I comes to terms with the fact that I don't think, feel, or live like an academic? Reading Nietzche is like being with a marvellous conversationalist, an aristocrat with the grounding of a peasant, Paul Fresnay and Jean Gabin rolled into one. Cendrars has that same range, and so do Melville and Thoreau. Kaufmann acknowledges that Nietzche writes far better than Kant and Hegel, but he has no interest in exploring what that means and can't wait to get back to "ideas." Nietzche says, by the way, that he can't even stand the sight of a reading room.

It occurs to me that we must have the makings of a whole volume of satire, what with your letters to the leading lights of the day, your dictionary of definitions and related pieces, my chlorophyll manifesto, abc of modern english studies, and now this mini picturebook. It's a volume worth doing, and it's amazing how little there is of it. *Heterodoxy* tries, but it's clunky and repetitive. There's a new collection of essays by Gertrude Himmelfarb and a book by Russell Jacoby ("Dogmatic Wisdom") that might be worth looking into, though the next step (or ten steps ahead) would be your collected letters to modern luminaries.

There will be problems with audience response, however. Serge tells me that he showed a copy of my chlorophyll manifesto to a colleague and that she took it seriously as an analysis of plantistic prejudice! He couldn't persuade her otherwise. I had a date with her last year. She was sexy and dismissive all at once. After half an hour, her sexiness wore off and I had a dismissive woman on my hands. So there you have it, a woman who brushes aside a real man but gets excited by something he wrote, which she believes is an exposé of false consciousness!

And most of them have been like that, although one was straight and nice but dull. Some choice - sexy neurotics vs. healthy bores. And no, I don't think the dull ones are boring <u>because</u> they're healthy (they're not all that healthy) or that the flashy ones are sexy because they're neurotic (they are neurotic). In any case, I don't have anything they want, even if they sometimes think I do. I had the same problem with my summer place. I must have had a hundred phone calls in response to my ads, but the people who finally bought it are one of a kind, and the place is absolutely right for them. They were going to buy the Bernhardt's unit, which is actually a little smaller than mine but has a porch view of the lake. Gail rented from me last summer and was renting again this July. Her husband told me that the Bernhardt deal fell through, thanks to Madame B., God bless her, who wanted payment in cash plus the year's maintenance. Tom said that when he and Gail went back to my place they felt they were home. He used to be Richie Havens' manager and was also close to The Band and other Woodstock groups back then. That's the kind of person it took to want my place - the kind that hardly exists in Lake Huntington Summer Community, Inc. The lesson I draw from this experience is that, given my character and the choices I make, whatever I want seems to border on the impossible. Beckerman's remark to me after my defense sounded the correct note: "For a minute I didn't think we were going to make it." In other words, I don't think of my past achievements as signs of future success but as clearings of underbrush to arrive at greater near-impossibilities. Nancy tells me, by the way, that Bill Bernhardt's wife is Impossibility incarnate and that he has his hands full with her. Serves him right for co-editing <u>Journal of Basic Writing</u> and for giving neurotics like Andrea Lunsford top billing (she's a certified harpy who attacks the idea of self-reliance as an act of "male aggression"). Actually, the situation with the Bernhardts had an element of pure poetry in it, since Bill's journal provided me with some choice lunacies by feminist teachers when I was working on "Text Production" in Pine Bush last summer. They'll get you every time, even in a Catskill bungalow colony. What am I saying? <u>especially</u> in a Catskill colony! Ah, Dr. Bernhardt, there's no escaping revolutionary plant consciousness.

8/15--it's done! Il Lago di Huntington recedes in the distance. Signed, sealed, and delivered, exactly a month since I returned.

> It was as if religion, princely
> power, saga, the myth and poetry
> of all times, his own family circle
> of close friends, even elemental
> nature, both in the animal kingdom
> and in the landscape, had turned
> confidingly to him that he might
> take them on his eagle's pinions.
>
> J. Burckhardt
> (RUBENS)

Steve

Responding to magical beings. These voices you hear (Ruth, et al.) - are they the audience you also write to? To appease? To satisfy? To quell? They are for me, and I damm them all. They are not in the world. Mine are grey-shrouded beings who have no pity and spit on me. They mock me, calling all I do into derisive question. They turn me around till I no longer know what I am doing nor why. From a great height they throw shit on me, and yet I remain center stage at the bottom of their ampitheater swirling about trying to answer their Roman hooting. I yell back to back to them into the wee hours of the morning hoping they will go away - then I realize I bought them lifelong tickets! They will stay as long I do! Where is the god-damm door out of here? (Even this question makes them slap their thighs in laughter.) Where is reality? Where did it go? I know it's there, just on the other side of the theater, but I can't get out of here. What I wouldn't give to see a tree, a blade of grass, another human face, I'd gladly "pay the fine" - but I have nothing to offer. If I put all my magical beings together they would weigh no more than a blast of stale air from an ancient, sealed tomb. Not enough to tip the scales even in the Bagdad of Ali Baba. Yet, they are all I have. (Perhaps this is where the "deconstructionists" fit in: they too are in an ampitheater talking to ghosts - and that's what irks me about them - I am of them. They remind me of myself and I rush in for the kill. Or is it I compete for their grey-shrouded audience. Can you imagine Foucault as mirror of my soul?)

Nonetheless, these monkish, faceless beings must be silenced! They can't even read! That's why they are always hooting. I want a literate audience which, after showering and relaxing on a sofa, will embrace me in their hands and read what I have written while eating an apple. Of course, that means I shall have to acknowledge their wants and needs (just as an apple does), step out from behind the footlights (or are they third-degreee lights?), as it were. Well? Oooo, Calico gal won't you step out tonight, step out tonight, step out tonight. Oooo, Calco gal won't you step out tonight and dance by the light of the moon?

But perhaps I read to much of myself in your letter.

I have three essays in the pot. Am writing like a demon - but can't figure out what or for whom. When I am not writing all I think about is: Why? Time burns like a potato in deep-fry oil. (Why does writing take so long? Why isn't it like going skiing, playing tennis, or eating out?) All this by way of saying: Sorry I have not kept up my end of the correspondence. It is soul churning time - and it's exhausting! (And then, of course, after *that*, there is real life.)

Received two, <u>bound</u> copies of my dissertaton from St. John's. Like Dagwood Bumstead rushing out from the maternity ward, I wanted to shout: It's a book! It's a book! and hand out cigars. But then I read it and want only to say: Shit, it's deformed. What does the doctor say, honey - can we try again?

The audience, the audience one writes for - that's the thing. If they are one's inner demons all is lost - they crap on everything, and rightly so. Battling ghosts deserves little else - some, according to your last letter, call this having an "inarticulate inner vision." But if they are not one's inner demons, who are they? Where are they? More precisely - where does one stand in relation to a real audience? Even more precisely - where am I in relation to mine? I thought I existed without differentiation from a world populated by demons and so wrote to them, but if I am to have a real audience, I must be somewhere in a world which is not me and has no demons. If there is a real audience, I must myself be different from them and somewhere else. Q.E.D. What a novel idea! Reality! So you see, if I can find my audience, I'll find me. One character in search of an audience which will tell him what and how to write. (Then the power to hold and sway millions by one's words can be savored - even if one is never published!)

To fight the deconstructionists one must deconstruct them - and that is the trap. One must write what they don't say, what they conceal in precisely the same way they do it to us. It becomes one myth fighting another myth; two non-realities battling it out. It is better to say what one means rather than how others have missed the only boat there is. To defend reality is pointless, and to defend it by pointing out what they don't say because they have a secret agenda is exactly what they do to us. Our reality, for them, is merely our unstated secret agenda to control them and all the other oppressed assholes in the world just as we, to fight them, say they have a secret agenda to control us who are self-reliant. So we both end up talking about secret agendas and we both miss the only boat there is - the joy of sublimating the world, i.e., reality. (Demons love secret things. This is the playground where they can come out and mix without being noticed.)

Enough of thoughts off the cuff!

You will be glad to know that the mutiny on the Bounty occurred because Captain Bligh "misunderstood the theatrical nature of shipboard life, especially his role as captain," not because the men were upset at being flogged. At least this is what Greg Dening author of MR BLIGH'S BAD LANGUAGE: PASSION, POWER AND THEATRE ON THE BOUNTY writes. More: "In the end, Melville recognized that the *realpolitick* of violent power in the navy was nothing more than the rationalization of the status, class and privilege of one set of men over another," and that, in Melville, violence "gets revealed for its social self-interestedness." Did you know these things? I bet you didn't. And so "our reflection of discpline and its texts leads us to a final thought. The violence of discipline was not necessary. Any captain could have known how to be a 'gentleman', how to manage the symbolic environment of his wooden world. Any captain could have been relativized by experiencing the otherness in his men's lives. . . . Any captain could have known how much he was the cause of the pain of those he flogged, how much he was the hangman of those that mutinied." But not Captain Bligh, he didn't know how to relativize himself - he didn't know what he could have been; he did not know his proper role on the stage of the Bounty. Perhaps he should have worn a T-shirt and sneakers and shouted his order while riding a tricycle from stem to stern.

When Nietzche writes (as you quote): *The only attraction of studying quasi-philosopers who follow* [Schopenhauer] *is to see how they land at once in a situation in which scholarly pros and cons, brooding and disputation are permitted, but nothing is - where, ablove all, one is not permitted to live,* he captures Dening marvelously: *Possessing Tahiti was,* he writes, *a complicated affair. Indeed, who possessed whom? Native and stranger each possessed the other in their interpretations of each other. They possessed one another in ethnographic moments that got transcribed into texts and symbols. . . . Each possession of the other became a self-possession as well. Pantomimes in this respect were no less significant than ceremonies, or acts of possession, of processions of hegemonic signs. Everybody is so busy possessing* no one lives! The world is a stage where on, just as actors on a real stage, no one is <u>really</u> the role they are playing; the roles are merely drawn from the pre-written script of the 'hegemonic' demons. Beneath the skin we are all the same and must relativize ourselves! Then we can really live! But not till then....Not until we are 'other'.

Dening also writes this curious passage: (believe me, I did not find this passage till long after I began this letter): *And you, the reader* [note the absence of "Dear"], *are in any case a figment of my imagination. I write for you, making decision on decision about what I select, what I leave out, wondering what you would know, what would tease you to read more. It cannot be that I just* [write for other scholars], *although they will know my licences. It cannot be that I write to make my readers* [note how he passes from the familiar to the 3rd person here] *equally expert as they or I about Purea* [some broad in Tahiti]. *I write to have my inventions join my readers' inventions. Poor impossible-to-reach Purea is not the mutual goal of our knowledge but the vehicle for our joined understanding. Her exemplarity is surely our shared invention.* This is not at all what I mean by finding my audience! I do not want "figments." I want to know who they are. And if they don't exist, tough shit for them. I want them to know who I am - I couldn't care less what they do. I do not want them to share their "inventions" with me, nor do I want to "invent" anything (like a new kind of screwdriver). I do not want to invite them to bed to make love, even if it is platonic love making as Dening seems to want - if can figure out if he talking to them or about them!

Whata life! I notice even when I am talking I don't know who my audience is though they sit three feet in front of me, looking into my eyes. I continue my conversation with my demons as though nothing has changed. I use the same tone of voice, with the same intent as I do when staring at walls - to prove something. Ah, these demons are so demanding, they never let me rest. I am always answering demon accusers, demon judges who know I am unworthy of even thinking I can defend myself. This is not the audience I have in mind either. This audience is truly a figment of my imagination!

Sounds like your CHLOROPHYLL MANIFESTO is chloroform for some your readers - a heavenly opium. I sent you a copy of my LAST MANIFESTO - what do you think that will do?

Il Lago di Huntington now fades into memory - congratulations!

May du Plexus de Pussy meet Andrea Lunsford - perhaps they will argue whether or not Colet possessed "self-reliance." Did Colet have a dick? I love that 'little mistake' - her confusing *la belle époche* with the time of the 1848 revolutions and the COMMUNIST MANIFESTO! Just a small one. Egads. (Too be fair, perhaps she meant it was a *belle époche* for the commies.)

Well, I see the sandman knocking at my midnight window, and so will depart till another morning dawns.

P.S. BATTLE OF THE BOOKS by James Atlas is pretty good, and Thomas Sowell's RACE AND CULTURE is even better. He's a mighty man, Sowell. Much to be admired - a scholar in the trenches!

THE LAST MANIFESTO

"A spectre is haunting the world. The spectre is
Capitalism. The forces of alienation, private property, and
materialism are rising among the people, overwhelming the
forces of oneness, community, and common property. We have
seen nations which oppose the monumental forces of Capitalism
collapse one after the other: Russia, East Germany, Poland,
Czechoslovakia, Hungary, Romania, Yugoslavia.... China and
Cuba will vanish as well, vanish as the stains of blood on
the stones of Tiananmen Square. The corpuscular arms of
Capitalism are reaching down into the very bowels of the
earth moulding the peoples without history into the free,
alienated makers of the future. American Indians are already
opening unrivaled gambling casinos. They are selling millions
of tax-free cigarettes for tribal profit as the tom-toms are
tucked away in forgotten teepees.. The fierce Yanomamo, the
bare-chested head thumpers and abductors of women in the
jungles of Venezuela, now buy clothes on VISA cards and sip
tea on Fifth ave. Soon, the despised minority of South
Africa, the naked Bushmen, will control the untold wealth of
fabled diamond and gold mines. Capitalism everywhere is
destroying the abject poverty of nations once held together
by wretchedness, communal property, respect for Mother
Nature, and ancient rituals which only sank them deeper and
deeper into their misery. Although some nations today are
stronger than others and take from the poor what they can not
yet afford, the cry of these impoverished nations and peoples
for freedom, private property, and alienated work will soon
be heard around the world as a cannon whizzing by our ears.
The word 'capitalism' now tumbles from their lips as
religious incantation, tomorrow it will be a deafening
thunder-clap bringing down the very gates of Heaven. They
hunger for liberty. Yes, the spectre of Capitalism is
everywhere, and its enemies tremble in their boots.
Comrades! join the struggle to liberate the down-trodden
through the forces of private property, alienation, and
materialism! Free the shackled from that which sustained
their centuries long poverty - selflessness, ritual, the love
of nature, and communal property. The Revolution is at hand!
Let us bring history to it's end once and for all! You have
nothing to lose but the illusions in your brain!

OKE OWEENGE
CRAFTS COOPERATIVE
SAN JUAN PUEBLO

OKE OWEENGE Crafts Cooperative of San Juan Pueblo, New Mexico displays and sells pottery, silver, jewelry, carvings in stone and wood, weaving, paintings and necklaces of over 100 pueblo artist members.

©1975 Eight Northern Indian Pueblos Council, Box 927, San Juan Pueblo, N.M. 87566

POST CARD

USA 20

Steve

re-read my latest letter
to you – sorry for the
terrible spelling and the
sentence which contains Hamlet.
It should have read: .... before
he knew that his mother, like
mine".... Haste makes waste!
It always seems as if I forget
to mention $\frac{3}{4}$ of what I meant
to say in my letter then
beginning another

Steve Cogan
Brooklyn, N.Y.

286

Dea *Steve*

In describing the life of Saint Joseph of Copertino,
Cendrars writes that on the high road to Bologna one day
Brother Joseph was "walking in such a weird manner that
people are pointing at him. Peasants in the field are
laughing at him. Some are throwing stones.   The further he
goes, the more conspicuous his unusual gait becomes. Women
stare after him, follow his footsteps. Brother Joseph
appears to be gliding, and, when they see that *his feet are
not touching the ground*, but move on without effort, his
sandals leaving no trace, no footprint in the dust on the
road, and that he walks miraculously, . . the women begin
crying out that it is a miracle." Cendrars comments, "Joseph
is still [among all the Saints] the only one who has
succeeded in flying backwards," then adds:

> *Until his death, at the age of sixty, Joseph of
Copertino was constantly being reprimanded. . . .At home, his
father, who was a cobbler, tried to teach the boy his trade,
but had to scold him repeatedly for his absent-mindedness at
work. . . . At last, [his parents] decided to send Joseph to
the monastery to get him educated. . . Early one Sunday
morning, therefore, the cobbler closed his little workshop
and, leaving his brood in the care of a neighbor, set out
with his wife to present Joseph to Uncle Anselmo after Mass.
. . . All along the way, the cobbler was berating his son:
"Walk ahead of us, you big dawdler. Can't you see you're
getting on our nerves, always lagging behind? We're ashamed
of you. Come on, get going, walk in front! Hup two!"*

Sartre would develop an entire biography upon such
admonitions - as he in fact did in *Genet*, but unlike
Cendrars, Sartre would see these as determining the biography
- 'man makes his own history, but not the history of his
choosing,' etc.. Freud would say the father destroyed the
ego of the son, and so his son flew away from humanity (i.e.,
himself), backwards into neurotic space. For Cendrars it is
merely the context in which the biography proceeds out of
Joseph's being. (Today, of course, Joseph's father would be
sued by a social-worker for child-abuse - such is the extent
of marxist notions that theory must precede reality.) But,
which is it? Sartre seems intellectual, Cendrars, a matter
of common-sense (I'll return to Freud in a moment). Sartre
brings theory to reality, Cendrars simply looks. But he
'looks' with eyes informed by 8000 years of history - in the
helter-skelter ways in which he was formed by looking at
streets, bridges, buildings, art, literature, plowed fields,
dammed rivers, etc., which embody those 8000 years. It is a

trusting of what humans did in history being reflective of human nature.. And he 'looks' with the eyes of someone in love, infatuated, with the way those eyes see and in what humanity has done with itself. (This, of course, is the precondition of art in my estimation.) It's as though everyone today is a Sartre and not a Cendrars. They make theoretical mountains out of real molehills every time they see a blip on the horizon. Thus, instead of seeing the molehill of beer-belly Pete they see the mountain "the white man," rather than seeing tight-ass Howard they see the social construct "gay," rather than seeing red-eyed Russell Means they see the incomprehensible "other," rather than seeing rapping SistaSoldier(?) they see the anger of universal oppression - just as Marx and Lenin saw everyone defined by economic class rather than as simply a clerk, a bank president, a homeless hippie, doing their own things. Now groups want rights to match their group-think, (called 'culture'), and everyone is now a sociologial abstraction. Indeed, this is the way liberals, commies and generalized pinkos have made Marx palatable to the American public - not by categorizing people by class but categorizing them according to "gender", race, and "sexual orientation;" all supposedly oppressed just as was the proletariat and by the same age-old oppressor: - the rich white man. God forbid that it should be just their own pissy selves. The barbarians!!

My way is the middle way, Freud's way.. Like Brother Joseph, my ego was reamed out of me and I can fly backwards. I no longer have enough weight to hold me down, in addition to possessing no sense of direction. But who shall canonize me? (Knock, Knock, I rap on the dungeon door to my past. "Whose there?" I don't know, I say, but I think you're me. Will you let me in? Then, of course, the sound of footsteps walking away.)

Was just pulled away from the computer into the living-room by Mahler tearing his heart out in the conclusion of the 2nd symphony. He was resurrected. Did he figure out why others would be interested in knowing this? I guess so. But perhaps he didn't care, and wrote it anyway. You see, I am back at the beginning - that is, my old question: can you imagine rounding up a hundred and fifty people and telling them to play your tune? (The amazing thing is, they do!) And there it is, your heart blowing out of the mouths of shabby, fifty bald men and a skinny flutist. And you are resurrected! Another kind of miracle!

Back to pounding on the dungeon door....

(Guess what - after I lifted Mahler's 2nd from the turntable, the radio was playing the 4th. So right now I am hearing that beautiful, bucolic mezzo voice while I write this dreck - the world is really a strange place.) I am like a surgeon who can't find the disease and so keeps cutting to the bone in different places. Remember the paradox: 'look and ye shall not find,' well, that one seems to fly over my

head. Didn't Mallarmé once prop a mirror in front of himself
when he wrote for fear of disappearing?. I think I'll do the
same just to make sure I don't start flying backwards

It's still to early to tell, but after reading the *Diary
of a Napoleonic Foot Soldier*, Jakob Walter, , and *Life of an
Indian Ensign 1833-43* [in India], by Capt. Albert Hervey, the
journals of American mountain men and scouts are so much more
vivid, fresh, and real. Can you imagine, for even a moment,
a mountain man writing the priggish: "The regiment to which
I now belonged was composed of a fine body of men, and I had
every reason to hope that all would be well with me. Having
commenced my military career afresh, as it were, with nobody
to blame but myself if I went wrong, I resolved to put aside
as much as I possibly could all boyish and griffinish [green-
horn] tricks; to attend strictly to my work; to fag hard, and
pass in languages; to gain a knowledge of my duty; to become
acquainted with my men; to do everything in my power to make
them like me as their officer; to try all I could to please
my commanding officer, and to make myself as agreeable as I
possibly could to those with whom I had become associated
probably for life." Hervey. (Imagine Nietzsche prefacing
Beyond Good and Evil with that paragraph! i.e., substitute
university for 'regiment', scholarly for 'military', my
colleagues for 'my men', philosopher-in-residence for
'officer', and Dean for 'commanding officer', and he would
have a fine preface.)

Or writing with such fatalistic, matter-of-factness:

*Finally, toward four o'clock in the evening, when
it was almost dark, I came to the bridge. Here [in Russia] I
saw only one bridge, the second having been shot away. Now
it was with horror, but at that time it was a with dull,
indifferent feeling, that I looked at the masses of horses
and people which lay dead, piled high upon the bridge. Only
"straight ahead and in the middle!" must be the resolution.
"Here in the water is your grave; beyond the bridge is the
continuation of a wretched life!" Now I kept myself
constantly in the middle. The major and I could aid one
another; and so amid a hundred blows of sabers we came to the
bridge, where not a plank was visible because of the dead men
and horses; and, although on reaching the bridge the people
fell in masses thirty paces to the right and the left, we
through to the firm land.*

*The fact that the bridge was covered with horses and men
was not due to shooting and falling alone but also to the
bridge ties, which were not fastened on this structure. The
horses stepped through between them with their feet and so
could not help falling, until no plank was left movable on
account of the weight of the bodies. For where such timber
still could move, it was torn out of place by the falling
horses, and a sort of trap was prepared for the following
horse. Indeed, one must say that the weight of the dead
bodies was the salvation of those riding across; for without
their load, the cannon would have caused the destruction of*

the bridge too soon. Jakob. (One can see the coming of *The Good Soldier Schweik* in this.)

Compare the two passages above to the vigor of the American:

> *Our party celebrated the Fourth of July, 1874, on the dividing ridge of the Rocky Mountains...at least 13,000 feet above the level sea. There we loosed the American eagle, and with polysyllabic speech and patriotic song moved him to soar and scream. We straddled the back bone of America, sat down on the ridge pole of the continental water-shed, ate sardines from California and crackers from Boston, and drank from two ice-cold rivulets which flowed from the same snow-bank, the one to the Atlantic and the other to the Pacific. The Occasion was inspiring. Of course we did and said all those patriotic things which are customary on such occasions; the speeches being the result of a geometrical progression beyond ordinary patriotic remarks in proportion to our elevation, and proving us the greatest, freest, wisest people in the world. Whether the British lion howled and the effete despotisms trembled, is not known, but it is to be presumed they did. The real enjoyment was in the trip to the summit.* J. H. Beadle, *Western Wilds and the Men Who Redeem Them, 1877.* (Sacco and Vanzetti would never have, <u>could</u> never have written this! Nor, alas, would my father - unless, of course, he was sitting on top of the Caucasus'.((Paul Johnson would call him a "Dupe"))(((Should that make me angry?)))(((((Where is he anyway?)))) (((((Reality was buried in the coffin with him!))))) (((((((In an unmarked grave!!))))))))((((((((Embryo sputter)))))))). This last bit should be read as though one were taking apart one of those wooden, Russian eggs.

A bit of a difference no?

And yes, I know, Nietzsche had ancient, white temples in mind when he wrote of the dry climates of the intellect - but I saw him running barefoot up the hills of Judea deliriously shouting "This is it!! This is truly the City of the Sun - Phoenix - home of the joyous mind and letters to Stanley Fish!" (He was mistaken, of course.) Then he was swallowed in the cloud of dust he himself had stirred, and, ascending in faintly visible patches of blue, pink, and moustache hair, dissolved in the desert wind. I was the only one to see this. Moments later, smack against a mesa wall, 2000 ft. up, Fredrick Remington appeared seated on a director's chair, brush in hand, easel before him, painting the "The Expedition of Francisco Coronado" - from life! I ran toward the Conquistador, serape fluttering, sombrero bouncing, waving like a peasant, and lifted my friendly canteen. Skin flaked off his lips as he smiled down upon me from his lofty steed. Rocks scattered down the canyon wall as Remington stood up in anger. Then I awoke, parched and in need of a glass of French wine. (And yes, the misspellings in the letter to Fish were added for authenticity. Subtle.   Or Stupid?)

The view from my letters: I imagine myself sitting in an aluminum lounge chair over-looking a vast garbage dump, the debris of which creates huge hills and valleys.. The sun glints off this or that thing in the far distance which I then describe in a notepad perched on my knees. Sometimes I raise binoculars to my eyes, sometimes I take a sip of tea from a glass which sits precariously on a chipped, but highly decorated Wedgewood saucer, which itself leans against a dusty, masonite print of the Mona Lisa. Everyday the trucks keep arriving, adding more and more garbage to the heaps. I can not leave until everything has been described. (God may be infinite, but so too am I!)

Rockin-an-rollin' with the West (from here on out this phrase, the West, is an abbreviation for the Wild West - not the Big One over there in Europe). Perhaps I can soar along the gulches, mountains, valleys, and sandy deserts with Bierstadt, Schreyvogel, Farny, and Russell. Perhaps, tagging along with my painters, mountain men and scouts and searching this ancient, wonderous landscape guarded by plants which attack and savages which seem inhuman, we can also find my soul. For like those intrepid explorers wandering in an unknown center of the universe, who, when they lift their sights see things incomprehensible, so too do I when I lift my eyes to the bathroom mirror. We share the experience of the unfamiliar.

I don't care how you slice it, Clinton should not go to Normandy on June 6. Refusing to fight for his country during the Vietnam War fatally compromises him. His motto: "The Man Who Would Never Be in The Position of Shouting: My Kingdom for a Horse." Some King. He should stay home and bear the brunt of his actions, and let the nation suffer for having picked one who would not make the sacrifice - but then again, do-gooders never believe they must suffer for their actions. After all how can doing good have wretched consequences? Everything for them is "abstract".

Rebel Angels

Lo, and Behold!

PARADISE

PARADISE  PARADISE

PARADISE

FIRST PHOTO OF THE UNIVERSE IN MOMENT OF CREATION
(and before Yacub got to it)

PS: This clearly proves that Africa had the camera long
before the whites did.

Dear Steve

At night, when the moon shines on my swaying palms, I
watch naked midnight nymphs climb my garden walls to frolic
in my pool. I watch them diving and rolling in the water,
breasts as white as the moon, legs as limber as the swaying
palms. Blowing smoke into the hot night I witness the
mysteries of life yet am consternated by the ordinariness of
my own. I can not square the two, and remain paralyzed in my
chair.
    Day in and day out the earth revolves about the sun.
It's quite a habit. But then, everything in nature is a
habit. Oceans curve on the horizon, bears wake up in the
Spring, and stars fall through the night. Always they are
endlessly repeated. It is only we, to ourselves, that seem
to break the spell of the Eternal Recurrence. On some days
we go shopping, on others not. Yesterday I used a pencil,
today a pen. Everything is in flux, nothing remains the same
for us - except our minds. In there the same eternal play is
staged every conscious day and sleeping night. Here is where
we experience the Eternal, one act Nightmare of life. It is
our one link to Mother Nature. But we must be down in the
mouth, and caught like a fly on the saccharin flypaper of
childhood to experience her. It is then, and only then, mouth
stuck to the yellow glue, that we can live the true brutality
of nature. We can experience the same destructive will to
remain eternally recurrent, heedless of the pain and
suffering it may cause, even if it rents our own souls as
nature does when she hurtles her bowels up through mountain
tops, or lacerates her skin with deep, wide gashes. First
hand we can experience the elemental, the primitive, the
swamp of existence. Between the ears putrid bubbles called
thoughts pop on the surface with monotone regularity, blip,
burp, and wheeze, feeding the miasma. Ah, the sick mind!
Once a clean *tabula rasa*, now as though ten, farting giants
spillng wine and gravy ate upon it, afterwards bringing their
bare bottoms to its edge and defecating.
    Whata life!
    I feel I was one day was brought to my knees by a
series of emotional knock-out punches which sent me into
cuckkoo land. I can no longer reason, merely feel the bruises
of defeat and the pulp of humiliation. With an inner rage I
set out to prove some cockamamie notion about the world:
namely, that it doesn't deserve the right to exist. That's
what I've been doing all my life: trying to prove that only I
have the right to exist. I have soared high upon the spiked
bat-wings of revenge and resentment. The Romanian version of
the botched and bungled.

LETS SAY I WRITE SOMETHING AS THE FOLLOWING:

SUICIDE AS SALVATION

In deconstructing the 'author' in 1978, Michel Foucault inadvertently, but more importantly, deconstructed the audience. "The auhtor has disappeared," he ambigously wrote, but if the 'author' is gone the audience also departs. Walter Benjamin had written the same a number of years earlier. The consequences were that both men were forced to write books to themselves under the pretense, as Benjamin put it, that "No poem is intended for the reader, no picture for the beholder, no symphony for the listener." anyway. In time, their narcissism took its toll, and both committed suicide. The world, however, went on. Their intellectual progeny, the ones whose volumes fill bookstore shelves labelled "Post-Modern Writers," have not been willing to pay this intellectual price prefering instead to have the reader do it for them. As Greg Denning explains; post-modern authors do not write to or for an audience. Their books are to be read by any one who freely chooses to do so and at any time of day. Our books, he writes, are as New Age music; there is no begining to them nor end. Post-modern writers, he says, merely ask their readers upon reading their books to give up the notion that they are doing so to communicate with another human, but are there rather to have their imagination given a new direction. On this accounting of the writing profession, writers do not share their thoughts and feelings with their readers, they only display them in order to spark readers to conjure up their own in endless, parallel monologues. These thousands of non-authors writing for non-audiences form an army of the published living dead. To read them one must except their premise: human commication is impossible. It is a self-destructive premise.
In an age strong with national identity, slopisistic thinking was a curious novelty which excited the intellectual imagination of the likes of Berkeley, Hume, and, Descartes, but in our anomic times it has a psychological twist and invites one not to festive delight in the powers of the intellect, but rather to a cozy party where everyone, while talking and dancing, self-annihilates for lack of human contact. A finding of salvation through social suicide. It is no wonder then that post-modern writers wear red ribbons in their lapels; fuck only your own sex and wipe out the species their ribbons tell us, end the painful charade of existence.

NOW - To whom have I writen this and why? It's a mystery to me.
Otto Friederick can write 40 2000 page biographies in a matter of weeks (I exaggerate), because he wants to. His research falls into place, is ordered, indexed, and he ends up telling a story, or rather, the story he wants to tell

because he is humanly normal. In comparison, my story
telling is contentless, shapeless, and defies indexing; it
flows like wet shit. It lacks being the expression of
desire; it's irrational venting. It is a public service as
it were. But my public is the rude horde of commuters in
Grand Central station rushing to get home on a dark winter
night. So . . . I end up writing to myself in a mood of
resentement and spite. Actually, it's more like vomiting
into a city sewer.

Between my ears is where the disorder lies. It's all a
jumble in there. My brain is like forty million ringing and
lighting pin-ball machines being played simultaneously.
Complex but no depth. No self.

I send you a recent, candid photo of myself (Rousseau
did not take it. I think it was Freud one night sneaking
round my back window):

But enough. It has been such a long time since I have written to you - and so much has come from you! Life on the desert is strange. But that is not it entirely. First Kathy Abelson visited for nearly two weeks, then Oliver came for nearly a month - a visit which was broken up by our having to drive to LA to take care of our mother, bless her arthritic soul. Things have been normal for barely a week now. But that is not it entirely either. Doldrums. Waiting for a wind to pick up my sails. Simply floating is what I am doing. Everything interests me and nothing interests me. I start something, but within an hour I am bored with it. I want to read this and I want to read that, but then again, something over there on the mantle intrigues me, but I am too lazy to walk over to it - and so I read nothing. Then a mysterious Gulf current jostles me and I turn on the TV only to meet the same indecision: channel 5 for two minutes, channel 50 for ten, etc. Then, surprising myself, I find myself painting my mother's garage. I am sweating - something I did not want to do.

All of this is related to my becoming aware that whatever I have written has amounted to no more than letters to myself. I have never experienced an 'audience' looking at me. Unlike Odysseus, I am at a complete loss. I can not see myself. I am not Greek, only Romanian.

To answer one question directly - no, I do not know that teacher at Eastern District - Gene Mann - but I bet he was quoted out of context. My sense of it is that he was saying 'if one doesn't pay graduation fees, then one can not attend graduation,' One must "pay to appear." Do not trust the article. The reporter knows nothing about how schools operate. 1) Students have never received their actual diplomas at graduation - only later in the guidance office. 2) Schools have been graduating unqualified students for at least twenty years - affirmative action graduations - to make them, as the Good Superintendent said, feel good about themselves.(The reasoning is: if the student can earn the necessary credit or two over the summer, why make him wait until January of the following year to attend graduation.) 3) Students request 'early' graduation, none are coerced. 4) Yes, students who fail summer school are not expected by those who do not know they failed to be on the Fall register 5) Mann overstates the case, but known loosers will continue to lose, and generally hang out in schools to sell drugs, shoot people, make contacts, piss in the halls, or simply to ward off lonliness. Schools have been trying for years to get rid of two or three year 'seniors.'

In response to your last letter, however - well, those which we pick to read these days seem to be all paranoiacs. Clever, but loco en la cabeza. We must learn, as you and Spengler write, to see them as ignoramuses "incapable" of figuring out what Mont St. Michelle is. Then, of course, we shall lose interest in them. Until then they feed our own paranoia; with all our might we fight their firecrackers and fists from within our room, curtains drawn. Neither of us

escapes this daily battle. After school they they wait for
us, you know, they linger on the stoop waiting for us to come
out smug and confident that we have defeated them, made fools
of them.   Unlike Napleon who marched to Russia, we march to
uor room and think Russia.   Peripheral vision fades when we
write.   The world disappears and we feel at home when the
mind gazes in upon itself, upon its angers and resentments.
Comfortable now, the very universe can gush from our pens.
Far from the inhumanity of man to child, of those who would
crush us, we can roam unhindered in the dark corridors of our
brain, imagining the world perfectly, secure that we fight
the forces of Evil.   I don't know about you, but my audience
is God.(Grading my malaise there are times when I feel that
if Len teaches those in the 15th and 16th grades, and you
teach those in the 13th and 14th grades, I teach those in the
9th grade. An appropriate scale don't you think?   A measure
of our grip on reality.)

But where is the Olympian Chateaubriand and Tocqueville
in us?   Why can not we spit on these hair-brained, shallow,
uneducated, mean, narrow slopsists in public?   Throw out our
chests in a remarkable show of superiority, and tell them
they have the minds of ants?   And then go on and write of the
beauty of flowers, the dissolution of empires, of fragrant
Spanish gardens, of things they are incapable of even noting
as having occured. I watch naked nymphs frolic in my pool yet
choose to dwell in my over grooved brain.

To "prove" reality is, as you say, pointless.   Yet what
else is it we do?   There is no audience for this pointless
task. Only ourselves.   And how many times can we do this?   At
last count I reached four billion.   As Garguilo said, still,
we are an audience for ourselves, but if this all we do our
'proofs' are not only pointless, they are absurd. (To speak
to myself is something of which I am incapable - I speak when
I am alone, but it is to nobody.   Or, rather, it is as though
I am dying and uttering my last words to an approaching
darkness. When I come to, I have forgotten what I said.)

Ah, Gilman and Nehamas! Reading them is like listening
to Charlie Brown play Beethoven.   Is this what the world has
come to? Or have we fashioned a world in which we can not
live?   I have thought about this one.   I have made the world
a party I did not want to be invited to, a festive meeting of
multiculturists held in a penthouse without elevators.   To
respond to Gilman or Nehamas is like being forced to danse
with Catherine MacKinnon.   To refuse them, to first explain
to them that they don't know how to ·danse, they will only
switch partners muttering "Who is that social misfit?"   So to
whom shall I explain the nature of dancing(reality), everyone
at this party is now avoding me. (But none of you know how to
dance I want to scream. Witness the very first sentence of
MacKinnon's *Only Words*: "Imagine that for hundreds of years
your most formative traumas, your daily suffering and pain,
the abuse you live through, the terror you live with, are
unspeakable - not the basis of literature."   As you would
ask, whaaa? That's not the Samba, the Continental, the

jitter-bug, the waltz, it's not even a dozy-dough.) Shall I explain the basic two-step to those who agree with me? If so, then they want to hear quartets, not how Gilman and Nehamas can't danse. I should be at the first floor soireé across the street. Gilman, Nehamas, Takaka, Rogin, Denning, MacKinnon, etc., are the "froth of events," the Saint Laurents, the Giglis of the intellectual world, or the Sorel's, the Gentile's of the forgotten Futurists whose country left them in the dust. Next season styles will change - and so my explaining would stick out of the old rags in the garbage cans of Seventh Ave.

My last pilgrimage was to the High Gate(?) cemetery. Here is a photo recording my ascent:

It was a dead-end. There was no sacred healing there as in the chapel dirt at Chimayo, just a nose broken by a bomb. No abandoned crutches or rusitng wheel-chairs littered the scene, testimony to forgivness. It was more like the roped-off lower-class living room of an unforgiving, immigrant father. A different kind of shrine altogether. It was my version of attending a Black Mass - I reversed reality and kissed the ass of Satan. Culminating my ascend from childhood I had managed to find the tomb of Hell, and entered crossing over from sanity to inanity. From then on life became an unwilling, boring struggle against inexplicable, gratuitious forces of oppression. A Calling, but the voice was an echo from my childhood drawing me deeper in to the canyons of myself. In to darkness, away from the light.

Two postcard photos adorn my window sill. One is of Tolstoy, an old man dressed in rags holding a bend stick for a cane, about to journey forth to find God. The other is of a handle-bar mustachioed Puccini, chest thrown out, a felt, white derby cocked jauntily to one side - as though he were ready to seduce a pretty bar-maid. Which shall it be?

"Behind the world in which we live, far in the background, lies another world, and the two have about the same relation to each other as do the stage proper and stage one sometimes sees behind it in the theater. Through a hanging of fine gauze, one sees, as it were, a world of gauze, lighter, more ethereal, with a quality different from that of the actual world. Many people who appear physically in the actual world are not at home in it but are at home in that other world. But a person's fading away in this manner, indeed, almost vanishing from actuality, can have its basis either in health or in sickness. The latter was the case with this amn, whom I had once known without knowing him. He did not belong to the world of actuality, and yet he had very much to do with it. He continually ran lightly over it, but even when he most abandoned himself to it, he was beyond it. But it was not the good that beckoned him away, nor was it actually evil - even now I dare not say that of him. He has suffered from an *exacerbatio cerebri*, for which actuality did not have enough stimulation, at most only momentarily. He did not overstrain himself on actuality, he was not too weak to bear it; no, he was too strong, but this strength was a sickness. As soon as actuality had lost its significance as stimulation, he was disarmed, and the evil in him lay in this. He was conscious of this at the very moment of stimulation, and the evil lay in this consciousness."
                                        Kierkegaard

Ah ha!

Well, the cattle are restless and it's time to move on. I shall try to write more often from the trail, but the cowboys wicked temptation - under moonlit skies - is to stare at the stars and howl with the coyote.

                    Yours to trails end

Note: Check out one Stanely Crouch - another black scholar in the trenches. I send you a slightly modified *Last Manifesto* - hang it where Ruth can read it. By the way - how are your classes going? School in general? Your health? David? You see, important things are the last thing on my mind.

escapes this daily battle. After school they they wait for us, you know, they linger on the stoop waiting for us to come out smug and confident that we have defeated them, made fools of them. Unlike Napleon who marched to Russia, we march to uor room and think Russia. Peripheral vision fades when we write. The world disappears and we feel at home when the mind gazes in upon itself, upon its angers and resentments. Comfortable now, the very universe can gush from our pens. Far from the inhumanity of man to child, of those who would crush us, we can roam unhindered in the dark corridors of our brain, imagining the world perfectly, secure that we fight the forces of Evil. I don't know about you, but my audience is God.(Grading my malaise there are times when I feel that if Len teaches those in the 15th and 16th grades, and you teach those in the 13th and 14th grades, I teach those in the 9th grade. An appropriate scale don't you think? A measure of our grip on reality.)

But where is the Olympian Chateaubriand and Tocqueville in us? Why can not we spit on these hair-brained, shallow, uneducated, mean, narrow slopsists in public? Throw out our chests in a remarkable show of superiority, and tell them they have the minds of ants? And then go on and write of the beauty of flowers, the dissolution of empires, of fragrant Spanish gardens, of things they are incapable of even noting as having occured. I watch naked nymphs frolic in my pool yet choose to dwell in my over grooved brain.

To "prove" reality is, as you say, pointless. Yet what else is it we do? There is no audience for this pointless task. Only ourselves. And how many times can we do this? At last count I reached four billion. As Garguilo said, still, we are an audience for ourselves, but if this all we do our 'proofs' are not only pointless, they are absurd. (To speak to myself is something of which I am incapable - I speak when I am alone, but it is to nobody. Or, rather, it is as though I am dying and uttering my last words to an approaching darkness. When I come to, I have forgotten what I said.)

Ah, Gilman and Nehamas! Reading them is like listening to Charlie Brown play Beethoven. Is this what the world has come to? Or have we fashioned a world in which we can not live? I have thought about this one. I have made the world a party I did not want to be invited to, a festive meeting of multiculturists held in a penthouse without elevators. To respond to Gilman or Nehamas is like being forced to danse with Catherine MacKinnon. To refuse them, to first explain to them that they don't know how to danse, they will only switch partners muttering "Who is that social misfit?" So to whom shall I explain the nature of dancing(reality), everyone at this party is now avoding me. (But none of you know how to dance I want to scream. Witness the very first sentence of MacKinnon's *Only Words*: "Imagine that for hundreds of years your most formative traumas, your daily suffering and pain, the abuse you live through, the terror you live with, are unspeakable - not the basis of literature." As you would ask, whaaa? That's not the Samba, the Continental, the

Dear Steve

> The man who, in order to understand
> the inner world of a cannibal tribe,
> has partaken of the practice of
> cannibalism, has probably gone
> to far: he can never quite
> be one of his own folk again.
> T.S.Eliot

As usual, I carry an Everest of words on my back and they all want to come out at once.

First, let me thank you profusely for the gifts. *Noa Noa*, in this edition, is a delight simply to hold, and Casper the Friendly Ghost brings back complicated but pleasurable memories of <u>A Perfect Day</u>. They both hit the spot.

Reason for delay in responding: my mother had a heart attack. I drove to LA, met Oliver who flew down, and we both stayed with her for two weeks. She feels better now after an angioplasty(phonetic spelling?). In any case, her heart took me away from myself - I was there in Sept. for over a week just before fulfilling childhood obligations - and I always need time to recuperate from another's illness. Whenever I am away from my self I require time to come home: I confuse being with others with absence from myself.

Self-Portrait after an absence

In the meantime, I have been carousing between book covers - mostly George Steiner(*After Babel*), Robert Pattison(*The Triumph of Vulgarity*, *The Great Dissent*, and *On Literacy*), Harold Bloom, yes, Harold Bloom(*The Western Cannon*), Frederick Karl(*Franz Kafka*), J. Derrida(On Grammatology), Kenneth Cmiel(*Democratic Eloquence*), Robert Paul Wolff(*Moneybags Must Be So Lucky* - an essay, get this, which attempts to prove that *Das Capital* is a "literary work of genius" "The text," he writes, "is rich in literary and historical allusions to the entire corpus of Western culture. The argument is twisted, convoluted, obscure, and terribly difficult to follow. Marx invokes religious images, Mephistophlean images, political images. He writes now mockingly and scornfully, now soberly and with proper professional seriousness, now angrily and bitterly. He swings with baffling speed from the most abstruse metaphysical reflections to vividly sensual evocations of the suffering and struggles of the English workers against the oppression of their bosses. At one instant he is a polemicist, writing to the moment. At the next, he is a pedant, calling down authorities in six languages from twenty centuries to confirm his etymological and analytical speculations." "What is going on," Wolff asks, if not a great literary artist at work! Never mind that all that Wolff attributes to Marx would make a normal person put *Das Capital* back on the shelf, what is the quirk in Wolff's mind that makes him believe obscurity, convolution, and twisted ways of writing make for literary genius? There is much to be made of this freudian slip), to name but a few. This is not to say that I endorse them like wonderous Gene Tierney puckering Merle Oberon Tropical Heat lipstick, yet they have all become a part of me and now subtly flavor my words as SenSen - or is their presence detected more as odors of perspiration? (It seems very thing falls into me just as like carrots, potatoes, and celery fall into a boiling pot.)

Ah, yes, and Borgmann. I now agree with you. He is all head. I thought he might have had something in the concepts of 'eloquent moments' and the 'existence of the world', but the concepts are vapid, bordering on Hallmark inspiration. My frantic search for relief was squandered. I should have paid more attention the writing. As you put it: "ugly work is generally incorrect." I stand corrected. Yet,.......

if they are such ugly writers why is this recent Duke
graduate whose dissertation, <u>Phallocentrism and the Fall of
Rome</u>, so pretty? (Fish took the snap.)

Is it a question of Beauty and the Beast?

"Where were the fathers?" you ask. Fighting in the trenches of Anzio, Normandy, the Black Forest? Or guiltly sitting in Parisian cafés with bérets tilted to one side? See if these Spenglerian inspired quoted words do not conjure up a bitter solace:

"Unfortunately, nothing will ever be the same because the art and passion of reading well and deeply, which was the foundation of our enterprise, depended upon people who were fanatical readers when they were small children. Even devoted and solitary readers are now necessarily beleaguered, because they cannot be certain that fresh generations will rise up to prefer Shakespeare and Dante to all other writers. The shadows lengthen in our evening land, and we approach the second millennium expecting further shadowing.

I do not deplore these matters; the aesthetic is, in my view, an individual rather than a societal concern. . . . Literary criticism is an ancient art; its inventor, according to Bruno Snell, was Aristophanes, and I tend to agree with Henrich Heine that 'There is a God, and his name is Aristophanes." Cultural criticism is another dismal social science, but literary criticism, as an art, always was and always will be an elitist phenomenon. It was a mistake to believe that literary criticism could become the basis for a democratic education or for societal improvement. When our English and other literature departments shrink to the dimensions of our current Classics departments, ceding their grosser functions to the legions of Cultural Studies, we will perhaps be able to return to the study of the inescapable, to Shakespeare and his few peers, who after all, invented all of us.

What interests me more is the flight from the aesthetic among so many in my profession, some of whom at least began with the ability to experience aesthetic value. In Freud, flight is the metaphor for repression, for unconscious yet purposeful forgetting. The purpose is clear enough in my profession's flight: to assuage displaced guilt. Forgetting in an aesthetic context, is ruinous, for cognition, in criticism, always relies on memory. Longinus would have said that pleasure is what the resenters have forgotten. Nietzsche would have called it pain; but they would have thinking of the same experience upon the heights. Those who descend from there, lemminglike, chant the litany that literature is best explained as a mystification promoted by bourgeois institutions.

... I urge a stubborn resistance whose single aim is to preserve poetry as fully and purely as possible. Our legions who have deserted represent a strand in our traditions that has always been in flight from the aesthetic: Platonic moralism and Aristotelian social science. The attack on poetry either exiles it for being destructive of social well-being or allows it sufferance if it will assume the work of social catharsis under the banners of the new multiculturalism. Beneath the surfaces of academic Marxism,

Feminism, and New Historicism, the ancient polemic of Platonism and the equally archaic Aristotelian social medicine continue on their course. . . . We are losing now, and doubtless we will go on losing, and there is sorrow in that, because many of the best students will abandon us . . . They are justified in doing so, because we could not protect them against our profession's loss of intellectual and aesthetic standards of accomplishment and value. All that we can do now is maintain some continuity with the aesthetic . .

Here they [the New Historicists, Feminists, Marxists, Lacanians, Deconstructionists, Semioticians; i.e., the School of Resenters] confront insurmountable difficulty in Shakespeare's most idiosyncratic strength: he is always ahead of you, conceptually and imagistically, whoever and whenever you are. He renders you anachronistic because he contains you; you cannot subsume him. You can not illumine him with a new doctrine, be it Marxism or Freudianism or Demanian linguistic skepticism. Instead, he will illuminate the doctrine, not by prefiguration but by postfiguration as it were: all of Freud that matters most is there in Shakespeare already, with a persuasive critique of Freud besides. The Freudian map of the mind is Shakespeare's; Freud seems only to have prosified it. Or, to vary my point, a Shakespearean reading of Freud illuminates and overwhelms the text of Freud; a Freudian reading of Shakespeare reduces Shakespeare . . . *Coriolanus* is a far more powerful reading of Marx's *Eighteenth Brumaire of Louis Napoleon* that any Marxist reading of *Coriolanus*.. . .

The silliest way to defend the Western Canon is to insist that it incarnates all the seven deadly virtues that make up our supposed range of normative values and democratic principles. This is palpably untrue. The *Iliad* teaches the surpassing glory of armed victory, while Dante rejoices in the eternal torment he visits upon his very personal enemies. Tolstoy's private version of Christianity throws aside nearly everything that anyone among us retains, and Dostoevsky preaches anti-Semitism, obscurantism, and the necessity of human bondage. Shakespeare's politics, insofar as we can pin them down, do not appear to be very much different from those of his Coriolanus, and Milton's ideas of free speech and free press do not preclude the imposition of all manner of societal restraints. Spencer rejoices in the massacre of Irish rebels, while the egomania of Wodsworth exalts his own poetic mind over any other source of splendor.

The West's greatest writers are subversive of all values, both ours and their own. . . . If we read the Western Canon in order to form our social, political, or personal moral values, I firmly believe we will become monsters of selfishness and exploitation. To read in the service of any ideology is not, in my judgment, to read at all. The reception of aesthetic power enables us to learn how to talk to ourselves and how to endure ourselves. The true use of Shakespeare or of Cervantes, of Homer or of Dante, of Chaucer

or of Rabelais, is to augment one's own inner self. Reading
deeply in the Canon will not make one a better or worse
person, a more useful or more harmful citizen. The mind's
dialogue with itself is not primarily a social reality. All
that the Western Canon can bring one is the proper use of
one's own solitude, that solitude whose final form is one's
confrontation with one's own mortality."

Two former Westerner's trying to recapture a sense of the
solitary.

And in direct response to you and Ruisdael, he writes:

"The motives for reading, as for writing [or viewing a landscape], are very diverse and frequently not clear even to the most self-conscious readers and writers [and museum goers]. Perhaps the ultimate motive for metaphor, or the writing and reading of figurative language [or the positioning of oneself before a Ruisdael], is the desire to be different, to be elsewhere. In this assertion I follow Nietzsche, who warned us that what we can finds words for is already dead in our hearts, so there is always a kind of contempt in the act of speaking. Hamlet agrees with Nietzsche, and both might have extended the contempt to the act of writing [but not to viewing]. But we do not read [or view] to unpack our hearts, so there is no contempt in the act of reading [or viewing]. Traditions tell us that the free and solitary self writes [or engages a Ruisdael] in order to overcome mortality. I think that the self, in its quest to be free and solitary, ultimately reads [views] with one aim only; to confront greatness. That confrontation scarcely masks the desire to join greatness, which is the basis of the aesthetic experience once called the Sublime: the quest for a transcendence of limits."

I won't tell you who wrote the above - though you probably already know or can easily figure it out - but it surprised the hell out of me. I do wish his writing were better - although I am not quite sure what I mean by that - - the experiences he points toward surpass the reach of his vocabulary, his metaphors? Music and the plastic arts are not encompassed by him as by you in noting the "musical motifs" in Schopenhauer, Nietzsche, Spengler,etc,. Nietzsche, of course, he's not. Spengler he's not either (especially when one gets into the body of the work which is often near incomprehensible) - but he's better than Borgmann; the guy is an ordinary mortal trying to make sense of <u>his</u> exhilarating experiences (trying to rationally convey what only art can convey). (John Adams' review of the book in the NYR is dreadful.) I remember Bobby Thomas once telling me that for a long time the most fightening experience for him was letting himself go on the drums; he couldn't do it though he knew that only by doing so could he become great - a true drummer. Objectivity, for a writer, is a similiar compromise with greatness: the Great Fear of abandoning oneself in the fountain of metaphor (a word, a brush-stroke, a musical note) which is oneself and where only the Devil and God know what might be heard or seen.
Nihilism and Me: My Childhood and World History, or The Prefiguration of World History in Enlarged Female Bellies, or

Coincidences of Futurity in Deficient Placenta and Periods of Decadence in World History.

Your essay arrived today. I will jump in to it after second reading knowing I will probably regret not letting sit within me for at least a week. Do not let me offend you; chalk rudeness up to self-despair and ignorance to ignorance.

Surprised, without warning, we stumble over a fallen Nietzsche brought down by de Man's misreading of a few sentences - the Great Nihilist caught leaving a Wagnerian porno store with operatic hope wrapped in paper - then we see Nietzsche upright, cleansed of the Wagner episode, and chatting in the company of Goethe, Constable, and Spengler, a great "aesthetic reader" who shames de Man's lifeless and irksome scholasticism. But the Wagner episode is confusing - why does it take Spengler, reaching back over his shoulder, to drag Nietzsche out of the porno shop? Indeed, why does it take the entire 19th century to drag him out of there? Is it because de Man says he found him there? Rid yourself of de Man. Nietzsche is to great to be prefaced by him! The music of your writing begins on page 4. Now we soar - though N's relations with Wagner and Germany continue to lack clarity for me; it is difficult to tell when N. felt what: Faust dies in Goethe, but what "solar orbit" swirls around Bach and Wagner, and when is the "inaccessible abyss" the heart of Germany?

Your 'argument':

> We want to hold fast to our senses and to our faith in them - and think their consequences through to the end!
>
> The existing world, upon which all earthly living things have worked so that it appears as it does (durabable and changing slowly), we want to go on building - and not critize it away as false!
>
> Our valuations are a part of this building; they emphasize and underline it.
>
> One must understand the artistic basic phenomenon that is called "life" -

the words of Goethe, Nietzsche, Spengler, Constable, Blake, Wodsworth, Whitman, Melvilee, Dickens, and Dostoevsky are as the clarinets, bassoons, drums, French horns, and violins of an historic playing of Ravel's Bolero begun at the opening of the 19th century and rising to a crescendo at its close. All of Europe is their symphony Hall. (A 2000 piece orchestra to 'prove' that Nietzsche writes of more than "mere formal symmetries devoid of thematic weight.") Yet, the music remains on the other side of 1900 - it is the music of the dead. You hear them from a great distance - from in your rooms on Henry Street, but what of it? "So?" Bertha asks, "You conduct a great sounding symphony. What have you got to say?" Ay, there's the rub! Like me, you quail before the abyss. Others can feel a greatness - but we dare not feel its rumbling within ourselves. We will only point to the great. "Mira! Mira!" we will cry, "look at what they can do. Now leave me alone." But we can't walk away, just like that. People want more than directions from us when they are not lost De Man may be lost, but it is not for us to assume that all our readers are mere replicas. They need not be chastised. We are like Kierkegaard's sign: "Trousers pressed here" - after a while even we won't buy it.

Brick wall, I tell you, that's what the world is, a brick wall.

What we need are sentences such as: "We possess the Canon because we are mortal and also rather belated." Or, "The study of literature, however it is conducted, will not save any individual, any more than it will improve society." Or, "Tradition is not only a handing-down or process of benign tansmission; it is also a conflict between past genius and present aspiration, in which the prize is literary survival or canonical inclusion."   That is, sentences which limit us to ourselves, not sentences wherein others are used to point to our inarticulate greatness: we must articulate ours ourselves even if we fall far short of ... it (as Bloom above - even though he is right)! Is it that Marty Maisel made his airplanes while we struggled to make somebody's idea of an airplane?

Or do I misunderstand you? Am I talking to myself? God knows I wish I could write as well as you. I just can not refrain from thinking 'something is missing' - as I do with my own stuff. It would not surprise me if you write back saying I smother you in foreign debris carted in from Chicago. I should keep it on my side of Appalachia. Are we moved to write only to correct faults, but not to lengthen and improve upon greatness? i.e., join the <u>march</u> of humanity.

Well, I could go on and on. Will pick up where I left off in the next because I do want to get something off to you. For Noa Noa I send you Lenny Bruce, he brought the South Seas North.

Lou

z

309

Nov. 18 1994

Dear Steve

   In your last letter you speak of - what?!!! - would you
believe it, I can't find your last letter. I had it right
here, besides me at the Mac! Did I mail it back to you?
(You now see what a rush I can get into!) Oh, well, if I did
parcel it to you please dispatch it on back - as you, I enjoy
re-reading or re-writing them when I'm feeling in need of a
pick-up or ever so slightly deconstructive.
   As I was about to say: in your last letter - according
to memory now - you wrote of your ever inceasing disgust with
Paul deMan. Have you read D. Lehman's book *Signs of the
Times* (at least Part 2)? Try it, your disgust will really
increase. (If you don't have a copy - if you like - I'll send
reproductions of pertinent pages.) DeMan is *Dr. Criminale*
down to the hair on his balls - only worse. Indeed, it would
not surpise me if Bradbury did not use him as his model.
Derrida's defense of deMan, as quoted by Lehman, also reveals
Derrida as a charlatan. The most telling argument occurs
when Lehman points out how Derrida defended himself against
critics of his defense of deMan by claiming his piece was
misread, i.e., claiming authorial interpretative supremacy!
As you or I have said, they are both no more than wavey-
haired Ron Hubbards waving good-byes from the front seats of
Jaguars (although deMan's hair is probably a mess by now) -
which is quite a bit actually. Gurus and predators of and in
an age susceptible to the Memory Loss Syndrome which
Frederick Crews speaks of in the last two isues of the NYR, a
syndrome which is really not the result of repression but of
the result of a loss of ego, i.e., the reality principle. The
collapse of which Gibbon writes we are now witness too - a
civilization in the process of losing its identity/memory.
It's an inner thing, insidious and creeping; egos are popping
out of existence all over the country, one by one. We are
becoming a nation of rudderless humans - although the last
election results show we will not go down.without a fight.
In the recent issue of the Atlantic Paul Kennedy writes that
by the year 2025 the improvished of the world will innundate
the West, pillaging it for its goodies. Of course, that
means 5 billion boat-people wearing Gucci tank-tops wet with
Chanel #5 and KFC chicken breasts dangling from their mouths,
dancing to boomboxes in the White House - until, that is, the
generators stop, trains run into each other, and the snow
falls. If we allow it.
   I did not mean to sound curt or brusque in my 'critique'
of your essay which you shared with me. It just seemed to be
so much more than a reaction to the shit of deMan. We needn't
prove our case, or be on the defensive. The challenge, for
us, is not to be defensive! I know I rush to feel
beleaguered, set upon to vindicate whatever it is that will

offer me salvation. But then the "it" overwhelms me, my ego submerges itself in the 'cause' and it is not me that I give voice to but the world as seen aright in the vision of others. I become the voice of Truth - against my will! How litle ego strength I have is amazing. But am I blinded by my weakness? Do I see it everywhere, in you, willy-nilly? This I am not sure of. So pardon my brash preempting of your head.

In an interview which appeared in <u>The Historian</u> Stephen J. Pyne, in response to the question: "Do you think about your audience when you write?" - said, "I start with voice. How do I want my book to sound? Do I want it to be ironic? Authoritative? Playful? An outline, endlessly reworked, decides the nature of the plot - narrative, thesis, chronology, informing metaphor, whatever the logic of the argument is. Fixing the voice solves lots of the minor problems, such as transitions and emphasis." Simple, no? It's finding that dammed voice! Not a reactive voice. But one's own voice, loud and clear, no matter what's going on in the world.(It's not a matter of voicing to the world what's already in it only not clearly percieved or forgotten, but expressing something they have never heard before, oneself! A passion which needs no preface or excuse for being.) It seems that when I write I wish to convince the reader not that I am right but that what I know is right. Thus, I deflect the reader from me onto the 'content'; it is not me that they must agree with but the 'content.' Like the Wizard of Oz I prefer hiding behind a curtain. The greatness of Nietzsche is that he flings open the curtain as the Wizard whom everyone is waiting for.

Nietzsche never argues - until he gets mid-way into *The Will To Power* (which I shall come to later). Sentences proceed out of sentences, each one elucidating/expanding the last. The first is dredged up out of the depths of his soul; the crystallization of a feeling in words which are its perfect expression, and therefore, our reality. It is beyond dispute. From the initial sentence certain things follow; it is massaged like the belly of a pregnant women until it gives birth to further perfect crystallizations, and so on until a "book" is completed and the feeling is mature and exhausted. We close the last page suspended in the sounds of words yet an anvil is falling through our dark soul as heavy as the atom from which the universe was created. <u>Serious</u> philosophers do not crystalize their feeling but the feelings of others or those of the world spirit. Amassing idiosyncratically choosen actions of individuals or of humanity in general and assigning them various historical/emotional weights, they crystalize history, revealing it for what it is. <u>Practical</u> historians quantify and measure the actions of humanity asigining them powers and emotional weight relative to their numbers, reducing the arbitrariness of selection of <u>serious</u> philosophers like Hegel. They argue their points. <u>Serious</u> philosophers can only be questioned by <u>practical</u> historians, but their desultory spears either fall

short or fly off the battle field. All the time Neitzsche lies
with the Queen of Sheba, stroking her hair and pointing to the
stars.

And this, I take it, is the thrust of your essay: art uber
alles! Nietzsche, Goethe, Spengler, as well as other 19th
century giants, train one for an "integration of intellect and
life," not to cultivate an interest in the mechanics of
"cultural decline." But, if I may say so, you seem to slide over
to quickly the difference between Spengler's unrelieved
pessimism and Nietzche's: "Briefly: the categories 'aim,'
'unity,' 'being,' which we used to project some values into the
world - we *pull out* again; so the world looks valueless." and
..."the universe seems to have lost value, seems 'meaningless' -
but that is only a *transitional stage*." Which is not at all
Spenglerian; for N. all does not lie in the seeming. Nihilism
seems a 'psychological disease' for Nietzsche, not an historical
phase. Spring is not for us and unlimited mental health is
always possible.

Late in life Nietzsche wrote: "I once saw a storm raging
over the sea, and a clear blue sky above it; it was then that I
came to dislike all sunless, cloudy passions which know no
light, except the lightning." and then sat down to contemplate a
Lorrain landscape. (Taken from Heller in <u>The Artist's Journey</u>
<u>Into The Interior</u>.) Heller says that N.'s philosophy is like a
human face "on the features of which are inscribed,
disquietingly, the destines of souls; or like cities rich in
history. . . . 'Do you understand Nietzsche?' is like asking 'Do
you know Rome?' In a sense, Nietzsche takes us back to
ourselves, stripped of excuses to live, grounding us in the
naked joy of living. It is not the search for truth, to know
the logic of God's creation, or to believe that we live to make
life better for all - to rid the world of want, need, scarcity,
ugliness, and pain - that pushes and sustains us in living, but
only that we want to be alive to be ourselves, to flower, to
realize that all the tools of our culture - our languages
(music, literature, art) are for us to make pleasure by
discovering ourselves in and through them as a flower through
its color, mesmerizing scent, and shapely petals. (For Spengler
our contemporary nights should be spent in honky-tonk saloons,
not on the banks of the Nile.) Understood this way, under the
course of world history there is a worm burrowing another
history: the struggle to be at peace in ourselves, to *accept*
making the universe *our* home, pleasure without pain. Nihilism
is the revealing penultimate chapter of 100,000 years of this
underground quest to free ourselves of the need for salvation
whether through the blessings of God or through intellectual
cleansing by Truth. The question is: will we, as humanity (as
oppossed to individuals who have already passed beyond nihilism
both today and in the past) reach the last chapter? (Of course,
what does all this mean must be grasped first. I don't think I
know.)

I suspect that Alexander, John D. Rockefeller, Ghengis
Khan, the Empress' of China (indeed, perhaps most women),

perhaps even Shaka Zulu, as all great movers and shapers of history, knew Nietzsche's dark secret all along. "He who does not *wish* to see what is great in a man, has the sharpest eye for what is low and superficial in him, and so gives away - himself," Nietzsche says. Which reminds me that in my twenties I either ran across or invented the idea that knowledge was a product of *wishing* to know what one knows. Knowledge was a *moral* choice for me. For thirty years I had forgotten this 'insight' - do I merely recycle myself? Is my version of the Eternal Recurrence simply obsessive neurosis?

Yet, if language has no referent, if there is an ontological hiatus between the signified and the signifier - if the "dancer" can be separated from the "dance" and be left on the stage scratching his head as deMan imagines (a neurotic dream) - than I doubt if humanity would have made it through the last 40 thousand years of its history. It is inconceivable to me that perpetual motion 'language machines' could sustain human life for that length of time without succumbing to the law of natural selection. Why would the tool of language which did not meet real, objective needs (pardon me if I sound Marxist for a moment) not be discarded just as blunt stones would be discarded as a tool for separating deer skin from deer flesh? Would not those who truly used non-referential languages, just as those who truly used blunt stones, soon starve of nutrients

But Nietzsche also says we live in a "language machine," albeit, a "false" one. A true language would recognize that life cannot be captured in the logical fallacies of 'cause and effect,' 'right and wrong,' 'meaningful or meaningless,' purposeful or purposeless,' but only as "a question of the absolute establishment of power relationships; the stronger becomes master of the weaker, in so far as the latter cannot assert its degree of independence - here there is no mercy, no forbearance, even less a respect for 'laws'!" From the elephant to the molecule each life form, he says, is itself, working out its being without benefit of motivation or purpose in a reality which our present language is ignorant of. Only "false" logic and grammar have led us to believe otherwise. It is the human task to now give back meaning to this discovered chaos beyond language - where even effects are not the result of causes and egos vanish as grammatical fictions. We must invent an inarticulate language to reflect our joy in biological being. He even writes: "'Subject,' 'object,' 'attribute' - these distinctions are fabricated and are now imposed as a schematism upon all the apparent facts. The fundamental false observation is that I believe it is I who do something, suffer something, 'have' something, 'have' a quality." To which list he might just as well have added written something, composed something, sculpted something - for we are dumped into the world of deMan and Derrida by this "fundamental false observation". " Tremendous self-examination: becoming conscious of oneself, not as individuals but as mankind," he even writes! How different is this from "There are no authors, only language writing

itself"?   N. Also writes "Parmenides once said, 'one cannot
think of what is not'; - we are at the other extreme, and
say, 'what can be thought of must certainly be a fiction.'
I'm having a lot of trouble with the last half of *Will To
Power* - indeed, I am finding it revolting. What is coming to
me is the thought that it is nihilism-as-path-to-revelation
that is false. Nihilism is perhaps just nihilism and as such
must be shaken off as one would a hairy tarantula. To take
nihilism seriously is to take a neurosis seriously. Do I
sound like an ol' fuddy-duddy?

George Peter Murdock has sorted the 1,264 world
societies coded in the 1971 Ethnographic Atlas into 150
"cultural provinces," 25 in each of six world geographical
divisions, and each distinguished within its region by
linguistic and cultural idiosyncrasies. Lets assume that of
all of them, only the circum-Mediterranean people possess a
language which "psychologically considered [entertains] . . .
certain perspectives of utility, designed to maintain and
increase human contructs of domination - and [that these
constructs] . . . have been falsely projected into the
essence of things." (N. *Will To Power*,p.14) Resulting, of
course, in brutal world domination by the West through a
perpetual motion language/dream machine made in Hell. The
hypothesis is absurd. All surviving languages "falsely"
project their dominating perspectives into the essence of
things.   Only the projections are not false, if they were
they would not survive, or not survive for long. Reality
allows for many adaptations to it, not infinite, perhaps 150,
and some throw out more 'essences' than others, but the one
requirement that all cultures must have is a referential
language, i.e., a subject who knows there are objects and
that if he kicks a rock it will hurt. If so: did not Karl
Polyani and M. Mead trace the impact of industrialization
upon the 18th century rural English countryside and later
upon various primitives in Africa and elsewhere - calling it
"alienation," "anomie," or the impact of gesellschaft upon
gemeinschaft? But did these people not experience the need
for the transvaluation of all values, i.e., nihilism? The
American Indians were known to have committed suicide out of
stark confusion and resentment. Those that survived did they
merely pick-up a different language (a different reality)
which they believed was referential? i.e., did they surmount
nihilism by falling dupe to yet another language machine or
did they actually learn something about a fuller, richer
life? This is not to say that Nietzsche was wrong, merely
that our nihilism is, perhaps, nothing new under the sun
though it be self-inflicted. Our world is transforming
itself, perhaps to a greater, deeper extent than the
transformation Chateaubriand experienced. The ice that
Spengler spoke of is perhaps chilling us to the bone and the
deconstructionists and "postmoderns" are mistakenly blaming
the past for the nauseous disgust such a chill can make us
feel in ourselves. We no longer belive in our language and
it is seeking a new vision which will encompass yet change

our present world as Greece did Egypt, Rome Greece, Europe Rome, and America Europe, but not by claiming the former was all a bad dream. On this reading of the times, perhaps deconstructionists, by replaying all the old forms over and over again, re-writing the history of the world all over again in all its detail (they are Medieval archivists, you know, collecting and preserving 8000 years of trivia, doing conservationist work while looking in a mirror), are only delaying the final horror of the New World - not because it is horrible, but because it is new.

Perhaps we are the End of History. As H. Bloom says, Shakespeare said it all. What we suffer now is boredom, relieved only by aesthetic readings of the past. The juice is spent; we can only drink old nectar. Boredom with ourselves, not nihilism, is our fate. Nihilism today is foppish; it is the resentment of the young against boredom. We wish we were nihilists, but we know that our values are the right ones; we are simply bored with them because there are no others. We are simply nasty, brutish, materialistic, and greedy and we have devised a perfect world for ourselves - this we know in our heart of hearts. We just can't bear to have reached the end. We may have fed ourselves lies to get here, but so what. And if our language doesn't reflect reality - well, who cares? (And who's to say?) We have our TV's, central heating, running water, food on our plates every night, a doctor around the corner, and a pain pill in the medicine chest - what else is there? Nihilism? What for?

No. That doesn't sound right either. Where am I? How is it I can talk like a river in flood yet never seem to say what I want? I always forget to mention the important stuff. Where am I in all this?

The stronger my thoughts, the weaker I am. The less I feel connected to reality. In rising I fall. Rather, as my thoughts rise in the understanding of life my ego falls in direct proportion. Thus have I adjusted to my fundamental collapse - an inability to reconcile my thought with life. 37 years ago I was defeated - near fatally. The difference between what I thought ought to prevail and what in fact did prevail proved to be almost beyond my powers to reconcile. I drowned in myself to avoid the humilation of being (wrong). I forgot myself and became invisible to mirrors. I struggle not to be a talker to myself on the vast, unbroken steppes of Central Asia for thought to me is most often rumination. I still do not remember myself without great effort. I do not even have the nerve to decapitalize "I" as did e.e.cummings. For 37 years I have reached for the grape of health I dangle in front of me, but unlike like Tantalus I don't know if it's not the bannana on the other side I should be going after.

Someday I shall write to you on the ontological status of being on retirement pay. It's like nothing you've ever felt before. It's like God smiling down upon one.

Have you looked at the H. Bloom book? I can understand the first and last chapters, but only thirty of the 400 pages in between. He is an 'idea man' (the Eliza Doolittle

complex): as profound as he tries to be he lacks that ol'
European depth. He would never, for example, write of
himself, "I have at all times thought with my whole body and
my whole life. I do not know what purely intellectual
problems are. . . . You know these things by way of thinking,
yet your thought is not your experience but the reverberation
of the experience of others; as your room trembles when a
carriage passes." Bloom retains his individuality severely;
he rides the carriage, seldom hearing his tea cups rattle.
His own life or that of the world does not depend on his
soundings of their reverberations. He's the one who makes
the streets tremble. After writing a passage on Montaigne
one can imagine him strolling out to buy a non-fat yogurt and
licking his chops, just like that. (But what would Spengler
do? claw the walls as a desperate prisoner of time?) He
writes of the coming of the Age of Theocracy - meaning by
that a time ruled by virulent do-gooders refifying a Decadent
Age - but he is curiously distant, the prediction only
inspires elegiac feeling in him. He lacks historical
urgency. But, one can disagree with him without going crazy.
And this brings me to Amy Tan-in-Hollywood and the <u>The Joy
Luck Club</u> - a marvelous movie as well as a tear-jerker. (I
recommend it.) Her characters grow out of life experiences,
i.e., they experience events and change. True, they all
learn self-love, self-worth, dignity, and gain power over
their destiny - for life in-itself, for her, is a ritualized
crushing machine - but how do they do it? Where is the
leviathan struggles of Nietzsche, Wittgenstein, Spengler,
Dostoevsky waged in tenements overlooking fancy boulevards
where carriages are soon to be replaced with thundering
elevateds? Tan's characters accomplish life's tasks
emotionally mugging each other under the tracks, salvation is
theirs if they best their opponents and the world can go hang
itself. Indeed, it must go hang itself if salvation is to be
found. These are personal issues for them. Is this the
difference between Europeans and Americans? Why the
Demanian, Foucaultian, & "Derridadaism" anti-European grasp
of nihilism landed on such fertile ground in America: because
it is levelling and democratic in spirit? Is this why so
many Americans thought they could understand it without
having to become French or German themselves? Has America
finally reached into the very abyss of Europe via the joy of
ingesting Big Macs under bright lights? Is this the deeper
resentment that Malraux had against American cultural
hegemony - that it would stop Europeans from dancing to the
distant rock-n-roll of history through gastronomy and neon as
Columbus did with glass beads and iron to the Indians? Is
this why I flounder in America? - by putting my ear out the
window to hear history in a land of individuals who attain
self-worth, dignity, and strength precisely by strolling
under my window jangling my tea cups? Is Amy Tan more
assimilated than I? And what does all this have to do with
my childhood?

I leave you with all these questions because I have no answers. (You need not answer them, though if you have a diferent take on the last half of the *Will*, please let me know.)

I apologize for making you read this 'letter' - if, in fact, you did. To translate from the Latin: "a voice from the desert" calls out. A blearly-eyed hermit that wishes to be over heard.

Hours after receiving your really most recent letter:

Thank you for asking about my mother. And yes, she is doing much better.

Speaking of "tone," I am certainly enjoying the 'tone' of your letters of late. They sound positively strong, manly. Something must be going right even if your ears are being boxed by the world.

What a strange feeling it must be to receive photos of women posing for your appraisal! Like women climbing out of a canastoga wagon in a small town on the western frontier before a crowd of spitting men. Basic, but real. It's what it's all about, Alfie. Democratic yet not levelling - like maidens filing into the court of the Sun King, ruffling their skirts and raising their bared perfumed bosoms before noble cod-pieces. It's too basic to be levelling. Choosing one that knows how to cook, now that's basic!

Are we all merely *enfant terrible's* grown older? Is philosophy the horses' ass - though I can't stay away from it? Kafka always summoned only himself. He may have had a ideas but they didn't come out that way. He had humility, not an epistemology. (A fancy word for finding an excuse for being?) But without an epistemology what am I? Why do I think the right idea will save me? There are no ideas for me, only emotional dreams. Egos coming to terms with the real world. Ah, now scientists and engineers they are something else; they finger the world, enjoying the corners, the stretch, and fatness of things. They don't need epistemologies either. (Like Goethe, but harboring guilt, is the very late N. also rebelling against the dessication of science, searching to slip into another dimension - beyond the illusion of 'cause and effect' - where distinctions don't apply? Is he feeling "I am great, but it is not for me." Does he believe that he can fight his nihilism by running through it as a gauntlet hoping to emerge on the nether side cleansed and reduced to being a mere undifferentiated mortal like everyone else - taking everyone else down with him? Is this not similar to plunging in and through a neurosis believing it has an escape hatch - when we know it is a Bosch bubble floating along the bottom of deep seas?) The West has nothing to be ashamed about least of all its grammar! On the other side of langauge is feeling as on the other side of notes lies music. Words, as music, gives voice to feeling;

they are not made up whole cloth out of words themselves. To reduce the world to words and grammar is to put it on a gurney and wheel it into the brain. And if primitives did not grasp themelves as feeling individuals but as mucous in large amoeba floating between trees or lying flat on desert landscapes, so much the worse for them! It used to be called superstition. But we knew they still felt anger, love, happiness, greed, etc., only that they expressed these differently than we.

We need not relativize the world to save the artist. The cost is too high and unnecessary. By the end of the 19th century the artist felt very threatened, Goethe had not saved them from the ravages of science, Mach, Planck and Einstein walked all over him. The artist could not adequately explain the world, only numbers could. To reduce the world to feeling - to "culture" in modern jargon - somehow entailed and entails the loss of reality. Actually, the murdering of reality to make way for dreams. The death of God does not mean however we are abondoned creatures who create post-mortem dream worlds of words that deduce universes from grammatical axioms! And then there was democracy - every one could become educated - and the masses, given their druthers, perhaps now came to believe they made it all, from the pryamids to the universe. The only thing they had to give up was being real - a fitting feeling for those who resented their betters (Goethe never went that far - the man who directed his actors to never turn their backs upon the audience never would). But the creation of nothing ex nihilo could backfire. Frederick Karl, in his biography of Kafka writes: "Conrad attempted suicide at twenty with a revolver, Hesse attempted suicide; Mahler thought of suicide, and his brother Otto, succeeded in it; later, Alban Berg atttempted it, as did his sister, Smaragda. Wittenstein, whose three older brothers all killed themselves, himself played on the edge of madness and suicide. In the public sphere, the apparent suicide at Mayerling, near Vienna, of Crown Prince Rudolf in 1889 was, as we have seen, the most sensational of what seemed an epidemic of self-destructivness. To this list, we can add . . . Otto Weininger, Walter Benjamin, Stefan Zweig, Georg Trakl, Ludwig Boltzman, Kurt Tulcholsky, [and] Ernst Toller" - and he leaves out the mass suicides of WWI. Karl follows this up with a cryptic remark of Durkheim: "If we follow Durkheim's theories near the end of the nineteenth century, then any phenomenon that increased potentiality and expectations of power or promised energy would also lead to suicidial impulses." (Is this a variant of my reading Nietzsche as saying: 'I am great, becoming greater, but it is not me.'? Arrogance and Christianity do not mix. One had to give. So everyone became Christ! In his newest movie Woody Allen (superficial as usual) posits art as a Mafia killer. But whom does it crucify? The artist or the world? According to Allen it's both. The option is to build white picket fences in suburbia, raise children and go bowling. But this is a nineteenth century problem, old enough for even him to understand (the theme reclines limp on the celluloid and possess no urgency) - I am not sure it is ours. Art must go back to creative memesis - joy in itself - and not take up the sad revolution of changing the world by committing suicide.

On the shores of lake Michigan, under yellow and green clouds spewed out by steel mills jutting into the waves, I used to play in the sand. I can be that way again.

Another Idol becomes complicated! Like me, nothing is simple.

Like Mallarmé I now have something to look at when I write - perhaps my next letter will be readable!

as always

Ilse und Maria

kunstverlag michel co., bertramstr. 73, 6000 frankfurt/m., tel. 553146.

foto-
grafik

Hold on to this one –
this is one of my favourite sexual fantasies –
couldn't resist – and yes, one does say
holding you or me in my or your mouth

This is like the movie Belle du Jour
in which a woman is being offered to a
man & her coming to enjoy her it in
spite of her initial horror.
Love

fotografik
printed in west-germany - imprimé en R.F.A.

Dear Ted, (read PS first - this is punched in on 11/20 after unsealing the letter)

This is a quick letter in reply to your "Everest" but not of words only (keep those paste-ups coming!), since the midterms will effectively seal me off from most of myself for the next few weeks. Your "debris from Chicago" sounds a lot like my own from the vacant lots of Ditmas Avenue, so we're in tune. Something didn't sit right with me either about my opening pages on De Man. Once I was done, the beginning seemed wrong, but since it got me to the rest, I'm not sure what to do. Either I say it more quickly or start again, since I too feel that fault-finding is the wrong way to begin, especially here, though it's a classic approach ("How about a romantic approach?" says another voice).

I'm not in accord with your idea that mankind is on the "march," however, although Time certainly seems to be on fast forward. I persist in thinking that humanity is already there. I'd simply like to join it instead of feeling that I'm on a railroad siding in Kafka's universe ("I was once the director of a small railway company in the middle of Siberia"). Somehow I can't own up to my deepest beliefs and therefore come out half-way towards <u>somewhere</u>. I have about ten versions of the essay, all of which were garbled attempts to sort out my thoughts on Nietzche and left me drained. This is the only one that's allowed me to stand back and look at the material without getting lost. But yes, something is off, and I knew it the moment the idea of Dürer's knight popped into my head, which rang a chord in me and seemed the best thought in the paper, though I'm not sure how I can square it with <u>The Stillbirth of Tragedy</u>, which I also like.

I think that what Nietzche first heard in Wagner was a sound that pointed toward himself. There's something beautiful about his love of <u>Tristan</u> and about those early hopes as well. Nietzche's sister, the dread Elizabeth-Förster, put together a Nietzche-Wagner correspondence that isn't half-bad and gives a year-by-year account of the changes N. went through. Perhaps when he says "inaccessible abyss," he means his own life energy. In any case, as you know, he ended up seeing even Beethoven as a "German phenomenon," unlike Mozart, whom he called one of the last Europeans, but the peculiar thing is that there's so much Mozart in Wagner. I've just started reading "The Magic Flute." The parallels with "Parsifal" are remarkable (have I already written this to you?), including Papageno not knowing who his parents are (Parsifal uses his exact words) and the whole idea of redemption through magical objects, i.e., flutes, xylophones, portraits, swords, rings, and finally holy temples and Grails. (It's a little like Bogart's secretary in "The Maltese Falcon" telling him that the story of the "black bird" is "wonderful," to which he replies, "Or ridiculous.") To complicate matters, Wagner had the same effect on others along their road to themselves as he did on Nietzche. This includes Mann, Spengler, Jung, and a whole host of painters, like Kandinsky, Munch, and our own Albert Pinkham Ryder. Wagner as everybody's magic ring. It's an issue I wanted to avoid.

As for Katherine J. Mayberry, she of the mute, inglorious "African-American" panel, it serves her right for wanting to be "included." I alternate between wanting to stroke her head and hit it with a frying pan. If she's lucky, she'll fall apart herself. By the way, what if some wag started writing "Afrikan-American"?

All this is off the top of my head, but, to get back to the essay one last time, I think that Dürer's knight may help me with the beginning, though I'm not sure how much more I want to do. In any case, I'd like to hear anything else you care to say about it, Chicago debris and all. As I said, it's close to the Brownsville school of aesthetics, although I see De Manians under every rock whenever I go into the Black Forest. I wish I could laugh at them, as Nietzche does. "The exhausted are attracted by what is harmful: the vegetarian by vegetables."

And speaking of Nietzche's knight of the pitiless gaze, I can imagine him riding past Fish, while the Duke-thinker is standing next to his Jaguar snapping a model as she hula-hoops on the Seine (La Femme Moderne, Paris, 17 Novembre: "Wanda Lovelace âpres avoir publié Le Phallocentrism et La Chute de Rome"). You had me there for a minute. I actually found it believable, but then I remembered that Danielle doesn't hula-hoop.

I've stopped firing off any more salvos to idiot journals and taken a new tack by writing directly to women instead, and even better, getting them to write to me. This project started last month when the idea came to me to put an ad in The NY Review, which I promptly did (the image of Mort happened to run through my mind one day, Mort of the seventy-five interviews a month, who said he was too cheap to put in an ad himself when I asked him why he didn't). It's been an interesting experience, to say the least. Mort really meant it when he said he was cheap, since the ads don't cost a lot if you keep them down to the minimum, which is all it takes, and I get to do my shopping at home, since NYR sends me the replies in a manilla envelope once a week (I asked for photos and mostly got them too). Something I hadn't planned on was seeing the whole business from the other side. What power. Let them show you who they are for a change. Amazing. Some write from Reno, Santa Monica, Miami, and even Pocatello, where Penelope Reedy publishes The Redneck Press, a journal of cont. western writing, having recently lost her cattle-ranching husband, she herself a one-time teacher in East New York. Then there are all those women in Manhattan. I've never had it so good lining up dates, but I can't tell you how queasy I felt opening the first letters and looking at those photographs (talk about self-made artsy porno shops). Now I open them in my cozy recliner and just say hello. The manilla envelopes are still coming in, so there's quite a pile. It struck me once again (for the millionth time) that I completely bury my own interests, in this case, by not having called the one woman whose picture attracted me the most. Luckily, I caught it, and, sure enough, her opening words on the phone were more engaging than anything the others said in a couple of hours over drinks. I do not do fifteen-minute Mort-like interviews, but I have yet to meet this interesting-sounding creature and will have to wait till the holiday weekend is over.

My calendar is booking up. I also began a correspondence with an art historian in Amherst, a pretty lady of German parents, raised in Beverly Hills, like Frieda, though not of the U-Boat patrol, at least not on paper. She says she has good friends on Schermerhorn and is "not glued" to Amherst. This one I will pursue, since the parrot on her hand ("Papagena," no less), plus her face, was a major attraction. The life-stories alone are a trip.

I also asked Sal for a new stove, which I promptly got. He was really good about it. I can't believe the shit I've put up with. I haven't talked to Clover since last spring, by the way, and my silence may stick this time if she doesn't call, since I allowed her to start the merry-go-round in '89. As you once said, she resumed contact as a way of plowing me under for having stopped seeing her in '82. Hopefully, she has someone else to nail to the cross. It's so damned frightening to discover what matters to me and that it's not being born to a French industrialist (Danielle), to the head nurse of Bennington College (Allison), to the chief financial officer of American Tobacco Company (Janet), or the entourage of Kay Boyle and Peggy Guggenheim. Art historians from Beverly Hills are probably wrong as well. The woman whose photo I buried sounded nothing at all like these types. It stuns me to see how consistently I've run away from the only women in my life who cared for me. So what else is new, right?

Your "Everest of words" indeed. You see what happens? I read them, and down comes an avalanche of my own. As in everything else, Hamlet has a lot to say about mountains of words (after Laertes jumps into Ophelia's grave and cries out that they should bury him with her until the mound reaches the heights of Olympus, Hamlet reveals himself. It's fantastic: "Who is it whose grief bears such an emphasis? This is I, Hamlet, the Dane!" At which point, he leaps in as well, crying out that if Laertes will "prate," then let them both be buried under "millions of acres" until Ossa looks like a "wart."

By the way, I don't believe that "The West's greatest writers are subversive of all values, both ours and their own," though Bloom's points on reading are good. Who said that values can't include "armed victory" and "societal restraints," and since when do the humanities exclude being human? I think that Bloom is confusing values with what Eliza Doolittle's father calls "middle-class morality." In any case, Dostoevsky does not "preach anti-Semitism, obscurantism, and the necessity of human bondage." No. You've really got to hunt for anti-Jewish remarks, and, as for "obscurantism," that's exactly what the socialists said. It's a Marxist put-down of religion and it's crap. I'm not sure about his views on Wordsworth or Spencer either. As for Dante "rejoicing" in "the eternal torment he visits upon his enemies," they did exile him from Florence, not only personally but also permanently. And why make <u>Coriolanus</u> the measure of Shakespeare's politics when he also says in <u>Lear</u>, "Poor naked wretches, that bide the pelting of this pitiless storm"? I hear Bloom catering to the radicals. He has a valid point, excellent, in fact, but he doesn't make it judiciously, so it comes out wrong. He has all the makings of a real affirmation but avoids it (am I any better?).

Your epigraph on Eliot's experimental cannibal was right on target and, among other things, reminded me of T. E. Lawrence's disturbance about crossing the line when he went "native" in Arabia. Eliot saw his whole generation running off to find other scenes ("In a world of fugitives, who can tell who is running where?" something like that. Real Joseph Conrad material. Yes, research cannibalism certainly is "a bridge too far" (it works the other way too, à la Mayberry, who thinks that she has to be understood by cannibals).

You'll be happy to know, in closing, that we're not as smart as we think we are, according to Lawrence A. Hirschfield of Ann Arbor. In fact, we'd best not think of anyone as being intelligent ever again:

> The bulk of research in recent years suggests that there is no such thing as general intelligence — a singular capacity to think abstractly about any problem, whatever its content. More and more, researchers agree that the mind is not a general problem solver, but a collection of special-purpose devices targeting specific domains of thought and reasoning. Similarly, intelligence is increasingly seen as comprising multiple and distinct kinds of intelligence.

(Sunday Times Book Review, 11/13)

Got that? There's no such thing as intelligence, even though there is (since "distinct kinds of intelligence" must have something in common called "intelligence"). Perhaps we should revise Hamlet:

> To be or not to be, that is the question.
> Whether 'tis nobler in the collection of
> Special-purpose devices targeting specific
> Domains of thought and reasoning to take arms
> Against a sea of troubles, or by opposing end them.

I'm enjoying the Lenny Bruce, though Kofsky is not critical enough for my taste (Socratic decadent that I am). All the same, it's a treat to see so much of Bruce on paper and to hear his voice come alive in my head, as in, "I'm not gonna buy any time for Radio Free Europe. Frig that. The disc jockey: "And that was The Coasters on the flip side of Two Up and Two Back and the Hully-Gully, and how bad do you hate Communism? Why not? 'Cause I have nothing to tell Europe." A great pleasure. Many thanks. And write early and often. Your reading list shows me what I'm missing by still teaching, grrr.

PS I was about to send this off and realized I hadn't said a word about your mother. I'm sorry to hear the news. I knew I was thrown by your remark about confusing being with others with absence from yourself - not thrown, but I became concerned for you, plus it echoed so strongly in myself that it pulled me into a dream. That line kept reverberating, but I didn't become aware of it till now (only a day late). Powerful paragraph indeed. Hope she's better.

Steve

Tuesday, Nov. 15, '94

Dear Ted,

Will words and _things_ never stop beating a path to your door from Henry St?[1] But didn't you send me an all-black postal card a while back, the one with the Derridean or Eagletonian void? I must have read it as "anything's possible," or, to put it another way, I'm taking advantage of a momentary lifting of the fog to see what's what wherever I can.[2] I've only been telling myself to send your records off for, what is it, ten months now? I make mental notes to myself every two months to do the things I either want or have to do, which I promptly forget, and then they return as though for the first time, yet also tired and stale (which leads me to bury them once again). Sometimes there are no notes, nothing more than nagging pain, from which I keep myself remarkably detached, like setting my alarm-radio to NPR at 6:30am when I have to get up for school, though I _can't stand_ the station, especially not their morning format: 10 minutes of self-righteous reporters interviewing incoherent Hatians, pre-med students of color, etc., followed by "in-depth" news on some hot government issue (Clarence Thomas again, Whitewater revisited), a 10-second report of local traffic by a woman who slurs her words, and, around 6:50, readings from yet another memory of grandma planting radishes in the back yard or interviews with gay opera composers. This has gone on for I don't know how long. And then, last week, miracle! I don't know what came over me but I set the dial to QXR and woke up the next morning to real music. Ever since then, I can hardly remember having listened to NPR at all.

So this has been a period of some clarity, including one face-off with two guys in my remedial writing class, whom I've been telling to shut up for six weeks now. This morning I walked right up to them and told them to leave the room, walk around the 7th floor, and think about whether or not they wanted to come back, because if I they distracted me one more time, I'd call the counselling dep't. and ask to have them expelled. I can't tell you how great it was to have them out of the room. Some time later, I don't even know when it happened, they were back in their seats and doing the work. Unbelievable. And I could have done it the first day they bothered me, because it's never real fog, as you well know. In fact, everything is all too clear. I left your records by the foot of my TV and saw them there every day. I even _felt_ their presence. And sending them off was something positive that I wanted to do. But reasons and motives don't matter. Pain or pleasure, it's all the same. Where feelings count, I just don't see. Total blackout. In other words, your postal card.

Steve

---

[1] As we now know, Theory reveals no connection between words and things.

[2] "Nietzche claimed there are endless perspectives from which to view events" - (The New York Times, Nov. 10, 1994). Thank you, Dr. Nietzche.

Dear Ted,

I can't help it. I can't measure out my responses to you and hold back so as not to scare myself with proofs that I exist. You must appreciate that I have a kind of psychological measuring device that signals when my time is up. So many responses alloted per day, per week, per life. I think I mentioned Chateaubriand on this point once before, if not several times: to Napoleon, a gnat that flew without his permission was a rebellious insect that had to be crushed. OK. So once again, I'm over my head. And you too! Fabulous! I just got your last letter today, as I was about to send this one off. Some day I may discover that I was always present in my life. Remember Cronkite's "You Are There" and his sign-off tag? It went something like: "What kind of a day has it been? A day like all days, filled with those events that make up the fabric of our time, and YOU ARE THERE."

I caught "Garden of Evil" on AMC the other day and wished you were there to see it with me. Do you know it? Eastwood made a study of Cooper's work after '45. The mythic element in "Garden" is very strong, and the dialogue gets better and better as it goes along. I love the opening. It's like something out of the *Odyssey* and must have been a common story in those days. Jennings has a similar description of hopping a freighter in Galveston and ending up in a port town in Honduras on a July 4th, where he runs into O. Henry in a cafe later that day. Then come the adventures up through Mexico and their capture back in Texas.

I caught the tail end of a Discovery Channel documentary on western painting - some professor saying that the new historians were right to call it a product of fantasy (cavalrymen were never gallant, as they are in Remington, cowboys were never heroic, as they are in Russell, etc. etc., ad nauseum), but that the art nevertheless captures the "*hopes and aspirations of westerners in a way that more accurate accounts cannot.*" In other words, it was false consciousness but more precise than reality. Such is the idiocy to which people have been reduced. Your image of egos going out one by one all over America is poignant and true. I had a cab ride the other day with an old time Jewish cabbie, almost a dead breed. He gave me a real hello and I told him I wasn't used to it from cabdrivers. "Nuttin's the same any more. It's all a lot of crap." He was Brooklyn-Jewish and born in Brownsville too. We reminisced all the way up to BMCC. He had a real love for the old neighborhood - the knish sellers by the school yards, the movies on Pitkin Ave, 12 cents was all it cost to get a kid out of the house for a whole afternoon. "Ya got de news, cartoons, a double feature. It was a nice life." He said that he and his wife felt there was no place left to breathe. He was so damned appreciative of our conversation. And I was too. We spent about five minutes just naming our favorite actors. He had no problem with greatness, and he paid attention to celebrity passengers, Claudette Colbert's son most of all ("I told him ya mudder was a great actress"). And sharp, in the old way. He said that Barry Gray was pissed at being recognized. "I apologize," he said, "that I got you angry because I said something nice to you."

It's amazing how far one can get if one speaks up and has brains to boot. I spent two hours today with teachers from the CUNY Writing Centers Association going through 55 proposals for our upcoming conference. I've known them for six years and done the same work with them before, but this time, I really heard them: the sarcastic semi-queers and the catty prima donnas, all babbling away to each other incessantly (it amazed me to realize that this was how they always were). This time around, I forced them to explain their choices to me, and I nearly always got the vote changed. Fearless Fosdick. I was really pissed but stayed clear as a bell. After about an hour of my contrariness, one of them said to me, in that snotty-queer way of his, "You say yes to all the proposals," to which I shot back, "That's not true. I just say yes to a lot of the ones you reject." I had an even better revelation a minute later: "How come you give the same reasons for ones you reject and others you accept?" Whereupon one woman accused me of wanting consistency. I told her I just wanted clarity. They looked at me as though I were speaking Urdu. At some point, I became aware of the fact that no one had asked me a single question (there was another Steve there, but not one "What do you think, Steve?" was directed at me. I missed that one. I should have started talking). When I went to the bathroom, it dawned on me that they had all read my article last spring. I was tickled pink with myself. And two hours later I was having drinks with the art historian lady from Amherst at the Cafe Clinton. Nice person. Her eyes were starting to melt, but she had a train to catch (this is the Beverly Hills lady of German parentage but not like Wolfpack Frieda at all). It was a nice day.

I've been looking through *The Nietzsche Legacy in Germany: 1890 - 1990* by one Steven Aschheim, who's stupid but informative, and just found out that there's a '67 edition of Spengler's essays, trans. by Donald White, which includes "Nietzche and His Century":

Goethe's life was a full life, and that means that it brought something to completion. Countless Germans will honor Goethe, live with him, and seek his support; but he can never transform them. Nietzsche's effect is a transformation, for the melody of his vision did not end with his death . . . Nietzsche's type of vision will pass on to new friends and enemies, and these in turn will hand it down to other followers and adversaries. Even if someday no one reads his works any longer, his vision will endure and be creative. . . . In an age that does not tolerate otherworldly ideals . . . when the only thing of recognizable value is the kind of ruthless action that Nietzsche baptized with the name of Cesare Borgia - in such an age, unless we learn to act as real history wants us to act, we will cease to exist as a people. We cannot live without a form that does not merely console in difficult situations, but helps one get out of them. This kind of hard wisdom made its first appearance in German thought with Nietzche. . . . To the people most famished for history in all the world, he showed history as it really is. His heritage is to live history in the same way.

It's the best statement in the book, but Aschheim says that it expresses "a brutalized will to power." Why wasn't I allowed to

get away with that kind of shit? I had good quotes too when I
first started working on my thesis.

Did I tell you that someone in the department lent me his copy
of Dietrich Fischer-Dieskau's *Wagner and Nietzche*? Nietzche says
that *The Birth of Tragedy* captures the perfect world that he and
Wagner and Cosima shared in Tribschen on the shores of Lake
Lucerne. Wagner was there for six years and Nietzche with them the
last three, before Wagner went on to build Bayreuth, which was the
turning point for Nietzche. He describes going through the house
with Cosima on the last day - Wagner was somewhere else - and the
two of them feeling that paradise was over for good. Nietzche says
that their conversations gave him a grounding for life and that
the house was filled with the spirit of Goethe, Schiller, and
Beethoven. He *does* talk about the house itself, but, all the same,
I felt that something esential was missing. All of it seemed
wonderful: the Alps, a lakeside villa, the young Nietzche coming
to the door for the first time and hearing Wagner working on
Siegfried at the piano, yet something was wrong. Cendrars had
similar intensities with people, and so did Pissaro and Gauguin.
They all did, in fact, but when you read Cendrars or Gauguin, you
feel that they're part of the world and that everything matters,
whereas Nietzche, Wagner, and Cosima could just as well have been
on Mars. It's as if Lucerne were only there to provide moonlight
reflections for rapturous insights into art. Thoreau would have
gone on for pages talking about the weather and the insect life,
with Wagner and Cosima thrown in for good measure. Goethe would
have too. Even when Flaubert writes back to Bouilhet that Rome is
like a world of art lifted from the everyday, he sees everything:

Antiquity does survive in the Campagna - fallow, empty, accursed
as the desert, with its great stretches of aqueduct and its
herds of large-horned cattle. That is truly beautiful, the
antique beauty one has imagined. As for Rome itself, in this
respect, I haven't yet recovered from my first impression, and
must wait until it has subsided a little. What the wretches have
done to the Colosseum! Stuck a cross in the center of the
circus, and built twelve chapels around the arena! But for
pictures, statues, the XVIth century, Rome is the most splendid
museum in the world. The number of masterpieces in the city is
dizzying. It is certainly the artists' city. One could spend
one's life here in a completely *ideal* atmosphere - outside the
world, above it [how like Yeats' Byzantium!]. I am overwhelmed
by Michelangelo's *Last Judgment*. It partakes of Goethe, Dante,
Shakespeare, merged into an art that is unique. It is beyond
description. Even the word "sublime" seems to me inadequate:
shrill and over-simple.

I have seen a *Virgin* by Murillo that haunts me like a
perpetual hallucination . . . I enclose some flowers I picked
in a lupanar whose door was marked with a phallus in a state of
erection. There were more flowers in that house than in any
other. Sperm from the pricks of the ancients had perhaps
fertilized the ground. The sun was blazing on the gray walls.

This is the kind of writing I adore. By contrast, Nietzche's idyll
is turned almost entirely inward. I'm curious to see if this is

part of what he rebelled at in what he came to call the "disease" of Wagnerism. But I appreciate (and this is very hard to spell out in detail) that everything about the later Nietzche comes out of a musical intensity, as though music were his touchstone, in the same way that Spengler is never so moving as when he speaks of Rembrandt and has more references to Art, Culture, History, and Goethe in the index to Volume 1 than to any other subjects. What to make of it all, I do not know, except to note that these are *not* the ways that professional historians think about the world. Then again, as you're suggesting more and more, who gives a rat's ass about how they think? I was at the new exhibit of early impressionist painting at the Met last week and saw some Courbets and one Manet that sent me through the roof. When *will* I say adios Casablanca, "where they wait and wait and wait and wait"?

Stay well —
Steve

Nov.21 1994

Dear *Steve*

What is that here? an ear
What is that here? a nose
What is that here? a hand I do not love.
                                Nietzsche
(from a soliloquy on a stoop in ancient Athens)

to which Pericles responds:

Your . . . hand ... must be borne with resignation,
that of the enemy['s] with fortitude; this was the old way at
Athens, and do not you prevent it being so still. Remember,
too, that if your country has the greatest name in all the
world, it is because she never bent before disaster; because
she expended more life and effort in war than any other city,
and has won for herself a power greater than any hitherto
known, the memory of which will descend to the latest
posterity; even if now, in obedience to the general law of
decay, we should be forced to yield, still it will be
remembered that we held rule over more Hellenes than any
other Hellenic state, that we sustained the greatest wars
against their united or separate powers, and inhabited a city
unrivaled by any other in resources or magnitude. These
glories may incur the censure of the slow and unambitious;
but in the breast of energy they will awake emulation, and in
those who must remain without them an envious regret. Hatred
and unpopularity at the moment have fallen to the lot of all
who have aspired to rule others; but where odium must be
incurred, true wisdom incurs it for the highest objects.
Hatred is also short lived; but that which makes splendor of
the present and the glory of the future remains forever
unforgotten. Make your decision, therefore, for glory then
and honor now, and attain both objects by instant and zealous
effort: do not send heralds to Lacedæmon, and do not betray
any sign of being oppressed by your present sufferings, since
they whose minds are least sensitive to calamity, and whose
hands are most quick to meet it, are the great men and the
great communities." so spoke Pericles to Nietzsche. For he
saw that the past had become hateful and loathsome for him
because of his relationship with his hands.
    In parable and aphorism do we lose our historical
strength? Is it the literary version of the
'phenomenological method'? Is it nihilism raising its head
between paragraphs: bits and pieces of a phenomenal self held
together by nothing more than blank spaces on the page? A
self incapable of meeting the past revealing moments of
intense clarity? But of what? A universe in shambles? Of
dreams full of sound and fury signifying nothing? Without a

self glorifying its history what else is there to write
about, i.e., without the strength to welcome the past
history goes up in aphoristic smoke. Burnt to a crisp. All
we get is a deconstructed reality and a blank future.
Revolution.

Passages of stridency (and probable ignorance):

Jack Flamm, in a recent NYR, mentions that one of the
differences between pre-impressionist painting and
impressionist painting is the way in which the human figure is
treated. In the former, humans are clearly more important than
the landscape in which they move, in the latter, they often
disappear into it. (Even the Medievals placed humans in the
foreground; peasants tilling castle grounds, Christ suspended,
hunters bringing home the game in wintry twilight.) What so
irritated the impressionists was not the style of the
"academics," but the humans who commanded the landscape - they
were to powerful for them to look at! Humans humbly sowing for
their lords, giving milk through voluptuous breasts, martyring
themselves on crosses, or posing as heroes in ripped, blood-
spattered costume, revolted them. Such strength only inspired
resentment, envy, and the will to destroy. But look at what was
destroyed - that which blocked the clearing leading to Warhol!
The 19th century begins to paint humans as background figures
though spitefully they often are in the foreground - the brush
strokes themselves cover their humans beneath layers of pigment
which diminish their subjects self-importance - blurred as they
are into the landscape or smoked in the fires of the mind. And
there it is - nihilism on canvas. Artists commenting upon life
rather then expressing it (or shall I say, expressing
themselves in a world which is, to them, no longer
comprehensible?). The ego begins its disappearance from the
world's stage, and dreams of that which is not fill the head;
humans gain meaning on demonic Parisian boulevards, alongside
purifying lakes, in fields of flowers more beautiful than they,
or in the rough, analytic texture of pigment. Gone are the
women of Vermeer's The Letter who are given human skin and are
surrounded by furniture, walls, and light which they
illuminate, The Jolly Toper of Frans Hals dressing in the style
of the reality he creates and loves to live in, and what about
the festooned ladies all pink and red who folic in make-believe
forests made just for them by Watteau? Even the gnarled roots
of Ruisdael express the wonder of nature in a human. (In Nausea
it is a protruding tree root which catapults Roquetin into
nauseous nihilism. As though Nature has a non-meaning all its
own!) Why did the ego become so hateful? Why so frightened of
its powers? The artists sucked the ego out of the world, ego-
evacuated it till it crushed them - like a vacuumed tin can in
a HS science class. (Or does my intelligence falter? Do I
reduce the impressionist, etc., to my limited grasp of reality?
How can I, whose one claim to fame is to not possess a self,
dare speak of those who were productive? I see through a
tunnel darkly.) The Greeks, the Romans, the Medievals, and the
Humanists filled the world, puffing it up with blowing silk,

wine, cinnamon, gods, and shining shields; we have pulled back and scratch in dark caves. It is strange that in a God created world man is supreme, in the death of God era we become despicable and impotent. Nietzsche noticed this, of course, but only because the former, he says, were a sham. Somehow, he says, we have seen through the illusion of our greatness built at the feet of the gods - finally. Now we are permitted to realize we are shit. (Do novels tend to do the same? i.e., make the context more important than the characters; use the context to explain the characters rather than vice versa? Heller writes that is was the realistic and psychological novel which revealed to Nietzsche the "epoch's utterly pessimistic idea of its world," and its "loathing of 'reality'." But not in Flaubert: *Salammbo* and *Bouvard and Pecuchet* are escapees from contexts - those are people novels. Though greatness is restricted to the past in the one, and in the other greatness is made absurd.)

I do not believe that masters in the past where less aware of the meaninglessness of man - Nietzsche's illusions - but they had no time for it. There were more important things to do; namely, be. Nihilism was for children, effetes, and other assorted weaklings. Perhaps they understood it better than we. Understood life better than we. I don't think the *Jolly Toper* would blink twice in the presence of Derrida's mouth. We suffer from a loss of nerve, nothing more. (Perhaps as war became more democratic after the French Revolution and the ordinary man had to go through rigours once reserved for the nobles, the common man broke down - he wasn't willing to pay the price which maintaining a reality with real boundaries required - why should he? Yet, the Greeks and Romans used the common man, and they gloried in battle!) On this take, postmoderns are those having dreams of finger-fucking God while the other hand is up to mischievous.

Perhaps I am an idiot.

I am so tired of reneging on every sentence I write. I pull myself down into the depths of neurotic nonsense (my version of world nihilism). (Perhaps with good reason!) As indicated in my last letter, I purchased a mirror which I placed before me at the Mac. But I am finding it difficult to look into. The "reasons" are curious. I literally do not want to see myself. Do I find the difference between who I am and what I am writing incomprehensible? The experiment will either save me or drive me mad, provided I can summon the courage to look! It is as though I do not want to see myself screaming - remember yourself!!! Mallarmé did it to prevent himself from disappearing, I do it to call myself into being. The tension is horrific. So far I have not looked. Perhaps, as your Mac, it needs to sit around a year or so - unopened by an image.

An historical interlude:

In the 11/3/94 issue of the NYR David R. Godine makes
the point that the words 'aristocrat,' 'aristocratic,' and
'aristocracy,' did not exist in pre-revolutionary France
(they are not in Johnson's *Dictionary*, for example), 'noble,'
'gentilhomme,' and 'noblesse' were used. It is anachronistic,
he writes, to use the "a" words in describing pre-
revolutionary France because they "anticipate the guillotine
and the pathos that grew up round [them] in the nineteenth
century, [and thought] of 'aristocrats' as a homogenous and
beleaguered group." Which Age suffers myopia? Here is the
crux of relativism. Both Ages can cite the same "facts," but
under what guise? Unselfconsciously with strength and joy,
as they did, or with a self-conscious twist as we, from a
reformist, nihilistic distance? Those who lived during the
time lived the times to the hilt unselfconsciously, those who
came after, we, unable to live our own lives, can only
interpret those times - the head comes into play. The
commentaries begin. The spinning of endless possibilities of
interpretation - each more dark than the last - begins. But
have <u>we</u> lost the ability to live our times unselfconsciously?
Or do we merely pretend to live in unspecified times, times
devoted to self-conscious commentary on the unselfconscious
lives of others. Are we pretending to be still busy getting
rid of our past in order to live in a better time - clearing
out time, as it were, so that we can live in good
unselfconscience? Do we remain in the Revolting Age,
divesting ourselves of history, and instead see ourselves now
brimming with aphoristic clarity and parable vision which
will, by further application, bury it once and for all? But
what if we only think we live critically and in clarity, but
are in fact as 'unconscious' as those in all other ages?
That 'commentary' is our way of living life to the hilt, and
we are going nowhere but up our own assholes? Then we are in
the Age of Parasites, in the Age of Grub-Worms eating our way
through our own minds thinking we burrow through the
universe. As Hamlet in his "nut." The thing is, if this is
so, we preclude being happy - this becomes our historically
unique claim to distinction. We can not even be angry, sad,
or ecstatic - merely maniacally depressed. And, if each
"age" must lead its own unselfconscious existence to the hilt
then historical self-conscious is a chimera and Spengler's
advice falls always upon deaf ears. Do you not feel the
compulsion to evaporate in thought? Who today, without
shadow, could say of the McKinnon's, the Derrida's, the
Foucault's, the Marxists, that their "mandates, . . .
protests, . . . petitions, etc. etc. arouse not the
slightest curiosity in me; I am profoundly indifferent to the
matters of which they treat and besides they are couched in
such paltry verbiage and in such false fine thoughts as to

make one sick to death," and then add that all conversations should be conducted with "rigorous frivolity" - as did Madame de Deffand in the mid-1700s? All we can ironically say is "Ah, there but for the grace of God go I." 'Irony' because we believe, as we must, that we are better than she, more advanced. But, Lo! we are not, and nihilism crumbles, succumbs to unselfconsciously living our lives to the hilt without joy. How do we get out of the Grub Age, where is the escape hatch? Reality is indeed what we make it, but why can't we make one which in which we have at least the possibility of happiness?

Madame du Deffand also writes to Voltaire:

> You do not know and cannot know from personal experience, the condition of those who think, who reflect, who have some activity, and who are at the same time without talent, without passion, without occupation, without diversion; who have had friends but who have lost them without being able to replace them; add to that a delicacy of taste, a little discernment, a great love of truth; put out those people's eyes [she was blind late in life], and place them in the middle of Paris, of Peking, in fact of anywhere you like and I maintain that it would be happier for them not to have been born.

But this does not even smell of nihilism. It's ol'time depression. Life with the ego. She probably loved Boucher, Chardin, Watteau, and LaTour. Today people complain about others, or their lack of self-esteem, or their abused childhood's. They yearn to live in a New World - a world without history - to be free of having to posses an ego that must be talcumed and pleased: the world itself will be cozy with a little more weeding, they say. The ego is a fart, an ill wind from the Time of Work. Voltaire responded well to her:

"It is not," he writes, that nothingness does not have much to be said for it; it is merely that it is not humanly possible to love nothingness, with all its good qualities. A human being is not master of himself to that degree. One curses one's existence but one loves it too; one's will is not one's own." (Did Nietzsche overlook this? Though gods may tumble, self love never will Voltaire seems precipitously to say. But, has it? Is Voltaire wrong? Some have said that of which Voltaire speaks is the candle of God burning within us. Is this the deeper meaning of the death of God for Nietzsche? With the death of God is the possibility of self love extinguished? How and from where would one ever get the energy then to take a shit let alone make an unbermensch of oneself if that "tiger, tiger burning bright" within oneself is torn out, shot, and left for the buzzards? "I do not love my hands." On this reading, does not the death of God <u>mean</u> that man, head hanging low, must lead himself down the plank in to the Chicago stockyards and, while mooing, patiently wait? The 19th century is then the great watershed in history, replacing BC and AD with BSL and ASL, ego with non-ego. But if the ego was false how can its absence be real? Nietzsche says what appears as a bloody hole appears so only in the after glow of the egos illusionary former presence, but just as in passing from a room of light bulbs to the blaring desert sky we are apt to mistake the sun for darkness so too do we mistake the new light emanating from our rented body; it is a brillant light, he says, a thousand times brighter which is bursting out. But is <u>this</u> possible? Something tells me it is not. Nihilism dead-ends in death or in Europeans wearing turbans and sputtering nonsense - as Lautrec mimed so well from the balconey of his apartment. (Or turns up as a footnote as in: "For example see: Nietzsche, p.4." for two sentences in the writings of Bernard Lewis: "The interesting questions are not why [the West set out to conquer the lands of Islam, Africa, and Asia] but why they succeeded - and then why, having succeeded, they repented of their success as of a sin. The success was unique in modern times; the repentance, in all of recorded history.") Is it what Proust meant when he wrote: "But really it seems that all those who have been too superhuman, who have committed the crime of Prometheus or Nebuchadnezzar, must end up eating grass like Nietzsche, or becoming besotted by a crackpot religion like Comte."? (Heller has Zarathustra feeding "on barren fields.") Can we love ourselves without the existence of a god? Perhaps not. Nietzsche writes: "Let us consider this idea in its most terrifying form: existence as it is, without meaning or goal, but inescapably recurrent, without a finale into nothingness. . . . Those who cannot bear the sentence, There is no salvation, ought to perish!"

It is wrenching to imagine Nietzsche running around an insane asylum wearing an "institutional hat" murmuring "I love myself. I do not love Friedrich Nietzsche." {Killing God does have consequences! Like in the exposing of the Covenant in <u>Raiders of the Lost Ark</u>, ghostly forces fly out of the chest.} Was he after what I sometimes think I pursue: a rekindling of the inner candle history has blown out - all by myself? - without a god (the world on the other side of psychology) - without the help of reality? As Nietzsche, do I want to love myself because I love myself, not because of and through the love of others which is its true source and endless fountain of reality, but which was denied me because I proved unworthy of it? Thus, do I "eat grass" alone on the path of my redemption. Ah, where is my Pericles?) To which she probably responded: 'Ah, the drudge! He takes me too seriously yet offers no sympathy! The Olympian speaks - away with him!'

I feel as though I am running at break-neck speed through a desert city glittering with neon - avoiding the mirror behind me. I cannot stop and must catch whatever sights I can while on the run. Where I am going is unknown. What will happen when I reach the outskirts and night slaps my face? That too is unknown.

Of course Madame du Deffand also heard the cries of Eradice in *Thérése philosophe* (1748) as she (Eradice) is buggered from behind by a Jesuit priest who convinces her that it is the cord from the robe of St. Francis which is penetrating her:

> Oh, father!" cried Eradice. "such pleasure is penetrating me! Oh, yes, I'm feeling celestial happiness; I sense that my mind is completely detached from matter. Further, father, further! Root out all that is impure in me. I see...the...an...gels. Push forward... push... now... Ah!...Ah!... Good... St Francis! Don't abandon me! I feel the cord... the cord... the cord... I can't stand it any more... I'm dying."

"Further, father, further!" is delicious. And Deffand also knew of the *Histoire de Dom B...*, (1740) a rascal who concludes his novel of sado-masochistic incestuous escapades with:

> Here is plenty of food for thought for readers whose glacial temperament has never felt the furies of love! Go ahead, Messieurs, think away, give full vent to your moralizing! I abandon the field to you, and want to say just one thing: if you had a hard-on as unbearable as mine, who would you fuck? The devil himself!

(Both quotes taken from the 11/22/94 NYR) She knew of the beast in men: THE UNCONTOALABLE PASSION TO FUCK WHEN THE DICK FEELS LIKE CONCRETE EXPLODING - and it doesn't take much if the time is ripe - when the dick is red-hot look out sisters, mothers, brothers, little girls, sheep, and knot-holes in fences! (At least back then!) And at a ripe old age she scampered over the continent seducing a reluctant H. Walpole. You see, you see what nihilism did? It took the fuck out of dick! My next book will be *The Deconstruction of the Erection In Mountain Men of the Wild West* - although McKinnon is probably working on it right now (with a differing intent!).

Can you imagine Nietzsche bringing an aphorism to an end with the cry - as Comte de Mirabeau did in his introduction to *Ma conversion ou le libertin de qualité* - "May the reading [of this] make the whole universe jack-off."? And I can imagine Madame Du Deffand looking up over her fan and into Mirabeau's eyes and saying, "You sweet thing, how ever did you guess what I was doing?"

How did I end up here? Under Madame du Deffand's skirts
wiping wetness from her blubberly thighs? I am running too
fast. (Actually, I'm not running at all, but seated before my
Mac, sipping at my cup of coffee and occasionally raising my
head to look out onto the morning garden - but not the
mirror.) Obviously, I feel myself the ant crawling under one
of Nietzsche's toe tails. It is how I approach myself, unable
as I am to square myself with being human, normal, a part of
things. I prefer to think of myself as possessing a
separating illness, a Richard III deformity, a fatal, fetal
incomprehension of life. Do I not also have a strange
relationship with my hands which I do not love, but which
move about anyway? (Is this what Nietzsche was trying to
elucidate all along? The ontology of such a relationship
does defy all reason and philosophy, and would, if it ever
could be expressed and be true, bring down all previous
ontologies! It would be an ontology which could explain the
existence of the Cheshire Cat.) I must go back to the
Genealogy, *Daybreak*, etc., to regain my perspective. (By the
way, in tune with one of your recent letters, any author who
could write; "In the nineteenth century this tradition
reaches *some type of height* in Germany with the publication
of J.P. Echermann's conversations with Goethe," (italics are
mine) needs "acoustic recordings" for writing is not his
forte, nor does he understand why he is writing. I love the
way, on the next page for example, where he puts the word
'false' in quotes then offers a definition of another,
unmentioned word which has little to do with the word 'false'
but is precisely what he does mean - but doesn't ever tell
one the one word he defined - 'not.' Is he hiding words(his
penis)from his mother? Is English his fourth language?)
More on SEX in the next installment of *Sitting Next Too the
Sun or Moon, Depending on the Time of Day or Season of the
Month*.
        The OED contains the THE history of the world - what
else is there to know? What else can be known - other than
the use to which one puts it's words? I imagine I know
perhaps two pages of the it - there is a lifetime of
happiness before me! (But, ah, the mirror, there it sits
unopened! Is it a Pandora's Box or a box of Grandma Maud's
chocolate? Sometimes I think of it as a pool - yes, yes,
Narcissus - into which I can plunge never to emerge, at
others as a mirage hovering above desert highways. But all I
do is think - I don't actually look - except furtively, as a
criminal. Me, myself and the world will one day coalesce.
On Cities:(A phenomenonal approach)

        A normal city is a hub where people gather to arouse
themselves to anger, love, hate, remorse, mysticism, and
excitement. They masturbate in bathrooms, withdraw
revolutionary or Talmudic books from the library, piss in
ally-ways, wear pearls to the Met, stab one another with pink
hair, throw haughty, spiteful glances across bars, and sleep

on church stairs with a gun at their side - then look wildy
into each others eyes pretending nothing has happened, or
daring something to happen. Policemen enforce boredom and are
avoided. An aberrant city, as Phoneix, occurs on a vast
plain where people stop to water their horses. They stay a
bit longer and fashion a life from rock and sand. Nihilism is
illuminated in a bright sun - it is one of the few emotions
that is - so they drink beer in the shade. Policemen break
the monotony. I have walked the streets of both hunched,
looking for Thesesus' thread.

From whence does Henry Fonda get the strength to cary
himself so erect, staight as an arrow, eyes poised an exact
90 degrees parallel to earth?   If man is the measure of all
things, he must be erect and possess such a geometry when the
measurement is taken. Izzy, the tailor, would say no
differently.

If there is a frontier between self and reality -
picture me as the man crawling the desert sand, head slightly
raised, and one arm stretched out, reaching. "Water, water,"
he gasps in the classic image. Only for me the words would
be: "the border, the border."

Note: Thank you for the return of the records I had forgotten
them. But they did remind me to think of Wittgenstein's
Letters to Eckermann(?) which I think you still have. Why is
it that H. Bloom makes me feel the total igonramus while
Heller enlightens me? The "thesis" I get, it's the stuff
inbetween that eludes me. Sometimes I think he, H., believes
words mean things all by themselves, that they do not have to
be given a meaning by the author. Is that it? Or am I just
ill-read? - and compared to him I am. (I have not read half
of what he has and certainly not twice as he also has.) Is
his a book for <u>experts</u>? Or is it written from the other side
of the frontier? Beyond my ken?

What is a letter!? Why do people write them? The answer
to this too, eludes me. Sorry to take up so much of your
time - my hands, they are tireless.

You see what retirement does? It brings out the
emasculated philosoper in me. A one who writes from within
the soul, not with his hands.

Love from the ol'

The Women's movement in Phoenix

Monday, Nov. 14, '94

Dear Ted,

Am I imposing or sharing? Always a tricky feeling when I mean the second but attack myself for doing the first. The truth is that I wanted to show you what I've been rummaging through these past few months. I've come to believe that De Man is even more hideous than Foucault or Derrida, if that's possible. They seem almost naively idiotic by comparison, or, rather, they're somehow up front insane, whereas he's truly corrupt. And I've only spelled out the half of it. The only other piece by him that I know is one on the De Manian art of reading (you can imagine). Anyway, this is the piece I'm sending off to that guy in Michigan. Tell me what you think of it, if the spirit moves you to comment. There are parts of it that I like a lot, but, in the end, I feel as though I'm speaking in a language that's deader than Greek or Latin. The Nietzsche commentary that I've read is truly pathetic. The Times ran a piece on him last week. His home town had sort of a 150th commemoration of his birth (130 villagers - like being born in Dogpatch). Some prof. from the U. of Texas at Austin was there, telling the reporter that Nietzsche shows us how words and things don't go together, that "there's no coherent self," and that there's "no continuity between temporal events." What was that marvellous passage you sent me? "I relate what is coming in the next two centuries, what cannot come differently: the advent of nihilism." This is now called "no continuity between temporal events." He also calls Goethe "a totality," but as we now know, "totality" means "fragment." Why not? De Man says that reading is writing, and Foucault and Barthes say that writing is reading, i.e., when we read, we "rewrite," and when we write, we "inscribe tissues of quotations" that we've read. They also say that Nietzsche taught them there's no such thing as "a totality," and anyone who thinks there is or who writes as if there were is guilty of "totalizing." Balzac and Racine are really big totalizers, according to Barthes. Do you remember "Trouble in Paradise" and the radio jingle of "Colet & Co."? "Cleopatra did it with her little atomizer." Kay Francis' eyebrows are more intelligent than the combined skulls of De Man & Co.

Anyway . . . I'm done for now with the piece and am looking forward to reading The Three Musketeers, which I picked up for a buck on the street and which I never read. A lot of the really good books are unknown to me (I'm reminded of the times when you were reading Ivanhoe and Uncle Tom's Cabin and how exhilirated you were to see what they were all about). I wonder if I'll have visions of Louis Hayward and Gerard Phillipe. I read The Count of Monte Cristo last spring and, like you, was amazed to find that these old standards really have a punch to them. From the postal card I sent you, you can imagine what critics must be doing to these books now: Edmund Dantes and Masculine Totalizing / D'artagna, Portha, and Arima: France's Hidden Female Musketeers / The Countess of Monte Cristo, etc. etc.

I taped a wonderful episode of Inspector Morse, "Masonic Mysteries," which uses "The Magic Flute" as the context for the story. It's amazing, by the way, how much of "Parsifal" comes out of Mozart, down to exact lines; in fact, how much of Mozart is in Wagner altogether. Up front, though you'd never know it by the music alone.

That's it for my teaching day (I'm typing in my office). Your letters have long-term effects. I keep them in a pile near the Mac and periodically go back to something you've said that caught my eye on the first go-round. Hope all is well.

Steve

Dear Ted,

Re Borgmann - I dunno. These postmoderns make me so crazy that the only acceptable criticism to me would be an outpouring of fury, bile, and ridicule. Those people are just plain stupid and nasty - awful, awful types. Stage-prop Marxists and a genuine Nazi at Yale:

> Still more than Rousseau's <u>Discourse on the Origin of Inequality</u>, <u>The Birth of Tragedy</u> is indeed a discourse, a harangue that combines the seductive power of a genetic [teleological] narrative with the rhetorical complicity of a sermon. . . . The complicity between the "I" of the narrator and the collective "we" of his acquiescing audience functions relentlessly, underscored by the repeated address of the audience as "my friends." The orator has our best interests at heart and we are guaranteed intellectual safety as long as we remain within the sheltering reach of his voice.
>
> (<u>Allegories of Reading</u>, '79)

Postmodernism's finest hour.

I'm not sure about Borgmann. I'll look again. Maybe I got him wrong. It's been a while since I read your letter, but if I remember right, he was trying to make sense of the postmoderns and I was having trouble with the attempt. I can't even say the word any more without feeling like retching. It's like saying "African-American" or "post-coloniality" five thousand times.

Yes, here it is: "Despite its benificence [salutary effects???], the transformative power of postmodernism is in doubt [how about destructive? and I have no doubts] because it has failed to resolve the ambiguity of individualism" (What else could it do but fail at anything it tried? It tried to resolve something?). He also says there are parallels to the shift from modernism to postm. in "a respect for Native American wisdom [oh yeah?], from White-Anglo-Saxon-Protestant hegemony to ethnic pluralism [it's WASPS that took in all those ethnics], from male chauvinism to many kinds of feminism" (does he <u>believe</u> this? I know what they say, but I don't believe a word of it). And what's this about postmodernism making the grade up to the point of "having considered critically the modern arrogation of reality"? He gets better, though when he says that pm. "accepts naively the legacy of that arrogance, namely, the disappearance of reality" (all this could be said much more cleanly and directly, though I'd say that whatever pm. accepts, it does it stupidly. In fact, I'm not sure it "accepts" anything. More like blindly assumes). And: "Worse, postmodern criticism gets caught in dogmatism when it restricts the postmodern conversation to humanity" (this had me a foxed - I like to think that humanity is everything). "Eloquent things" is not bad, all by itself. Keats' "Ode to a Nightingale" is an eloquent thing. But wouldn't Flaubert et. al. find it an impossible idea that things could speak to us? I prefer your following paragraph on "eloquent reality." In fact, I notice you changed his term, for the better. Plus, you say real things - Callas and a Vaught-Corsair taking off already make me feel happier. Yes, he's not slopsistic. This merits an A for effort. But the prose is much too much in the head. Reading Nietzche, on the other hand, is benificent. He really is an athlete. A heavy dose of Nietzche and a lot of crap falls by the wayside. The man is a champ. And funny as hell. In the same breath he can talk about Kant, the labor question, and the virtue of drinking strong tea for breakfast. Not in one breath, exactly, but that's the effect. I opened Daybreak at random last month and my eye fell on a sentence about people who crash into their railway carriage seats as opposed to people who sit down straight and those who stand up, and a few paragraphs later, he's talking about horseback riders and the power that comes of breeding and discipline.

I'm still trying to plow out from under and come up with some pages on N. that will make some sense. De Man is a sick son of a bitch (I'll send you some of my essay soon). I almost prefer Derrida's lunacies. I'm sure that my reactions ultimately stem from my relationship to my father: why didn't he protect me better than he did? Why didn't he tell me the truth and draw a boundary line between me and my mother's lunacy? Why didn't he protect himself against mother's craziness and Marxism? Where were the fathers when Foucault, Derrida, and De Man hit the graduate schools and university presses? That's one of my deepest reactions to the postmoderns: where were the fathers? This business is wretchedly confusing. Peter Shaw, of Academic Questions, saw the whole thing happening in '68 at Stony Brook and it galvanized him to start writing and speaking out, yet he seems so aborted to me. Our whole generation seems aborted to me. I don't know. Spengler tells us to throw away our pens and brushes and learn physics and economics. "We no longer live in a Phidias or a Mozart time." But when I stand in front of Ruisdael's "Entrance to a Village" or read Balzac's description of the concierge going up the staircase to the lawyer's office in Cousin Pons, I am in a Ruisdael or Balzac time. I suppose that Spengler would say it didn't matter and that I was living in "the zeitgeist of the week before last." Henry Miller loved him but said to hell with it. Jump into whatever it is and have a good time. Borgmann is unhappy with this whatever it is (he'd be better off if he thought of "eloquent things" that way, i.e., "or whatever they are." Basho speaks of having conversations about right and wrong with his silhouette. You can't beat that). But Borgmann says that these brush strokes and ink traces "would be forever silent were they not embedded in a communal context wherein they invite and instruct the reader to call forth a certain reality." What if I were the last man in front of "Entrance to a Village"? Would it matter? When I'm at the Met, the world falls away. What if I were the last man fucking? I'd be glad I were doing it. The negative and positive are really incompatible, and the little bit of each in the other takes care of itself. I already feel like the last man anyway, with a few exceptions, notably you. Spengler has a disturbing end-of-the-culture passage in Vol. 1, in which he sees the last page of Mozart and the last self-portrait by Rembrandt fluttering in the breeze - unread, unseen, and meaningless. The same life that brought organic unity brings death. Nihilism, for him, as for Nietzsche, is a symptom of old age, a <u>late</u> life - cold, hard, and soulless, the first step toward dissolution. So what else is new? John Webster says it beautifully in <u>The Duchess of Malfi</u>: "All things must have an end; / Churches and cities, like to us, / Must have like death that we have." What else is ancient epic about if not the destruction of "the topless towers of Ilium"?

In your last few letters, I've been listening to the <u>tone</u>, or rather the tempo. I hear my own flailings. I've always been under the gun of feeling chaotic and inarticulate. I used to watch Marty Maisel make perfect airplane models and perfect drawings, while my own fingers were covered in glue, my design sheets were full of holes, and pieces of balsa wood stuck to the paper. In the end, my planes and drawings were just as good, but I always felt terrible about my lack of clarity the endless time it took me to complete my work. Have I talked about this feeling before? It's never left me. I feel that same scatter-shot confusion in your letters. A thousand thoughts and feelings explode in all directions. Intense clarities, intense repetitions, wonderful humor out of negativity, negativity out of wonderful intelligence and sensitivity. Details, confusions, perceptions, knowledge - I feel the same tempo in myself. Not so much a tempo, maybe, as jangled nerves, an intense rush to "say it all." In my senior year in college, as I once wrote to you, I just wanted to crawl inside Conrad's prose and speak from there. Now I'd be happy to crawl inside a woman in whom I could recognize myself, the way I do when I'm in front of Ruisdael. The images on MTV are in slow motion compared to those that fly inside my head.

Doesn't Nietzsche write beautifully? I just read a review of a new physics <u>cum</u> theology book, in which the author is quoted as saying that most work in physics that's correct also happens to be beautiful, whereas ugly work is generally incorrect. The same goes for writing. Flaubert tells George Sand that "The concern for external Beauty you reproach in me is for me a <u>method</u>. When I hear a repetition or a bad assonance in my writing, I know I'm floundering in the False." And doesn't it seem as if Nietzsche couldn't be writing to more than five people, tops? But he knew. In <u>The Birth of Tragedy</u>, he compares Kant and Schopenhauer to Dürer's knight travelling on horseback with his dog, accompanied by Death and the Devil. It's a wonderful passage and says volumes about him (he had another take on Kant and Schopenhauer afterwards and must have realized that <u>he</u> himself was the knight - This image will help me to tie my Nietzsche essay together with a nice bow on top, I hope). I love being in N's company. One feels recognized. And he's such a smart-ass. Right on top of things: "In the art of seduction, <u>Parsifal</u> will always retain its rank - as <u>the stroke of genius</u> in seduction. I admire this work. I wish I had written it myself; failing that, I <u>understand it</u>." He could be talking about Derrida: "Wagner is bad for youths; he is calamitous for women. What is a female Wagnerian, medically speaking? . . . Ah, this old robber! He robs our youths, he even robs our women and drags them into his den. Ah, this old Minotaur! The price we have had to pay for him! Every year trains of the most beautiful maidens and youths are led into his labyrinth, so that he may devour them." I bet you that Derrida's classes are packed with gorgeous females, only they're probably stupider than the Wagnerian women. Danielle would have been one of them had Derrida been around in her time. She found others. The scene nauseated me even then. And it was French, no less. Columbia had its Michel Riffatére in the mid-60s. He was in on it right from the start and apparently remains a real lunatic. Sleeps about four minutes a night. That's what I was told. "Astonishing powers of recuperation." For all I know, he said it to me himself at one of those hideous upper West Side dinner parties we used to attend. I was utterly lost, and I had the most beautiful woman on campus. The connective word should probably be "because."

I also hear something else in Nietzche. All the heavyweight Germans have it - Marx, Freud, Goethe, Burckhardt, Spengler, Hegel - that superb sense of language, the inevitability of expression, the idea of inevitability itself: "I describe what is coming, what can no longer come differently." I think that it either stems from German music or stems from the same source as the music. Nietzche and Spengler both call it German seriousness, in the best sense of the word. Borges speaks of Spengler's "virile pages," which is an astute observation. Nietzche says that Schopenhauer - I think it was Schopenhauer - wrote by hearing his ideas as musical motifs. And there's a great deal said about music in Nietzche and Spengler, isn't there? - about Bach and Beethoven, and Wagner, in particular. I have no doubt that, in the original, one can literally hear whole passages of Handel and Gluck moving through Spengler's prose. Pound says he hears the troubadours in Dante, and when I listen to William Byrd's Mass for Five Voices, the interiors of Gothic cathedrals rise up in my imagination. Spengler has beautiful things to say about the darkness of the cathedral making its way into Rembrandt's backgrounds and into the surface features of the Italian masters. Something to the effect of: "Raphael, Michaelangelo, and Da Vinci, each in his own way, attempted to recreate a Euclidean-static sculpture, but that was possible only once, in Athens. In all their works one feels the movement-quality, the tending to distances and depths. They are on their way not to Phidias and Praxiteles but to Monteverdi and Palestrina, and they have come there not from Roman ruins but from the still music of the cathedral." What was so wrong about Spengler to Collingwood? In terms of the scholars I had to read, he was ahead of his time in sensing the Gothic spirit of the Renaissance. Is it simply a matter of small minds recoiling at the sight of anything that's beautiful and true? According to Heller, that's what Burckhardt thought: " . . . the inability of mediocrity to expose itself to the impact of what is great."

The opening particularly impressed me in "Truth and Lies." Imagine Nietzsche's self-possession to be able to write out whole pictures of the universe with real belief, the sheer intimacy of the man and the intimacy with which he reads and writes. It's the same in Spengler: "This book is solely intended for those who are capable of living themselves into the word-sounds and pictures as they read." That's how these people read. That's how the painters painted. Leslie says that Constable used to sit so quietly sketching out of doors that mice used to creep into his pockets.

The cartoons are a treat. I know that Thurber well ("With you I've known peace, Lida, and now you say you're going crazy"). Yes, exactly. But it was the peace of the dead. Lida's reply was always the same: "With you, Steve, I've been going crazy, and now you say I brought you peace?"

The discs arrived. Many thanks. I haven't plugged them in yet - I'm waiting for the planets to come into proper conjunction, I suppose. Your description of Derrida playing with mental razor-blades in his baby-blue suit was so wonderful that I included it in my last letter to Tom Bertonneau in Michigan. He too is flailing around and is crazed by what he sees. He gets it first-hand, since he and his wife go to conferences, give papers, and make contacts, and then they vomit. He writes superb letters, a little too academic for my taste but a real mensch. Grew up in the Santa Monica mountains, by the way. I keep thinking that it would be marvellous if the three of us could meet.

Your newspaper collage is delicious. The <u>Peter and the Wolf</u> item is too crazy for words. I had my own run-in with the story in fifth or sixth grade, when the teacher asked us who wanted to act out the play in the auditorium by miming it, with the recording as background (I had it at home and used to listen to it all the time). I raised my hand and said I'd do the grandfather, and in <u>Russian</u>. I actually thought that this would be a plus for the performance. She looked at me sort of bent, the way most people did ("there goes that kid again"), accepted me, and said there'd be no need for language altogether. The word "pantomime" was a blank spot in my mind till we started to rehearse (Incidentally, my father remembered hearing those Roumanian wolves in the winter night when he went riding with his grandfather by sleigh.)

As for Anne Conrad-Antonville, the orchestra is in better shape without her. She ought to go live in a hermetically-sealed box, because it's the only way she'll never step on an ant. (Nietzche is so sharp. He says that nihilism is one step away from Buddhism - an "exhausted" life.) In fact, it's too late. She happens to be alive, and her immune system is killing microbes by the thousands every day. Live cells are replacing dead ones, and her whole body is a battleground. I can imagine a <u>real</u> lunatic attacking AIDs research for attempting to find a way to kill the virus ("Science teaches children that it's good to destroy micro-organisms"). This principle is already being preached, in fact. As for Garlo's idea that he doesn't want human fingers to rub off the molecules of wood from his guitars, CD's are probably a petroleum derivative, and if he makes a hit recording wind humming through the strings, he'll degrade the biosphere a million times more than Segovia ever could. Note the idiotic "only the wind will <u>touch</u> the guitar strings." It's old hat, by the way. I met a "composer" at Dave Hopkins one night (I can't believe someone actually said this to me) who put bells on fifty cows for the same purpose of a "natural" performance. This is what comes of treating life as oppression. Myra Jehlen, writing in an MLA publication, says that Melville only gives us a linguistic construction and that "there are no natural states in literature." I wrote to Tom that Jehlen seems to think that Moby-Dick would be "true" if she opened the book and water spilled out. Even this has been tried. Ernie Kovacs did a wonderful half hour silent skit ("Eugene's World"), in which Eugene is in his library opening books, and each one he opens gives its sound effects (Camille coughs, etc.).

One final point, about Nietzche's "prediction." I think what happens is that the times move through us as we move through them and that Nietzche simply saw himself in the age. That's the conclusion he comes to about Wagner. He says it occurred to him at one point that every time he said "Parsifal," he was already saying "Zarathustra." He's such a marvellous registering instrument because he carries nihilism inside himself. All artistic sublimation seems prophetic or mirroring to me in some way. You can hear the music of William Byrd and the music of Gluck to Wagner in Shakespeare. Which may be another way of saying that the feeling comes first, though that feeling is already filled with the life of the times in a hundred million ways. And standing in front of "Entrance to a Village" is also a living experience, whereas postmodernism is not. It's born dead. It was meant to be dead, and it is. It won't predict anything, the way Marx doesn't predict anything, even with his ringing declarations. For all I know, his writing is probably worse than the other Germans I mentioned. In fact, I'd bet on it.

Here's a real thrill: Yesterday (10/24) I noticed that AMC was having a one-hour special on Gene Autrey in the afternoon - a bio narrated by Johnny Cash, who opens with a wonderful rendition of "I'm Back in the Saddle Again." Then you see kids flocking to the movies, and Cash starts talking about what Autrey meant to him as a ten-year old. "A poor country boy" seeing a man on a horse who sang and could set things right. What else was he if not a Grail knight, American style? Really wonderful. And Then! The story of Autrey's life starts, a country boy himself - Oklahoma Territory at the turn of the century. My skin starts to pop and I think, Al Jennings! This is the closest I've gotten to him outside of his book and Cendrars' translation of the story Jennings wrote for him about Dogtown, New Mexico, 1875. And then there's the hero of the story, Jim Stanton, the foreman of Ranch 101 in Colorado, known as the best shot from Colorado to the Canadian border. And not two minutes into the bio there's a film clip of a western shoot em up scene of cowboys and Indians, and Cash is saying how the people in those early silents were the real thing, and next thing a clip of Buffalo Bill's Wild West Show, and there it is, a poster advertising "Miller Bros. Ranch 101" travelling show, and then . . . Autrey, now in his 80s, starts talking about outlaws and him Cash says the magic name, "Al Jennings" - and the next clip you see is the man himself, Jennings, starring in "When Outlaws Meet," 1919. Unbelievable. Just ten second worth, but it was all there. Jennings in dark suit knocking on a shanty door, goes inside, grim scene like a Walker Evans photograph but fifteen years earlier, a

woman buttoning up her blouse with a baby at her breast, <u>exactly</u>
like Jennings' descriptions of the lives of the convicts he met in
the Pen in Joliet; and, in fact, I'd been thinking about those
descriptions recently. They're the best I've ever read about the
harshness of those lives. Cendrars calls him the Dostoevsky of an
American prison house, and he's absolutely right. After all the
Mailers and Malcolm X's and all those "proletarian" writers Jenkin
reads are done, no one tells it better than Jennings (Jenkin kept
lumping him in with his own reading list - something about
"sentimental realists." I kept saying no, but he didn't hear me).
And I could feel it in those ten seconds of film. I instantly
believed everything Cendrars said about him - that he was called
in to work on westerns because of his eye for the truth, and that
Hayes got him out with the new censorship rules, which according
to Cendrars, had something to do with the realism of his films and
filmscripts themselves. I'm planning to call AMC and find out
who's there who might want to see the story I translated and what
I found out about him. It should go to Cash, shouldn't it? Those
ten seconds were true grit. It was stunning. Jennings, by the way,
looks exactly as Cendrars describes him, only younger. <u>Through the
Shadows with O. Henry</u>. The title alone makes it a classic.

10/29

I'm up to my eyeballs in school work and feel terribly pressed for
time, though that feeling may be a function of how I feel about
the whole scene in the first place. Everything blurs. Nothing gets
done. Administrators announce one crazy plan after another,
students don't study, committees don't commit, and nothing
happens. <u>The Sunday Times Book Review</u> just ran an article on a new
study of CUNY. The community colleges come out in the basement as
usual. We're the perpetual ground-zero of every attack on the
four-year schools, and CUNY is coming in for some pasting now as
never before. Zombie-like, I stagger through the days, with a
voice behind my eyes saying that I don't like anything I see. A
constant, low-level hum. I'd prefer those Rhinemaidens you blow
smoke at during the night by your swimming pool, but then again,
they rise up before me as well, and in the most unlikely places.
They're just my mother singing "hoyatoya," with Janet, Clover, and
Lee waving their spears in the air. No, those are the Valkyries.
They're all the same. Nietzche says that if you take off their
helmets and underwater Rhine clothing, they're all Madame Bovary.
Wish I could gab with you for hours.

Hope you like the book. Don't recall if you have it. We went on
a trek for it one day. It's not the same edition I had but close.

*This letter is undercovered by the repeated thought of its audience
as my friend —*

Steve

open Casper's clip and slip it under a hallow —

Eat when hungry
sleep when tired
bathe when dirty
swing when swung at

these are epiphanies

Creating nihilism out of illusion
is like creating nothing ex nihilo-
no great feat

Language is the metaphor of being
without it there is merely existence

There are two varieties of nihilism;
cloaked and uncloaked
the one conquers friends
the other, nations as well

For some nihilism is self-imprisonment,
For others, it is an excuse to put
the world in prison.
Thus, nihilism can produce either art
or holocausts

A good writer makes sense of words,
A great writer rearranges them

Women have always lived
on the other side of nihilism;
they are content eating grass on
plains with jealous eyes.
Must men live with them?

For some, to remember the past
means giving up who they have become

To catch up to Nietzsche, the artist
must abandon his tools as excess baggage

Looking into the eyes of nihilism
one sees the absence of reality

ON GAY IDENTITY, PLEASURE, & NIHILISM

One could stuff all nihilism
in a "rats ass" and still have room
for homosexual relations -
first things first!

Aphorisms from myself

Dear

Steve

THE
REVOLUTION
OF NIHILISM

In his *Fin-de-Siècle Vienna* - a strange book which
considers narcissism, nihilism and the collapse of a liberal
middle class society in Vienna street by street - Carl E.
Schorske gives a précis of a novelette written by one Leopold
von Andrian zu Werburg (Ringstrasse Mietpalast, Apt. 3C), *The
Garden of Knowledge*. (Coincidentally, you send me a movie
called "The Garden of Evil"!) The hero's name, sadly, is
Erwin (about as exciting as 'Ted'). The story is not
concerned with "the outer world of social and physical
reality," Schorske writes, "but the inner scene of [Erwin's]
psychic life. The social and physical world exist merely as
stimuli to or symbols of the hero's feeling." For Erwin,
Schorske goes on, "the world is a flow - now viscous, now
torrential - whose liquid elements blend into each other and
into the self. [He] cannot find the way into the world
because he sees rational self, outer reality, and personal
feelings as an undifferentiated continuum." (Hofmannsthal
said this well: "And the three are one: a man, a thing, a
dream.") . . . "The liquidity of the boundary between self
and other meant that the search for '*the other*' was condemned
to futility. Even scientific knowledge Erwin drew into the
vortex of self-infatuation. After a year of scientific
study, it . . . '*became clear to him that he should not
search for his place in the world, for he was himself the
world equally great and equally unique. . . . But he studied
on, for he hoped that if he knew the world, out of its image
his own would look back.*' Erwin's hopes went unrealized.
Separated from the world, he could not use it as his mirror.
Merging with it, or ingesting it, he felt his selfhood
threatened. Only in ceremonial or aesthetic experiences were
ego and world bound together in a rhythmic unity of feeling.
But this unity lacked both strength and durability. The
shudder at the poetic word, in which heaven and Hell flowed
together in an ambiguous, sublimated ecstasy, '*full of
trembling glory*,' brought neither clarification to the
understanding nor satisfaction to the instincts. Life, which
began for the sensitive Erwin as '*an alien task*,' ended
without the direct and meaningful experience of engagement.
The aesthetic aristocrat remained the devitalized Narcissus,

hoping as a dying man that a dream might give him what life had failed to provide: contact with *'the other.'* . . . Andrian's Erwin, unable to find the secret of life by direct engagement, turned inward and *'bent deeper and more anxiously over his past.'* His recollections of past experience became not merely moving but *'exalting and priceless.'* As in Marcel Proust, Erwin's remembrances became his life. Again desocialization accompanied internalization. Human beings acquired worth for Erwin only insofar as they contributed to his memories; that is, *'they moved him only because he had lived of them.'* The past recalled became more significant than the present experienced. Thus the narcissistic hero imperceptibly shifted not only from a life of engagement to imprisonment in the self, but also from a life not yet lived to a life lived out. . . . When death came for Prince Erwin . . . it came not, as to Narcissus, as moral retribution, but as *'psychological necessity'*." At the end of the story Andrian reminds one of the curse Tiresias placed upon Narcissus for the last sentence reads that Erwin dies *'without knowledge.'* (Schorske makes no mention if the novelette is a pleasure to read or a drudge. A significant omission which I will pick up on later.)

Why, you may ask, do I repeat this decadent tale? A number of reasons. It has to do with hands, frontiers of reality 50 years long, nihilism, narcissism, self-imprisonment, art, and your having pointed to me an Indian path winding its way between them' (a debt I repay, unfortunately, by punishing you with my long letters). Two things fascinate me about it: 1) what has narcissism to do with nihilism and art with either, and 2) what is my place in history; i.e., what is the 'milieu' in which I, blind and deaf, make my way through reality as through a crowded Viennese café? I wish this letter could be written in sections with headings to ease the pain, but clarity does not reign in the kingdom of Ted. The wandering Prince remains without compass and snow swirls through the forest.

Another myth.....(or, Back to Basics)

When I was a eleven, two weeks after a friend told me God was dead (which I believed), I took a small BB rife to my bedroom window, pointed it at squirrel casually making its way up a tree and fired. The creature jumped straight out, vertical to the ground, landed back on the tree a few feet down and fled to the leafy branches above. I too jumped straight back, thunderstruck by what I had done. Then a fearful self loathing descended upon me. I both feared and disgusted myself. I had become a cause of suffering. My habit of using twigs, leaves, petals, and blades of grass as succulent gum to commune with nature was tainted. I wanted to beg the squirrel's forgiveness, but as in the human kingdom, after the death of my father, it was too late. With the death of God there was now no forgiveness to be had anywhere in the universe. I detested my unforgivable existence and felt I had to cast the demons of desire out; let them fly into the world, I cried, I want nothing to do with them. I will not accept that I can be the cause of suffering in others. Without a God to judge and forgive, evil(being human) is unbearable. Others, testing for death, would throw me from quarry cliffs for their experiment, but I would know the gesture was fitting yet pointless for I had erased my face, plugged my ears, blinded my eyes, and plunged my hands into my pockets. Salvation could be mine as long as I remained in myself. If, in giving up being the destiny of other men I had to also forfeit their being mine, well, so be it! What was being human to me? All could do with me as they please. All, on the other hand, hosts to my demons, also consigned themselves to perdition in a reality without the possibility of redemption. For, for me, it was not "forgive them for they know what they do," it was, damm them, for they possess the unforgivable urge to bring suffering into the world wantonly. They are willing to live damned yet undammable lives.

Is this, or is not, a form of nihilism? Was I not "ashamed in front of myself, as if [I] had deceived myself all too long"? Had I not "lost faith in [my] own value when no infinitely valuable whole works through [me]? And finally, did I not "pass sentence on this whole world of becoming as a deception and [set out] to invent a world beyond it, a true world?" as Nietzsche said? I lacked only the last ingredient, the "last form of nihilism," the "disbelief in any metaphysical world and [did not] forbid [myself] any belief in a true world." I could not forbid myself "every kind of clandestine access to afterworlds and false divinities," and could not bear the thought of not being able "endure this world though [I did] want to deny it," as Nietzsche says the absolute nihilist must. Perhaps that was too much to ask of an eleven year old. So I did invent a true world, a world wherein I was my own Christ, I became my own forgiveness by evaporating. Is this not at least a slanted reaction to a dim apprehension of nihilism? I do think that the "candle of self love" blew out in me upon hearing of the death of God - it was chilling news that my friend Paul brought me that day. Clinically, I think its called, "reaction formation," rather than "reactive nihilism," however.

If, for Hofmannsthal, to avoid the cul de sac of Erwin, the urgent question was "How shall art transcend mere passive rendering of beauty to achieve a fruitful relationship to the life of the world?", for me the question was: How shall I transcend a destructive relationship to the life of the world and achieve a selfless rendering of existence?

Cast-out anger is a terrible thing - but how does one, once one has blinded oneself, plugged one's ears, and plunged one's hands into one's pockets, fit into history, relate to the State, the Weltgeist, the temper of the times? With anything at all? Such a one seems a bastard child of history, nameless (except, perhaps, clinically), and wrong in any century. As with Erwin, separated from the world it was no longer my mirror; when I looked I saw only others bathing in what I loathed about myself. A narcissism of self-abasement trapped in an inexplicable (dammed) world. Even their flesh was mine. They possessed my face, my eyes, my ears, and used my hands to sow havoc and destruction. I was now surrounded by five billion people who reflected what I hated in myself (even my own reflection was of 'the other') - and all their names were Ted. They gave me not a moments rest. All I could do was placate them - succumb to their every wish - for they knew my deep-dark secret - that they were me and I would be forced to reveal this secret if I turned aggressively upon them, i.e., sucked back into myself my destructive forces and unleashed them upon a godless world. Does this sort of self-loathing, on an evolutionary scale of emotional development, predate both the sloth of narcissism and the tyrannosaurs rex of nihilism? Was I a brainless trilobite for fifty years? A dry geek in the drunken circus of life? "Ahem!" says the professor, "lets not make philosophy too personal!"

How does Nietzsche get from nihilism to the will to power? Why don't we simply stop at nihilism? What's the push from Apollo to Dionysus? (At one point, Nietzsche speaks of "philosophy" as <u>wanting</u> "to cross over" from the negation to the affirmation of life.) More likely though, Nature won't allow self-destruction. Nature asserts its will to pure life, which we, till nihilism hit us, for 8000 years, had cloaked with false psychology and housed in Apollonian civilizations we could stroll through as kings. I don't believe it in either version. Nihilism is a dead-end disease, a turning of the cannons upon oneself and firing. (As Nietzsche said: "I want to teach the idea that gives many the right to erase themselves.") No "Overman" can arise from these ashes. Unless, of course, one confuses one's self destruction with true fullness of being - but then one ends up in a mad house. Is nihilism, in other words, simply involuted anger grand-standing itself - as such anger is so prone to do?

Old fashioned "nihilism" (formerly called cynicism, or opportunism) is wonderfully captured by Burckhardt in his description of Constantine the Great: "In a genius driven without surcease by ambition and lust for power there can be no question of Christianity and paganism, of conscious religiosity or irreligiosity; such a man is essentially unreligious, even if he pictures himself standing in the midst of a churchly community. Holiness he understands only as a reminiscence or as a superstitious vagary. Moments of inward reflection, which for the religious man are in the nature of worship, he consumes in a different sort of fire. World-embracing plans and mighty dreams lead him by an easy road to the streams of blood of slaughtered armies. He thinks he will be at peace when he has achieved this or the other goal, whatever it may be that is wanting to make his possessions complete. But in the meantime all of his energies, spiritual as well as physical, are devoted to the great goal of dominion, and if he ever pauses to think of his convictions, he finds they are pure fatalism." The word "nihilism," in other words, used to be reserved for those who unleashed their full humanity upon the world, anger and all, in a quest for dominion and self-fulfillment which they found by either magnifying or purifying the course of world history or their street corner, depending on the amount of genius or anger within them. On seeing the Ringstrasse for the first time, Hitler wrote, "From morning until late at night, I ran from one object of interest to another, but it was always the buildings that held my primary interest. For hours I would stand in front of the opera, for hours I could gaze at the Parliament; the whole Ring Boulevard seemed like an enchantment out of the *Thousands-and-One-Nights*." But it wasn't his! Unlike Constantine who aggrandized himself by enlarging the Empire, however, Hitler had first to purify the empire (by eradicating evil) to get it. He never tasted victory, whereas Constantine relished every morsel. But reality did not flicker for either of them. Isn't this old fashioned nihilism? A use of the world for one's own ends, where the non-nihilistic opposition is the ideal of subsuming oneself under a cause and the making of oneself a pawn in someone else's great design? - yet both can be redeemed if things go wrong. Arrogance versus humility? One can not be arrogant and feel a Nietzschian nihilism it seems to me - he never did himself by all accounts. He was not a nihilist! He was a kind, gentle, and "good man." Much like me or you he stooped to be kind and never bothered anyone excessively - until the end when he was unaware of doing so.

But back to me and history:
    If Hermann Rauschning was correct in believing in 1939 that the National Socialists embodied nihilism (actually, Rauschning should say they embodied the "Dionysian" world of man as "beast and superbeast") and that what they wanted "was a *tabula rasa*, a complete liberation from the past, on which to build a totalitarian despotism," and Hitler was Dionysus himself who, taking Spengler's advise, surrounded himself with murderous, Roman "legionaries sworn to personal allegiance to the new Cæsar," thereby fulfilling Nietzsche's historical prediction, but only to be followed, after defeat, by "structuralism,' "Foucaultism," and 'deconstruction," i.e., polite nihilism, nihilism minus a Dionysus world (mad-house nihilism), did I sidestep this latter history, content merely to murder fathers, shoot squirrels, feel the loss of a redeeming God, and retch at the sight of human flesh? Was I out of the loop? With five billion people breathing down my neck, it was difficult enough finding a bathroom to masturbate in let alone pausing to wonder if I were in step with those eagerly tearing down the edifices of Western civilization or were merely an hemorrhaged appendix. ("Ahem!" again the professor says.) Was I the only true nihilist among them? Spiritually broke and expressionless?

Others were wondering about such things; but they felt in history, taking it for walks in the garden at twilight, corresponding about it through letters addressed to others who also paused to think while sipping café coffee, lounging in the ivy halls of academia, leaning upon the Arch de Triumphe, or gesticulating in the corridors of government. They wondered about their loss of faith in civilization, Prospero's machinations, the lost messages of the Yanamomo, the intrusion of psychology between language and reality, and what all this had to do with the death of God, the ego, and being published, but they did not suffer a loss of faith in themselves. In my 50 year long frontier of myself and history; where was my contact point? If history went North, it seems I went South. It's true that for me as well the world was a glaze of false consciousness sweetening rapacity, but still it was a different rapacity than most people understood. Only I knew its name and it wasn't nihilism but Teddiness. Can nihilism be anything other than personal? It's not exactly an intellectual apprehension.

What is it to actually feel nihilistic? Need it not take a gut form of self-hatred which blindingly separates one from history, reality, the world, as did mine? Nietzsche talks as one who has **gone through it,** sees it swirling around him, but what did he feel in the throes of it, before he could speak of it? Or was his a purely intellectual deduction based upon musings and reading; a healthy insight into what, till the insight, seemed healthy; i.e., was he in possession of a strong, domineering ego in love with itself on both sides of the insight? Was it a passing from one healthy state to another without ever once slipping from the log into the swamp? Or was it that Nietzsche had not **gone through it** at all, but had merely universalized his Nietzscheness, confusing casting it upon others as having **gone through it**, till five billion people who hated themselves and named Nietzsche drove him to the mad house? What if after fifty years of seeing his demons cavorting in the world and finally looking at them from his window in the sanitarium in Jena, he could let himself surface: "I lived in Naumburg a lot, because I was good.... I was very fine because I live in a house. I write letters everyday to very good people and to his Majesty. I was very fine and give a house key to my mother everyday. ... But I was excellent my mother was very fine because she loves very much, *pour le mérite*. ... I loved someone very much, myself. ... I did not love Friedrich Nietzsche at all. I lived in many good places. I liked very much to be in one place, née Oehler. I read very much. I liked to live in a house it was really a good house. I liked to go out of house. I didn't love anyone not even one person. ... What is that here? an ear. What is that here? a nose. What is that here? hands I do not love." What if this was Nietzsche at his most articulate? What if this is what he wanted to say all along, but had first to rid himself entirely of his demons? (His mother's *mérite* (?).) Would Kane have sputtered differently had he not died upon clasping his "rosebud"? And what was Nietzsche's connection to history while wearing a dunce cap in the Jena sanitarium? The modern version of a medieval monk proudly displaying his bleeding stigmata, an example of an inchoate illness of the times which rolled over him like a steamroller? Pullman left his tracks and a twinkle in his eyes! (Of course, Nietzsche also wrote: "My struggle against the *feeling of guilt* and the projection of the concept of *punishment* into the physical and metaphysical world; also into psychology and the interpretation of history." In my ill-prepared reading of him, he failed in that struggle, much as I did though I would have used the word 'fear,' not 'guilt'. You see, like Zelig, I can turn up even at Nietzsche's writing desk.) Am I then to join history this way - wearing a dunce cap, an historical freak? Was becoming a teacher a country bumpkin's imitation of Cecil Rhodes? A Napoleon for the weak? (I received an "exemplary teaching" award from the UFT. It should have been for "St. Michael in the Projects".) Must I die feeling that others have lived my life, while I was given the miserable task of living it out as a hermit? If one, in brief, truly lives Nietzschian nihilism, can one be productive and walk with history as a friend? I do not think so. Thus, those who are structuralists, Demanians, Foucaultians, deconstructionists, etc., and are productive and possess flowing hair, are self-lovers, their candle has not flickered out, and the glide into nihilism for them is an amusement, or rather, an excursion into self-advancement - i.e., they exercise the old nihilism as did Constantine and Hitler, or as does the teenage Mafioso spitting outside Vito's coffee shop. (Some, of course, are truly sick, and how they get published is beyond me.)

My Debt

Imagine my wonderment then when, years later, through conversations with you (without benefit of acoustic recording *Touché!* for future verification, however), things began to change. I began to see my long forgotten ears, nose, and hands from a side-long glance. It is not possible! I cried from the desert streets of Brooklyn. What have I been doing that I should see appendages? Let me talk again with Steve, I told myself. And I did. You spoke of reality with unwavering confidence that it was there, you spoke of great men and art as signposts you measured yourself by, you spoke of ideas as being more than ruinous ruminations, and you spoke of a world which was different than you; you drew distinctions between yourself and the world. Though you wavered on some things - women, teaching, writing - your immersion in self was not as profound as mine. You were a giant to me, my first true mentor. I listened closely, desperately sorting your strengths from your hesitancies to find *loss of Hands - my cabin* my way. Slowly my hands came back to haunt me, wiggling before my eyes, tingling with desire. What do they want of me? Is it possible the world would accept their presence? Were they beginning to acknowledge, through my conversations with you, that they hold the destiny of other men, that my self suffers because of them just as it is the cause of suffering in others and that that is the way things should be? Nihilism hovers on the horizon like a huge, black bird but a candle begins to shine next to it, however dimly. It remains dim, but it is there!

|Anti-Social Patrol Agency MEMO,#204,<DEPT B/24> >2nd FL<
|>Office Of Disintegration<|
|Memo Advisory:<BEWARE OF ANYONE LOOKING HUMAN ALL TOO HUMAN>
MUG SHOTS OF RENEGADE NIHILISTS
(for purpose of stereotyping)

Yet Science Goes On

Can art be transformed from "an ornament to an essence, from an expression of value to a source of value"? Is that what industrialization did to art, took away its gaiety, made it serious? The New Order destroyed the old traditions, and art succumbed on the promise, or so it thought, that it would be granted an even larger ego, a world encompassing ego, an ego freed of tradition to speak the raw Truth outside tradition. It gave up the joy of expressing a world everyone knew and loved; the joy of life. Art made a bad deal. It passed from the particular to the general - always a great temptation to the intellect. Had Constable taken all this seriously his aesthetic question would have been: "How do I make my paintings comment upon the universal impact of the New Order upon the countryside, humanity, and the human psyche?" This aesthetic would have been a great loss to his art, as it would have been for all the great masters down to Phidiås. This transformation also occurred in philosophy - the philosopher/artist as scientist of the soul. The psyche is rummaged for universal Truths in mock imitation of physics and comes up with idiosyncratic myths which violate the Truths others have discovered. The War of the Artist/philosophers begins. In aphorism, non-representational art, and cacophonous music - the purely generalized idiosyncratic - relief is sought to drive home the point, with much obscurity, that the individual contains the universal comment. A dead-end, and anti-democratic. So Language - the general in the particular - is posited as the Great Tradition that binds us in a common life, this time inescapably - the Gothic, Medieval, Renaissance, Baroque, Louis XIV, Victorian ages only seemed to possess traditions which artists had warmly expressed, but what binded them all together in an even greater, more encompassing tradition is: Language. All artists, from time immemorial, were serious imperialists, creating epistemologies of life - only they were unaware of themselves as doing do: Language, once it has an alphabet writes itself. However, the price paid for <u>this</u> universal Truth is the loss of reality. The Age of Impotency is inaugurated, nihilism raises its head. But perhaps today the artist finally realizes that he had no business reacting to the Industrial Revolution and must go back to expressing the joy in life that he and his friends share - perhaps without patrons. Does this Art strike us as frivolous? As "ornament" and not as source of value? Mahler remained untouched by the I.R.. He never spoke for anyone but himself -

like Flaubert & Kafka & Gauguin.   This was the other way and had little to do with the world.

SCHORSKE

"Elsewhere in Europe, art for art's sake implied the withdrawal of its devotees from a social class; in Vienna alone it claimed the allegiance of virtually a whole class [the liberal-bourgeoisie which was losing political control to the anti-Semitic Christian Socials and the Pan Germans] of which the artists were a part.   The life of art became a substitute for the life of action.   Indeed, as civic action proved increasingly futile, art became almost a religion, the source of meaning and food for the soul." p8-9

COMMENT

We are all pedestrian and there is no metaphysics. Only the State makes us think so, for it gives us our external dimension.   <u>After</u> the State comes psychology. (The ego is really another name for the State.)   When the State is changing for the duration, the out group suffers an 'objective malaise'. A crisis in reality.   Chateaubriand, Goethe, and Tocqueville saw it coming but they were born to early to feel it in their bones.   In the case of Europe, it was capitalism's engulfing the State after 1850 that precipitated the crisis - the final, finishing touch was given the aristocracy by a generation that had no desire to ape it, did not even know what it was.   Madame du Deffand became one with the Louis XIV chairs she sat upon, no longer the quintessence of an Age, and all Europe felt the loss as wax images of her holding court in them adorned period piece rooms in museums.   Even Kafka mourned.   He would have visited her sålon.

————————————————

The nihilist conquers the world by default: he never leaves his room and the path leading to his door he erases.
The Minotaur can not reach the nihilist for he has removed the labyrinth and sits at home pondering his mirror image.
Nietzsche does not write, he talks. He is very biblical that way. That is the secret of his style.
Nietzsche thinks he knows everyone better than they know themselves, so he talks to us in a kind manner.   He explains our unhappiness, centering it in our own souls. We are relieved it is not political. But then we are told we must destroy the world to attain happiness - the happiness of a beast in heat.
Is nihilism an active state or a passive state?   Those who built civilization for the past 8000 years were not nihilists, according to Nietzsche.   But those who realize it

was all an egotistical sham - the nihilist of today - what do
they do? Purge themselves of the psychology of civilization
builders while eating a Dunkin' donut and sipping coffee? Or
do they, as Lenin, Mao, and Hitler, literally tear down the
past to rebuild a better, more true civilization? But if so,
they are not nihilists, for there are no *true* worlds to build
for them. Mussolini would have build nothing after destroying
all, a true Dionysus, but he was a fool. And Zarthustra,
what did he do?

Nihilism was a godsend for Marx. He used it as an excuse
to write we needed Communism; a world he controlled. Had he
lived, Lenin would have locked him in the British museum.

Fin-de-siècle Vienna - a temple for the readers of
Wagner and Nietzsche. Hauptmann, Schnitzler, Hofmannsthal,
Zweig, Kraus, Wolf, Schonberg, Berg, Kreneck, Schiele, Klimt,
Freud, Kokoschka - all wandered in the shadow of the
Cathedral of St. Stephens with eyes cast down on the writings
of those two. Mahler, who found Nietzsche musical and set
Zarthustra to melody, however, could not stomach the
"overman" and for the opening of his monumental 8th symphony
chose the lines:

> *Come thou, Infinite Creator*
> *Let thy spirit visit us*
>
> . . . .
>
> *Inflame our senses with Thy light*
> *With Thy love fill our hearts*

Had Nietzsche been alive he would have croaked.

The Imitation of Christ

Brother Zeitunseen approached the Masters ancient wooden
door with trepidation. True, he knew that because of the
Order's rule that no shoes be worn, he could not be heard
approaching, but still, he knew they were awaiting him,
barefoot, lining the walls of the room with the Master
himself sitting at the desk and illumined from behind by the
stained glass window overlooking the courtyard. Today was
his day, the day he would be canonized, elevated to Sainthood
though he thought himself unworthy. He also knew that most
in the room, including the Master, detested him. They would
not be encircling his neck with the golden image of agonized
St. Sebastian were it not for the Pope who, the previous
week, had concluded his reading of the thousands of monk
evaluation sheets that had accumulated upon his library
shelves for these past twenty years. It was not that he read
a hundred glowing reports of Brother Zeitunseen's devotion
which had him confer the honor, but that he had not
encountered the Brother's name once! With great perception

he realized that a man who had gone unnoticed for twenty years - in an age of computers! - must indeed be the most humble of all. What he did not know is that upon the day following his canonization Brother Zeitunseen would be booted out of the monastery to the loud cheering of his fellow Brothers.

From nihilism (defined perfectly psychologically) N. wants to deduce an ontology. He wants to say our combined psychologies made a world which does not exist - then he wants to say what the world is really like on the other side of this psychology. But this dehumanized world can only be the absence of our initial error, barren, which leaves us with biology since all else that can be thought of must be jettisoned. This is too harsh, too earthy. It smacks of women. It's like advertising we enjoy life the way a tree enjoys life - without thought, without psychology. Isn't that a woman? See if I'm wrong.

Imagine a perfectly efficient factory, each section separated from the others, producing pieces to an exactitude that no caliper can fault. Then imagine that this perfect factory is entirely automated, not a single human in it, and that all the pieces, from first to last, have accumulated for 8000 years in a heap at the long end of the assembly line - for the factory was never programmed to assemble them. That is reality today.

Using words comes close, in some strange way, yet is not actually me speaking; they are more like what I think I would be saying if I were writing what I wanted to write. They come that close. Like sparks, off a flint, which always fail to light the fire.

Have you ever felt you were an affront to nature?

AND NOW, POSTMAN, DELIVER THIS MESSAGE TO STEVE

Dear Ted,

Your last letter put me in mind of Frost's "The White-Tailed Hornet." Do you know it?

. . . He stung me first and stung me afterward.
He rolled me off the field head over heels,
And would not listen to my explanations.

That's when I went as visitor to his house.
As visitor to my house he is better.
Hawking for flies about the kitchen door,
Trust him then not to put you in the wrong,
He won't misunderstand your freest movements.
Let him light on your skin unless you mind
So many prickly grappling feet at once.
He's after the domesticated fly
To feed his thumping grubs as big as he is.
Here he is at his best, but even here -
I watched him where he swooped, he pounced, he struck;
But what he found he had was just a nailhead.
He struck a second time. Another nailhead.
"Those are just nailheads. Those are fastened down."
Then disconcerted and not unnanoyed,
He stooped and struck a little huckleberry
The way a player curls around a football.
"Wrong shape, wrong color, and wrong scent," I said.
The huckleberry rolled him on his head.
At last it was a fly. He shot and missed;
And the fly circled round him in derision.
But for the fly he might have made me think
He had been at his poetry, comparing
Nailhead with fly and fly with huckleberry:
How like a fly, how very like a fly.
But the real fly he missed would never do;
The missed fly made me dangerously skeptic.

Won't this whole instinct matter bear revision?
Won't almost any theory bear revision?
To err is human, not to, animal.
Or so we pay the compliment to instinct
Only too liberal of our compliment
That really takes away instead of gives.
Our worship, humor, conscientiousness
Went long since to the dogs under the table.
And served us right for having instituted
Downward comparisons. As long on earth
As our comparisons were stoutly upward
With gods and angels, we were men at least,
But little lower than the gods and angels.
But once comparisons were yielded downward,
Once we began to see our images
Reflected in the mud and even dust,
'Twas disillusion upon disillusion.
We were lost piecemeal to the animals,
Like people thrown out to the delay the wolves.
Nothing but fallibility was left us,
And this day's work made even that seem doubtful.

It's all there, isn't it? Currier & Ives with a little Hamlet thrown in. And unerringly fine, the Nietzchean way: ". . . That really takes away instead of gives."

I was talking with David and Pierre Bourgeois over dinner last night about my revulsion over my colleagues in the CUNY Writing Centers Association, and they said they've had the same weird conversations with their colleagues. When Pierre tells lawyers that justice is still the name of the game, he either gets a blank stare or they start talking about self-interest, politics, and winning cases. According to both of them, most everyone in their fields seems positively afraid of the old ideals, angry or afraid. To which I said that the world has always had its quacks and legal monsters but that without any values all restraints are gone and independent thought itself goes out the window. No higher values = no self and no humanity. David's been reading an author named Patrick or Peter O'Brian, who writes historical novels about the British navy during the Napoleonic wars, and he's surprised at all the codes of honor that were strictly enforced. Your point about the democratization of war reminds me of Nietzsche's analysis of rationalism as nihilism, as in the citizen-army, under the banner of "all men are created equal." Goethe himself equates abstraction with formlessness. It's all there in Burke's reflections on the French Revolution, but I wish that he hadn't been such a Jew hater, because his analysis of the revolution is so prescient. For Nietzsche too the Jews are the arch-destroyers of the organic, or, rather, Jews, Christians, and "Socratists." Spengler felt that everyone was chasing after explanations, including Nietzsche, who couldn't face the fact that organicism means decline as well as growth and that there are no supra-historical categories - no Greek reality that anyone destroyed - merely the life-cycle of a culture running its course. It's curious, isn't it, the way Spengler removes individual agency and yet leaves humanity intact, precisely because he is so pitiless, unlike Marxists, who create "iron laws of history" and then preach utopia. In this sense, Spengler has nothing to do with "History" and underneath it all is mystical (he has great respect for the German mystics in *The Hour of Decision*, and Nietzche and Mann also mention them with praise):

> Imagine Columbus supported by France instead of by Spain, as was in fact highly probable at once time. Had Francis I been the master of America, without doubt he and not the Spaniard Charles V would have obtained the imperial crown. The early Baroque period from the Sack of Rome to the Peace of Westphalia, which was actually the *Spanish* century in religion, intellect, art, politics, and manners, would have been shaped from Paris and not from Madrid. Instead of the names of Philip, Alva, Cervantes, Calderon, Velasquez we should be talking to-day of great Frenchmen who in fact - if we may thus roundly express a very difficult idea - remained unborn. . . . The Incidental chose the Spanish gesture for the late period of the West. But the *inward logic* of that age, which was *bound* to find its fulfillment in the great Revolution (or some event of the same connotation), remained intact.
>
> This French Revolution might have been represented by some other event of different form and occurring elsewhere, say in England or Germany. But its "idea" - which (as we shall see later) was the transition from Culture to Civilization . . . was necessary, and the moment of its occurrence was also necessary.

This is the point at which Heller accuses Spengler of inhumanity or what you call the conundrum of historical inevitablity, in which "historical self-consciousness is a chimera and Spengler's advice falls always upon deaf ears." But the wonder of the aesthetic imagination is that it is at once supremely in the world and supremely separate. Spengler's "necessity" is frightening, but that just may be its saving grace. Marxism has a seductive escape hatch and gives its believers a way of seeing themselves as the bearers of "history," whereas Spengler requires one to live in reality. Nietzsche would approve his vision of Necessity, which is thoroughly Greek, precisely as you put it when you say that chaos was once embraced, whereas now we seem clobbered even as we think we've surpassed it all. Homer would have understood Spengler perfectly, and so would Shakespeare and Ruisdael:

> "Mankind," however, has no aim, no idea, no plan, any more than the family of butterflies or orchids. "Mankind" is a zoological expression, or an empty word [Footnote to Goethe: ""Mankind? It is an abstraction. There are, always have been, and always will be, men and only men."] But conjure away the phantom, break the magic circle, and at once there emerges an astonishing wealth of *actual* forms - the Living with all its immense fullness, depth and movement . . .

And the following lines (orchestration by Bach, Beethoven, Wagner, or Mahler, take your pick):

> With the formed state, high history also lays itself down weary to sleep. Man becomes a plant again, adhering to the soil, dumb and enduring. The timeless village and the "eternal" peasant reappear, begetting swarms of children and burying seed in Mother Earth - a busy, not inadeqaute swarm, over which the tempest of soldier-emperors passingly blows. In the midst of the land lie the old-world cities, empty receptacles of an extinguished soul, in which a historyless mankind slowly nests itself. . . . And while in high places there is eternal alternance of victory and defeat, those in the depths pray, pray with that mighty piety of the Second Religiousness that has overcome all doubts forever. . . . Only with the end of grand History does holy, still Being reappear. It is a drama noble in its aimlessness, noble and aimless as the course of the stars, the rotation of the earth, and alternance of land and sea, of ice and virgin forest upon its face. We may marvel at it or we may lament it - but it is there.

Why *are* we so blown away by events when we respond to the same facts in art and literature so thrillingly? Is there something special about "the march of time" that somehow excludes what everyone from Homer to Melville so clearly knew?

> . And now, concentric circles seized the lone boat itself, and all its crew, and each floating oar, and every lance-pole, and spinning, animate and inanimate, all round and round in one vortx, carried the smallest chip of the Pequod out of sight. . . .

> Now small fowls flew screaming over the yet yawning gulf, a sullen white surf beat against its steep sides; then all collapsed, and the great shroud of the sea rolled on as it rolled five thousand years ago.

Sometimes when I am at my most depressed, I feel that I am utterly alone among the beauties that I see, a lost Ishmael hearing the great choral music of the masters. I look at Ruisdael's massive architecture of clouds, fields, and giant oaks and hear the thundering organ notes of Bach's chorales. I speak and feel an ancient language, and yet I heard it plainly enough one afternoon while wandering through Notre-Dame when suddenly the organist began practicing a Fauré organ piece for an upcoming concert and I was almost knocked off my feet. David has gone through about ten of O'Brian's historical novels. I told him that I bet he had a following, and David said that there was, in fact, a society of O'Brian lovers and that he had been writing his novels for the past twenty years. David has a patient who's done the man's publishing, who said that those were the most successful works his company ever did. As we walked out of "Bar Six" on 6th and 13th, I felt a glancing blow against my mind to hear of yet another man who had simply gone his own way and had allowed himself to become involved in a world of his choosing - a real Sir Walter Scott, apparently. One of his appeals to David is that he has a central figure who's a naval surgeon. David's checked out the medical lore and finds it completely accurate.

No, I don't "feel the compulsion to evaporate in thought." I spent 1966-67 in a dingy apartment on 26th and Lex trying to do just that. It was the year after my divorce from Danielle. I moved away from Riverside Drive (and Columbia) to 26th and spent months sitting cross-legged on a beat-up couch scribbling mantras to save (or escape) myself. After a year of this despair, I met Cynthia Reid, and we screwed our way to the coast, where I finally blew out all my wiring and ended up in a snow drift in Vermont. She was my first adult experience of feeling in the world on any level, and I've never been the same since then. Now I agonize and plod.

Or maybe I'm misunderstanding you. I know that on some profound level I would love never to think again. I don't need it. I need to live. You follow that question with a marvellous quote: "I am profoundly indifferent to the matters of which they treat . . ." And I don't mean the *libertinage* of which Robert Darnton had so much to say in NYR. It was all I could do to restrain myself from writing yet another outraged letter. It's all a con, the latest wave of criticism as pornography / pornography as criticism. I didn't count, but he must have said at least a half a dozen times that we can't know what those ages felt, in which case, why bother to read them? And in the same breath, he kept thanking God that we no longer have the sensibility of those strange men and women, whose humanity is barely recognizable to us. I hear professorial repression in it all. How can you possibly thank your lucky stars for no longer possessing a view of life you say you cannot comprehend? It's that philistine pomposity disguised as Olympian detachment which drives me up a wall. Darnton is no Nietzche, Spengler, or Thomas Mann, just another "Professor of History at Princeton," according to NYR, yet he comes on as if he has all the answers without needing to experience his material. And that's all that's wanted nowadays, more scholarly noise, another MacNiell-Lehrer talking head, full of claptrap "expertise." I *know* what someone sounds like when they're honestly trying to make sense of a subject (the voice of Erich Heller, for example, as opposed to Bloom - and the hell with how many books they've read. Nietzche was probably sustained by not more than twenty authors, and Lincoln made do with the Bible, Shakespeare, and Plutarch, which is not a plea for ignorance, only for *aesthetic* judgment. Bloom could read another thousand volumes, along with writing his incessant introductions, and still remain ill-read, whereas Melville, who *did* read a lot, never came anywhere near Bloom's bibliographies - assuming you believe him - yet Melville conveys the impression of a truly encyclopedic mind and invites one because he integrates his readings so compellingly). I *know* the voice of curiosity, exploration, and discovery, the voice of a man like Constable, who thought that Turner's skies were "too yellow" until he realized that every creator stands on the edge of his own individuality. Nietzche was never so disgusted as when he thought about the "educated":

> . . . perhaps there is nothing about so-called educated people and believers in "modern ideas" that is as nauseous as their lack of modesty and the comfortable insolence of their eyes and hands with which they touch, lick, and finger everything; and it is possible that even among the common people, among the less educated, especially among peasants, one finds today more *relative* nobility of taste and tactful reverence than among the newspaper-reading *demi-monde* of the spirit, the educated.

In other words, the very same "common people" who would express genuine disgust over something like "Sophie, or the Rape of a Chambermaid in Confessional," would be *the very same people* who would tell these kinds of stories. My father and his cronies had whole repertoires of jokes about the Rabbi and the Whore or the Rabbi and Mrs. Goldberg, not to mention tunnels of love between convents and monasteries, yet he chewed out Mrs. Labavsky's son for smoking on the Sabbath in her presence, knowing how bad it made her feel. Darnton speaks of the anti-clericalism of the "Hell books" approvingly, and that too disgusted me, perhaps more than anything else. I've seen its results in the ruined monasteries of France. The greatest Romanesque cathedral of them all, at Cluny, the center of the Clunaic reform, was almost entirely torn down during the Revolution, and Normandy is littered with ruins, from the same people who destroyed Chateaubriand's family. And all the time I was reading the article, I kept remembering Spengler's passage in *The Hour of Decision*:

> It must be stated again and again that this society, in which in our own time the transition from Culture to Civilization is taking place, is *sick*, sick in its instincts and therefore in its mind. It offers no defense. It takes pleasure in its own villification and disintegration.
>
> . . . In all such times there is a priest-rabble which drags the dignity and faith of the church through the mud of party politics, allies itself with the revolutionary forces, and, by sentimental talk about loving one's neighbour and helping the poor, eggs on the underworld to set about destroying the social order - that order with which the church is irrevocably and fatally bound up. . . .
>
> At the beginning of the French Revolution we have, besides the swarm of degenerate abbés, who for years had mocked at authority and rank in their writing and preaching, the runaway monk Fouché and the renegade bishop Talleyrand, both of them regicides and thieves *en grand*, Napoleonic dukes and traitors to their country.

I felt a double blow in Darnton's "professionalism," namely, his sexlessness and his own brand of irreligion. He has it all figured out. For him, the "Hell books" are an intellectually sexy step on the road to Progress ("Yes, yes. In! In! - ah, Monseigneur, I see light at the end of the tunnel! THE RIGHTS OF MAN!"). Darnton is overjoyed to tell us from his Olympian heights that pornography was more, much more than Catherine Mackinnon would have us believe about porn, when, in fact, *anything* that 17th-century writers talk about has more than one could ever think possible in any given genre. On the Duke of Buckingham's homosexuality and colossal naval failure at La Rochelle, William Drummond writes to the king:

> Charles, would yee quaile your foes, have better lucke;
> Send forth some Drakes, and keep at home the Ducke.

Any historian of the period worth his salt should know that sex, politics, and religion are interconnected in the Baroque. And what was so terrible about keeping the books locked up for special reading only? France was a Catholic country, even after the Revolution, and it did preserve the books, damn it, though the mobs did their best to destroy the churches.

Not to put you off at all, but Flam's distinctions between traditional painting and the Impressionists don't add up either, since they also painted women reading books, arranging flowers, sitting with children in marvellous interiors, etc. and were fascinated by group portraits, indeed, whole crowds of people. Why "spitefully" in the foreground? (The NYR got the attributions for the Grenouillére paintings wrong side up as well. The Monet is the one on top.) Flam is an idiot: "We know very well that no dog posed for that particular gesture any more than Monet could have made sailboats stand still so that he could paint them." Did this distinguished professor never hear of sketch books? Did he never hear of artists training themselves, as Hogarth and Daumier did, to *remember* what they had seen in the streets? But no. Flam has to build a theory based on learned nonsense: "By such methods the Impressionists suggested that their paintings were done more quickly, more spontaneously, and more naively than they really were." But they *did* paint fast. And who thinks that they painted "naively"? Or does he mean that an image of a dog about to leap into the water or leap back is *not* a momentary scene? Or that it is but that *painting* it to look momentary makes it calculated? Then what about Constable's dogs? He even has them splashing in water. And he painted slowly, even though his dogs also look like they're moving. Was he being doubly calculating? Signorelli's "Annunciation" in Volterra has the archangel's filmy robes blowing in the wind. Would any sane person think that Signorelli was trying to fool us into believing that he tried to freeze the garments in mid-air in perfect billowing folds? Is Flam believable? Did he never hear of *Art*? Did he never see a Chinese or Japanese painting of birds in flight or fish swimming? Did he never hear that Japanese prints had an incaculable effect on the Impressionists? "The departure from the conventions of perspective and the emphatic flattening of the picture space serves [*sic*] to flatten out human relationships and narrative content as well." Ergo, the Japanese, from whom Degas and the others derived so much, lived flattened lives, and the Cubists had geometrical relationships with people? The little bio says that "Jack Flam is Distinguished Professor of Art History at Brooklyn College and at the Graduate Center of the City University of New York." The learned pedant, first, last, and always: "In the end, despite our desire to put a convenient label on their work, their diversity makes it difficult to characterize the individual artists primarily by their relationship to a group." Brilliant. First you try to squeeze a way of life into a word, and then you announce that it can't be done. Meanwhile, Monet, Renoir, Pissaro. et. al. not only *were* a group but even took lessons from each another, from Pissaro most of all. Flam's "In the end," by the way, is no different than Gilman's "this tradition reaches some type of height," also known as "ultimately," as in Lewis Dodley's Channel 1 comment on 6 o'clock news that "Dec. 7 marks the anniversary of the Japanese bombing of Pearl Harbor, which ultimately led to America's entry into the war." I was fixing supper in the kitchen and couldn't believe my ears. America "ultimately" entered the war the next day! It's unbelievable, Ted, from TV to the CUNY Graduate Center (where I meet with the Writing Center people and where the elevators always become hushed when an Obviously Important Person goes riding up or down with us). The arrangement of the show that Flam is so happy about followed the same mentality of the Pissaro exhibit of street scenes that we saw in Philadelphia. The pictures themselves were gorgeous (I don't know what he's griping about - it was meant to be about the origins, not the high point of Impressionism, or "Impressionism"); but my friend John at one moment pointed out to me that all the pictures were arranged "thematically," that is to say, by subject matter, at which point the effect became ludicrous: ten tree pictures in a row, another ten of water reflections, children with musical instruments, etc. It was a beautiful show, *but*. And as for the article, it doesn't have a spark of artistic understanding. Is there a single remark by the painters themselves?

Experiment: I just took out my copy of Pissaro's letters to his son Lucien to see what he has to say, and, as you'd expect, one sentence by Pissaro is worth the whole art criticism industry:

> Old Corot, didn't he make beautiful little paintings in Gisors, two willows, a little stream, a bridge, like the painting at the Universal Exhibition? What a masterpiece! Happy are those who see beauty in the modest spots where others see nothing. Everything is beautiful, the whole secret lies in knowing how to interpret.

Does Flam even mention Corot, whose moral and aesthetic influence and sheer presence were enormous (he died in 1875)? As for "The New Painting" about which Flam has so much to say (taking his cues from Duranty's essay of 1876), I too feel intimidated when these scholars start drawing fine distinctions and marshalling their facts and arguments like a Roman phallanx in the field. We lose ourselves. That's all. We become frightened, like children, and the fact is that we're meant to be intimidated. "Where, above all, one is not permitted to live." These people have careers to build, museums to advise, fathers to obliterate. There isn't a thing that Flam offers in the way of a new interpretation that I haven't heard before, either in Rewald or half a dozen other works. "The New Painting" indeed:

My dear Lucien,

   . . . Are you drawing? - Don't waste time, try to improve your work, remember the drawings of Holbein you copied, he is the real master.

What a man. What a superlative human being. The same spirit as Constable's, right down to the ground.

My dear son,

   To give you an idea of what I mean by *done*, I sent you those Daumier lithographs. You received them, of course, but could not have felt them deeply. You have not said a single word about them, but they are "marvels" from any point of view. . .

   My dear Lucien, do not vex yourself about doing something *new*. . . .

   Your mother is upset because of my letter. She claims I encourage you to concern yourself with art, whereas you should think of earning a livelihood. I do not know whether my advice is good, but in any case, for the present, I urge you only to draw often, and to acquire strength by drawing the nude. When you are strong you can do as you like. But perhaps I am wrong.

"*But perhaps I am wrong*." And Pissaro is one of the giants of the age, a man from whom Flam draws his livelihood by writing learned articles about the "Impressionists."

The other side is no better. According to a current *Sunday Times Book Review* article, the Marxists "are correct" to say that Impressionism is a bourgeois invention, since it focuses on the middle-class scene. It's all a lot of drivel, all of it, no matter what they say, because none of it *begins* in love and wonder and therefore all of it is tendentious, if not political hackwork of some kind. The truth is that the Dutch probably have just as many paintings of people in the background as in the foreground and just as many bourgeois as rural scenes. You wouldn't expect background figures in earlier periods before the landscape came into its own with the Dutch. As for the brush-work, up close, any late painting by Titian, Hals, or Rembrandt similarly dissolves the figure in a mass of paint. All the great westerners, from Titian through Monet in the 1920s, including Michaelangelo, Beethoven, and Shakespeare, dematerialize boundary lines. That's the "musical" element in western art that Spengler writes of so beautifully. Nietzche, by the way, sees Delacroix on a par with Wagner, another "virtuoso of plebian instincts," and no doubt would chalk up Impressionism as yet another sign of French decadence, but brilliantly so. In many ways, Pissaro is a quiet Nietzche and no less keen when it comes to the corruption of the times. But then again, so are Van Gogh, Gauguin, and Cézanne. The photographs of Pissaro show a man of true 19th-century character - flowing beard, rooted body, a head like Moses.

Yes, of course there *is* something irreligious about the Impressionists. Ruisdael and Watteau create metaphysical landscapes, whereas there's always a railway station near an Impressionist site, as Spengler (and Gauguin) say. Then again, the Dutch genre painters also create postal cards, but the *colors* are a giveaway.

I just finished reading *Responses to Rembrandt: Who Painted* The Polish Rider? - by one Anthony Bailey, a novelist and non-fiction writer. It's a look at the whole new de and reattribution issue in contemporary art scholarship, which has been going ahead full steam since the 1960s, along with "restoration," and is especially pronounced in Rembrandt studies, in part because of the enormous sums of money involved in all the deattributions that have taken place under the Dutch Rembrandt Research Project, established in 1968. Bailey is very fair-minded and seems to give a good thumb-nail sketch of the whole controversy surrounding "scientific" analyses of painting. As you'd expect, it's the old story of science vs. aesthetics, and if Bailey is accurate in what he says, the art scientists are deplorable in their lack of judgment and finesse. His citations from the Project sound monstrous, and Bailey mentions many authorities who disagree with it along a wide range of objections (many of which are in keeping with 19th-century views of Rembrandt and are surprisingly Spenglerian in character), although the "connoisseurs" do not have the aura of the members of "the Project," which, here as well, seems to stem from the weight of intimidation that is brought to bear on the audience. But Degas wasn't intimidated. His is the clearest voice of all in the book:

> "What do I want?" he demanded. "I want them not to restore the paintings. If you were to scratch a painting you would be arrested. . . . Time has had to take its course with paintings as with everything else, that's the beauty of it. A man who touches a picture ought to be deported. . . . To touch a Rembrandt!"

That's the voice of life, it seems to me. Keep your nauseating fingers off it. Let it live and breathe and grow old and die, and meanwhile live with it, absorb and grow by it and give it "the pathos of distance," to borrow Nietzche's words. It's amazing how little we know of Ruisdael's life - of Shakespeare's even less - and yet we feel them to be so terrifically immersed in the life of their times, precisely because of all we do not know, even as their works loom out of the past. What we don't know they didn't care to tell, and there's an air of monumentality about every fact we have: Ruisdael's trip to the German border, guild records for Bosch, Ruisdael, and Hals, a note from the French Royal Academy calling for Watteau to submit his candidate's painting, which was five years overdue ("The Voyage to Cytherea") - fragments of a real social order and a whole form of life. The old masters were felt as immensities in their own time as well, since their audiences were comparably as profound as they. Degas is absolutely right. There's nothing to be "improved" upon, ferreted out, or "discovered" and every reason to be frightened by the power of "science" when it puts its hands on art. We clean the pictures, make a big noise about de or reattribution, jazz up the museums with glass pyramids and shiny exhibit halls, jam the shops with glossy books (see Flam's note 5 about "The public's insatiable thirst for things Impressionist"), swell the crowds to tens of thousands, and pretty soon we have the conditions I saw at the Louvre in August, '92, where one could almost feel the destructive power emanating from thousands of mouths and prespiring bodies, a deconstructionist nightmare, in which the whole spirit of art seemed to be crumbling right before my eyes. I'm convinced that these are all deliberate attempts to destroy art, the way you felt that the Board of Ed was bent on destroying children, and I also believe that no scholar who loved painting would write as Flam does and no museum director with integrity would allow hordes to tramp through his galleries, would actually *invite* them to create a mob spectacle through mass publicity (the noise in the last room of the Impressionist show was deafening - people had had more reality than they could bear and couldn't wait to get out on the streets). The Frick, which Bailey says is highly respected among scholars and connoisseurs, fought off an attempt to have the place democratized (cafeterias, children's areas, God knows what).

The irreligion of the Impressionists is a thorny question. Spengler sees Constable's transformation of traditional landscape as a step from "Culture" to "Civilization" and away from the metaphysical. It was Constable who placed a violin on a lawn and said that the grass was green, not brown. All the same, he learned deeply from the Dutch, and not just painting. This is just the kind of "shrewdness" of which Nietzche accuses Wagner, the shrewdness of a great artist who drinks at the source but is "plebian" all the same, *cannot* help but be garish, even in his exquisite understanding of music, drama, and psychology. I don't know. It's a little too pat. Maybe Nietzche heard Wagner and Spengler saw Impressionism the way we regard the doing away with Armistice Day and the downfall of teaching. I saw "The Strange Love of Martha Ivors" again the other night, and Van Heflin's acting in the taxi cab with Lizabeth Scott was more than Kevin Kostner could do in two hours or a dozen films. The scene itself was superior to most of Hollywood today, I kid you not. When all is said and done, I end up with a headache trying to understand what it's all about, which is a very different experience from actually standing in front of a Monet *or* a Ruisdael.

You've got to watch these professors like a hawk. David Godine's point about the words "aristocrat" and "aristocracy" is true, but not entirely. He says they're not in Johnson's *Dictionary*. Maybe not, but "aristocracy" is current in English in the 16th century and stands for rule by the choicest people, different from, though not necessarily opposed to monarchy, although the terms start to slide together later on. Godine is right about "aristocrat," though, which does have the flavor of a cant term and, as Nietzche would say, came into being the moment it was all over for an organic culture in the west. He has a lot to say, as you know only too well, about aristocratic vs. plebian social habits. That *vs.* has been the bane of our existence in many ways, hasn't it? Orwell says the lower middle classes in England also struggled with conflicts over "the right" and "the wrong sort." Hence John Osborne's sardonic title of his autobiography, *A Better Class of People*. All I know is that I was raised to be a proper courtier to my mother. And yet, there was something real in America called "class," which now seems deader than a dodo. I sometimes feel as if I make noble gestures to a vacant space, as though I learned to ape the trappings of style and avoid the heart of it. A fearful classy person is a monstrosity.

That took guts to put the mirror next to your Mac. My feeling is that it's OK not to look as long as you can't. I myself can't bear more than an instant when I'm shaving, and now that I use an electric, I don't have to look at all. Think of Rembrandt's self portraits. What an astonishing act. What was it with the Dutch? Van Gogh has it too. Even their landscapes are portraits of a soul. But at least you have the mirror next to you. Start by kneeling, says Pascal, and you'll end by believing. I'm grateful when my students can still repeat the words about television stunting the imagination. The better ones do know the right words, which is more than I can say for the CUNY Association and the proposals that they loved:

> I will argue that it is [the students'] thoughts that are important, and not necessarily the language in which their thoughts are expressed.

> Recent literature suggests that writing centers are not keeping pace with the adoption of "writing-to-learn" activities in the classroom and continue mainly to help students learn to write.

Yes, the country has had enough of these lunacies, but unless I miss my guess, there's a cruel joke coming down the road. Then again, what the hell do I know about "the country"? I couldn't even see that Janet's walls were peeling, even though I was staring at them every day. My solution? No relationships in the past five years, and the only woman I was attracted to in all my recent dating gave rise to another bout of agonizing. Meanwhile, Claudia Nagy, in the Science department, leaves me hot little notes in my mailbox at school, which I stare at in bewilderment. Schopenhauer as a Dürer knight indeed. "I cannot imagine him at a university," writes Nietzche. "The students would run away from him and he himself would flee from his colleagues."

Nihilism one last time for today. This from Tacitus:

> When the slaughter of Brutus and Cassius left the state without an army, when Sextus Pompey was crushed in Sicily, and when the relegation of Lepidus and the death of Antony had left Augustus sole leader of the Caesarian party, he dropped the title of triumvir and advertised that he was consul and content with tribunician authority for protecting the people. And when he had enticed the soldiers with largesse, the people with grain, and everyone with the sweets of repose, he rose by degrees and concentrated in himself the functions of senate, magistrates, and laws. None opposed, for the most spirited had fallen in battle or proscription, and the remaining nobles waxed in wealth and honor according as they were complaisant to slavery; revolution had exalted them, and they preferred the safe present to the perilous past. Nor did the provinces dislike the innovation; rivalries of potentates and rapacity of governors had rendered the rule of the senate and people suspect, and the laws, subverted by violence, intrigue, and bribery, were powerless to protect.

> The state was thus revolutionized; not a shred of the old morality was left. With equality gone, all looked to the emperor's bidding, and there was no apprehension as long as Augustus was in his prime.

Fantastic, isn't it? *The Joyful Wisdom* #23 and *The Decline*, II, "State and History," viii-x, rolled into one. Keep those letters coming from Sitea U. Here at Koganschule I read them with *avidity*.

Many many Thanks for the driving!

Gene

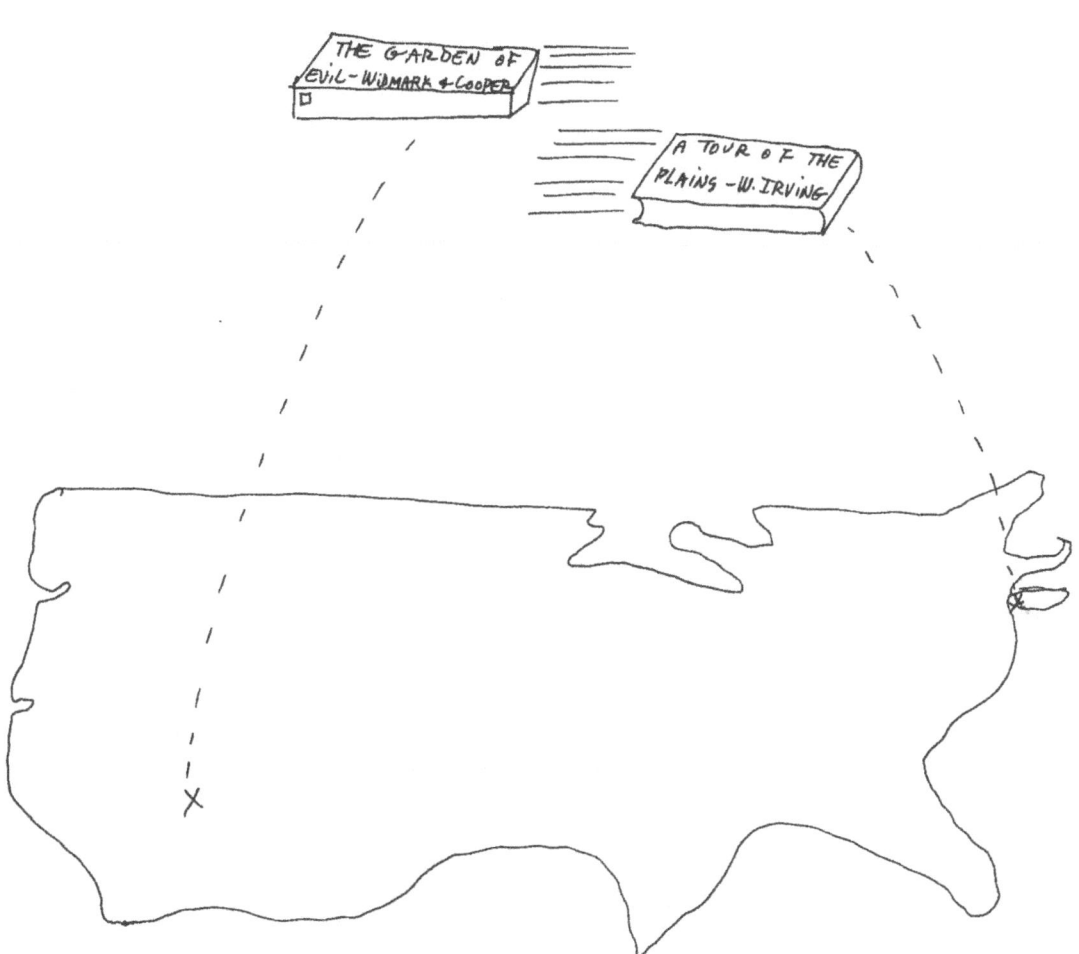

THE GARDEN OF EVIL - WIDMARK & COOPER

A TOUR OF THE PLAINS - W. IRVING

Of course the old convoluted, labyrinthine self-doubt is still there. In a diary entry from 1922, he notes . . .

Dear Ted,

Maybe the spirit of nihilism is like Scrooge's take on Marley's ghost, a bit of undigested cheese or underdone potato. Nietzche also says that "the constipated bowels betray themselves." The truth is that I loved *The Christmas Carol* right from the start, which I first read in a big fat book when I was eight or nine years old. It also had "Tales of Robin Hood," "Adventures of a Brownie," and "Alice in Wonderland," with lots of gnarly engravings I wish I had today. I walked around with it the way girls carried their dolls and guys their baseball gloves. I used to look forward to the Alistair Sim version of *The Carol* every December, along with a Russian film cartoon called *The Snow Queen*, which was superb. I once saw it in color in a theater, but it's long gone, and *The Carol* wasn't on TV at all this year. One station carried the Reginald Owen, and once only, buried late at night. It's too sad for words. I showed the Alistair Sim to downstairs Kathy a few nights ago. She brought up some Christmas cheer (hot cider, popcorn, etc.), which was nice, but, then again, her bloodstream's filled with Prozac, which may be good for her but is otherwise distancing. I met a nice woman out of my pile of NYR responses a week ago, which has at least restored my faith in *possibility* (but also confirmed my awareness of its rarity), and will see her again next week. An architect, no less, and very WASP. Janet Revisited, but altogether different, except for that Nordic face, which I still find exotic. Maybe it's got something to do with what Joyce called the "Celtic twalet."

Another neat parallel, this one for the books, *from* the books. Your letter arrived yesterday (it's now Christmas eve) amid wonderful holiday mail, which included a letter from Marsha in LA and a manila envelope from Jenkin with a copy of *Introducing Kafka*, text by David Mairowitz, illustrations by R. Crumb (The Kitchen Sink Press, '94). I recommend it highly. Superb drawings, and the text is intelligent and filled with choice passages from all of K's writing. I told Jenkin it could just as well be called *Summing Up Kafka*. Right after reading your last sentence ("Have you ever felt you were an affront to nature?" - answer: yes), I opened Mairowitz's Kafka and saw this for openers:

> Throughout most of his life, Franz Kafka imagined his own extinction by dozens of carefully elaborated methods. Those set down in his diaries, amongst mundane complaints of constipation or migraine, are often the most striking: "To be dragged in through the ground-floor window of a house by a rope tied around my neck and then to be yanked upwards, bloody and mutilated, as if by someone not paying attention, with no consideration, through all the ceilings, furniture, walls and attics, until the last torn-off bits of me drop from the empty noose as it crashes through the tiles and comes to rest on the roof."

Knocked out by this direct beginning, I began flipping through the pages and found the following. Note paragraph 3:

This wasn't the only time Kafka would arrange to have himself SENTENCED TO DEATH. It had to be that way. Suicide wasn't in the cards.

"YOU, WHO AREN'T CAPABLE OF DOING *ANYTHING*, YOU WANT TO DO *THIS*, OF ALL THINGS ?!?"

But Death itself took too long. For Kafka, there would always be another way: making himself "DISAPPEAR".

There were many variants on this theme, although it would always be a matter of making himself SMALL. His existence, as such, was an offence against nature. He saw himself as an object, for example, a wooden clothes-rack, pushed into the middle of the room.

"MY LIFE HAS SHRUNK AND GOES ON SHRINKING..."

Or: "A picture of my existence . . . would show a useless wooden stake covered in snow . . . stuck loosely at a slant in the ground in a ploughed field on the edge of a vast open plain on a dark winter night."

Kafka's relationship to his native Czechoslovakia was (and still is) ambiguous, to say the least. If Prague was the centre of his universe, the place where he was born and spent nearly all his life, it hardly ever figures in his works as itself. He NEVER names it or describes it in his fiction.

In one of the rare stories where he seemingly alludes to it, **The City Coat of Arms**, it is in the following terms: *"All legends and songs originating in this city are filled with nostalgia for a prophesied day when the city would be smashed to bits by five blows in rapid succession from a gigantic fist."*

376

Mairowitz seems to touch on everything, and with just the right priorities. Getting it in the mail together with your letter is wonderfully appropriate, particularly now that I've started reading *The Will to Power* (K. "Every day I need to have at least one line of writing directed against me"). I need quiet time to sort out all of this material and to see what else I might make of my essay. It was only on the last page of your letter that your many comments on *hands* finally came through to me. Yes, I know only too well what you're talking about. It was the theme of my second session with Gargiulo in Nov. 1970. The problem began the day I finished my cabin in the fall of '68. As I stood there looking at what I had made, I literally began to feel dislocated from myself and lost all feeling in my hands, which only started coming back to me in the first months of analysis. I told Gargiulo I knew I was in trouble as I'd never known it before. What the hell was I doing on a hilltop in Vermont when I was a graduate student specializing in Renaissance court theater? Or conversely, what the hell was I doing with an incomplete dissertation on the masque when I could be starting another life? There was nothing left of me. I poured myself into my hands and they turned me into a ghost. Gargiulo called the cabin "making mother well." I had a student in the early 70s who went through the same experience in Vietnam. He said that everything was fine until a helicopter landed his platoon in a rice field somewhere and he suddenly found himself in a trance. He said he didn't know where he was except that it wasn't Long Island.

12/26

In the backwards-inside-out life that I lead, it was only when I started working with Gargiulo and hearing insights instead of being physical that I was able to start feeling my body. It took reality to make me feel myself. And what if there had been no Gargiulo, no analysis? Did I simply luck into the right moment and the right man, like the first people to get Jenner's and Pasteur's vaccinations? Or, even more strange, in keeping with my analogy, did I simply luck into the right vaccine, when I could have gone on floundering? I was so wired in those days that I wouldn't have stayed a moment with anyone who wasn't talking straight. This too was confounding, because my sickness was the healthiest I'd ever been. Gargiulo himself said "I think we can work well together," which bewildered me, but in a very different way from all my other confusions, because he brought me right back to the four year-old I'd been on Riverdale Avenue, who spoke a foreign language and had no idea of what was going on. Session by session, I felt my body return, which had the paradoxical effect of enraging me against everything that drew me to him, his clarity, common sense, and intelligence. About the sixth month, I exploded, "I want to hear my voice! My voice! Not yours!" And that's when things really became excrutiating, and my anxieties tripled in intensity ("You want to feel yourself! Go ahead! Feel yourself, but don't come back again!" - as though I ever did go to my mother - as though there had ever been a word of comprehension between us - and all the time my father saying that everything was normal, if only I'd adjust). Mairowitz: "He imagined his father's body spread diagonally across a map of the world."

378

> I could only live in those areas not covered by you or out of your reach. But, considering my idea of your magnitude, there are not many places left.
>
> > (Kafka, unmailed letter)

That's the way so many people whom I've ever loved or admired have appeared to me, from Marty Maisel to Spengler and Cendrars. My father's travel stories literally spread themselves in exotic scenes across the map, from Jasi to Marseilles and points between. The color-tinted photograph of a praying bedouin, which hung in our foyer, was a constant reminder that he had *been there*, while all the time I was trapped with *her*. From then on, anyone who seemed "equal to the world" had the same effect of transporting and trapping me all at once. I still remember the passage in *The Decline* that drew me in when I first read the introduction in my sophomore history class in '57:

> Amongst the Western peoples, it was the Germans who discovered the mechanical *clock*, the dread symbol of the flow of time, and the chimes of countless clock towers that echo day and night over West Europe are perhaps the most wonderful expression of which a historical world-feeling is capable.

Yes, you're right. It's his realism that carries me away, carries me off and boxes me in. Boxes *us* in. "The dread symbol of the flow of time." But is it his box or life's? In kicking the props out from science and its "theoretical optimism," does he give us exhilirating life-glimpses at the cost of putting us in a prison-house? Is it a prison-house or the price of "tragic wisdom"?

> The habits of the scientific researcher were eagerly taken as a model, and if, from time to time, some student asked what Gothic, or Islam, or the Polis *was*, no one inquired why such symbols of something living *inevitably* appeared just *then*, *and there*, *in that form*, *and for that space of time*.

The historical is the only sense of form, of limits, left to us, he says. It's *The Birth of Tragedy* all over again. We believe it in *Lear* or *Oedipus*. Why not in history? "The drama of a number of mighty cultures" (did you note the transition from culture to civilization in *The Will to Power*, #121?). He even calls the scene a stage.

> It is not a matter of choice - it is not the conscious will of individuals, or even that of whole classes or peoples that decided. The expansive tendency is a doom, something daemonic and immense, which grips, forces into service, and uses up the late mankind of the world-city stage, willy-nilly, aware or unaware.

Nietzche's precision has the same effect on me. He reads the 19th century in people's postures in railway carriages, but it's never just the concept that matters for either of them. It's the events themselves that count, seeing the depths in the surface. Spengler gives you the broken lamp itself hanging by a wire. It's not "hardened" by a concept but more like Nietzche's embrace of "tragic knowledge" (and whenever N. illustrates that idea, his writing becomes especially vivid). Same difference as Ishmael on this score. Queequeg's coffin has to leap out of the Pequod's bubble just for him, because that's how Ishmael meets experience. He's always open to the world, so thoughts, images, and coffin life-buoys are always springing up for him. He *swims* in life and gives it shape and meaning by the immediacy with which he sees and relates to analogies. And without any desire to get to the bottom of it all, which is Ahab's lunacy. In one of my Spengler essays I wrote that from Melville through Joyce and Mann we have the symbolic novel, so why should we be surprised that someone came up with a symbolic view of history to counter "scientific" history? Ishmael makes his choice to go whaling by picking up on hints and suggestions, which is what the world is to him anyway. That's all it is for Spengler too, isn't it? "A glimpse," he calls *The Decline*. And yet, as Ishmael says in Chap. 1, his little part was written down from the beginning of time in the book of providence: "War in Afghanistan" - "Voyage by One Ishmael." It was all set down and yet it's all free and alive. I don't agree that with Spengler "Nothing is by chance" or that we're on the "Necessary march," or rather, I agree, but the opposite is also true, since the very patterns that happen by necessity also happen freely. Have you noticed that his details never get swallowed by "ideas"? His verve and eloquence are proof that he has no "system" and that "men and only men" are enhanced, not trampled by a "law" of birth and decline. All the same, I grant you that it's not a happy picture (neither is the *Iliad* or *Lear*), and I too wonder just where Constable's delight at seeing his boys get dirty in a blacksmith's shop "fits in":

> I see, in place of that empty figment of *one* linear history . . . the drama of *a number* of mighty Cultures, each springing with primitive strength from the soil of a mother-region to which it remains firmly bound throughout its whole life-cycle; each stamping its material, its manknd, in *its own* image; each having *its own* idea, *its own* passions, *its own* life, will, and feeling, *its own* death.

Yes, there *is* an oppressive conundrum at work, insofar as "*its own idea*" has to happen, as an organic necessity, i.e., a "destiny," yet there isn't one fact of nature that he doesn't regard as a "living" metaphor, and he's stunning in his choices:

> Regard the flowers at eventide as, one after the other, they close in the setting sun. Strange is the feeling that then presses in upon you - a feeling of enigmatic fear in the presence of this blind dreamlike earth-bound existence. The dumb forest, the silent meadows, this bush, that twig, do not stir themselves. It is the wind that plays with them. Only the little gnat is free - he dances still in the evening light. He moves whither he will. . . . This midget swarm that dances on and on, that solitary bird still flying through the evening, the fox approaching furtively the nest - these are *little world of their own within another great world*. . . . Servitude and freedom - this is in the last and deepest analysis the differentia by which we distinguish vegetable and animal existence. . . . A herd that huddles together trembling in the presence of danger, a child that clings weeping to its mother, a man desperately striving to force a way into his God - all these are seeking to return out of the life of freedom into the vegetal servitude from which they were emancipated into individuality and loneliness.

What could he possibly have in common with academic historians, when he himself may well be that child *that clings weeping to its mother* or the adult *desperately striving to force a way into his God*? (I think of Van Gogh wanting people to look at his works and say, "That man feels deeply, tenderly.") These men amaze me by the courage of their humanity. Flaubert doesn't care if documents were to turn up proving that Tacitus was wrong from beginning to end. "What would that do to his glory and style? Nothing at all. There would simply be two truths: that of History and that of Tacitus." Nietzsche calls it the residue of art that's out of the reach of science, the way Goethe read Spinoza to calm his mind. That's the Rhinegold. It's only good if you play with it, as Ishmael does. Maybe Spengler is too much the Ahab, too much the Flying Dutchman, blown ceaselessly through symbolic history, like those midget swarms that dance on and on. Then again, so is Ishmael, yet for him it's a wonder and delight. He was a school teacher too but preferred a captain over him to lording it himself. Wouldn't Spengler have liked him? He who called Goethe "the eternal child"?

Freedom in the necessary - real freedom, real necessity. (Am I babbling at this point? I remember from the first loving Dante's "In His will is our peace.") "Necessity" is also to be taken in Spengler's and Nietzsche's sense of art as a necessity. But would we have felt comfortable among those liberals of whom Schorske writes, or would we have felt that they too were part of the sickness? Would we have looked at them and said, like Prufrock, "That is not what I meant. That is not what I meant at all"? And necessity for Spengler moves through the incidental, as Mandelstam says it does for Dante. "In His will is our peace" is not a resignation for Dante nor an escape into art and religion but a "living into" them. Here's where the ethical-aesthetic gets as precise as mathematics. Mandelstam can't stand academic Dante criticism, with its glowing praises for Dante's "sculptural" quality and "perfect" system, in which every image is described as if it's bolted into a machine ("text production"). He read *The Decline*, by the way, and liked what Spengler had to say about Dante's *intuitive* vision. He also says that Dante creates his "stereometric" universe as he goes along (the mathematics of the *Comedy* are exquisite), like bees building a hive, with more and more bees spontaneously attracted to the work as it develops. Spengler is particularly nice on the fateful innocence with which Lear and Othello enter their plays. Other moments could have worked themselves through to similar results (those "unborn" Frenchmen), yet *these* are the ones that happened. The events happen freely, and all their resonances emerge freely as well, exactly like a work of art - alive and fresh, yet also inevitable (I'm sure that *Zarathustra* speaks of this conjunction). But at what height, exactly, does one have to be to see the Gulag as a work of art, as a spontaneous necessity? Yet Solzhenitsyn derives strength from seeing the camps as the inevitable conclusion of Marxism. Even more, he sees them as something *sacred*, exactly the way Cendrars speaks of the First World War as an experience that put him into the midst of reality (at the end of one chapter, S. blesses the camps for having made him whole and then says that he can hear the dead mocking him, "That's easy for you to say. You're still alive," which is just the kind of awareness that makes him ring true to me).

Or to put it another way, just what is a work of art? Or to put it yet another way, at what strict point of "soul" does one have to abide in order to see Ruisdael as a height and Constable as a decline? Is this the strictness of a Dürer knight or medieval monk? (I'm reminded of how few doctorates those Germans at the New School let through). Constable wanted to do the Dutch over from nature, as Cézanne said he wanted to do Poussin, and it's just this "from nature" that Spengler sees as as a loss of the metaphysical. Perhaps we're so far in rot, as you say, that these distinctions don't matter any more. From our perspective, perhaps anything that still smacks of soul is as good as any other. But it does seem true that Constable stands out in his own sublime humanity where others in his mode painted postal card effects, whereas even the second-rate Dutch have a spark of Ruisdael. Then again, I turn to my copy of Leslie's Constable (1845) and find that these people are all quiet Nietzcheans and Kierkegaardians:

> I remember to have heard him say, "When I sit down to make a sketch from nature, the first thing I try to do is, *to forget that I have ever seen a picture.*"

> He was struck with a remark of Dr. Gooch, that he found "every individual case of disease a new study."

> "The deterioration of art has everywhere proceeded from similar causes, the imitation of preceding styles, with little reference to nature" [i.e., the Dionysian?].

> And Leslie: "Nine years have elapsed since these observations were made and the tendency of taste is still more confirmed in the direction of which Constable speaks. The present age, distinguished as it is by the advance of the other sciences, has become, in all that relates to painting, sculpture, and architecture, little else than an antiquarian age. It is well, in all things, as we go on, to look behind us, but what advance can we hope to make with our faces constantly turned backwards?"

Isn't the following a lot like Spengler praise of "Nietzche's questioning faculty"?

> In some points of Constable's character a striking resemblance may be traced to that of Hogarth. Though their walks of art were wide apart, yet each formed a style more truly original than that of any of his contemporaries, and this, in part, prevented each from enjoying the fame to which he was entitled. They both incurred the imputations of vanity, perhaps from much vainer men, because they vindicated their own merits - Hogarth expressed in a witty etching ("The Battle of the Pictures") his sense of the injustice he suffered from the connoisseurs, and Constable spoke his opinions openly of the critics; and with point, truth, and feedom, as did Hogarth of contemporary artists, and each by so doing, made bitter enemies. In conclusion, they were both genuine Englishmen; warmly attached to the character and institutions of their country; alike quick in detecting cant and quakery, not only in religion and politics, but in taste and in the arts; and though they sometimes may have carried the prejudices of their John Bullism too far, they each deserved well of their country, as steady opponents to the influence of foreign vice, folly, and bad taste; in which, however, Hogarth's class of subjects enabled him to exert himself with far the most effect.

Spengler also speaks of Hogarth as a giant, just as Constable did, and they both have that same keen eye for northern art in relation to the Italian Renaissance. In matters of judgment, Constable goes right to the heart. Have I mentioned this line to you before?

> *They* do not in reality feel how much more the Dutch painters have given to the world, who wish for more; and it may always be doubted whether those who do not relish the works of the Dutch and Flemish schools, whatever raptures they may affect in speaking of the schools of Italy, are capable of fully appreciating the latter: for *a true taste is never a half taste*.

Yes, I'm sure that Constable saw it all coming. He speaks of his love of old canals, old bridges, and mouldy timberwork, citing Edgar's lines from *Lear* on "poor pelting farms, sheep-cotes, and mills," and says that the picturesque is rapidly disappearing from England, by which he could just as well have said the loss of tragic wisdom, since it's Edgar's world that crossed his mind: madness, poverty, and the threat of death, from his father, no less, all made good through art, through *madness in disguise*. It occurs to me that I never heard a critic wonder why the son of a Duke should instantly think of throwing away his power in order to survive ("the country gives me proof and precedent of Bedlam beggars." Isn't that too a blessing in disguise? "Poor Turlygod. Poor Tom. That's something yet. Edgar I nothing am."

And what would "the living" be for me? Yes, living was quite literally not permitted at Columbia, at least not in the graduate school, and they kicked out every young college instructor who *was* alive, enamoured as they were with the new breed of Edward Saids. I'm a witness to the fact that not a single feeling was allowed. My friend Dennis Flynn, who was the most outspoken of all my friends, dared to say something one day in Mazzeo's graduate seminar about what Donne was getting at in the *Anniversaries*, and he was immediately trounced for his pains ("Mr. Flynn, you're engaging in the intentional falllacy" - Mazzeo, the liberal Renaissance humanist, who put on his elegant coat and hat and pushed me out the door even as I was in the middle of talking to him about getting back in the doctoral program in '71. He had been the one to give my two-hour grilling on my make-up exam after my orals in '65, where I acquitted myself perfectly, though he claimed to draw a blank, and, after all, "What do you need a doctorate for, Mr. Cogan? You have a job"). As for Dennis, I never heard another word about poetic expression again as long as I was at school. All this was of a piece with my mother, as Gargiulo once put it so well: "To be with her one had to die a little." Yes, I too feel that there's a part of her in my involvement with Spengler, but then again I die a little every time I come upon something that I love. My pleasure turns into a "this you cannot have." This is the devil according to Shakespeare, Milton, and Melville: "Capable of seeing the good but powerless to be it." How close to Spengler's "We no longer live in a Mozart or a Phidias time." But is this any different from tragic wisdom? Ruisdael's shaft of sunlight that will soon pass into shadow? Those blowing clouds? "In the Temple of Delight, veil'd Melancholy has her sovran shrine." Is Spengler just a hard-edged Keats? Would Mozart, Phidias, and Nietzche have understood each other perfectly?

383

It's a curious situation to wake up and find that there are no more degrees to get, no more institutions to satisfy. Then we took the plunge into what you so aptly call "post-thought" and got smacked in the head (though maybe the smack was worth it, if only for my laughter at "post-thought people"). It certainly did bring us up close to ourselves. What an amazing moment that was when you first came to Henry Street. If I remember right, the dam burst the first night you were here. The talk began immediately. It all seemed so right and it all happened on the fly, the necessary in the incidental. It certainly stopped me dead in my tracks as far as needing any more life teachers was concerned, à la Jenkin, Len Allison, and Janet. How soon after her was it? About two years, I think. I was still whirling around. I think what we did was to help bring each other back to earth. *La Vita Nuova* indeed. I am moved by your remarks concerning my effect on you and am hugely enjoying your pictures on the tour through your words (and what I like to think of as your Rhinemaidens who float through it all). Your image of nihilism hovering "on the horizon like a huge black bird" reminded me of a passage in T. E. Lawrence, who could be right up there among your gallery of "Likely Candidates." He's got the sterile landscape, the torment, everything:

> . . . the efforts for these years to live in the dress of Arabs, and to imitate their mental foundation, quitted me of my English self, and let me look at the West and its conventions with new eyes: they destroyed it all for me. At the same time I could not sincerely take on the Arab skin: it was an affectation only. Easily was a man made an infidel, but hardly might he be converted to another faith. I had dropped one form and not taken on the other, and was become like Mohammed's coffin in our legend, with a resultant feeling of intense loneliness in life, and a contempt, not for other men, but for all they do. Such detachment came at times to a man exhausted by prolonged physical effort and isolation. His body plodded on mechanically, while his reasonable mind left him, and from without looked down critically on him, wondering what that futile lumber did and why. Sometimes these selves would converse in the void; and then madness was very near, as I believe it would be near the man who could see things through the veils at once of two customs, two educations, two environments.

Colin Wilson calls the desert Lawrence's "symbol of purity; of escape from the human," which is true, but he doesn't give enough weight to *sterility*. Lawrence went so far as to say that children themselves are responsible for original sin, because the idea of the unborn provokes the urge to procreate. Somehow or other, they all shadow-box with phantoms, don't they? First lesson of religion and psychology, says Spengler: contempt of the world. That's exactly what the schoolmen called it, *contemptus mundi*. Not the last lesson, but the first. Melville, as always, puts it beautifully: the Israelite prophets saw right into the heart. "And who were they? Recluses, mostly." He was nauseated by the idea that so much wisdom should come from such sterility, and his tour of Jerusalem didn't help. Nor did his walk across the bridge at the Bosphorus, where he was sickened by the human ant heap down below. Is Spengler healthier when he says that the swarm of life is proof that "the living" can never be encompassed by thought? Does he mean by his "glimpses" what Whitman means in *Specimen Days* when he says that "The Real War Will Never Get in the Books"?

Meanwhile, English teachers beat their heads against the wall seeing students who have not the slightest interest or courage to experience a thought. Is this any different from the Wallersteins? I was reading Wilson's section on Nietzche in *The Outsider* last night. He mentions Kierkegaard's contempt of academics: "professors of men who have suffered."

A timely coincidence tonight, the 29th, in the way these things often happen to me: A & E "Biographies" did a two-hour program on Lawrence, with wonderful footage and reminiscences by one of his brothers and some real old-timers, plus the usual idiotic commentary by licensed chatterboxes, including one "authorized" biographer, whatever the hell that means, and Columbia's very own Edward Said, looking gray and intimidating, as I remember him, but with the right touch, Derrida-like, in a perfectly-tailored suit, not like Spengler's up-front severity, not your Robert Mitchum kind of authority, but *frightening*, all the moreso for being petty and insidious. It was truly amazing to see Said in comparison to the men who served with Lawrence. After a while his dwarf-like, pitiful nature became unmistakeable. Here was a man who could not say one good thing about anything, i.e., *Seven Pillars* should be read as "literature," not as history, since its so-called facts are really Lawrence's projections. After all, according to Said, Lawrence said, "I wrote my will across the sky in stars / To earn you Freedom," so *obviously* the book can't be real. Got that? If you proclaim your self, you can't be telling the truth, even if you are. On top of which, Said says that we should take Lawrence at his word when he said that he wanted to write an epic. But in that case, why shouldn't we take him at his word when he said that he was writing a history as he saw it day by day? Then there's his account of the beating he received by the Turks at Deraa, which Said, along with all the other muckrackers, says was a fiction (although one of the soldiers who hung out with him in Surrey remarked on the scars across Lawrence's back when they went swimming one day); and, yes, you guessed it, Said couldn't resist saying that Lawrence was a racist, because he spoke of "the Arabs," since "Arabs" are really human beings and therefore infinitely particular - "men and only men" - like infinitely different snow flakes or grains of sand, each one of whom is being grossly maligned in the purity of his humanity. Said has eyes like microscopes to detect the slightest hint of a stereotype, a kind of perverse romantic, if one can imagine Constable attacking his contemporaries as "leafists," because they painted trees with less freshness and spontaneity than he did, and, after all, he did say that "No two leaves on a tree are alike" (this also assumes that Said writes more precisely about "Arabs" than Lawrence does, which he does not, by the thundering balls of Allah). It gets really looney, doesn't it? As in his attack on western literature and scholarship in *Orientalism* (precisely the same mechanism that's at work in Sweeney), Said accuses Lawrence of diminishing the Otherness of Arabs, reducing them to a stereotype of his own imperial prejudice, hence maligning precisely that which makes them Arabs! In other words, "I can call them Arabs, but you can't." Drawing a line against this insanity, one ex-ambassador called the charge ludicrous, because if Lawrence had been a racist, the "Arabs" would have seen it immediately and sent him packing instead of following him to Damascus. Another point, from the book itself, is that Lawrence is always making fine distinctions, down to the village level, as you'd expect (compared to which, Said is literally ignorant), but of course Said doesn't mean "racist" in relation to the world, including Lawrence's knowledge or anything he has to say about the anguish of his double allegiances (which are also deemed lies by his detractors), even though Lawrence rejected the Victoria Cross and Churchill's offer of a major position for him in the middle east, subsequently enlisting in the RAF as a private under an alias. All this too was supposedly a scam (my mother all over again: the world is a lie, and only she tells the truth). After a while, I felt again how *embarrassing*, how *sick* it was to be associated with my profession and how true and beautiful were Lawrence's own words and those of the people who knew him. In a letter (not cited on the program), E. M. Forster said he didn't give a shit whether Lawrence lied or not. All he knew was that he felt completely safe with him; and the 70 year-old son of one of Lawrence's closest Arab chieftans, who was on the film, simply said that Lawrence had done great and brave things and that people who said he "wasn't good" were "not right." I think of Said as another product of the times, a real "product," a PLO man with lofty academic titles, Columbia's patrician version of Leonard Jeffries, like Kurt Waldheim, a Nazi presiding over the UN when it passed the resolution that "Zionism is racism." There was, in fact, a sizeable Nazi influence among Arabs in the Second World War, and that poison is right there in Said. I bet that somewhere he detests the west for having defeated Germany. Meanwhile, Lawrence ended his career by doing far-sighted work on air-sea rescue operations before his death in the 1930s.

Your remarks on our Zippos, by the way, was refreshing. Nice touch, and right on target. I got it in the cigar store on Christopher and 7th Ave. I stood there feeling both lighters in my hand and went for the "Classic" even though, and perhaps *because* the edges were hard on my skin, conscious that I was rejecting the smooth, comfortable feel of the other. And something about the machine-tooled lines across the surface also attracted me, and the tombstone effect. Your "battle-cruiser" image is apt. I've often used it in thinking about the women in my life. I used to imagine Danielle and Allison moving like dreadnaughts off the coast of Normandy or some god-foresaken island in the Pacific just before an invasion, their giant turrets moving slowly back and forth, the big guns lifting and lowering, scanning the shores, and then all hell breaking loose as they softened up the shore. Now I flick my Zippo and have a miniature heavy cruiser all my own, or better yet, Nelson's HMS Victory.

No, I didn't mean to fault your readings of Darnton, Flam, and Godine (shades of Beckett's Fartov and Belcher, Testew and Cunard). It would have been more accurate of me to ask you what your drift was, though sometimes I go off on a thought that you've provoked, apart from what you've said. As for *NYR*, *The NY Times*, et al. ad nauseam, more and more I find public discussions on current "issues" intolerable, if only for the tone. That's a consequence of our talks and of reading Nietzsche frequently. They were amazingly strengthening, weren't they? Anything to break through the gag rule of childhood: thou wilt have no other reality before mine. I was reading through the latest *NYR* and wondering how much longer I was going to put up with still another article that made me gnash my teeth, having opened to Updike's essay on Martin Johnson Heade, where I read on p. 10: "With an honesty remarkable in a pre-Freudian man," and promptly closed it for the day. The next night I thought I'd give Simon Leys' piece on Balzac a try and plodded through the first page, wincing at

> Yet even popular women's magazines have their editorial standards, and one doubts they would ever have been willing to publish the passage in which Lucien is in his loge and Coralie is on stage, behind the curtain which is still down, and "suddenly the amorous light flowing from her eyes, *pierced the curtain* and flooded into Lucien's gaze."

Yet on the very next page, and without seeing the connection at all, Leys writes that

> Later in life, [Balzac] explained: "Whenever I like, I draw a veil over my eyes. Suddenly I go back into myself, and there I find a dark room in which all the accidents of Nature reproduce themselves in a form far purer than the form in which they appeared to my other senses. . . . Balzac would constantly resort to these "wilful hallucinations,"

which is exactly the energy that Balzac gives shape to in his writing, the exact same experience that allows the "amorous light" from Coralie's eyes to pierce the stage curtain and flood into Lucien's. What in God's name do these people think they're dealing with? They give you the facts and then deny that they mean anything. Why do I still read this shit? I seem to have forgotten, or never taken seriously, all I know about the words "bourgeois" and "philistine." Nietzche calls scholarshp itself a herd mentality. Actually, I was almost ready to stop after I read Ley's idiotic remark about the standards of women's magazines and how keen the ladies' press would have been to strike out a moment of hallucination in Balzac (and he's nearly *all* delirium, just as Cendrars says he is). Then I turned the page:

> By a cruel contradiction, however [here I was starting to go off into slumber-land], if he wrote novels to win women, he also had to forsake women in order to write novels: he firmly believed that every man had at birth a finite store of vital fluid and that the secret of creative life was to hoard one's energy.

Second reason for the slumber coming on, apart from "cruel contradiction, women/novels, novels/women": in a footnote, Leys says "these views may appear odd to Western minds but they were commonly held in China" and that Balzac read a lot of Chinese lore. Forget that he also read a lot of Christian lore, and by all means hype your field. The fact is there's nothing odd about it to "Western minds." Any good study of Donne will tell you the same, and it's a commonplace in Nietzche, Van Gogh, and a hundred other Europeans. But then, altogether inadvertently, Leys woke me up:

Sperm was for him an emission of pure cerebral substance - once, after having spent the night with an enchanting creature, he turned up at the house of a friend crying: "I just lost a book!"

I burst out laughing, while Leys went on with more of Balzac's suffering. It was the best moment I'd had all week. It occurred to me that every article I'd read for months had brought me to the same impasse. I respond to life, and these people are dead. Maybe it's all a replay of the moment that led me to break with the men's group and much else besides. I had the same feeling last week while leaving school, probably after another moment of blood-letting with Nancy, when the thought crossed my mind that this was the same kind of flailing away I had been doing at Gerson for two years until my feelings came through loud and clear. Do you recall that scene at my house? "I don't like you," is what I said to him

Another of Leys' gems that he presents in a passage fit for nothing better than upscale suburbia: Baudelaire's remark on genius as the capacity to summon one's childhood at will. It would be better if they kept their traps shut and let people find Baudelaire on their own, *if they needed him*. But since that's not likely to happen, better if I were to stop listening to all this yammering instead of gorging on junk. I may be just plain scared of spending even one week reading nothing but wholesome thoughts. Then again, I read yesterday that John Osborne died. An angry man, indeed. The few quotes were a pleasure, one to the effect that words were all that were now left to connect us to God, and another asking what was the point of living to 110 without smoking and drinking. Both Nietzche and Spengler at various points paint the image of a wise old Chinaman who sits somewhere far off and knows exactly what is going on. Miller and Singer seem like that to me. Their characters put a new slant on the "monuments" of thought, the way Herman, in *Enemies*, hits upon a remark by Nietzche while all the books and bodies are falling through his mind. The big names suddenly seem small compared to him and all that he's experienced, not small, exactly, but far off:

Herman turned left onto the street where Masha lived with Shifrah Puah. It had only a few houses, separated by empty lots overgrown with weeds. There was an old warehouse, with bricked-up windows and a gate that was always shut. In one dilapidated house, a carpenter was making furniture that he sold "unfinished." A "For Sale" sign hung on an empty house whose windows had been knocked out. It seemed to Herman that the street couldn't make up its mind whether to remain part of the neighborhood or to give up and disappear.

Shifrah Puah and Masha lived on the third floor of a house with a broken porch and a vacant ground floor, the windows of which were covered with boards and tin. A shaky stoop led to the entrance.

Herman climbed up two flights and stopped - not because he was tired, but because he needed time to complete a fantasy. What would happen if the earth were to split into two parts, exactly between the Bronx and Brooklyn? He would have to remain here. The half with Yadwiga would be drawn into a different constellation by another star. What would happen then? If Nietzche's theory about the eternal return was true, perhaps this had already occurred a quadrillion years ago. God does everything that he is capable of doing, Spinoza wrote somewhere.

Ginsberg touched that maniacal mood in "Howl," but there was
something there I didn't believe, not the way I believed Miller or
Singer. Lawrence was a beatnik too, for that matter, and it was no
big deal. One of his tank corps friends used to spend time with
him at Lawrence's cottage (the one who saw his scars) and said
that the house was always filled with people coming and going,
eating, sleeping, reading, talking, listening to records, doing as
they pleased at all hours, with Lawrence stocking up on canned
goods and everyone opening tins any time of the day or night.
Lawrence had no use for regimens either, but all the more to *work*.
Singer's Bronx is no less beat than Ginsberg's, but there's no
moaning and groaning, and Herman's just as lost. So how is it that
he's an immensity and Ginsberg's people zeroes? I saw "Picnic" for
the first time since it first came out and once again marveled at
another 50s film that showed America as a real place, with real
people, and a real aesthetic at work - that wonderful plaintive
music, part "Grand Canyon Suite," part "Appalachian Spring," part
jazz, Broadway, and orchestral-operatic sound. And always real
people with real concerns. There's a great moment in "On Dangerous
Ground" (Robert Ryan and Ida Lupino), where a fellow cop is
telling Ryan that he's headed for nowhere if he keeps up his
brutality and isolation. Ryan talks about the human garbage they
have to deal with every day, and the other guy asks him "What did
you expect from the job?" Ryan asks him, "How do you do it? How do
you live with yourself?" and the guy says, "I don't. I live with
other people. To get anything out of this world, you have to put
something into it, from the heart." Seems like a dead language
nowadays. Meanwhile I read about another police suicide. I think
they're the highest of any group in the nation - nearly fifteen
this year in NYC alone. I don't know how they stand what they see.
I was actually thankful, if I didn't tell you at the time, when
you refused to go over to Nancy's any more because of how the
neighborhood churned you up inside. I was there a couple of
afternoons one summer, helping her move some stuff, and distinctly
felt an atmosphere of *sickness* all around. It wasn't a reflection
but a whole response. That's exactly what goes on in the "inner
city," and Spengler is perfectly right, even in a clinical sense,
when he says that we offer no defence. I have a theory that the
Nazis poisoned all our instincts at the well. They made such a
fetish of the language of human "vermin" that they crippled us
even more than we were before. Any healthy standard and conviction
is now treated as a piece of fascist brutality. Looking over the
Kramer / Rosen letters (9, not 11/22), your point that "One
immediately knows that what Rosen says is true" applies to everything they say. Kramer's "traditional self-containment," "a
traditional notion of musical meaning," "I argue that music is
radically enveloped," "the kind of ideal totality he invokes,"
etc. are all meant as propaganda and self-glorification, the
language of "now we know," which is a dead giveaway: "Younger
musical scholars, like those Rosen ignores, know better." They
know everything. Even Spengler, for all his trumpet blasts against
the professors, never once says "now we know." And what they know
is suicide, but not real suicide, like those fifteen city cops,
not their own, but *yours*, as you once said Derrida desired from

389

his audience: "They recognize that prescriptive forms of musical experience may be questionable, opaque, or self-deceived, even in music we care for deeply." That says it all. They'll call anything fascist that holds to reality. Yes, the gays have won. And Nazi-like, they lie through their teeth. They can't help it. They don't mean anything they say. Can you imagine being involved with someone who says that his experience "may be" doubtful or self-deceptive, *even if he deeply cares for it*? It's pure license, a step away from Svidrigailov, if it weren't so vulgar. One language fits all - new historicism comes to musicology: the experience of music "is dependent precisely upon the contingent assumptions of perceptibility and significance that it seems to validate." This is the "theoretical" line that education simply confirms ideology. People who value *War and Peace* over Donald Duck only find their own prejudices confirmed in it. Nietzsche for everyone. Whoopee! There are no more facts. Except that the problematical and "contingent" (they love that word) now becomes absolute. It's the boiler-plate character of the language that makes it formless. That's what's so bizarre. You can tell that Rosen has all his marbles and is pissed at Kramer for trying to scramble his brains: "I do not wish to prescribe the way music can be listened to. Kramer does. He even knows how the dead listened to a work." And: "This is what I meant by overemphasizing trivial points: the detail will not bear the weight Kramer gives it; nothing in the score sets it into relief, and dragging it out of context detaches criticism from the act of listening - and I do not mean anything lofty or transcendent about listening." (Translated: You're either lying about what you heard or you're just a fucking moron.)

> Jan. 2 - the new year! ("the old quarrels, the old troubles" - Wotan sees Fricka approach)

I'm suddenly feeling the flood of my words. I can't believe I've written so much. It just pours out in response to you. I don't know what to make of the death of God. It's so easy for me to write my mother's will across the sky. Maybe I just assume that the gods are there and that it's up to me to find my way about. Everything is there, if only I could find a way to myself. That's the way it's always worked for me. "The candle will re-ignite and new glories will come, but again, not from us." Literally, not from you and me? Keats said that this world was not a vale of tears but a vale of "soul-making." Nice point you make: loss of faith in oneself is a mark of irreligiousness. But there is "soul-making," isn't there? Let's assume you did say, "No thanks, I think I'll stay home and paint landscapes with my soul." And let's say it wasn't what "the age demanded." You could end up making crackpot religious pictures, the naive American kind that Jenkin hangs on his walls, or you could make Burchfields, the kind I like. Or you could find a form to write all you want to say, the way you did your doctorate, except that now it would be all up to you. "Overcoming the times in ourselves," as Nietzsche says. Now that does sound more positive than Spengler, yet he overcame them too, didn't he? Borges says that *The Decline* is remarkably free of the *hatreds* of those years. Meanwhile, historians consider him a freak. In *The Nietzsche Legacy*, Aschheim gives an approving foot-note for his remark about those, who, unlike Spengler in his 1924 lecture on Nietzche and Goethe, "continued to regard [Nietzche's] Germanness as central but interpreted its meaning in terms far removed from the politics of a brutalized will to power" (Nietzche and Spengler, supposedly). Then the note:

> The cultivated Nietzchean [??] Count Harry Kessler, for instance, was appalled by Spengler's rumination in that lecture:
>
> > For an hour a fat person with a fleshy chin and brutal mouth . . . spouted the most trite and trivial rubbish. Any young worker in a Worker's Educational Association who tried to inform his fellows about Nietzche's philosophy would have done better. Not *one* original idea. Not even *false* glitter. Everything uniformly shallow, dull, insipid and tedious.

And on the previous page, as I believe I quoted in my last letter, these remarks from the lecture: "Nietzche's effect is a trans-formation, for the melody of his vision did not end with his death. . . .His work is not a part of our past to be enjoyed; it is a task that makes servants of us all. . . . unless we learn to act as real history wants us to act, we will cease to exist as a people." As for Hitler's rallies and youth brigades, he thought it was all dangerous romanticism and says somewhere that "we sing around our fires because we're afraid of the dark." If I know this, and I'm not an "authorized" Nietzche scholar, how much *more* should Aschheim know? Who is this Graf Harry Kessler, this "culti-vated Nietzchean"? Why does this hatred of Spengler persist, he whose "virile pages, written between 1912 and 1917, were never contaminated by the hatred peculiar to those years"?

I too get derailed so easily. But maybe we're just using or helping each other to detox, so all the poison, of necessity, has to come up. I too have felt the strengthening effects you speak of in your letter, though, in this, I think that I have a harder time than you in acknowledging my needs and gratitudes. What I was going to say, before the cultivated count exploded in my mind was that it doesn't take a Nietzche or Spengler to "overcome the times." Lodge and Bradbury didn't do so badly either, and I think that you "push around reality" a lot better than Jenkin does. I saw them over Thanksgiving. Curious reversal. He was genuinely pleasant, whereas Romona kept bitching at him all the time, which made me seriously uncomfortable. I wondered what was going on, since I'd never seen her that way before (a case of married couples sucking each other's juices until both are drained?). As for us, we've both come out amazingly clean. I *know* this comes from mucking in shit up to our ears, so maybe it's the others who have it backwards. I met Betsy yesterday in front of the Met, and while waiting for her saw thousands of people going in and coming out. I saw truly gorgeous women going by, the well-fed and the well-bred, and all those interesting men, and the young girls and the well-tailored elderly, and then one guy in a shiny blue baseball jacket with his family stomping down the stairs: "I don't care what dey got. I'm not going in." But the Islamic rooms were nearly deserted, and there was a surprisingly quiet gallery of Greek gold jewelry, c. 400 BC, which was truly superior, just as you'd expect of the Greeks. It was a world apart, nothing like any other jewelry I'd ever seen before. Perfect tiny figures of the gods on everything - tritons, mermaids, Eros figures, Athenas - all in perfect human forms no bigger than your nail or thumb - along with several oak-leaf crowns in beaten gold, whose shadows in the cases looked exactly like foliage, down to the rustling as each leaf vibrated when people passed. Then again, seeing these beauties in the mass-world of the Met only drained me all the more, and I was grateful for the coffee shop we found.

Enough, enough. I continue to feel that I burden you with words, and quotes, and pictures, though I cannot help but respond, being so pleased to get *your* words, and quotes, and pictures. The back of your manilla envelope looked for all the world like a piece of mail out of Prague or Vienna, circa 1910, with Nietzche in a wreath and flanked by engraved demons in torment, "First Class Printed Matter" stamped above, and rows of inexplicable tiny rectangles printed front and back, all of which gave the effect of the envelope having crossed numerous duchies and principalities.

As ever,
Steve

A quick PS. Have you made or thought of making a catalogue of your library, at least your rare books, soft cover as well, i.e., hard or impossible to find? I ask because someone told me that my home insurance would not cover a fraction of the worth of my books unless I had it all down on paper, as precisely as possible.

Is Western Civilization Worth $20 Million?

In 1991, Benno C. Schmidt Jr., then president of Yale University, accepted $20 million from Lee M. Bass, the Texas investor, to start a course on the history, literature and art of Western civilization. But some say the money could be better spent elsewhere because more than 100 courses at Yale cover the same territory.

Susan Harris for The New York Times

There are better ways to spend $20 million at Yale than on more courses on Western civilization, says Serena Parker, 21, a philosophy major from Manhattan, who wants to write a thesis on African philosophy.

Ms. Parker said she had taken plenty of Western-oriented courses on thinkers like Plato, Kant and Rousseau but could not name a single non-Western course in her department.

"I'd like to write my senior thesis on African philosophy," said Ms. Parker, a 21-year-old senior. "But there isn't anyone in the department who knows about it."

Steve

OK, ok, so I am brought up short again. Why do I find your letters so illuminating? I suppose because they are.

Thank you for the Frost - which I did not know. Yes, yes, yes, and yes again! Your memory is as musically sharp as ever - and your insights are in scherzo time.
We play with heavy instruments.
Yes, your quote from Spengler is right on target: *It must be stated again and again that this society, in which in our own time the transition from culture to civilization is taking place, is sick, sick in its instincts and therefore in its mind. It offers no defense. It takes pleasure in its own vilification and disintegration.*
But isn't this the "candle going out," that ember of self-love which the "gods and angels" implanted to remind us of their presence and our worth? Isn't that it? The snuffing of the candle? ("No higher values = no self and no humanity," right?) Who else could shamelessly vilify themselves if not those abandoned by the gods? Yet, for Nietzsche, it was not in shame we that meet ourselves, it is with humiliation and embarrassment, for we were not abandoned by the gods we slaughtered them. Naked and raw we stand cold on deserted plains, no 'nestling' in the ruined cities of departed and exhausted souls. Our home, Eden, too, is gone. So are we without redemption. We enter history parentless, from nowhere without possibility of going anywhere and must build our happiness out of dirt - endlessly. (Some 'supra-historical category'!) How much more horrendous, on second thought, is Nietzsche in comparison to Spengler. Spengler offers hope - but not for us. The candle will re-ignite and new glories will come, but again, not from us. That is something! Both are dismal to be sure, yet Spengler does not leave us staring at red meat. Isn't there an air of the necromancer about Spengler and Nietzsche? Neither, it seems to me, could reproduce the tempo or cadences of a joyful Schubert, Mahler, or Dvorak. They are always the opening of *Das Reingold*. The Pequod sinks into an old, repetitive sea, but Ishmael floats away. Isn't <u>that</u> the difference between Spengler and Melville? No one floats away from civilization.
I was not really interested in what Flamm, Darnton, or Godine had to say - they are post-thought people. As you say, "They have it all figured out." They "flatten out human relationships and narrative content as well." It's all part of the shameless vilification. But I did clumsily use them to put art and <u>everything else</u> in the context of:

> As our comparisons were stoutly upward
> With gods and angels, we were men at least,
> But little lower than the gods and angels,
> But once comparisons were yielded downward,
> Once we began to see our images
> Reflected in the mud and even dust,
> 'Twas disillusion upon disillusion.

there is no ... other world ... is all a meaningless round ... so we must see it - that when are all that's left ... for him -

As you say, "It may all be too pat." It certainly feels
so. But still, the question nags - if not that, what the
hell was nihilism, relativism, and the death of God all
about? Who really felt them? Perhaps just a handful.
Likely candidates:

The Ecstatic Devil is playing their tune

Perhaps you said it best of artist in transition from culture to civilization: "Even their landscapes are portraits of a soul." But from whence does this soul come if the gods and angels are dead? In both Spengler and Nietzsche souls (and Reality) hinge upon the existence of the gods, and for both He has exited. And still later, Van Gogh, Gauguin, Renoir, Pissaro, etc., are not "plebs" though they painted their grass green - sometimes. Perhaps Luther saved them all from the ravages of modernity and they never went along with all that nihilism stuff. They had the strength to fly over history, directly into the heart of God. In our time the pollution is too thick.

And yes, Spengler is mystical, as you say, but Nietzsche is psychological. Yes - "It's curious, isn't it, the way Spengler removes individual agency and yet leaves humanity intact." - but Nietzsche - he emphasizes the individual and leaves humanity broken.

"Mankind," however, has no aim, no idea, no plan, any more than the family of butterflies or orchids," "men and only men" possess ideas and plans. From there how do we get to the "organic" which sweeps up mankind in huge clumps of men and only men and dampens them together in various stages of leafing and desiccation? If we can now know precisely where we came from, where we are, and what is in store for us as a whole, is this not our joining "mankind" on the Necessary march (even though individually)? Does Spengler know this through an exercise of his "aesthetic imagination" which is "at once supremely in the world and supremely separate? Is this what you, in the case of Spengler, mean by "mystical"? But in detecting the essence of Constable's tell-tale violin does he not miss the spontaneity of Constable, the joy of being Constable in strength, freedom, and maturity as Heller says? Maybe not. Does the coming and going of flowers replace the blossoming of different Gods?

True, he does "place us in reality" with a carpenters "T". So precisely that our fingers turn blue from tracking the blueprint. Everything falls into place but leans in a cockeyed direction. Nothing is by chance; the poor quality of paint in our homes, the faulty design of plumbing running beneath the city, the broken street-light hanging by a single wire, the installation Christs crucified on Volkswagens in city parks with a pinned note reading "I hate you," the ruminating inanity of Philip Glass pounding in one's ears, the fear of bright mirrors, the increase of traffic accidents, Vermeer oils bubbling in the sweating heat of crowding tourists, women of high fashion combat clothes with frizzled, multi-colored hair stalking the cities, artists perched atop Offal Towers not knowing whether they are in command of themselves or its about to commit suicide, students leaving school knowing less than when they entered, people forgetting their manners and therefore forever not knowing who or where they are, and minute by minute biographies of seers in order to capture their souls in

trash. Its all there, and much more..... We <u>can</u> see
ourselves trapped in a spiral Necessity leading directly to
Hell.

The Anti-Pope at the gates of Hell Waiting for Us

Spengler may certainly have felt capable of gripping
this monster by the throat and dragging it triumphantly with
him into the future, but I can't nor do I think I want to.
Ah, how I wish I could be Ruisdael and now say: "No thanks,
I'll think I'll stay home and paint landscapes with my soul."

It's Spengler's insistence upon reality you like -
nihilism with reality (and nihilism remains). In Nietzsche
everything goes up in psychological smoke (and nihilism goes
with it). What for Nietzsche is a sham is for Spengler a
necessity.

A possible explanation for the differences we have on
our "takes": the Zippo I bought is small, sleek, shaped to
move quietly, and camouflage gray. Yours is large, sharply
squared, bruises as it moves, and is flashy, brilliant
silver. The differences between a submarine and a battle
cruiser?

Within an hour of God's death the gun sounded and there
was an Oklahoma rush to stake claims in reality.

For me, the "step from culture to civilization" is the
step from "love and wonder" into "tendentiousness" (from the
business of fulfilling oneself to the business of squabbling
over the nature of reality) - to jumble your words. It <u>is</u> a
matter of irreligiosity - a loss of <u>faith</u> in oneself. And,
of course, humanity.

What is so impressive about your letters is their tone - I strike myself as so amateurish, so intellectual, in comparison.

"Sometimes when I am at my most depressed, I feel that I am utterly alone among the beauties that I see, a lost Ishmael hearing the great choral music of the masters. .... A fearful classy person is a monstrosity." These sentences haunt me. A reflection: Spengler did it to you. He's boxed you in. He rendered your 'classiness' a monstrosity. You have not the visage, the staring eyes under that bald dome. Depression saves you from historical insanity. The only refuge of an individual in a rendezvous with disgusting history. Would Kafka turn this into a parable of his existence and then explain to Felice why he can not marry her? Trapped in a parable of history? They still haunt me.

Ach! This was meant to be a brief acknowledgment of receipt of your 12/10 letter and introduction to my enclosed letter. But so much has happened since I opened yours, so many feelings came up, that, as you see, I have begun another even before I send the last!

Can we love ourselves without gods having made a world for us to live in? Can we love ourselves without being loved, without the immortals on Olympus looking down, making sport of our passions in their Eden? Unlike Beethoven who clenched his fist toward God, Nietzsche and Spengler turn on their heels and walk away insisting on the Greatness of Man. But where do they go? And what do the gods do? Just watch? Have they become depressed? (In order to kill them they had first to reduce them to historical or psychological size - no bigger than an epoch or a buzz in the brain. After that, it was easy for gods can't lift a finger.)

O, hell! I've fenced with nihilism long enough. Lets talk of cabbages and kings.

The singing

Ex.Note: This is a good example of how the mind of post-thought people works (or rather, doesn't work): (from a letter by Lawrence Kramer in the 11/22/94 NYR):

> Even more crucial is the threat of mutilation which Rosen identifies with my "weak grasp of the experience of music." Here I must pause to rehearse his impassioned claims that I have little "sensitivity to the ways music can be perceived rather

than analyzed on paper," and that my "inability to
distinguish insignificant details from important ones"
leads to a "pretentious expansion of triviality."
What do these lofty terms really mean? Why should
readers be expected to accept their authority? What
assumptions about music make Rosen seem to think that
not hearing what he does is the definition of having a
tin ear?

One immediately knows that what Rosen says is true and
that Kramer is sacrificing reality to save himself. "Lofty
terms," "accept their authority," sure! - Reality is all a
matter of interpretation, but is _really_ false when
interpreted in "lofty terms," i.e., as being real! The last
sentence is a dead give away - why should not hearing music
as music mean one has a tin ear indeed. (Lawrence never does
tell us what these lofty terms mean. Just their being
'lofty.' transcendental, is enough to render them
meaningless. Can we please take the 'dental,' the bite, out
of reality? Reality as biting vagina - the gays have won
the day!)
I think what drives the post-modern mind crazy is the
use of words to describe reality rather than the contents of
a mind. It's at that point, when words are used as a
transition into the world, they they tune out. Words lose
their meaning for them, so used are they to living in their
heads non-psychologized words throw them. Words sudenly
sprout wings and fly away, become "lofty" and without
referent. And indeed, when words are employed to describe
the world they do take flight, they create worlds which the
reader may not want to exist in, worlds that must compared to
one's own - for better or worse! - and worlds which one
didn't know existed or would rather not exist. H. Bloom may
be right after all when he says that one of the marks of a
great writer is the "strangeness of the world" he creates (of
course, we must interpret the word 'strange' here liberally
and with benefit-of-the-doubt thrown in).
Words _are_ scary. Take the word "monster" - if is used to
describe demons of the mind it is one thing, if it is used to
describe an object in reality it is another ball of wax
altogether. Do Kafka's interlocutors really exist? But is it
any different with grecian urns, claws scuttling across ocean
floors, or white-tailed hornets? The worlds these words create
are really there, phantom like, but out there all the same.
Just as they are in a Ruisdael, a Monet, a Giotto (but not a
modern "installation" which is the head objectified: one's
personal psychology in a Macy's Christmas window. The nerve of
them!) Diversity does rule.
In my theory, poetry would be the first form of writing
to lose comprehension in a nihilist world - to many worlds to
cope with for one trying to make a living at Princeton.

More:
A flirtation in the history of nihilism & art:

399

Brassaï, in an interview with Lawrence Durrell, said: "My own little film is all movement, and in order to underline the sovereignty of movement, I cut out all words, all commentary . . .. A little music to accompany the movements of the animals, that was all. I even went so far as to prevent myself consciously from trying to 'compose' beautiful photographs; I snuffed out the still photographer in myself in remembering that the cinema is *movement*."

Ach, ach, and ach du lieber!!! I can't shut-up.

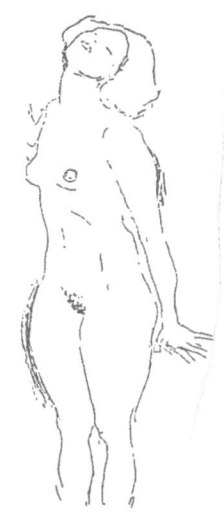

"The Pirates of Penzance"

December, 1995

Dear Ted and Ruby,
Let us try to be as Mousquire
Scott, Earley, and Clooney in the
New Year! — Am looking
forward with tingling toes to
see you in January.
Love to all,

Gene

Dear *Steve*

On the afternoon of Nov. 6, 1821, after sight-reading manuscripts of Mozart and Beethoven, the child Mendelssohn received a kiss from the impressed Goethe who had heard Mozart play in 1763. "Think of it!!" Felix writes a friend, "In the afternoon I played for Goethe for more than two hours."

On another day, Wagner turned towards Cosima saying, "Such a shadow as Mendelssohn does not grow. It can only vanish."

Felix, however, "deliberately" mutilated and debased the score of the Tannhauser overture in Leipzig bringing out howls and the cessation of its playing.

On yet another afternoon in 1832, Constable walked into the Academy's exhibition the day before it opened and discovered that Turner, whose work hung next to his, had been there just before him to add a bright red seal upon his stormy, gray scene which made the reds in his <u>Waterloo Bridge</u> look weak. Turner "has been here," said Constable, "and fired a gun."

On a hot afternoon in a saloon in Dodge City a few years later, an Englishman offered to buy a Texan a drink. Taking out a coin to pay for it, the Englishman said, "You see the head of his Majesty the King on this coin? He made my grandfather a lord." The Texan, reaching into his pocket, promptly replied, "You see the Indian Chief on this penny - he made my grandpappy an angel."

Several thousand years earlier, but still in the afternoon, Herodotus noted the following: After conquering Egypt, Amasis was despised by the people. He gained their favor, however, by fashioning one of their gods in pure gold whereupon they worshipped it and him with the utmost reverence. He then told them that he had obtained the gold for the statue from his foot-pan, wherein he had been want formerly to wash his feet, vomit and piss. "And truly," he went on to say, "it had gone with him as with the foot-pan." (Who in the crowd would not rush up and kiss his feet?)

Edward Fitzgerald once described one of Constable's painting as having a "felicity in execution which gives one a thrill of good digestion in one's room, and the thought of which makes one inclined to jump over the children's heads in the street." - such is the secondhand effect of these scenes upon me. Living oneself to the hilt I call it. They have mastered the art of living - such is my ant's view of mental health.

On an excursion to Deep in Pomerania on the Baltic coast on July 11 of 1928 Feininger saw a curious structure at the top of a cliff overlooking the sea. From the beach below he made this charcoal sketch:

July 11, 1928

Drawing closer he drew:

Closer still, he saw this:

And closer still::

July 11, 1928

On top of it now:

July 11, 1928

But one month later, and no longer looking:

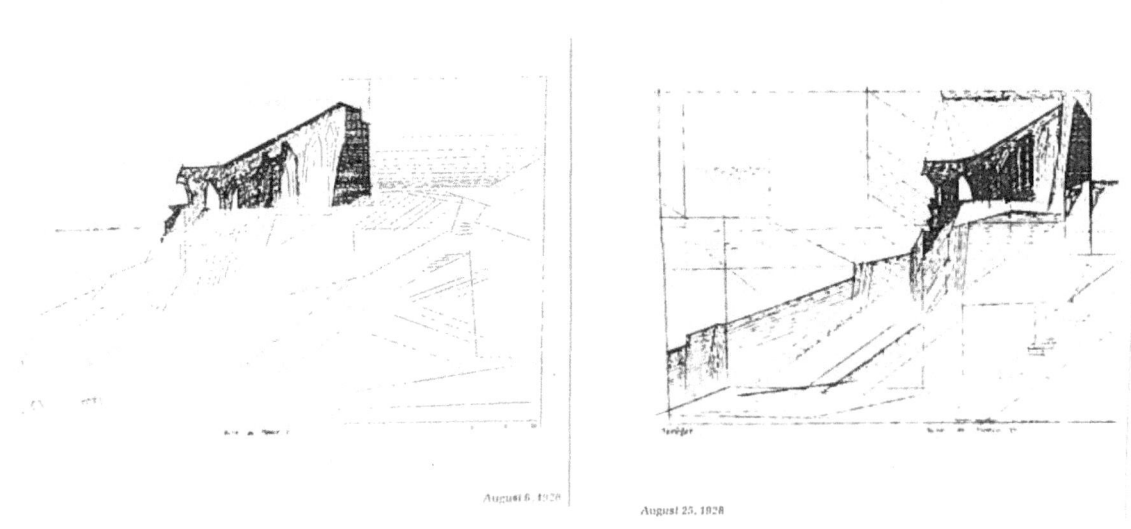

August 6, 1928

August 25, 1928

And two years later at the easel in his studio:

Physical distance and spiritual distance.

It's all in the strolling approach, the slow examination. The meticulous curiosity betrays the coming interpretation, the dissolving of reality into self. A method radically different than say, Constable's. The initial sketch in Constable contains the finished product. It is not curiosity which draws him to a dark ruin which he then sketches at a distance of a hundred yards, then fifty, then twenty, but the ruin itself, each perspective containing the whole: he does not use himself to interpret reality, it reveals itself in him. Feininger is a meat-grinder, Constable eats nature raw. Fieninger gives meaning to the world, Constable imbibes it.

What is physical distance to Constable? What is spiritual distance to Feininger? What is the distance from sketch to easel for either? The worlds they inhabit are irreconcilable. Is it the death of God which divides them? Were they to stroll down the Baltic coast together - if one could dislodge Constable from England - what would their conversation be?:

"What is that?," Feininger asks pointing toward the cliffs.

"See the somber clouds swirling round the ancient ruins and the gleam of light thrusting from the Gothic arches?" Constable exclaims.

"Interesting." says Feininger. "From here, dark geometric shapes appear on a wind-carved landscape. Its rather remarkable"

"From here beauty appears to excite the soul." Constable says with a hint of scorn.

"No. no. It's not beauty we see. We must endlessly jot down our nebulous, chaotic conception of what's up there then evolve them into the finished painting in oil."

"Rather we must ecstatically gather up this sight with delight as we would a loved child to our breast and draw now what we must later paint."

"You assume too much, dear friend. Nature does not offer up experience like a maid in a pub, it is rather a whore that must be fucked till one explodes. The body of nature is a virgin one, spread legged like a constellation in the night sky, knowing itself only after it has been penetrated, translated, transmorgified, then destroyed in the perspectives of a self. That is why our sighting of her must be approached from the North and then from the East, from above and from below, from a telescope and from a microscope just as one does a women one is disrobing, approaching her from all sides, savoring the curves. All views deconstructing her body to its essential nothingness, its point of penetration, its hole, then fucking it till she produces a reality never before seen. Thus revealed, the fetus takes shape and clamors attention from all who are lost and waiting to see new realities. It is one human in the world opening his bedroom door for another to witness the secrets of life; the birth of this ruin by the sea."

"Would you dash experience in favor of creating the world afresh upon each easel, fashioning it in the image of yourself? Is this your 'secrets of life'? If so, the creation is fleeting, for unlike God you do not create for eternity and is fragily finite, perhaps fatally so. Condemned your picture, is it not, like nature, to silence - for who can understand it? Circling your painting as we would an alter of God we must ask why this rather than nothing, and if not to be loved, nay, adored, why else would it be? What, in other words, on your canvas, is revealed and why? Why should we peer into your bedroom? At best, it harbours the stains of your spent semen of feelings, at worst, a chair of philosophy. You create a world true, but at the moment of completion, when the last brush stroke lifts from the canvass, does it not shatter like glass into a thousand pieces? I paint what I see, until my eyes nearly fall out. That is all. I count for little.

At that moment who should be paddling up the Baltic but Gauguin, blown off course by a tempest at the Gates of Hercules. Alighting from his bamboo craft and bending to put on his worn scandals he approaches our friends on the beach:

"The waves are wonderful conduits of sound," he says, combing the salt from his tussled hair. "They brought to my ears every syllable of your discourse. I come from the south where all realities dissolve in the sun - see, even my dick is indistinguishable from the tan of my thighs.

"Your name, sir?" asks Constable.

Ah, yes, my name. It is Gauguin, and I too am a painter. I'm one of the artists whose work causes the greatest astonishment, if truth be told. This is so because I do not destroy to reconstruct, nor use color to delineate or replicate,

forms, I paint only colors and use form to to display them. I do
not know if you know of Mallarme,the famous French poet of the
symbolist school, but he once said of me that I am the only artist
who paints mystery on open air. A bright red which is a dog is a
mystery to behold. Just so a patch of bronze hiding a muscle. You
put all the right colors together on one canvas and there, behol ,
you have the greatest mystery! Inexplicable! I am neither God
nor creature - but a mixture. I do not think when I paint nor do I
feel - I am! Color is pure. Color avoids philosophy and feeling.
Even symbolism!"

"Ah, yes. Was it not you VanGogh had in mind when he
said that the future of painting lies on the warm islands of the
south seas? Or did he mean you at all?" Feininger knowingly
inquires.

"Poor Vinny! You know of him do you? Poor man. The
half-light of Arles got to him. The primaries appeared weak,
unable to dictate form. He went mad believing things had color
rather than color possessing things."

"This is all too much for me," exclaimed Constable
throwing his arms up into the air. "Don't artists just paint
anymore?"

"It's not simple anymore," Feininger and Gauguin said
simultaneously.

"Oh, but it is," shot back Constable. "If you believe
in the world.... While you were talking I took the liberty to
paint a seascape ruin from memory. Here, look at this:

Is this not a painting? "

"My dear, dear Constable didn't Ruskin once write that you had a vulgar mind and that you 'perceive in landscapes that the grass is wet, the meadows flat and the boughs shady; that is to say, about as much, I suppose, might in general be apprehended, between them, by an intelligent fawn and a sky-lark.'?"

"O, that's good. Very good," laughed Gauguin.

"See here," Feininger went on pointing at Constable's work, "what is on the canvas that a skylark can't spy and shat upon? Where is its sense, it meaning, not for the world but for you? Surely you are not so dogmatic as to claim that you see things the way they truly are for all and sundry?"

"And you claim you can see it all by yourself? asks Constable with a twinkle in his eye. Nature in all its richness and beauty is what I see. It's your ego that blocks your vision not philosophy. Know that if a skylark happened to shat while in flight over this ruin, I would paint that air born droplet too! Why if all painting were up to you every skylark would be constipated for lack of where to let go! Moreover, I don't hem and haw about my ruin being there, really there, not in my mind. My paintings are full of life, propagate life, and provide humanity with home and hearth. They are paintings of solace and love. Yours are of extraterrestrial monster worlds, or of forbidding color codes beyond deciphering. Interior worlds where only the dessicated can live. No one would want to hang their hat in them even if they could find a peg, I dare say."

"But that real world does not exist, or no longer exists! And the hat-rack an illusion!" shouted Gauguin.

At that very instant, however, as though the gods had been suddenly reminded of something, Constable popped out of existence. Vanished without a trace. Merely a circling skylark squawked above them.

Feininger and Gauguin looked at each other. Who would dare repeat the words of Gauguin to the other first? Why? And where, if at all, would they reappear? In the meantime, the distant ruin by the sea continued to suffer the crashing waves, and the skylark, smiling, shat upon Feininger's sketch.

Nietzsche's annotated foot as it appeared to me high in the sky while on route to Wal-Mart, (visions are not nearly as deluxe as they used to be. Of course, neither are the destinations.):

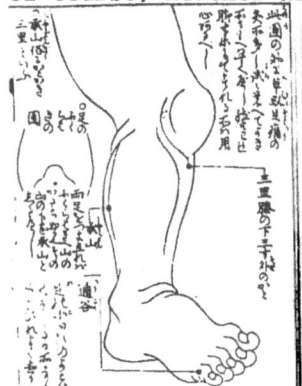

But I went anyway. I wanted those plastic garbage can liners come nihilism or hell and high water.

   A real dream; I am sitting with my stepfather Lloyd on front porch stairs   the desire to call him Dad and ask how he feels about the the long ago death of one of his sons   I know we have never talked this way and I hesitate   the hesitation is important for during its momentary passing he notices that the glass portion of the screen door is hanging loose   he gets up   I follow   he appraises the situation   I rush to fix it   he reluctantly helps   I push a little to hard and the glass shatters spraying us both   he is cut on the face and back   so too am I   some one rushes out to care for his wounds   I lie alone I feebly utter: I too am bleeding   no one hears or they hear but do not respond   the despairing feeling is 'it's fitting I'm not heard.'
   And so it is.   I remain unforgiven.   The nature of the sin which contaminates me, however, eludes me. Did I hesitate in order to have Lloyd be distracted from me?   If so, did I wreak revenge by pretending to be of practical assistance but spraying him instead with splintered glass - for which I then had to punish myself?   Or do all my attempts to join the world result in calamity one way or the other simply because it is I who attempt them?   The question is; why do I hesitate?

Received your letter today: 1/10: a response

   A young man arises this morning, washes himself, clothes himself in the modern mode and as he holds his mother's cheek in one hand to give her a gentle kiss, with his other he puts on his bowler and crosses the threshold for work. This day, as the insurance agent he is, he visits the famous Gedunken Plant where he had been summoned. Though intensely annoyed by the din of banging hammers and the clatter of metal sheets, he listens to the story of a worker whose hand was crushed in a kantian machine of gears.   He listens sympathetically, and though he truly can not determine from the labourer's story whether the lack of safety devices caused the accident or simply inattention to its dangers, he writes in his note pad that it was the exposed gears which took the mans hand and holds the company at fault. After all, he reasons to himself, the routine nature of working at such a machine would put anyone to sleep in no time at all. Placing his pen back in his pocket and closing the note pad he rises, extending his hand for the farewell handshake, only then noticing that the man's right hand is loosely wrapped in piles of bloody gauze. The worker apologizes as does he, then both turn and walk away from each other as those beginning a duel. That evening,

after a dinner of boiled potatoes and sausage which his mother
has prepared, he says good-nite to his father and retires to the
bedroom. He loosens his tie, removes his shoes, and sits before a
small desk resting his face in the palms of his hands. Instantly,
as though he had waited all day for this moment, he imagines
himself dragged through the ground-floor window of a house by rope
tied round his neck and then yanked upwards, bloody and mutilated,
as if by someone not paying attention, with no consideration,
through all the ceilings, furniture, walls and attics, until the
last torn-off bits of himself drop from the empty noose as it
crashes through the tiles and comes to rest on the roof. Then,
scarcely moving a finger across his cheek, he imagines himself
stepping upon a loose sewer grate and falling into a vast,
underground tunnel while the grate, a moment later, lands upon him
firmly pinning him down in a slow flow of fecal water at the
bottom. The pressure of the grate upon his chest, a corner of
which leans heavily on his lower lip, and the greatness of the
depth prevent his voice from being heard at the surface. In a
matter of months his body is indistinguishable from the fecal
matter, and bit by bit empties out into the river where children
throw rocks at his pieces. Shifting his weight from one foot to
the another, he then imagines his bones neatly stacked in the
shape of a pyramid and serving as one of many guides to nomadic
Bedouins trekking across the desert.

The next morning he clothes himself with a shirt his mother
has laundered and a fresh suit, making sure to place the note pad
in the vest pocket of his coat. He walks to the agencies'
headquarters seven blocks away, stopping at a cafe for coffee and
a glance at the morning newspaper. His co-workers welcome him
cordially, genuinely glad to see him after his days absence. He
places a small rose upon the secretaries desk while her back is
turned, and slips into his office. "In regards to case #221456,"
he begins, "the state is at fault if".......

Your letter was read with great enthusiasm and pleasure - the
longer the better! - I awaited it anxiously. (I especially liked
your Herman reflecting on Nietzsche while climbing tenement
stairs. Yes, is that not precisely how all the "monuments" must
be incorporated into ourselves - otherwise they remain dumb,
stared at as one stares at ancient, stone pictographs?) Now I must
digest it carefully and get back to you - this letter already
attaining too great a length.

Ezra and Josh recently left with the holidays, but Oliver is
scheduled to arrive on the 14th, at which time we will depart once
again for LA for about a week's time. To check on my mother.
Expect a hiatus.

I am 10th character!

Dear Ted,

I just got my annual convention preview for the '95 Conference on College Composition and Communication, the famous "4 C's." I think I sent you some samples of last year's convention, but this is the craziest I've seen them yet. Two possibilities, or a mixture of both: 1) they feel beleaguered by criticism, 2) this is the natural progression of any psychosis going out of control (the AFT in the latest issue of *The American Educator* seems to have opted for reality, but it feels like a political con just the same).

I just finished Christopher Lasch's newly-published *The Revolt of the Elites* (he recently died, sad to say). I have problems with his call for a new populism, but he's got a real mind and a real voice (unlike the NCTE, which doesn't seem to understand what these words mean - see last page). Lasch puts it nicely in discussing the raceclassgender mongers when he says that people with obsessions are not quite the ones you'd want to turn to for making sound judgments. He has the same bracing effect on me that Johnson had in *Modern Times*, and his *Culture of Narcissism* was one of the only works in sociology to have stayed with me over the years.

As for the 4 C's (should be 4 F's), since the conference is going to be in D.C., the cover page naturally had a photo from Martin Luther King's march in '63, with photos on pp. 3-4 of scenes from "Black Family Day" in DC in '94, and on the back page a photo of the Howard U. debating team of 1913. A comparable photo of the Yale or Columbia debating team would no doubt have brought shrieks of "racistsexistelitist." One wonders how long they can keep it up. Many of the workshop titles are incomprehensible, and Roger Kimball couldn't have made up a crazier agenda if he tried. I culled those listings almost at random. I couldn't find one normal session in the catalog. Lasch thinks of the new "expertise" as another version of class warfare and an assault against democratic values of plain speaking and honest competence.

Apropos that woman (?) you once mentioned who wrote about her lost Paris, I picked up a copy of Louis Chevalier, *The Assassination of Paris* (1970s, but just translated - somewhat awkwardly). He teaches or has taught in Paris and seems to be the acknowledged authority on its history. It makes for interesting reading in the light of French deconstruction, to say the least, and like Lasch's book, is refreshing in its realism. God help me. I may be weaning myself from the lunatics. Speaking of the plans that were in the making in the late 50s, Chevalier says of the "official projects" that "Even more to be feared than these bourgeois excesses were the extravagances of the technocrats, 'brain storms,' as they say in America, where they believe in organized frenzies of thought, where a gathering of sociologists is taken seriously only when it starts to resemble a madhouse." Chevalier is a real find, and I can't help wanting to speak to you through him, or with him, or next to him, if only for a moment:

If the Parisians who have known the Paris of yesterday, the Paris of an earlier time, forget, how much easier will it be for those who have never known it, the young, who are scandalized to hear me disparage a city that seems to them more beautiful than any of those they have seen. Today's youth are different, for they travel throughout the world and can make comparisons. In listening to them enumerate, in support of their views, their favorite neighborhoods, all that is vibrantly alive for them is moribund for me. I recite to myself the passage from *Les Misérables*: "The horizon, the trees, the green fields, the sails of ships at sea." In place of the beauties of nature which are vanishing, in my mind's eye I see those of the city, which give the same satisfaction, the horizon still intact, the fine articulation of the bell towers, "the ocean of clustered rooftops," as Henry Miller saw them around 1935, in *Black Spring*. "My eyes still see them. Darkness closes my eyes: night."

Vanishing, this is the theme of my book, the certainty that in a few years, easy enough to calculate, no one will have any idea of what Paris was. In barely fifteen years it will be gone except when we conjure up its image - always inadequate - from books. There will no longer be the faintest imprint of a footstep, as it was possible to find in an earlier time, no longer the smallest stone where one sat daydreaming or grafting the city's past onto one's own. Ineluctable intolerable oblivion. . . .

For a work of this kind, though, which lacks the chronological framework of traditional history, some authorization for the historian to begin, some point of departure, is needed, as with the three blows struck offstage at the theater to announce the raising of the curtain. There are so many difficulties for those who would set out on their own! The novelists, for example, have the same problem when they have a historical bent or write a historical novel. What pains Balzac takes in the opening lines of his novels when he fixes the action not only in space but in historical time - the year, the season, the day in relationship to the great events of the hour. . . . This is also so in Victor Hugo, and more dramatically, this obsession to establish a necessary correspondence between his story and the immensity of the moment: "1817 is the year that . . ." It is the year when *Les Misérables* opens, an insignificant year, "a year now forgotten," the year when this gigantic work begins. A minor circumstance of life, something so insignificant that one is astonished it determined such a choice, makes this year a point of convergence of events and an important date in history.

In what year, and why in this year rather than another, should I begin a narrative for which the traditional documents of history are less important than personal impressions and which history itself will undermine? In such an account anecdotes would dominate. Anecdotes are not, as Voltaire insisted, "this small field where one gleans what is left from the vast harvest of history," but rather lovely bouquets of history, at least when it concerns Paris, where the anecdote is at a premium. In such an account facts, usually thought to be of major importance - command decisions, celebrations, inaugurations, scenes worthy of the movies - would have a lesser role than the minor events, incidents from daily life - in a word, mundane details. "The details that are erroneously considered of little value," writes Hugo à propos of 1817, "are useful. From the physiognomy of the years is the face of centuries made." These details, as he imagines them, show us "Chateaubriand standing every morning at his window (27 rue St. Dominique) in trousers . . . his eyes fixed on his mirror . . ." Why am I not a novelist, able to describe this or that man in his undershirt? Why can't I invent? As far as I'm concerned, it is ungrateful to speak thus of a novel that gives such pleasure and embodies so much truth. Rather than invent, it is preferable, as Hugo himself had done, and without embarrassing myself any more, to choose some personal historical fact and begin.

It's the epic mode, no mistaking: the downfall of a city - only in this case the barbarians are the technocrats, "Visigoths in tweed" from the *Ecole Nationale d'Administration*.

> I will start in 1955, when I happened to make the acquaintance and to become the friend of the man who was, without doubt, the last prefect of the Seine, in the full sense of the word, the last prefect endowed with the traditional grandeur of the office, Emile Pelletier. . . . it is from this year that I find in my memories and in my papers a way of understanding approximately how these things happened.

Chevalier is puzzled to see how much a creature of habit he was and how, even as the new towers were going up, he still could not perceive what was happening, even though he was closer to the planning than most. He's the first west-European I've come across who sounds like Solzhenitsyn and the other Russians I've read, who also found themselves waking as though from a trance to discover their country stolen from under their feet and, even worse, that they had somehow participated in the theft. I always felt that people like Kopelev and Shostakovitch put the French to shame, so Chevalier is a rare find. I haven't heard anything like him since reading Cendrars on the suburban "projects" of Paris in the 1930s, the same venomous hatred of the "experts," the same love of the old Paris, and, like Cendrars, expressing it through the most graphic particulars of people, buildings, and streets. Chevalier is doubly puzzled, because the 19th-century transformation of Paris under Haussman did not suffocate its life, as the new gentrification has done. One common quality he notices among all the modern architects, Courbousier included, is their hatred of the past. But he stands up to them and knows their histories inside out. What impresses me most is that he can rise above "intolerable oblivion" and his own despair at not being Victor Hugo, on top of which, he has the strength of mind to see that it would be "ungrateful" of him to lay his despair at the foot of a work "that gives such pleasure and embodies so much truth." In this way, he puts Bloom's neurosis in perspective for me and helps me understand why I think that Bloom is posing under "the anxiety of influence," whereas Chevalier's despair is real *because* he fights it, because he has genuine humility and therefore could not conceive of himself as less than Hugo, and because he refuses to surrender his love of facts, of Chateaubriand looking at himself in the mirror on 27 rue St. Dominique. Stunning, isn't it? (I'm reminded, by the way, that Marty never said a word about the struggles for the soul of Paris that Chevalier recounts in detail, for all his twenty-years' worth of travel abroad.)

Browsing through the bookstores on Court St., I came across *The Sea-Wolf* and was knocked out again to see what the American novel used to be, but where Chevalier *uses* the past and is not afraid to feel alive in it, I only feel the loss. There's Jack London's narrator mentioning Nietzche and Schopenhauer, on the first page, no less, as he sails through San Francisco Bay, while I spin my wheels over the condition of academe. But maybe there's some life in me yet, since all I had in mind when I started the letter was to send you some paste-ups from the nuthouse, which now seem far away. Trieber calls it clearing the underbrush in order to get to the elephant, who stands there patiently all the time.

Steve

INTO THE LOONEY BIN WITH COLLEGE ENGLISH—
WELCOME TO 1995 —

■ World Wide Web
Choose 'open URL' on your web browser and enter one of the following addresses:

http://www.missouri.edu/~cccc95/online-intro.html

http://watarts.uwaterloo.ca/ENGL/nrandall/ccchome.html

I Sessions
2:45–4:00 p.m.

I.1 Classroom Performativity: Making It Strange
I.2 Beyond Justifying Ourselves: Projecting the Centrality of Writing Centers to Teaching, Research, and Service
I.3 Dreamwork and Responsibilities in Writing Centers: Freud, Pedagogy, Poststructural Feminism, and Technology

An Evening at Howard University

Thursday, March 23
5:00–10:00 p.m.

Come to the "capstone" of African American education! On Thursday, Howard University welcomes you to its campus for an evening of African American hospitality. The **Evening at Howard** will feature African American food, music, dance, drama, and art:

5:00 p.m. Once on campus, you may view the *25th Annual Faculty Exhibition* in the Howard University Gallery of Art, home of one of the most prized collections of African American and African art.

5:30 p.m. While browsing in the art gallery, you will be serenaded by the Howard University Choir, which is internationally renowned for its haunting spirituals and classical melodies.

6:00 p.m. Following the concert, dinner will be served (compliments of Allyn & Bacon Publishers) at the *Allyn & Bacon Soul Food Jazz Buffet.* As you sample barbecued ribs, black-eyed peas, sweet potato pie, and other African American delicacies, you may also savor the music of the *Howard University Jazz Ensemble.* (If you plan to ⸻ vour Evening at Howard

M.26 Power Lines or Lines of Power: Intersections of Writing and Gender in Electronic Writing Spaces
M.27 (Inter)Changing the Subject: Authority and Responsibility in the Online Writing Classroom
M.28 A Teacher Training Program Goes CD-ROM: Issues of Translation, Representation, and Authorship

M Sessions
12:30–1:45 p.m.

M.1 Death of Freshman Composition at the Liberal Arts Institution
M.2 No Neutral Ground: Three Positions for Feminist Teachers in the Composition Classroom
M.3 Canary in a Coal Mine: What Native Americans Can Teach Us about College Composition
M.4 'I Turned the Entire Course Over to the Students': Students as Teachers of College Writing

Sara Cytron "Take My Domestic Partner—Please!"

Friday, March 24
9:00–10:30 p.m.

Sara Cytron has performed her "out" lesbian stand-up comedy act for dozens of clubs, festivals, Pride events, and rallies. She has appeared on college campuses for many gay and lesbian and progressive organizations. The director and chief writer of Sara's act is Harriet Malinowitz, who last year won the CCCC Outstanding Dissertation Award.

"With economy and candor, energy and freshness, Cytron chooses to unfurl her gut rather than curry favor with straights."

The Village Voice

416

W.1   Beyond the Cognitive Domain: Classroom Practice in the Teaching and Learning of Writing

Sponsored by the Assembly on Expanded Perspectives on Learning, this workshop will explore a variety of innovative, noncognitive approaches to the teaching and learning of writing. The workshop format includes a panel presentation, interactive teaching demonstrations, small group discussions, and a special feature illustrating how breathing and movement relate to the writing process.

Enrollment Limitation: 75

    Cochairs: Alice Brand, State University of New York, Brockport, and Dick Graves, Auburn University, Alabama

W.6   Women in the Academy: Can a Feminist Agenda Transform the Illusion of Equity into Reality?

The 1995 workshop will explore how academic hierarchies affect women's choices. The academy privileges a "male" model of progress and success; quick conclusion of the Ph.D. with publications in hand; mobility in the job search; publications, committee work, teaching at a research institution, and gaining tenure. This model neglects the multiple realities of women's lives: the ways in which the dynamics of gender/family, gender/class, gender/ethnicity, gender/imaging, gender/politicking complicate women's progress. It will examine the ways in which this rather static hierarchical model not only creates material conditions which affect women's progress, but creates divisions of the haves and have nots of women in the academy. Constructed on collaborative, feminist principles, both the morning and afternoon sessions will focus on "cluster issues": **Family and Partner Choices and Consequences** (dual career partners, part-time mommy track, single women's issues); **Images and Consequences** (stereotypical roles and the imaging of women, ageism, and composition as women's work); **Perceptions and Realities** (sexual orientation, ethnicity, and class); **Inner Circles and Their Consequences** (graduate school, tenure track, composition vs. rhetoric, and administration).

    Cochairs: Mara Holt, Ohio University, Athens; Jody Millward, Santa Barbara City College, California; and Susan Hahn, California Lutheran University, Carpinteria

B.10 Feminisms: Women's Lives, Feminist Literacy, and Lesbian Theory

B.11 Rhetorical Practices of Three Nineteenth-Century African Americans

B.12 History of Literacy Practices: Untold Stories

C.20 Straight but Not Narrow: Heterosexual Teachers Discuss How and Why They Teach Lesbian/Gay Issues

C.4 Should Basic Writing Be Abolished, Transformed, or Maintained in Higher Education?

C.8 Professing in the Contact Zone: "Never Let 'Em See Ya Sweat"

C.9 (De)Technologizing Rhetoric: Foucault, Habermas, Baudrillard

C.10 Postcolonial Rhetorics

C.11 Negotiating Technical Communication's Past: The Clash between Technology and the Humanities

C.12 Theorizing Modern Composition: Historical Production of the Composer

C.13 Re-Presenting the Classroom: The Tales We Tell of Teachers and Students

C.14 Responding to Teaching: Feedback Methods for Professional Development

C.15 The Core of the Matter: Should Freshman Composition Service Higher Education

C.16 Multiple Literacies and Discourses: Changing Relationships, Conceptions, and Practices

C.17 Portfolios Are Necessary but Not Sufficient: Looking at Consequential Validity in Large Scale Writing Assessment

C.18 Applied Literacy: From Engineers to Cyberdwellers

C.19 Literacy, Technology, Responsibility: Collaborative Literary Projects in Detroit's Inner-City Schools

B.17 The Politics of Literacy Performance

B.18 College/High School Partnerships to Permanently Improve the Writing Skills of Urban Minority Students: Results and Assessment

B.19 Orality to Text to Orality: African American Discourse Performance

B.20 The Other Side of Generation X: Multiple Facets of Adult Literacy

B.21 The "Occidental" Tourist: The Politics of Teaching Difference

Half-Day Workshops

W.15   Practicing the Arts of the Contact Zone

In the field of rhetoric and composition, the idea of the "contact zone," as proposed by Mary Louise Pratt and developed by people like Patricia Bizzell and Richard E. Miller, has proved to be powerfully attractive as a way of reimagining our circumstances and possible modes of action. The purpose of the workshop will be to help participants to locate contact zone issues in their teaching and writing experiences and to explore different ways of practicing what Pratt has called "arts" of the contact zone.

    The speakers will give short presentations that will exemplify a range of issues that could usefully be imagined as contact zone issues. Then the participants will break into seven groups, each of which will be moderated by one of the speakers. The groups will write in response to the presentations and in an effort to locate contact zone issues/prob-

W.11   Revisiting Ethics in the Pluralistic Classroom

In 1990, CCCC participants from California to Newfoundland participated in an all-day preconvention workshop in Chicago on this topic. Five years later, the group would like to continue this dialogue, much of which now seems to have been prophetic given the increasing concern paid by the profession to the ethics of responding to "hate language" and other writing that does not conform to the ethical standards of a teacher or institution. We propose essentially the same format as in 1990. Each participant should bring to the workshop six copies of a student paper difficult to assess because its views differ profoundly from those held by the teacher (one, for example, the teacher considers racist, sexist, violent, or politically offensive). Participants will meet in small groups to read and discuss each other's papers, and later in a plenary session. If anyone who does not have such a paper wishes to attend the session, that person may bring, instead of a student paper, six copies of a one-page written description or an unresolved problem on a related issue.

    The aim is not to provide uniform solutions or procedures, but rather to expand, through dialogue, the possibilities available to teachers in responding to ethically diverse student writing.

MARXISM FOR NOBODY —

W.7   Textbooks: Respecting the Form/ Reforming the Discipline—Writers and Publishers Shaping the Future of Composition Studies

For all the criticism of textbooks that we hear on a regular basis—from the public, our colleagues, and our students—the greatest breakthroughs in theory and research mean nothing unless they get into textbooks, and into the hands of students. Yet the publishing process—from developing an idea to seeing that idea come to fruition in a successful book—remains largely a mystery to many teachers and researchers with significant and challenging ideas to share. Through this workshop, we hope to accomplish several goals: 1) to demystify the process of negotiation between potential authors and publishers; 2) to interrogate and map the changing roles textbooks have played, are playing, and will play as composition studies becomes increasingly professionalized; 3) to explore the expectations teachers have of textbooks and of publishers who will represent those expectations; and, 4) to examine the role of publishers in shaping the market as they conduct research in order to determine ...

— They know how to say demystify, map, and interrogate, but they have trouble with noun-verb agreements.

SW.8   Reading and Writing with Critical Linguistics: Interventions from the Outside, Stylistics from the Inside

This workshop draws upon the work of contemporary British linguists connected with the Poetics and Linguistics Association and the School of Critical Linguistics at the University of East Anglia to demonstrate a pedagogically useful series of deconstructive and reconstructive activities called "interventions." Writing is a process of active—often radical—textual intervention. Workshop participants will "subvertise" philosophical, commercial, and literary discourse; analyze dominant stylistic traits in their own writing after intervening intertextually in various kinds of writing about gay people; rewrite ideological "power plays" in government documents and news stories by reappropriating linguistic and typographical features that have been "co-opted."

— "To subvertise" — good college English for '95.

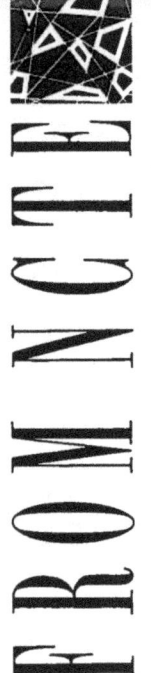

VOICES ON VOICE
Perspectives, Definitions, Inquiry

Kathleen Blake Yancey, editor

What is *voice*? Is it compatible with postmodern views of the self and of writing and reading? And if so, how can it be translated in ways that both respect students and challenge them? Those are the questions and issues that *Voices on Voice: Perspectives, Definitions, Inquiry* seeks to explore from a diversity of perspectives—from that of writers such as Toby Fulwiler; from readers such as Carl Klaus and Laura Julier; from scholars such as Peter Elbow; from teachers such as Paula Gillespie; from cross-cultural rhetoricians such as Gwen Gong and John Powers; and from the "unvoiced" world of the deaf. Other perspectives—the feminist, the Native American, and the postmodern electronic—situate voice differently still. That is, in part, the point of this work: We all hear voices, those we admit, acknowledge, and construct. How we listen to those voices—as individuals, as communities, as writers, and as readers—is the point of departure of *Voices on Voice*. 363 pp. 1994. Coll. ISBN 0-8141-5634-7. **No. 56347 $29.95 ($22.95)**

Toby doesn't read, and Carl doesn't write, and Elbow neither reads nor writes but does scholarship.

this is priceless

National Council of Teachers of English
1111 W. Kenyon Road, Urbana, Illinois 61801-1096

Dear Ted,

I mark the day down as well as the date, in celebration of coming out of a week's bout with the flu, or rather, let's make it a tentative celebration, since this creature has a way of doubling and tripling back on itself.[1] Yesterday's *Times* carried a front-page article on this latest *xhazerai* from Asia, a brand new strain called Shantung flu (sounds like Anna Mae Wong in a red silk sheath), which hit the city several weeks ago and immediately clogged all the clinics and medical offices. People found themselves completely spun out. After five days of solitary suffering, I took pleasure in other people voicing my miseries. No niceties of analysis from the doctors. "It doesn't matter what you call it. When you got it, you got it." All my instincts prompted me to work it out on my own. Steaming cups of hot mint tea with Jack Daniels, which worked fine for several days, until the virus *really* went to work, but David's reassuring voice confirmed what I already knew, so I just stayed put. Yesterday brought renewed craziness (every day had its own round of *tsouris*), reaching some sort of crescendo last night. Then, all of a sudden, like a super nova, it burst and was gone. Occasional flashes today, but I was able to shop and pick up the fixings for a gourmet chicken soup, now on the stove and filling the apartment with memories.

Your last letter, which arrived yesterday, was just what the doctor ordered, starting with the back of the envelope, "Grecian symposium drinking vessel very likely depicts a common male fantasy motif." Real educated nonsense (Lewis Carroll couldn't have done better), which they hide by saying "very likely" (trans. "It's bullshit and we know it"). I don't recall "Athenian prostitutes" in Plato, do you? Plus the high-fallutin' "common male fantasy motif," as in "Doric ivy motif." Is that what makes it a symposium *fantasy*? That there were no prostitutes in Plato's dialogues? Common male, as opposed to aristocratic male? Common male, as in 2,000 years of one unending fantasy? "Athenian prostitutes" a collective fiction, as in Stanley Fish's "John Milton," as opposed to John Milton? The *NYR* arrived that day as well and fit your point about my dismay over its writing perfectly. I'm thinking of the article on Saint Exupery by Alvarez, whose book on suicide or Auschwitz I read some years ago. These guys can babble about anything. Chevalier says that the "urban planners" would come into a meeting and fill the room with charts, diagrams, files, brochures, speeches, smiles, commands, and all the time the Municipal Council wondered what the hell they were saying (not yet realizing that the fix was in, even in '55, and that it didn't matter whether they understood or not):

> Who is this functionary, Bucaille asked, who is under the prefect's authority and obeys him, but is charged, at the same time to head a delegation appointed by the minister [of the Interior] who also appoints the prefect? He is able to give the prefect orders, in the name of the minister. And what is this coordination all about? Why create a functionary to find usable land, to discover polluted parts of the city - as if we didn't know where they were! . . .

1- which is exactly what happened - hence the delay in mailing this off to you.

These were the areas to be demolished, or what they hypocritically called renovated. From the Porte d'Italie, where they were already chomping at the bit, to the Porte de Clichy, an army of bulldozers leveled everything in their path. Only the beautiful west side of Paris was spared, but there would later be other plans for the west. The delimited zone thus corresponded to all the neighborhoods on the circumference of Paris, a zone they called, with a happy turn of phrase, "the Paris croissant." A croissant is, as everyone in the world knows who salivates just thinking of one, a crusty and flaky butter roll that the fortunate Parians eat with their coffee. This is a deplorable expression for a plan that literally sought to chew up the city.

These planners belong to the "educated classes," who can't keep their disgusting fingers off anything, as Nietzche says. I had trouble with Alvarez from the very first line. And turning the page, there it was: Saint Ex was a lousy pilot. I could have guessed. But then he gave it an incomprehensible twist: Ex's incompetence led to great literature, because he became absorbed by "the experience of flight" and its technically irrelevant data, such as wind stress, engine sounds, and starlight (The 2000 year-old man: "In those days we ate only what God intended - the organic, the natural - clouds, rocks, stars"); whereas "A natural flier would have simply got on with the job without noticing what was involved." The only sense I can make of this gibberish is that once again art is unreal. Or life. It doesn't matter which. With your envelope by my side, a litany went off in my mind: Greek philosophy was corrupted by sex fantasies (sex being nothing to fantasize about if one is true and good, which the Athenians weren't, hence their need to mask their vices by talking about the true and good, thus creating the language that subverted their etc.); Rembrandt painted twenty or maybe thirty paintings tops (the rest done by his pupils, as we can tell by analyzing his genuine brush-strokes, see statistical tables for a quantitative analysis of "authentic"); Saint Exupery was a lousy pilot; and T. E. got to Damascus mainly in his mind.

Your dialogue was a pleasure to read. Half way through I flashed on the very painting that you provided on the following page. It's truly a marvellous work. The French took to Constable right away and to the English watercolorists as well. Everything about him radiates health and sanity. It's the same spirit people admire in Goethe, but in a way so much finer to come across in a painter.* Yes, back to the 19th century, by all means. Spengler is annoyed at those who still see things from the *zeitgeist* of the day before yesterday. We seem to be looking at things from the *zeitgeist* of the *century* before ours. Spengler is so confusing the way he has things right and wrong at the same time, so much so that the figures and cultures he writes about with such verve and reality are three-dimensional and ghostly all at once, or so it seems to me today. I took out "Sink the Bismarck" two weeks ago, and one line gave me pause: the British commander is depressed about the prospect of the Bismarck on the high seas and its apparent invulnerability, but then he says, "Germans have to be right every day. That's their fatal weakness." *Iron necessity*. Why didn't French *esprit* rub off on Nietzche more than it did, who appreciated it so well? He seems so close, yet so far, whereas with Chevalier it registers in every line.

* I just read this line in Goethe: "We should talk less and draw more."

Here is what matters and it comes from La Fontaine. Life, but what is beautiful and touched by beauty, which is the same for Baudelaire as for Malherbe: "Beauty, my lovely obsession!" Life joyously and vigorously lived, not whined about. There are not many verses here about death. It's a peasant's healthy way of looking at death by not speaking much about it. With an almost joyous tone [Pompidou] told us at lunch about his father's death: "It was a fine death!" Proudhon spoke thus of his own father, an old kindling carrier in the forests of the ancien régime. "An old woodcutter completely covered in twigs and branches . . ." La Fontaine's *Death and the Woodcutter*. On the question of death, as well as all else, it is La Fontaine who has the most to say. "Death is a cure for everything / But let's avoid it as long as we can: Suffer rather than die / That is the motto proper to man." And God knows, when it came to suffering, Pompidou had more than his share. "As for myself, I am doing an apprenticeship in illness," he wrote in a letter to one of us who was concerned about his health. In contrast, we have all the jeremiads of Malraux, this endless funeral oration even delived over the healthy cradle of Brasilia, about the death of civilizations, the death of cities, pure hogwash.

Chevalier has complicated feelings about Pompidou (an old school-mate of his) but little good to say about Malraux, who was De Gaulle's minister of culture at this time; and he's right about Malraux's fixation on death, which was not the same as Hemingway's and certainly not the same as Cendrars', who was fascinated, not riveted. I think I may have mentioned to you that I heard him speak on the occasion of Braque's death - thousands gathered outside the Louvre - a rainy night - the funeral march from the *Eroica* - thousands of umbrellas - and Malraux: "I speak with a worn-out voice - *une voix usagé*." Chevalier notes that Paris hardly ever appears in Malraux's work, just as the requirements of *pleasure* never once appear in the plans of the technocrats. He has complicated feelings about Pompidou, however, for whom he cared a great deal and whose inhibition to follow his true bent casts its pall over the "assassination" of Paris. Chevalier says all this with great point and delicacy - he's really quite profound - and the way he separates himself from Pompidou is beautiful. You'll appreciate this:

> Between teaching and politics there was a life that he could have led, a "previous existence" in the sense Baudelaire described: "In a rapture of repose I lived there / Amidst the blue, the waves, the glories / and the naked perfumed slaves . . ." To put at ease those who never understand anything, let us leave the naked slaves with Baudelaire. As for the rest, who can deny that it better fit his temperament, his tastes, his way of looking at life, his culture, classical culture itself, which makes the enjoyment of life supreme, than does politics, with its perpetual and often long stretches of mediocrity and boredom.

Nevertheless, Pompidou presided over the destruction of the city, mainly through detachment, says Chevalier, citing a line from Valéry that Pompidou used as an epigraph for one of his books: "this curious inaction / so full of power." I was there with Danielle when it all began and remember being both elated and bewildered by Malraux's cleaning of the facades, which, according to Chevalier, diverted funds from much-needed repairs and thus sparked further losses. Malraux, one *hears* his voice, who pronounced, in August 1959 before the Brazilian authorities, a speech which more resembled a funeral oration than an appreciation: "Under the immense indifference of the clouds . . ."

Under the immense indifference of Malraux. I don't know what Brazilian ears heard any more than I know what the Parisian authorities understood who came to the meetings in the Elysée Palace to ask Malraux (Malraux who knew), his opinion about the future Brasilias in Paris. . . . What is certain is that he talked and, from the "immensity" of what he said - and his speech at Brasilia gives us some idea of that - the visitors, the would-be architects of towers, could always conclude that Malraux agreed with them. Was he in agreement or wasn't he? "Under the immense indif-ference of the clouds . . ." But if Malraux was in agreement that meant the Elysée Palace was in agreement.

Chevalier's ear is attuned to words in most fulfilling ways, and he gives us the "experience" of the destruction of Paris, *pace* Alvarez, together with the "technical" side of it. And he helps me understand all over again Degas' remark on Rembrandt restoration, which I mentioned to you some time ago: "What do I want? I want them to keep their hands off Rembrandt! Let the pictures age. That's the beauty of it!" Chevalier has only a few lines for the deconstructionists, but he says it all:

This is my situation. If at some last judgment a heavenly judge should question me, as a witness or a defendant - does one ever know which? - I would be hard put to say what I saw and heard, what I read (indeed the prose was unreadable), what I understood, what I knew . . . What a splendid subject for our young researchers interested in such things: the obscurity of administrative language. The more they concentrated on the prose of officialdom the less time they would have to pulverize Racine.

He speaks of the "freedom, confidence, and ease that was the natural climate of an epoch when the teacher was a friend, not a suspect instantly put in the dock." When *life* and literature were friends. "What if the Parisian's clairvoyants and card readers write their memoirs! They were, at least in the period I am talking about, specialized according to quarter. A fortune-teller of Strasbourg-St. Denis, from whom I have these anecdotes, excelled in the sorrows of love." Something must have rung a bell, because I pulled out my copy of Wyndham Lewis' *Francois Villon* (the other Wyndham Lewis, remember?) and reread his chapter that begins: "In the year 1436, when Francois Villon was five years old." Lewis takes us on a walk through Paris in Villon's youth:

And of a sudden the student observes a ragged, hag-like figure shuffling past him, and turns his curious gaze on her. The old woman is known throughout the Quarter as the Belle Heaulmière. She was a famous beauty and courtesan in the early part of the century and the mistress of Messire Nicolas d'Orgemont, Master of the Chambres des Comptes, who very scandalously installed her in his house in the precinct of Notre-Dame, whence she was evicted by the Canons. In Villon's day she is a mumbling witch of eighty; her lover has died long ago, in 1416, in the prison of Meun-sur-Loire, where Villon himself will be cast in due course. In the Lament for her hot, sweet youth which Villon will write in a few years, the figure of this poor old scarecrow is preserved like a mummy for ever and ever.

And that's Chevalier's point over and over, that there was a thread of life and art running through Paris, Paris in particular, from the 1100s till *1960-65*. Lewis corroborates Chevalier in the most precise, "physiognomic" ways. This is from his introduction to Villon's "Ballad of the Ladies of Times Gone By":

> One of the master-songs of the world, with its gentle rhymes in *-is* and *-aine*, the exquisite ache of its music, caressing and soothing to dreams, and its lovely refrain. . . . Observe the rhyming of *moyne, essoyne, royne*, and *Saine*. This was Parisian.

Parisian rhymes, no less. This is exactly what Chevalier means by the singular life of the city. And at the heart of it all, "the center of the center," is les Halles. Obvious, you'd think, isn't it? Food. The central produce market. And food in the Parisian sense. Chevalier is marvellous at reconstructing the city out of its life, none of which figured in the plans of the "developers," who destroyed it all, *deliberately*, for the sake of an *idea*.

> The main argument was the traffic jams, which around les Halles were stupefying; yet people involved in them, the truck drivers, coped amazingly well and were the last to complain. Then there were the traffic jams of the entire municipal area for which the market traffic was invariably held responsible, even though in the early morning hours on the boulevard Sébastopol (without parked cars because of street-cleaning) traffic moved well, which, paradoxically, was no longer the case once les Halles was moved. . . .
>
> No less astonishing was the economic argument. "The laws of supply and demand," declares a sacrosanct text, "cannot work in perfectly normal conditions in les Halles because the merchandise cannot be presented at the opening of the market and also, since the goods are not arranged and displayed by category, the buyers cannot make a quick survey of the available quantities." I suggest, timidly, that the telephone exists and one can know at any instant the price of wool in Melbourne or cod in Newfoundland. But it seems this was not possible at les Halles. The economic argument, no doubt because it was the most mysterious and the most obscure, as is everything connected to economic science, was most often invoked. Then there was hygiene, the legendary filth of les Halles. The foodstuffs left out in all seasons, exposed to the heat and cold, in sunshine and rain, in dust and mud, sitting on the sidewalks or the walkways, in the gtters, near sewer openings. Of course, I cite in no particular order the accusations as I find them in the speeches, without attempting to categorize them, arrange them as they do the produce at les Halles, the beans in elaborate careful piles which, in the dramatic artificial light, exude order, beauty, taste, and, of course, cleanliness. They are so fresh, so clean that it even seemed unnecessary to wash them. But filth got everyone's attention. It suggested disease and threatened public health. The fear is hardly credible if one is to judge from the robust appearance of those who worked at les Halles. . . . As for filthiness, those who worked at les Halles were adapted to the imagined unhealthiness of the markets, that is, their own uncleanliness, which they were used to and even appreciated. They breathed the smell with pleasure, a smell which was no more than the good odors of meat and cheese, of the country and the barn, and the less welcome smell of the day's catch, which forced the fish sellers to spend an excessive time under the shower so as not to offend their women. "It's incredible how much they can wash," their employers said. . . .

To make it more dramatic, they invoked the rats. The old medieval fear of
rats. "An army of rats," the word "army" making the danger more obvious.
. . . Even though no one had heard of any of the workers at les Halles
battling rats as Hugo's fishermen in *Les Travailleurs de la mer* are
described fighting the giant octopus, those who heard about the rats or
read about them in the newspapers got goose bumps. . . .

If it had only been a question of rats! But there was also the danger
of fire. The argument was curious. Since Baltard's pavilions were built of
iron the speaker explained rather obscurely, they rested upon wooden piles
which were "particularly combustible since over the years they had caught
fire and not been repaired." Here was a medieval vision of an army of rats
attacking citizens in the lurid light of fires, a veritable apocalypse of
epidemic! To complete this scene worthy of Gustave Doré, were the huge
prostitutes of Villon, shameless of course, some of whom displayed their
charms on the very steps of St. Eustache. Finally, there were the satyrs
and clochards who were lumped together and of whom it was said, according
to certain speakers who specialized in such things, that they joined and
mated in a witch's Sabbath. This was especially so in certain places:
"Around Beaubourg, where a disreputable population hangs out, given over
to the most immoral displays" (session of June 24, 1954). Hieronymous
Bosch at Beaubourg! This was a place predestined for art.

After the Louvre and that hideous reconverted railway station, I
had no stomach for the Beaubourg and never saw it. Chevalier notes
that it was renamed for Pompidou after his death, and he also says
that he avoids the new sites as much as possible.

But here's what's interesting: those thousands of sweating
tourists, who disgorge from giant charter buses and run screaming
through the Louvre taking flash pictures of everything in sight,
turn out to be a by-product of the developers' plans themselves,
because those masses have been squeezed out of the boulevards,
which simply don't have the interest that they had. Even in '63, I
could spend a day browsing along two or three streets north of les
Halles, but now in its place there's an underground mall of some
kind (I didn't go in), and the whole area north to Strasbourg-St.
Denis has been ghettoized by Arabs, Africans, Chinese, etc.
(another reason for tourists to avoid the old neighborhoods),
something, says Chevalier, that never existed before in Paris, not
because there were no immigrants but because they too became part
of the life of the city ("collective existence," he calls it, a
concept that French sociologists now deny, which he finds logical,
since they helped to kill the reality). He makes the fine point
that as France gave up its colonies it began to colonize Paris.
The new ambition was to make Paris the "office capital of the
world," signed, sealed, and delivered, "a culture fixed once for
all, certified with a diploma, tied up like a dossier, sealed like
a tomb. In that tomb is Paris." Above all, les Halles:

. . . it was necessary to understand this. The technocrats had failed
to do so or would have looked at me wide-eyed, like the fish staring at
one on the slabs in the seafood pavilion. Prefect Pelletier didn't need
to be told twice. Here was the evidence itself.

I didn't have a lot to say to him about the problem except that it
was more serious than he imagined and more serious than anyone in his
entourage imagined. Above all it was of another genre: it was not a
neighborhood problem but a city-wide problem. By studying the ancient

site of the markets and their evolution over the centuries one would understand the fabric of Paris. Just as the original location of the markets had inclined the city in a certain direction, a new location would abruptly reverse this direction. To change the location of the markets, even to alter the markets, was to run a great risk. To tamper with les Halles was to tamper with Paris.

I don't know if this opinion carried any weight. I don't think so. It had no influence some years later when Louis Vallon, no less hostile than I to moving the markets, in a critical debate cited as evidence what I wrote in *Les Parisiens* of the importance of what I called, not the center, but the center of other centers. The group of quarters that touch on les Halles, that branch off from the markets, that draw some of their life from the markets - from Châtelet to the gare de l'Est, from the Marais to the Place de la Concorde - make up the essential Paris. Was I completely sure if this contention was true? If nothing else, what eventually happened would prove that I was right.

Marvellous, isn't he? "If nothing else, reality proves that I was right." If nothing else. If you people can't understand anything, if Baudelaire's "naked perfumed slaves" are beyond the pale, think of all the demolished streets, buildings, neighborhoods, shops, vistas, restaurants, theaters, occupations, and riverfronts. And what happened to that "hardworking, easy-going" way of life?

Les Halles is the subject that closes the book, since that's where Chevalier believes the destruction of the city really occurred. And his conclusion, like his beginning, is bound up with Chateaubriand. I couldn't believe it when I came to it. Uncanny, isn't it? I mean all of it. I can still remember reading to you from the *Memoirs* in my first flush of excitement, and then you reading back to me. Where would I be with Chateaubriand locked up inside myself? But no, that's not true, either. It all happened because I stepped out of myself and went up to 79th and Columbus to see an old Carpenter Hill friend who was selling his candles at a crafts fair. Do you recall my telling you? And then I walked down Columbus one or two blocks, where I stopped at a booktable and Chateaubriand's name jumped out at me, for the one and only reason that I had liked an anecdote that Kafka recounts in a letter to a friend. It wasn't even the anecdote (it wasn't for Kafka either) but his response that drew me in. Yes, here it is, and Kafka says he got it from Flaubert! So who *am* I reading, ye deconstructionists, when each man confirms the reality and fulness of the other? And yet, beyond all doubt, each one is distinct. How *did* Kafka manage to hear them perfectly? By being himself!

One day Chateaubriand and some friends visited Lake Gaube (a lonely mountain lake in the Pyrenees). They all sat and picnicked on the same bench where Flaubert had breakfasted. The beauty of the lake enchanted everyone. "I would like to live here forever," Chateaubriand said. "Oh, you would die of boredom here," answered a society lady. "What would that matter," answered the poet with a laugh. "I am always bored." Actually it is not the wit of the story which delights me, for that is nothing special, but the cheerfulness, the almost majestic happiness of the man.

I read something of Chateaubriand's in college, maybe from *The Genius of Christianity* and from that American Indian romance of his. Maybe the *Memoirs*, I don't recall. I do remember being impressed by what was said of him, "great stylist, created French romanticism," etc., without understanding what any of it meant. But Kafka's response made him matter to me. I couldn't remember him using the words "cheerful" or "happy" before. I'm sure he does, but God knows where, and it's that exact remark of his which drew me to the book, plus the lakeside bench in the Pyrenees.

And here's the story Chevalier recounts, which is taken from the *Memoirs*, Chapter Five, "Soldier and Courtier." Chateaubriand had come to Paris from Brittany just before the Revolution, and, among his walks through "the desert of the crowds," was drawn to an old house near les Halles because of a strange event that happened there in 1606 to a friend of King Henri IV, the Marshall de Bassompiere. Bassompierre was to meet a woman who told him to wait for her between ten and midnight on the second floor of a house in the rue du Bourg l'Abbé near the rue St. Martin, "not far from a bathhouse," writes Chevalier, "where, still in my time, everyone from the markets came to bathe."

> When Bassompierre arrived, the second floor was aglow. Climbing the stairs he discovered that "this glow was the bed-straw burning, and there were two naked bodies laid out on the table." What had happened? "Had the plague (for there was plague in Paris) or jealousy arrived in the rue du Bourg l'Abbé before love? One's imagination can play with such a subject. Mix the poet's inventions with the popular chorus, the burial detail arriving, Bassompierre drawing his sword, a superb melodrama will unfold from these events."

"One's imagination can play with such a subject." For Chevalier that's the key to it all, "the heart of the mystery of Paris: the secret attraction exercised by so many apparently insignificant remnants of the past. Chateaubriand saw it." Exquisite, isn't he? "Chateaubriand saw it." He cites Miller lovingly as well, and, on the very last page, this from Julian Green:

> "Often I stop suddenly in front of some large window with artificial lace curtains, deep in an old part of the city, and daydream endlessly about what unknown destinies had unfolded behind these dark windows." But Balzac wrote of nothing else, and the Parisian chapters of his *Comédie humaine* should bear sufficient witness to the fact that he wrote what the city dictated to him . . .

As for me, I feel stymied by it all, by my mother, my times, my marriage to Danielle, my fears of daydreaming in deep parts of old Paris when I was there with her, my years with Clover, my trip to France with *her* as well, Man Ray's photo of Kay, and through it all, stymied by myself. This letter is one long pointing at Chevalier's book and saying, "This is what I mean. This is exactly what I mean." If you don't hear much from me here, it's because Chevalier brings me up short against my stammerings and, on the positive side, because he offers something simple and direct: follow your interests. It's Rabelais' motto on the Abbey of Theleme: *fais ce que vous voudras* - do what you want. Chevalier has a footnote on Lacenaire's writings, the Lacenaire of *Les*

Enfants du Paradis, a footnote that goaded me and reminded me again that it's been ten years since I had the idea of going to the 42nd St. library or the rare book room at Columbia to see if anything of Lacenaire's still exists, and I still haven't done it. This and a thousand other things, none of it useful or of consequence to anyone but me. Every time I do follow my bent, I come up with something fine, and then I hit that brick wall again. My flu kept me occupied with Chevalier and with myself all week. I told Trieber that this was a hell of a way to give myself what I want. The idea came to me that conflict, fear, and anxiety are backhanded ways of arriving at myself, in the same way that I was fired four years in a row and then got my certificate - fired into tenure - like my two dissertations as well - rejected on the first and given an award and publication on the second, as if to prove that with me impossibility means advance. (Lenny Bruce as small-town mayor watching the Lone Ranger disappear in a cloud of dust and a hearty hi-o Silver: "I dunno. Is he scared or involved? Did he lose or clean up the town? So he's the Lone Ranger. So what does that give him? The wife made coffee and he rides off, and I'm standin' here like a shmuck without a quarter.")

Meanwhile, whether it's just that I'm more aware of it or that it's happening more and more, the junk mail keeps pouring in at home and at school, my mailboxes fill with more and more pieces of paper with plans for BMCC (we have a new building, departments are slated to move, and Nancy tells me that the school had all the locks changed and that only the locksmith can give us keys, if you can find him). There are plans for CUNY, plans for the city, plans for medical care, changes in tax laws, incomprehensible phone bills, incomprehensible students, interesting-boring encounters with women, 1/100th of my intelligence of interest to hardly anyone I see. Hence these outpourings of my present mental life and my pleasure in your wonderful Ted tours of all and everything (I'm reminded of what Kerouac said about his favorite films by the Three Stooges and wonder if you're entering your Baroque period of letter writing). Do I know *anyone* else who would stick Constable's castle in the center of a letter to me? That picture in which you can hear the sea gulls themselves. One can't hear anything at the Metropolitan any more for the ringing of the computerized cash registers and, yes, those same screaming herds. One day in Paris with Clover (i.e., alone), I found myself walking in or near or behind or in front of the "Forum des Halles." I was completely disoriented. I had turned a corner on a street and landed on a giant manicured lawn northeast behind the Louvre near the church of St. Eustache (the whores are God knows where, in the Bois de Boulogne, I hear), with cheap arbored walkways, rock and roll bands playing at some sort of "pavilion" near the church (a short walk from Notre-Dame, both from the 1100s), students and tourists eating lunch and staring vacantly, and I suddenly see that each Lilliputian walkway is marked "rue" or "boulevard de," followed by some sop thrown to "French culture," à la "rue Jules Romains," and would you believe it, "Allée Blaise Cendrars" - all of which looked as if it had been laid down in a weekend - the shrubs, the lawns, the arbors - (they can do this now, as I saw for myself at the Shearson-Lehman building on the north side of BMCC). My first reaction was, "Hey, Blaise Cendrars." And my second, "Blaise

Cendrars? Here? He's buried here?" And Chevalier answers, yes, Steve, he's buried here, dead, buried, and destroyed.

> . . . Hugo tells us frankly, in *Choses vues*, how he found his ideas by chance, in the streets, often through unexpected encounters, not hesitating to rescue some girl in distress. He is speaking in *Les Misérables* of the unexpected in the Paris streets, of encounters that are not hallucinatory in his novel precisely because these streets are themselves the origin of these hallucinations.
>
> Inspiration was thus born in the city, the city of yesterday which in numerous places (and despite Haussmann) was still the city of *Les Miséra-bles*. This came about naturally, spontaneously, as a supplementary grace that no one could have imagined they would one day have to ask for, beg for, seek; something that no power would have imagined it would one day have to finance. To pay people from city funds to encourage them to have ideas or, as they say today, to exercise their "right to create" - to finance culture - would still have seemed, a few years ago, a mad scheme. To borrow money to create was to admit a lack of creativity.

And that about puts my own case in a nutshell as far as work, pension, etc. are concerned. I'll never get anywhere except by slogging it out in the boiler room, which is my preferred place as it has been yours, though I seem to do my best to deny it. I'm comforted by the fact that Chevalier didn't see it happening either. No theory of nihilism here, only lived experience, the pain of real discovery, and a thousand times worse for knowing that his old schoolmate, George Pompidou, who took first place in Greek translation, sat back and let it all happen, with the "Forum" and the tubular Beaubourg built over the desert where les Halles and its life-line neighborhoods had been. This is the big time, Ted, no mistaking. Better to go for your trash liners than sit as you and I used to do listening to Marty recount his high teas and lunches with radical friends in his oh so favorite quarter of the Marais, nearly all of it schlock, as I found out staying in the neighborhood with Clover in '92 - me walking around like an idiot wondering where were the army surplus stores, the crêpe-sellers on the streets, the bushels of oysters on street corners, where was Clover, where was I in my precious youth with Danielle? Why was I incapable of saying where I stood on anything, except for a bleat now and then? And it was not much different in '92, except that I'd built a weather-proof shack in the meantime and learned to take pleasure in tromping snow-covered hills on bright sunny days, the wind whistling snow crystals off my skin, and no one for miles around. That's what it was felt like to be in Paris, which was a step above being there in '63 with Dani, because this time I knew I was alive and that most of everything around me was dead, except where there were hardly any people around (Utrillo had it right), as in the Cathedral of St. Denis and the magnificent and almost deserted rooms of the Musée Guimet near the Eiffel Tower. The only new site I took in was the grotesque subway station museum, which still repeats on me, plus I. M. Pei's glass pyramid, which really has entombed the Louvre (one descends on an escalator, instead of walking *up*) and the "Forum des Halles," or whatever it was, which I simply stumbled on. I silenced a woman over drinks about a month ago when she started bad-mouthing Phoenix and I told her that she didn't know what she was talking about. No, she hadn't noticed the parks, the palms, the pleasant exchanges, the flower-lined freeways, the desert sky.

Your afternoons with Felix, Cosima, and Texans snapped me out of myself wonderfully. And Peter Reib (Reis?) was a treat, no matter where I looked. Afficionado as you are of really bright Americans, I leave you with an honest-to-God footnote by Poe to a line of his from "The Devil in the Belfry: "Everybody knows, in a general way, that the finest place in the world is - or, alas, *was* - the Dutch borough of Vondervotteimittiss."*

> *"Touching the derivation of the name Vondervotteimitiss . . . Among a multitude of opinions upon this delicate point - some actute, some learned, some sufficiently the reverse - I am able to select nothing which ought to be considered satisfactory. Perhaps the idea of Grogswiff, nearly coincident with that of Kroutaplenttey, is to be cautiously preferred. It runs: '*Vondervotteimittiss - Vonder, lege* [read] *Donder - Votteimittiss, quasi und Bleitziz - Bleitziz obsol: pro Blitzen.*' This derivation, to say the truth, is still countenanced by some of the House of the Town Council. I do not choose, however, to commit myself on a theme of such importance, and must refer the reader desirous of information to the *Oratiunculae de Rebus Praeter-Veteris*, of Dundergutz. See, also, Blunderbuzzard, *De Derivationibus*, pp. 27 to 5010."

And this nugget from the mysterious wisdom of the east that I found in "How to Write a *Blackwood* Article," in which Poe speaks of "that exquisite passage in relation to the fitness of things, which is to be found in the commencement of the third volume of that admirable and venerable Chinese novel, the *Jo-Go-Slow*."

A priceless man, and he knew his Paris, somehow, didn't he, in those Inspector Dupin stories of his. The streets of Paris indeed.

God, how all this talk just pours out of itself. That's what happens when I receive envelopes with Nietzsche's portrait in a wreath and Athenian male fantasy motifs.

How was L.A.? Did Ventura and Malibu float out to sea?

Steve

P.S. Nice changes on the Nietzche paper. I'll show it to you when it's all done.

Dear Ted,

   I went downstairs to pick up my mail around 8 last night and
found your package snugly resting on the ground floor, like a reward
for having done footnotes all day to get the paper done. I took your
point to heart, and you were right, so Goethe got larger and De Man
got smaller. Seems better now, doesn't it? But it leaves me with a
nagging feeling, as though I'm fifty paces behind myself. Good
question you asked a while back: what *were* those men writing for if
their concerns evaporated? Who even cares about the 50s, let alone
Weimar, 1786. The world is now on CD-ROM. Instant replay anywhere.
Students can plug into *King Lear*, along with 50 essays, scholarly
visuals, and library access, while their teacher "interacts" with
them and they with each other all at once. Homogenized Balzac. At
least the guy in *Atlantic* likes *Pere Goriot* and *Lost Illusions*. It
would be asking to much for him to go to the real cruncher in *Cousin
Pons*. Thanks for the article. Your "oh, well" helped a lot.

   My notes are meshuga-large, but what the hell. I showed the paper
to Ruth, by the way, giving it to her with some dread. Typical Ruth
drama - she was upset that I had shown it to Nancy and someone else,
but this time I took the bull by the *cornuti* and told her I was
annoyed by her little scenes. She apologized, etc. etc., said she
really did want to see it, and actually read it with the brains that
God gave her before Marx scrambled them. She did a lot of editorial
work at one time and pointed out some spots that weren't clear,
which I think are OK now. Both she and Nancy said that there was a
book in it and wondered if I'd ever write it. I could do it in a
year, if I could give it to myself. I envy you your time and desert
skies, mainly by the Rhine-pool, where you blow smoke rings at
Voglinda and her sisters.

   I see that Wagner even has your squirrel, in form of dead swan.
It's about time I got myself Wolfram's *Parzival*. I've only known
about it for thirty years now. Wagner took the scene you mention in
your letter and made it Parsifal's entrance. Grail knights: "Why did
you kill it?" P. "In flight, I kill anything that flies." Between
you with your Herodotus and me with my Wagner, we'll end up like the
moody French soldier in *Grand Illusion* who sits and reads his Pindar
in the camps. And Gabin will come by and ask, with that endearing
twist of his nose, "*Que-est-ce que s'est, ton Wag . . . ner*?" Renoir
has the Chevalier spirit written all over him. Remember when they're
all sitting at Von Stroheim's table after being shot down? I think
that's the scene. Von S. asks Paul Fresnay how they're doing at
Maxim's now that the war is on. Fresnay says it's still packed, but
Gabin says, "Me, I like a nice little corner bistro." That table, by
the way, is exactly what Chevalier says was happening on the streets
by les Halles, where everyone could meet. The idea of "social
centers" seems to have caught on, with reviews coming out on Lasch's
posthumous book and one by Putnam (?), well-reviewed in the 1/22
Sunday Times Book Review. From what I make out, Putnam discusses
northern and southern Italy along the lines that Lasch interprets
the States and Chevalier Paris. I heard a lot of north/south talk

when I was there with Janet. It would be a real headtwister for our multiculties if they came up against Italian leftists, who make it a point of being socialist to accuse southerners of ignorance and welfare dependency. I never went south of Rome, so I have no idea what it's like. Wonderful, I'm sure. Italy has a knack for turning north vs. south into art. Florence vs. Naples. Veal Milanese vs. Pasta à la Siciliano.

I started reading Cantor. Will get to the tape in a while. Yes, a care package from America to Khartoum-on-the-Hudson. But changes loom. The axe is slowly falling and CUNY is bracing itself, as are all the big city-state agencies. So what does BMCC do, having already cut a few hundred sections from this semester's classes? It *raises* the enrollment. Logic: with fewer students, it loses grant money next year. Question: Why doesn't the school simply live within its means? "But answer came there none; / And this was scarcely odd, you see, / Because they'd eaten every one."

My classes are OK. I'm not depressed at all about the work, only about the time I wish I had, but it's a big question, and I've only just begun to consider it. Lots of flashes on my last two-three years in the men's group before I finally had it with Gerson and the passivity of it all. But I've got one guy in my Intro to Lit (Comp 2) who's giving me a hard time. Large and black and filled with the Truth. I assigned Al Jennings' story, told them I wanted to consider other places in America besides cities (i.e. "urban writers"), and received the instantaneous response, "America killed 14 million Indians." I said his number was debatable, to which he replied, "No. That's the number." I've been through these scenes before and didn't want him to become the focus of distraction. The students are pretty nice, for the most part. But he was at it again a moment later when I assigned Hemingway's *In Our Time* and told them a little about why I was assigning it. His hand goes up: "Why do we have to read it? I like to know exactly why I'm reading something." I asked him if he had heard what I said and then asked others to repeat it, which they did. Other teachers have used the book, by the way, but I'm a bit nervous, since Hemingway uses Negro/nigger a few times in "The Battler," and I have visions of 500 demonstrators beating at my door. The amazing thing, and it's all there right in that class, is that he stands out completely alone. No one else is remotely like him. A few have already read *Animal Farm* and *Dr. Jekyll and Mr. Hyde*, which I also assigned. And none of them complained that they read it before. In fact, they seemed curious to see what the books would look like now to them. Just by putting me on the spot by asking a question I had already answered, the guy managed to destroy the concentration I was building up over the hour. Multiply him by 600 feminist literature programs in the colleges, thousands of "sensitivity" workshops, and God knows how many required "Theory" courses, and you have the insanity that's going on today, all in the face of a majority that can't stomach these people.

Did I tell you? Tom showed my paper to his graduate advisor when they were at the MLA conference in San Diego last month - Eric Gans, ever heard of him? - he's at UCLA, I think - and Gans was impressed. HA! Tom says he wishes they'd had him read Goethe and Spengler

●

instead of the horrors he was forced to study, which I took as a compliment. The idea of reading the paper to a bunch of teachers at a conference fills me with dread. I can't believe I said yes, except that I wanted the opportunity to meet the guy and a few of his friends, who will also be reading. He says it will be low key and that I'll be comfortable with the other guys, but I dunno. My childhood fears are at their worst when I'm standing by the edge of the Grand Canyon or in a confined public space facing others (the subway is just as bad - here, that is, not in Paris or London, where seats go sideways - and not at the top of Mont St Michel, high as it is. There really is something to the issue of American *space*, isn't there?). And me with my own festering sense of what you call your swamp-like ignorance. In my terrified vision, I see thirty members of the Goethe Society staring at me as I begin to read. Thirty long knives waiting to be thrown. And all I have in my defense is, "No, I have no idea what De Man means by intra and extra linguistics or genetic narratives or diachronic and synchronic interpretation. When someone writes ugly prose and gets his facts wrong, I don't have any interest in learning his methodology."

Cantor. I had trouble with Cantor. I think you picked his best passages, and I see what you liked in him, or think I understand. You talk about his straightforward manner and breadth of knowledge, and I'm wise enough to you to know there's always something quite precise, some fact or nuance of feeling that you've seen when you point to something without saying just what it is. When you do, the observation always comes as a surprise, as though from deep in left field right to home, even though you pointed to the thing a moment before. But here you say you were "demolished," so maybe that demolition got in the way of Ted-sight. Or mine.

Before anything else, thanks for corroborating my feeling about "Inventing." After opening the book, it occurred to me that William Morrow & Co. thought it would be a bright idea to cash in on the five thousand "Inventing" and "Reinventing" titles that have come out in the last five years, because there's nothing in Cantor that speaks to the term as it's been seized upon. "Inventing," as you well know, means the subject is a fake, a phantom of race, class, and gender, or some such thing. For the post-whatevers, the subject becomes "provisional." For the new historicists, "superstructural." Alexander Nehamas says that the big treat in reading Nietzsche is to travel the long road to nowhere: "And, so long as Nietzsche's writing is being read, the question whether truth is created or discovered will continue to receive the essentially equivocal answer presupposed, as I have argued here, by his very effort to turn his life into literature." Into a post-modern text, in fact, which "can be interpreted equally well in vastly different and deeply incompatible ways"; i.e. Nietzsche was German. Nietzsche was a Trobriand Islander. It's Nietzsche peekaboo: "Come out, come out, whoever you are." For Gary Tayler, on the other hand, "Reinventing Shakespeare" leaves not a shred of doubt. There is no Shakespeare, and English imperialism is his name.

None of which is Cantor, a mercy in itself. But he irritates me, because his material is truly interesting and yet is filtered through a pedestrian and almost deliberately uncultivated style. He's so caught up in his data-bases and distinctions between vulgar, middling, and "infinitely" superior knowledge that I can't trust him even when I know he's right on target (I like your method better - the hidden outfielder - grabbing a smoke deep in left and firing the ball to the plate). I went right to his passages on Huizinga, Spengler, and Durham Cathedral. He's incredibly well-versed but keeps making pronouncements that stop me in my tracks. Why is Durham "a bleak northern town"? I was there on a day in January, on market day, in fact, and I'm still living off the memory. The setting is of unbelievable splendor. A castle-cathedral complex on a cliff overlooking a river, the whole town built on hills, the cathedral itself visible from different heights and perspectives everywhere you walk. From the train station in the early morning, it hovers in the air like a Monet haystack or cathedral. The other side faces into meadows, and the facade itself is pure Gothic ornament. You can hear the sacred music in the patterns of the stone. The whole setting evokes the presence of the Grail as I've never felt it anywhere else, not even in Normandy, though I say that gingerly. Cantor says that Panofsky wouldn't have found any literary texts to account for the "break-through" style of Durham but would "have had to look at the political ambitions of a frontier prelate." Goethe would say, "Open your eyes. Look at the facade. Feel the propor- tions. Listen to Wolfram and Chretien as they run through your mind. Consult records. Walk around. Sit. Measure. Contemplate. Look at Turner's watercolor. Look at old engravings. Read Sir Walter Scott. Stop this madness of hunting for 'causes' in the midst of life."

> It is a young and trembling soul, heavy with misgivings, that reveals itself in the morning of Romanesque and Gothic. It fills the Faustian landscape from the Provence of the troubadours to the Hildesheim cathedral of Bishop Bernward. The spring wind blows over it. "In the works of the old-German architecture," says Goethe, "one sees the blossoming of an extraordinary state. Anyone immediately confronted with such a blossoming can do no more than wonder; but one who can see into the secret life of the plant and its rain of forces, who can observe how the bud expands, little by little, sees the thing with quite other eyes and knows what he is seeing."

Is there something wrong with that? Am I off? Bannister Fletcher's ten-pound *A History of Architecture*, the basic textbook in the field, gives us the technical side of Hildesheim, but it amounts to the same thing, minus Goethe, whom about whom Mann says the following in "Goethe and Tolstoy": "It is a primary maxim with him that art is as inimical to purpose as nature herself; and this is the point where the follower of Spinoza sympathizes with Kant, who conceives detached contemplation as the genuine aesthetic state, thus making a fundamental distinction between the aesthetic-creative principle and the ethical-critical one." And then Mann cites Goethe:

> I have, in my trade as a writer, never asked myself: How shall I be of service to the world at large? All I have ever done was with the view of making myself better and more full of insight, of increasing the content of my own personality; and then only of giving utterance to what I had recognized as the good and the true.

Cantor says that Spengler wrote "in a strictly imaginative, poetic, unscholarly way." So? So what? Spengler says that this is precisely the way to look at history after "the spade-work" has been done. Somewhere in my notes I mention Spengler's citing von Ranke to the effect that "after all, *Quentin Durward* was the true history writing." And let's not forget Herodotus. Those passages are marvellous. And your distinction between him and Thucydides is on the money. Nietzsche says that T. is the last Greek in whom the discipline of the old culture can be seen. "One must turn him over line by line and read his hidden thoughts as clearly as his words: there are few thinkers so rich in hidden thoughts. . . Thucydides has *himself* under control - consequently he retains control over things" (*Twilight of the Idols*, "What I Owe to the Ancients," 2); whereas Cantor persists in ranking scholars by how close they come to ordered methodology, i.e. Emile Mâle "lacked systematic control of his material"; "French iconography is enthusiastic and romantic, the post-Hugo effect, rather than persuasively analytical and theoretically well grounded." Say rather, theoretically well pulverized. Melville puts it so nicely, so quietly: "There are some enterprises in which a careful disorderliness is the true method." I type it and start laughing. God damn it, he's wonderful.

Cantor's problem may be a function of doing "overviews." I've seen the effect before. With a lot of ground to cover, the tendency is to label and categorize, and Cantor fits many into the frame of "connoisseur, amateur, and popularizer," with Huizinga as rustic clown, Breughel-like, the "wise peasant," who "outfoxes the academic establishment and in absurdly quick time, with small effort, produces one of the classic books on medieval history. This is the image that Huizinga sees to have us retain of him." Maybe he's talking about memoirs, but that's not what I heard in *The Waning*. I heard something more like W. Lewis and Villon. Absurdly quick time? Poincaré opened up a branch of mathematics when he put his foot onto a trolley in Paris. Cendrars wrote some of the first major long poems before Ez and T. S. in single night sessions, and Van Gogh was churning out one vision after another day by day for two years. From Cantor's descriptions, Huizinga seems marvellous all the way around, but I have to read into Cantor to picture him, and I'm stopped by the fact that he doesn't help me to *see*. Then again, I felt I had a handle on some important facts when I read his account of Panofsky's career and that I was standing on solid ground, but only up to a point. It occurred to me afterwards that when it comes to most scholarship, one should consult it as one does a telephone book, encyclopedia, or shipping list, whereas one should read Hugo and post-Hugos as deeply as possible. I got a bit scared by Cantor. Am I one of those thousands of avid European amateur readers, who couldn't wait for another book by Huizinga or Eli Faure, all the time dwelling in my little circle of amateurishness? That's how Donald Kagan put down H. G. Wells and Spengler: "Each man and his work won considerable notoriety, but all were easily dismissed by professional historians." Meanwhile, Emery Neff told me more in the little book you lent me than half a hundred "professionals." Fritz Stern was a joke by comparison. Yes, and what does Neff call it: *The Poetry of History*. Exactly. It's one of the Nine Muses, that's what it is, right up there with poetry and dance. Doesn't Herodotus list them at the start of his book? Cantor comes close and then pulls it all away: "Huizinga was right in subtlely bringing attention to a parallel between himself and Van Gogh [I hit it on the head, eh?]. They were originally obscure autodidacts, awkward, amateurish at times [that word again], but their unique, idiosyncratic art prevails, hauntingly. There is something there that is much better than it ought to be." What does *that* mean? Van Gogh felt he *wasn't* as good as he ought to be, and who should know better? And why "idiosyncratic"? Van Gogh? Who absorbed Rembrandt, the Japanese, the Bible, Monet, and Pissaro down to his fingertips. Who was related to Anton Mauve and took lessons from him, one of the great 19th-century Dutch landscape painters. Whose brother was in the middle of the Parisian art market and worked in galleries himself. OK. I'll settle for unusual, but not idiosyncratic. The right word is *Himself*. And autodidact? Did Cézanne study Robert's Rules of Painting? He went to the Louvre, all by himself, and looked at Poussin. Is it possible that Cantor's heaviness has thrown you and made you too feel like one of those amateurish readers who barely knows what real scholarship means? Or more to the point, that his very real and absorbing narrative is confounded by his distancing effect, and that it's this mixture that has "demolished" you, unbeknownst to you and quite apart from his learning that you focus on? I once read a book on American Jews and Israel that left me totally depressed, just feeling awful about myself, until a light bulb went off and I realized that the book was playing on precisely those guilt feelings that many Jews have vis-à-vis Israel. It was one of my rare good moments. Cantor is much better, but . . . Here it is. I italicize:

> *No book written about the European Middle Ages before 1895 or so is still worth reading except for curiosity's sake because the data base was inadequate and because the phantasmagoric screen of now-obsolete Victorian assumptions shaped perceptions of the past that are too remote from the understanding of the late twentieth century to be worth bothering about (44).*

"To be worth bothering about." He can't mean it, can he? Our beloved 19th century? Many people say that Viollet le Duc's Gothic restorations are excellent, but he couldn't have done it without being part of a culture that still retained the Gothic temperament. Scott knew his middle ages, didn't he? I bet the old stuff is fabulous. And let's say Cantor's "data base" compiled every single fact, down to the last syllable of recorded time, every last clue into every last piece of iconography, coat of arms, and armor rivet. And teams of scholars published fifty folios of close text on "Chivalric History in Upper Burgundy, 1150-1160" alone. What exactly would we know? Would that team simply look at us and say, "This is it. This is chivalry in Upper Burgundy at the time of early Norman Gothic"? And we'd look at them and say, "That's it? What do we do now? We're confused. If those Victorian perceptions that '*are too remote from the understanding of the late twentieth century to be worth bothering about*' were clear to our grandparents' generation, what exactly is the point of knowing the assumptions of 1155? And how can we even dream of understanding chivalric Burgundians if we can't understand what people meant in 1895?" And here's the bugaboo again, same page: "Even such a work as Henry Adams's *Mont-Saint-Michel and*

Chartres, completed in 1913, reads today as naive and idiosyncratic, in a way that his great history of early-nineteenth-century American politics does not . . . all things considered, he never mastered the complexity of twelfth-century ecclesiastical culture sufficiently or asked tough enough questions about it to make his book useful today as other than an emblem of an artificial neoromanticism in early-twentieth-century Boston culture." Well, I'm not an artificial neoromantic early-twentieth-century Boston Brahmin, but I was reading Adams all through Normandy, and he was a wonderful companion. Useful is *exactly* what he was. The book doesn't pretend to be scholarly. It's an expression of his love affair with the Virgin and a good place to start. I just wish he hadn't made those ugly remarks about money-grubbing Jews. That's the only Boston I could find in him, if that's what it was. Cantor calls all these works "impressionistic." And the funny thing is that he is too. That's what makes him so readable. Forgive the barking. It's a treat to have the book, and he'll certainly show me things I know little about. I'm already enjoying the opening, "The Quest for the Middle Ages." I think it's your feeling undone that made me snarl. And Gouty, Neatsfoot, and Springer have given me a taste for style I never quite had before. It sets my teeth on edge to hear scholars put into boxes marked "retromedievalist," "German idealist," and "post-Hugo romantic." These labels make everything seem known in the same breath that they seal knowledge from view. Consensus is reached, and everyone can now go home. But Burckhardt stood alone.

That's my identification with Chevalier. Chevalier, no less - cavalier, horseman, Dürer knight. I see him sitting on some Paris bench, armed in his clarity, watching the last traces of the middle ages disappear, still in love with his Chateaubriand and Villon.

> There will no longer be the faintest imprint of a footstep, as it was possible to find in an earlier time, no longer the smallest stone where one sat daydreaming or grafting the city's past onto one's own. Ineluctable intolerable oblivion. . . .

What if we chucked all art-historical problem-categories to the winds? Mandelstam says it so well in *Conversation about Dante*:

> Imagine something intelligible, grasped, wrested from obscurity, in a language voluntarily and willingly forgotten immediately after the act of intellection and realization is completed.

> What is important in poetry is only the understanding which brings it about - not at all the passive, reproducing, or paraphrasing under-standing. Semantic adequacy is equivalent to the feeling of having fulfilled a command.

> The signal waves of meaning vanish, having completed their work; the more potent they are, the more yielding, and the less inclined to linger.

> Otherwise stereotypes are inevitable, the hammering in of those manufactured nails known as images of cultural history.

He's quite wonderful, was especially keen on Goethe, and says that Spengler did some superb writing on Dante, though sometimes from the perspective of his seat at the Munich Opera House while watching Wagner. You see what I'm getting at in my identification with Chevalier on that bench? Let's put it this way: you and I are just too intelligent to be banging our heads against our so-called limitations. Everybody raves about Mikhail Bakhtin - Bakhtin this, and Bakhtin that (exact contemporary of Mandelstam's). Bakhtin with his "subversive" readings, his theory of "carnival" and Rabelaisian "play" undermining the "canonical" voice, Bakhtin with his "no language is whole." They lap it up nowadays. Mandelstam? Dead silence. Absolute ignorance, even though North Point published his complete essays and letters while everyone was reading Fuckoff, De Monic, and Dairy Queen. His *Travels in Armenia* and *The Noise of Time* are infinitely more pleasurable and rewarding than Bakhtin's heavy simple-mindedness, and his *Conversation* ranks with the best of Eliot and Pound, better, in some ways. But you can't build a professional career on making theories out of it. Remember the Hallmark ad? "When only the very best will do"?

later

I think I mentioned to you that I picked up *The Sea-Wolf* in January (the flu hit me soon after and got me on a reading binge I haven't come off yet). It's amazing how many of the classics I never read. It would be just like me to go in reverse order, start doing my childhood over, and go back to Scott, Dumas, and London. Something crossed my mind today concerning Wolf Larsen's contempt for Humphrey van Weyden's soft hands, the hands of a "gentleman" living off his inheritance, "standing on a dead man's legs," as Captain Larsen says. It's this: Larsen refuses to bring van Weyden back to San Francisco after the ferryboat sinking, telling him that he needs a new hand now that an old one just died after a drunken binge in Frisco, and, anyway, that he's doing it to save his soul. The whole story takes it for granted that work is crucial to being a man, and you can tell from van Weyden's opening remarks about himself as a writer (shades of "Unforgiven") that he's soft somewhere inside (he's just published a plea for artistic freedom in *Atlantic*, which someone on board the ferry in Chapter 1 is reading before the collision, plus he's been thinking about "Poe's place in American literature). Then comes the disaster, and van Weyden finds himself floating in a pitch-black, frozen tide, having moments ago stood in a romantic reverie over the night-time fog. London's descriptions of van Weyden adrift sound a lot like Poe's dungeon descriptions in *The Pit and the Pendulum* and the scene in *Descent into the Maelstrom*. Priceless. At any rate, it occurred to me that while it used to be axiomatic to chide the "leisure" classes for not getting their hands calloused, no one accuses "inner-city youth" of being morally soft, although they don't even do the kind of work van Weyden did. A lot is said about jobs and "self-esteem," but who talks about hard work as a necessity? Larsen wonders if van Weyden would survive a day having to fend for food on his own. And London assumes that this is the natural order of things. In fact, van Weyden is impressed by the specialization of labor that he sees on board the ferry and the fact that there are captains and pilots who know how to transport thousands of passengers, while they sit there reading "A Plea for Artistic Freedom" or just gaze into the fog. Marxists confound everything and call the Van Weydens hard soft-people, oppressing the masses with their diabolically inventive yet lily-white minds, while the down-trodden are magically spared (mustn't be judgmental about the lower classes - mustn't even call them lower - though you must call them victims, which makes them actually superior because you've made them feel inferior, so much so that they've *taken on the semblance* of being lower, thus completing the vicious circle of false consciousness that only Marxists can decode). Meanwhile, Al Jennings has the finest prison scenes and deepest portraits of criminals I've ever seen in American literature - the greatest sympathy combined with the sharpest clarity - three amazing chapters on the Ohio Pen at Joliet, c. 1890 - and yet he's a zero in the new anthologies. But Cendrars recognized him as soon as his book came out. My experience has been that when good writers say something is worthwhile, they're right, while your marvellously-named "post-thought people" only point to dreck. Even on their own turf, De Monics and Fuckoffs have nothing to show for themselves. They can't get enough of hyping second-rate "marginal voices" while they avoid with absolute tenacity the truly wonderful unknowns: "the spontaneous disinclination of mediocrity to expose itself to the impact of what is great." The line jumped out at me when I was reading Erich Heller at your house one evening. It's either Burkhardt or Heller paraphrasing him. Yes, indeed, *spontaneous* disinclination. An organic, instinctive desire for sickness. That's what is so confounding about those tenured nihilists.

The exhausted are *attracted* by what is harmful: the vegetarian by vegetables.

And this gem in *The Will to Power*:

Finally, [women] are also inspired by their finery; their finery is their *third* intoxication: they believe in their tailors as they believe in their God - and who would dissuade them from this faith? This faith makes blessed! And self-admiration is healthy! Self-admiration protects against colds. Has a pretty woman who knew herself to be well dressed ever caught cold? Never! I am even assuming that she was barely dressed (807).

The real Nietzsche will never get in the books.

Many thanks for the tape and the book. Your jiffy bags are a treat to come upon. They sit there quietly waiting, after Maureen has sorted the mail. I open my door at 386 and find peace, order, and harmony, like Zhivago coming back from Siberia and finding Lara's neat and sunlit kitchen.

Gene

P.S. Am reading Mountain of Victory - a life of Cézanne - by one Lawrence Hanson (London: Secker and Warburg, 1960). Truth to tell, I didn't know a thing about Cézanne himself, but he's his own man, every inch as revealing as Gauguin or Van Gogh. Hanson says he lacked Gauguin's worldly confidence and Van Gogh's appeal but is every bit the poet and human being that they are. A solitary beyond the bounds even of the other two. Mont St Victoire turns out to be the center of his childhood landscape, as the Stour Valley was for Constable. I bought the book from our strange County St. lady bookseller. Amazingly, she sprang to life when I showed her what I was getting, and we rapped for a good fifteen - twenty minutes. That Cézanne should help break a wall of silence is unusual in itself.

439

Dear Steve

Seeing this reminded me of you –
I think of these lovely women as Catlin,
Clover, Pam and Nancy. You, of course,
are in the middle, delighted but unable –
not to decide which of them you want – but simply
to move; ~~[illegible crossed-out text]~~
~~[illegible crossed-out text]~~
~~[illegible crossed-out text]~~
~~[illegible crossed-out text]~~
~~[illegible crossed-out text]~~
~~[illegible crossed-out text]~~
~~[illegible crossed-out text]~~

(But the present is more than the stage upon
which the past in ourselves reveals itself (as a
microcosm of the macrocosm of the infinite past);
it is more than their photograph, their car, their
picture, their sonata (now being played) carrying us
back into the past in order for us to gain meaning
and acceptance of them – it is also its own stage
where each player has a script, each prop
its raison d'être, and we must make our way
around them as new born babes floating on the

niagara of history.)

Whenever you attempt to join the past in the present with a seamless stitch called 'yourself', I am reduced to trying to find my past among the bric-a-brac of metaphysical speculations and the re-constructions of others. My quest is without meaning, without point and, like a moth, I keep circling the hole my past has fallen into.

Today the cranes are flying overhead - noisily making their way south. the sun is bright and all else is still

My Indians resemble your mother - sitting in their soft teepee light they hold their ancient spears and medicine circles and live among the ghosts and villages of remote time.

Miss you dreadfully —

Love

Ted

Dear *Steve*

"Herodotus is the father of history."

Cicero

"You see, friend, how he takes you along with him through the country and turns hearing into sight."

Longinus on Herodotus

"I devoutly wish that Herodotus' other characteristics were imitable; not all of them, of course - that is past praying for - but any of one of them: the agreeable style, the constructive skill, the native charm of his Ionic, the sententious wealth, or any of a thousand beauties which he combined into one whole, to the despair of imitators."

Lucian

"Herodotus sometimes writes for children and sometimes for philosophers."

Gibbon

"[We must admire] his inexhaustible interest, his insatiable curiosity, his infinite capacity for taking notes: his flair for a good story, his power of sustaining a continuous narrative, his delight in digression, aside and *bon mot* . . . the lightness of his touch, the grace of his language, his glory in human virtue and achievement wherever to be found; and withal the feelings of mortality, the sense of tears, the pathos of man's fate."

R.W. Macan

"Our guides described the life and guilt of each culprit; the severest torments were reserved for those who in life had been liars and written false history; the class was numerous, and included Ctesias of Cnidus, and Herodotus."

Lucian

"So little pains do the vulgar take in the investigation of truth {e.g., Herodotus] . . . I have written my work not as an essay to win the applause of the moment, but as a possession for all time."

Thucydides

Everyone knows Herodotus was a teller of fables.

Paraphrase of Aristotle

"It would be superflous of me to point to readers better informed than myself . . . how the medacity of Hellanicus is exposed by Ephorus, that of Ephorus by Timaeus, that of Timaeus by later writers, and of Herodotus by everybody.

Josephus

"His calumnies must be watched out for, like insects among roses."

Plutarch

Together, these are precisely the reasons to read Herodotus. He understands the nature of truth, letting, as he does, the world speak through him. As Goethe wrote: "The beginning and the end of all literary activity is the reproduction of the world that surrounds me by means of the world that is in me." He shows us himself thereby leading us into the richness of humanity. His is a subjectivism (like Goethe's) that does not swallow the world whole (reify itself), but insists on the difference between self and reality. The modern temper has lost this distinction (this sense of separateness), and has interiorized the world only to discover that once the outside is brought completely inside (every nail, thought, bridge, poetic cadence, punctuation mark, lover, handshake, etc.) there was nothing to bring in to begin with (a logical deduction) and is thus impaled on its own petard. The next logical deduction, lo and behold, is to say that the self doesn't exist either, merely an amorphous, unindividuated consciousness. It is not "I think, therefore I am," but "It is thinking, therefore I am not." Imagine discovering that once the world is reduced to self the self itself must be absorbed into an omnipotent yet powerless consciousness without individuation. A paradoxical quandary. The end result, of course, being schizophrenia; the intellect taking endless inventory of the number of thoughts it houses for and in a consciousness which is not one's own but which permeates the atmosphere as colored smoke.

Herodotus, on my accounting, was one of the ideal classical figure which the Romantics (Gibbon, Chauteaubriand, Goethe, Schiller, Mahler, et.al.) spiritually tried to keep breathing in the 19th century. Alas, he died with them.

Let's get down to specifics:

In the Jan.22 issue of the New Yorker Malcolm Gladwell insanely writes:

> *What if* [attempts to avoid future accidents] *don't help us avoid future accidents* [as scholars assure us they won't]? . . . . . *The truth is that our stated commitment to safety . . . has always masked a certain hypocrisy. We don't really want the safest of all possible worlds. . . . What accidents like the Challenger should teach us is that we have constructed a world in which the potential* [for accidents are] *embedded in the fabric of day-to-day life. At some point in the future - for the most mundane of reasons, and with the very best of intentions - a NASA spacecraft will again go down in flames. We should at least admit this to ourselves now. And if we cannot - if the possibility is too much to*

*bear - then our only option is to start thinking about
getting rid of things like space shuttles altogether.*

   Thus, the reason shit happens in America (e.g., car
crashes, train collisions, dams cracking, planes colliding,
space shuttles blowing-up, grandmothers falling off high
curbs, etc.,) according to Gladwell, is because Americans
don't care, and unless they fess up to this they should "get
rid of things like space shuttles" (as well as, I imagine,
cars, trains, planes, dams, and high curbs). Of course, if we
do fess up we won't want to makes "things like space
shuttles" etc., anyway for we would have admitted to the
possibility of becoming like Gladwell and dared to become
unAmericans who can care, and would do nothing mechanical on
grounds that if we did Shit would Happen.
   Skewered thought - thought unanchored in everyday life -
attains an abstractness unimaginable. True, I have
skeletonized his brief essay, but only to lay out the way its
bones articulate. These are the thoughts of a man who lives
entirely in his head, without a sense of history or reality,
writing that if we were honest with ourselves accidents would
vanish. He uses words which describe himself (his fear of
possessing a self) as descriptions of what others have
wrought in a world constructed by false consciousness, and
for which he takes no responsibility, preferring to moralize
and do nothing; i.e., to being passive and sinking back into
his own head to see what else is hypocritical with the way
others construct the deluded world they live in.
   Again, from the same issue, Paul Griffiths (on the
moment of death of Richard Versalle during the performance of
"The Makropulos Case" at the Met) writes:

   The ironies [arising between the opera plot and Mr.
Versalles' death] give a pattern to what happened, but that
pattern is a false one*. . . Other patterns would interpret
the event as drama or tragedy.* [But] *It was too little for
drama and too much. Only those close to Mr. Versalle, as
friends, family, or colleagues, can properly feel his death
as tragic . . .* [For others, like me, the most appropriate
pattern is] *that death is stupid. . . .*[The Met] *lost one
performance to catastrophe - since, following Mr. Versalle's
fall, surely the singers couldn't have gone on, and the
audience would not have wanted them to* ["rituals of disaster"
as Gladwell would put it, to hide the hypocrisy] - *Third time
lucky, the production opened last Thursday, and it wasn't a
surprise to find that the staging of the first scene had been
altered. . . . Ronald Naldi* [the new lead role] *. . . got us
through* [without interruption, thank God, and Emilia Marty
sang] *because that's the way of sirens.* [Of course, in the
future, there will be future deaths on opera stages just as
there will be future Challengers exploding over Florida.
Opera singers will again fall while dying for American stage
designers, like the engineers who built the Challenger,
refuse to fess-up.]

Here, Paul Griffiths images himself as living in a universe of hovering social "patterns" which, like other intellectual, psychological, philosophical, critical, artistic, or cultural "patterns" floating around him in the social ether, interprets events for him, descending prefabricated, as they do, into his mind - as they do into all of us (without minds of our own). Other "patterns" which hang-out in the social ether, may descend and interpret Mr. Versalles' falling from the scaffold as tragic - Richard's crying mother, for example, was obviously invaded by the 'tragic pattern'. For the rest of us, however, excluding "friends, family and colleagues," of course, death (like the explosion of the Challenger) is an example of the "senseless, sudden, irresponsible" pattern, i.e., the pattern which sudenly stops us from watching operas uninterrupted or witnessing successful flights to the moon.

These are microscopic examples of schizophrenia in action. Pandemic disemboweling of the self in public. It is what Nietzsche had in mind when he predicted what can come no differently - nihilism. (I know I have added a new word to my vocabulary, defining "nihilism" now one way, now the other, and finally, clinically, as schizophrenia, but there is a continuity to them all - bear with me, even if I project to much of myself into all of this.) Nihilism, it now seems to me, is the philosophic realization of how schizophrenia manifests itself in the real minds and factual behavior of individuals. Nihilism, after all, is the total abnegation of the self in self-hatred; a throwing of it away for nothingness - of thinking oneself as being pure thought which thinks itself, language which speaks itself, and as a universal conduit through which cultural patterns waft through. Uncontaminated by self-realized desire, sexuality, volition, or the love of smelling of one's own farts the self is lived as the arbitrary intersection of culturally constructed vectors whose center is everywhere and whose circumference is nowhere. That is schizophrenia - or at least as I have come to understand it through the writings of L. Sass (a clinical psychologists). It is a paradoxical way of living which goes a long way in explaining the involuted writings of the likes of Derrida, Barthes, Lentricchia, Fish, Greenblatt, etc., i.e., most of the recent spate of scholars who like to publicly show how they can crawl up their own assholes without getting dirty, i.e., emerging on the other side as selfless (i.e., grandiose on the universal scale yet humble in the specific).

There is, in other words, much to be said for looking at the entire 'modern,' post-modern,' and deconstructionist' enfabulation of the world as just plain sick and intellectually crucifying (not to mention, boring). In fact, these 'movements' are not intellectual at all. B. Russell once remarked that medieval theologians did not engage in thought but rather adumbrated fantasies ad nauseum. The same may be said of these well-dressed monks of devastation - they do not think but ruminate endlessly. Which is one reason why, perhaps, my former students (and primitives, according to Paul Radin) make such great 'philosophers' and catch on so quickly to what nowadays is called "critical theory" - it's as easy as day-dreaming. A ride through the wild side of the brain on a juggernaut headed straight toward psychological suicide and from which we (primarily, me) should jump off. The historical approach to these fellows and gals should be the same as the approach to Savanarola, Christian fundamentalists, the KKK, Skinheads, and Survivalists - as seriously lunatic. That is the proper perspective. One should be humanely interested in them precisely as a botanist is interested in man-eating plants - careful with one's fingers. To meet them on their own ground as do Dinesh, Sowell, Lasch, Lehman, Jacoby, Shaw, Bloom, Beichman, etc., i.e., as bona fide thinkers, is itself insane. Not a militarized approach which rushes to defend the entire Western heritage against hordes of dreaming Gauls, but a humane one on the road to add to that heritage - while one balances a cup of coffee and cigarette upon the arms of a recliner - is what is called for. (Not to be in this manner interested in them, as was I, can indicate, as it did in me, the presence of fear. The fear of being the mirror image of the barbarian and frightened of looking into it - hence a rush for higher ground, to scramble the mountain heights necessary for throwing spears into one's despised self in the darkness below.)

This, of course, for me, means leaving my knapsack of childhood decisions along the roadside and starting my journey all over again with a new, samsonite-clad self. (I can't explain to you how my encounter with Sass resembled my encounter with my first therapist who allowed me to see - O, so many years ago - that I had confused such basic words as love and anger, happiness and depression, health and sickness, selfless and selfish, etc., to such a pitch that I meant one when I spoke the other. The encounters resemble each other in being revelatory, but not in content. The first helped me to sort through feelings, the second, to place myself in a world populated by others - not merely as the sole tenant of my consciousness. My journey has been and continues to be a long one, even though I will end up where I started - myself. I am reminded of Valéry's writing that Leonardo reached himself by way of "detour through the universe," but I am not sure that that is what I mean, for all the while I have never left my armchair, in more ways than one. Valéry, of course, never did himself.)

Here is a photo of me putting nihilism through hoops while the world anxiously awaits the outcome:

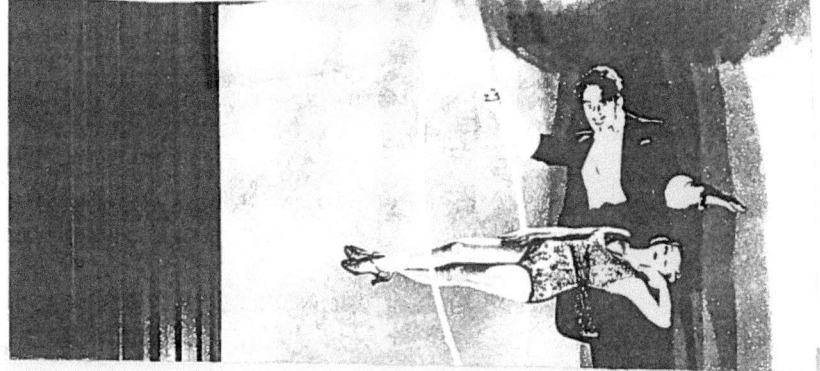

I will send you photocopied pages from Sass' book to help clarify my confession, if you like. Hopefully, they will be more assistance than my photo. I do, however, send you a copy of the recent cover to the MIT book catalogue as recent confirmation of what Nietzsche predicted and Sass adduces. A university press no less defensively firing back at its rational critics with proud claims to be able to invade minds with viral protoplasm and to take their readers "outta here," (tacking on the implication that the existence of the world depends upon one's mind). Really not much different in thrust than Gladwell and Griffths who I imagine also have eyes as bugged out as the employees at the MIT presses. All these scholars need is syncopated rhyme to write gangsta rap.

I hear from the weather station that you have been a bit chilly for weeks now. Ah, but here, in warm breezes(80°), the palms sway and sun light filters through the blue air like Ben-Gay for the soul. In any case, wipe the ice from your parka, shake the snow from your sneakers, put Orwell and BMCC on the radiator to keep warm, and write me a letter, a note, a sentence, or merely an exclamation mark! You must have read something of interest to me or to you which cries out for expression, which deserves a small trot out into the world!

Did you catch *The Final Cut* on PBS last week - a wonderful 2 day four hour program that was startling for its acting and writing? A few, minor comments (not to be read unless you've seen it in wonder, of course): the entrancing, devastating acting of Ian Richardson and the wonderfully crisp writing of Andrew Davies incidentally serves to glorify the peasants of the world who desire only the simple things in life: truth, honesty, and decency but have a hard time getting it from the ruling cosmopolitans who have closets so full of smelly skeletons they must . . . if the world is to get back on its wobbly feet. In the spirit of Rousseau and Shelly - viva the rural & righteous (Greek) peasant! (*The Final Cut* was preceded a year or more ago by two others in the series, the first one named *The House of Cards* & the second I can't remember. I saw neither of them, but Oliver has & advises that the first must be seen before the second if they are to be properly savored. At any rate, I am anxious now to see them both - perhaps Oliver will send me copies and then . . .

Dear Ted,   April 22, 1994

I'm on the job! Toujours à la qui vive. I found this notice in my college alumni magazine today and had a sinking feeling about myself for a few moments. In my worst despair in '68 before I dropped out, I felt there had been an almost solid bond between my childhood and Columbia, which I broke afterwards but still have not gone beyond into reality itself. Though glimmers are there. The Modern World-System — isn't that ludicrous — now of all times, when so much is falling apart. It's as though Wallerstein were calculating the measurements of the deck-chairs on the Titanic. I wonder what he has to say about Africa, expect that he seems to be from the blurb. Speaking of which, I taped the C-SPAN coverage of a recent Howard University "Black Holocaust Conference" the portion that included Jeffries and Khalid Muhammad. I toyed with the idea of sending it to you but was stopped by the feeling of not wanting to send you a piece of poison. It was truly frightening and insane, down to Hitler-like salutes. Jeffries is quite creepy, and Khalid almost murderous, though both remind me of what Hamil said in '29 concerning the coming "of a genuine paranoiac who will not be able to resist competing with the amateurs." Am reading the Count of Monte Cristo for the first time. What a fabulous book. Dumas! I never read him before.

Take care and accept no
substitutes—   Steve

Immanuel Wallerstein '51, Distinguished Professor of Sociology at SUNY–Binghamton, is chairing an academic commission that will propose a major reorganization of the social sciences as studied on the university level. Supported by the Fandaçao Calouste Gulbenkian, a Lisbon-based foundation, Dr. Wallerstein's 10-member multinational commission is challenging the traditional division of the social sciences into such discrete areas as anthropology, history, and economics by arguing that interdisciplinary approaches are eroding these distinctions. For this reason as well, the commission feels, the tripartite division of the arts and sciences into the humanities, social sciences, and natural sciences has also substantially eroded. The group hopes to issue its findings in a book-length analysis by 1995.

An authority on social change and a specialist in postcolonial Africa, Dr. Wallerstein has since 1976 directed Binghamton's Fernand Braudel Center for the Study of Economies, Historical Systems, and Civilizations, which is serving as secretariat to the commission. He was professor of sociology at McGill University from 1971 to 1976 and from 1958 to 1971 he taught at Columbia: during the 1968 student uprising, he played a leading role in the Ad Hoc Faculty Committee, which sought an independent mediating role between the University administration and the students. Dr. Wallerstein is the author of many articles and several books, among them Africa and the Modern World and the three-volume The Modern World-System.

NOT LIKE HIM, eh? →

Oswald Spengler in 1931

and certainly not →

Candias.

448

End notes

Since many of the letters in this collection were lost, not properly dated, or found with a missing page or two, there may be an occasional confusion in the reading of them. This can not be remedied. Nor can it be remedied that all the letters from Steve to me are tagged as "Carol Rusoff " as the sender – Carol and Steve shared the same e-mail account. I did my best to keep the chronology correct, but I assume all responsibility for any mistakes made. Believe me, Carol and I tried to find every letter Steve and I sent to each other. But, as neither Steve or I had any intention of publishing the letters, thirty-plus years of physical neglect have done their damage.

We were not, ala T.S. Eliot or Thomas Mann, creating a legacy. We were just friends.

Alfred Jacob Miller
"Breaking Up Camp at Sunrise"
©1989, The Anschutz Collection

Lightning Source UK Ltd.
Milton Keynes UK
UKHW050717070619

343971UK00001B/56/P

9 781366 7048